Drunk Driving
And Why The
Carnage Continues

Bob Mitchell

Copyright © 2009 by Bob Mitchell.

Library of Congress Control Number: 2009912546
ISBN: Hardcover   978-1-4500-0434-3
                 Softcover   978-1-4500-0433-6
                 Ebook   978-1-4500-0435-0

All rights reserved. No part of this book may be reproduced or transmitted in any form or by any means, electronic or mechanical, including photocopying, recording, or by any information storage and retrieval system, without permission in writing from the copyright owner.

This book was printed in the United States of America.

To order additional copies of this book, contact:
Xlibris Corporation
1-888-795-4274
www.Xlibris.com
Orders@Xlibris.com
71080

Dedication

This book is dedicated to the memory of Lynn Allard who only lived 14 years before her life was taken by a drunk driver. Although I never met her, she completely changed the course of my life when I saw her small lifeless body, sprawled in a field, clothes in disarray, on a moonlight night. The effect it had upon drunk driving enforcement reverberated throughout the State. She will never know in this world but she did not die in vain.

Acknowledgments

A very special thanks to my wife, Laura, for the many sacrifices she made so that this book could be written. She never complained though her sacrifices were many. Also, to my daughter, Cheryl, who was always available to provide assistance and advice.

I would be remiss if I didn't mention my lifelong friend, Jim Davis, who was my partner on the Montebello Police Department and, of course, Jerry Klippness, my partner on the California Highway Patrol. Both men were dedicated law enforcement officers who were more concerned in saving lives than just carrying out their regular duties and getting a pay check at the end of the month. Sergeant Klippness was indispensable in our fight to remove drunk drivers from the highway. His loyalty and dedication is more fully explained in the book.

And the book would not have been written if it were not for granddaughters, Heidi Row and Kate Best. Heidi kept insisting the book should be written and Kate was a motivating force during the two years it took to write it.

I also want to thank Terry Hennessey for editing the book even though he was extremely busy managing Senior Softball-USA during the same time. I know it was necessary for him to do most of the editing on his airline flights between tournaments but, being the professional that he is, he eventually got the job done.

Preface

On Sept. 11, 2001, terrorists affiliated with al-Qaeda intentionally crashed two passenger airliners into the the Twin Towers of the World Trade Center in New York City, killing 3,000 innocent Americans. The terrorists also crashed a third airliner into the Pentagon and a fourth crashed into a field near Shankville, Pennsylvania. There were no survivors from any of those flights, including the 19 terrorists.

Americans were outraged by this slaughter of innocent people and rightly so. The United States responded to the attacks by launching a war on terrorism. That fight has cost the lives of more than 4,500 brave Americans soldiers, at a cost of $10 billion a month.

What most Americans don't realize is there is an unrecognized war going on in America at this very moment and we are losing it. Since the Sept. 11 attack more than 113,577 Americans have lost their lives and an additional 2 million have been seriously injured or maimed by drunk drivers. The price to American taxpayers has been $357 billion.

While international terrorists are often the product of extremist views of destruction, drunk drivers often don't care or realize the danger they pose to their fellow Americans. But the dangers and the results are just as devastating.

Each victim of drunk drivers has a name and loved ones; and whether one is killed by a foreign terrorist or a drunk driver does not change the pain of the loss. In fact, it is hard to find a single adult in the United States who has not been touched in a very painful way by drivers under the influence (DUIs).

This book is NOT a campaign against drinking. It is a wake-up call against drinking AND driving. Consider the facts of this unrecognized war being waged by clueless, careless DUIs on American roads:

DUIs kill one person every 40 minutes, an average of more than 36 victims a day.

DUIs injure a person every 30 seconds. In 2002, (the latest figures) DUIs injured 1,058,990 of their fellow Americans.

In 2007, one of every three people killed in roadway crashes was the victim of a DUI. That translates into 12,998 Americans killed in DUI crashes in 2007.

Measuring this clear and present danger another way, Americans drove drunk 159 million times in 2002 and were only arrested on less than 1 percent of those trips.

In terms of economic cost, each DUI crash costs innocent victims $26,000. The direct total cost of alcohol-related crashes is an estimated $45 billion a year. In addition, the quality-of-life loss is estimated at another $70.5 billion a year.

This war against innocent Americans has been going on for decades with marginal progress.

Often a person does not realize just how devastating drunk drivers can be until after a loved one has been crippled or killed by one.

These are real people. On Saturday, May 14, 1988, Larry Mahoney was DUI. Mahoney drove in the wrong direction on an interstate highway in Carrollton, Kentucky, and collided head-on with a church bus. Mahoney killed 27 people, and seriously injured 34. Only six people escaped without significant injury.

Here are some hints to help you stay alive: Your chances of being killed by a DUI is four times higher at night than in the daytime. You are twice as likely to be killed by a DUI on the weekend. If you can, avoid the roads completely on the weekend between midnight and 3 am. That is when 75% of the fatal DUI crashes occur.

Just how ineffective has our war against DUIs been? By the time a DUI is arrested—or killed someone on the highway—he has driven 87 times DUI.

In California alone, 300,000 drivers have three or more DUI convictions. More than 40,000 have five or more DUI convictions.

The most dangerous DUIs are true domestic terrorists: One-third of the DUI drivers are felony, repeat offenders. And those DUIs are 40 percent more likely to kill someone on the highway.

In many cases the very people who are supposed to protect innocent victims—legislators and law enforcement officials—are part of the problem.

It is time the entire nation mobilize and declare war on these local terrorists, who are killing an American every 40 minutes. This book is designed as a gripping blueprint for the first national comprehensive strategy to effectively combat drunk driving.

This book is designed to light a fire under legislatures and law enforcement agencies to deal with a problem that continues to kill 12,998 Americans each year.

Bob Mitchell

Table of Contents

Part 1

Chapter 1:	Some Things are Worth Fighting For	1
Chapter 2:	Entering the California Highway Patrol Academy	5
Chapter 3:	CHP Commendations for Record DUI Arrests	21
Chapter 4:	California Legislators Reject Tougher DUI Law	41
Chapter 5:	DUI Blamed for the Watts Riot	53
Chapter 6:	Promoted to Sergeant and Transferred	79
Chapter 7:	Moving to Santa Maria	91
Chapter 8:	Harris Grade Fatal Changes my Life	115
Chapter 9:	Choice of Coffee or Arresting DUI	129
Chapter 10:	Battle Continues Over DUI Arrests	153
Chapter 11:	Firing Conspiracy Leads to Headquarters	173
Chapter 12:	The Day I Had Been Dreading	197
Chapter 13:	A Search for the Truth Begins	257
Chapter 14:	Big Win in Santa Maria	289
Chapter 15:	Assigned to CHP Headquarters	307
Chapter 16:	Transferred to Monterey	321
Chapter 17:	Attitude Toward DUI Enforcement Hasn't Changed	339

Part 2

Chapter 18:	How to Defeat America's Domestic Terrorists—Drunk Drivers	355
Chapter 19:	Resources for Combating DUIs	379
Chapter 20:	Celebrities: The Privileged Get a Free Pass	389
Chapter 21:	Victims of DUI	397
Chapter 22:	Fresno: A Case Example of How to Fight DUIs	407
Chapter 23:	Schemes Used by Lawyers in Court	417
Chapter 24:	The Substances Behind DUI	435
Chapter 25:	How to Identify a DUI	443

PART 1: *Chapter 1:* Some Things are Worth Fighting For 1

Chapter 1
Some Things are Worth Fighting For

I glanced up at the California Highway Patrol Hearing Officer. Thirty-one witnesses had testified for the CHP against me, and it would soon be my turn to take the stand in my own defense. Even as my hearing was entering the final phase, my thoughts drifted back to a dark ditch on a deserted road near the scenic Highway One that runs along the California Coast.

It was in that ditch, on a September evening in 1967, that unquestionably led to this day, in this hearing, in which I was fighting for my job, my reputation, my family. This fight was intensely personal, but it was also part of an overall quest to get drunk drivers off the road.

The full force of the California Highway Patrol and the Attorney General's Office had lined up against me and my partner, Jerry Klippness. The CHP brass had spent hundreds of thousands of dollars to make sure we went away. We had far fewer resources, but we were committed to the ideal that truth would win the day. Our futures depended on it.

The hearing room was daunting, as were the titles of the people who had testified against us: a deputy chief, captains, lieutenants, sergeants and a score of officers and several of the people I had arrested for Driving Under the Influence (DUI). The hearing had moved in starts and spurts—some days fast and others dragged—for two weeks. It was now in the waning days of November 1968 in the packed courtroom in the Santa Maria City Council Chambers.

Hearing Officer Robert Hill was seated at the Judge's Tribunal. I glanced to my right to the table across the aisle. Seated there were the men who represented the Highway Patrol and the California State Attorney General. This was indeed a David vs. Goliath struggle and it had captured the attention of the public. Reporters from the Los Angeles Times, the local Santa Maria Times and the Santa Barbara newspapers had been there for the entire hearing.

Television and radio stations throughout the state had also been covering it.

Our defense was simple, as their charges were complex. We were arresting drunk drivers—all drunk drivers, regardless of their positions in their community or their links to law enforcement. It wasn't popular, but we knew getting drunk drivers off the roads was saving innocent lives. We were hoping that the public would find out the truth and pressure the CHP and the Attorney General's Office. The word had to get out or we were sunk.

I have lived most of my adult life in the firm belief that the purpose of law enforcement is to protect the public from harm. This isn't some textbook belief. It became very real very quickly as I dealt with the carnage left by drunk drivers in the form of broken bodies and shattered dreams.

To some not in law enforcement it may seem strange that decisions made about violent, bloody acts are made in a tidy courtroom following very civilized rules of law. Now, I was being judged on the way I protected the public from violent deaths on roads made dangerous by drunk drivers.

Again, my mind drifted back to that one night I'll never forget. The night I knew I would lose my job.

It began on a typical California evening when two young men decided to have some beer and go for a drive. By early evening the driver, Greg Collier, and his young friend were already drunk and on their way to get some more beer in Lompoc. Two 14-year-old girls were walking down the sidewalk when Collier and his buddy drove by.

They stopped alongside the girls and asked them if they wanted a ride. The girls said they were going to get a malt and the boys said if they would get in the car they would take them to the malt shop. The girls got in the car

PART 1: *Chapter 1:*   Some Things are Worth Fighting For   3

but instead of buying malts the boys stopped at a liquor store, bought more liquor and sped away.

Collier and his friend opened the beer they had just purchased and continued to drink and drive at high speeds. The girls became very frightened and begged Collier to stop and let them out. Collier refused.

While continuing at a high rate of speed, Collier missed a curve. The car soared over an embankment, smashed into a ditch, and flipped over.

I was working the evening shift when a call came out that there was a possible "11-44" (fatal accident) on Harris Grade near Highway 1. I acknowledged the call and advised the dispatcher to send two beat units because of the location and the probability of it being a fatal accident. When this type of a call goes out, especially at nighttime, units respond code 3 (red light and siren) because of the need to get there as quickly as possible.

The units responding are also supposed to give their location at the time they receive the call for a couple of reasons. The fact that all the units are running code three and so the dispatcher will have an idea of our arrival time. Sometimes a closer unit will volunteer to take the call. It is Departmental policy that a supervisor also respond. Both units with two officers in each car acknowledged the call but did not give their location. I gave my location as southbound US 101 near Betteravia, which was about 12 miles from the accident scene.

When I arrived, the headlights from the patrol cars and the ambulance illuminated the overturned car. That's when I saw Lynn Allard sprawled in a field, clothes in disarray.

Her girlfriend was seriously injured. Collier and his friend, who were obviously intoxicated, were less seriously injured. All three were loaded into ambulances and taken to a local hospital.

I immediately asked the officers on the scene why the young girl had not been placed in the ambulance and taken to the hospital as well. Officer Short remarked that they wanted to take a few pictures first and "besides she's dead anyway." I must admit the young girl appeared to be dead and investigators do like to have photographs to assist them with their investigation but somehow it just didn't seem right. She had just been killed by a DUI and she deserved more respect than just to be left lying there for the sake of a photograph.

I had a daughter her age and I would want her in an ambulance being rushed to an emergency hospital. I told them to let a doctor make the final decision. The ambulance attendant who was previously standing by his ambulance removed a gurney and placed the victim upon it. She was taken to the Valley Community Hospital where she was pronounced dead upon arrival by Dr. Riehle.

Seeing Lynn Allard's crumbled little body laying in a dirt field through no fault of her own (other than to believe someone was going to get her a malt) touched my heart to the point of saying enough is enough. I'm not going to stop actively arresting DUIs regardless what happens to me. If I get fired, I get fired.

Chapter 2
Entering the California Highway Patrol Academy

My road to this courtroom started 10 years earlier on a much happier note. I had been working in the Montebello Police Department for five and a half years and had just accepted an appointment to the California Highway Patrol.

I received a notice from the California Highway Patrol that I was scheduled to attend the CHP Academy in Sacramento on January 6, 1958. I kissed my wife and three children goodbye. Steve was now 7, Cheryl 6 and Bob Jr. was 4. Steve and Bob Jr. would both become law enforcement officers. Cheryl would work for the California Department of Justice.

I reported into the CHP Academy in Sacramento after driving 474 miles from Pico-Rivera in Southern California. We received three months of basic training, which included motorcycle training. At that time, everyone entering the CHP had to learn to ride a motorcycle, known as "riding motors."

I had been riding motors for five years as an officer with the Montebello Police Department. It was there, in fact, that I began specializing in arresting DUIs—and it had everything to do with basic human suffering.

Investigating traffic accidents can be painful and horrifying because of the things you see and are involved in doing. A part of your job is seeing people horribly maimed and in severe pain. Some are dead and others burned beyond recognition. Please note that I didn't say "get used to" seeing people because you can never get used to that part of the job. And, of course, children and babies are always the most devastating sights.

It was during my first several months on the Montebello Police Department that I came to the conclusion that this carnage is unnecessary. It's caused by selfish and unthinking individuals under the influence of alcohol or drugs (DUI). Some of the DUIs are drunk but they're all DUIs. And it's important to remember that you can be under the influence without being drunk.

Most people are not aware that driving under the influence is so devastating; they even joke about it. How many times have we heard some driver boast about how drunk he was but still made it home without having an accident. But most people never have to see the blood and mangled bodies and screams coming from the children trapped in crushed cars.

That's reality. It's not a movie or video game. Emergency doctors and nurses know how real it is. Oh! And let's not forget the coroners. So, I decided that if DUI is that important then why not concentrate my enforcement efforts toward that violation. Not to the exclusion of other violations or duties because they are also important and necessary. I just made it my *priority*.

From that point in time, early in my career in Montebello, I put priority on arresting DUIs. And, of course, the more experience you gain in doing something, the more proficient you become or should become.

Because I had five years experience riding motors in Montebello, the CHP trainers at the Academy called me into the office and asked if I would be willing to serve as one of the motorcycle instructors, which I was pleased to do. Needless to say, I became very popular with the rest of the 79 cadets in class. I never dreamed I would be one of the instructors in the Academy that I was attending.

There were those trainees who were anxious to be certified and then there were those who wanted to be disqualified so they would not have to ride a motorcycle. They preferred four wheels over two. An officer would not lose his (females were not eligible at that time) job if he couldn't ride a motorcycle, the Department just wanted to know who was qualified to ride one. Even though assignments out of the Academy to an Area were based upon seniority, the need for motor officers could be an overriding factor.

PART 1: *Chapter 2:*   Entering the California Highway Patrol Academy

No one was killed during our training but one trainee was killed in an earlier class. We were also trained in driving a cruiser at high rates of speed. If a cadet was able to drive at a high rate of speed without spinning out, then a cruiser with special tires driven by an instructor would deliberately spin the cadet's cruiser out so the instructors would have a better sense of how an officer would handle a cruiser in that type of situation. If a cadet could not handle the cruiser proficiently then he would be "washed out" and sent home. The motorcycle and cruiser training was outstanding and extremely beneficial as was all of the training in the Academy.

Our regular training classes consisted of all the subjects you would expect, with a lot of emphasis on arresting drivers under the influence of alcohol and drugs. One part of the DUI training consisted of viewing a large number of photographs of actual DUI victims as they appeared at the accident scene. The photographs were of mangled bodies, including children, people burned to death with their charred bodies still behind the steering wheel.

One shocking photograph, that I still can't get out of my mind, was a body half way through the windshield with the driver's brains exposed. A couple of the cadets closed their eyes and a couple left the class room because of the horrible and tragic sights. Of course, those cadets would have to prove that they could endure these types of tragedies and still do their job. It wasn't necessary to fire a cadet for not viewing the photographs; they would quit on their own.

Some people have asked me how I was able to cope with seeing such horrifying sights and still carry out my duties. I did it by telling myself that the people that I was looking at were already dead. There was nothing I could do for them and they were no longer suffering. But, as you know that is not always the case. Some were still alive and still suffering. I had no problem with the ones still alive because I could help them. This may not make complete sense to everyone but it did to me.

But to take it to a higher level, I had a job where I could prevent these types of atrocities from happening. I already knew that if every DUI was removed from the highways 25,000 people would not have to go through this hell and another 150,000 people would be spared serious injuries. Fatalities were higher in the 1960s than now.

Fatalities were not limited to civilians. During the cadet training our instructor told us that two of us would "be killed within one year." That was the average number of new CHP officers killed in the line of duty. It seemed like everyone in the class was trying to identify who the two might be—and it was pretty uncomfortable because I realized they were looking at me the same way I was looking at them, wondering who might be killed. Unfortunately the prediction became reality. Two of the cadets in the classroom were killed within the first year. One was killed at the scene of a traffic accident and the other was shot to death during a traffic stop.

Ironically, the night before our graduation, two of the cadets were caught drinking beer in the parking lot with their girlfriends and were fired the next morning. No intoxicating liquor was permitted on the Academy grounds, but more importantly, police agencies look for individuals who follow the rules. A State Highway Patrolmen, as well as other Police Officers and Deputy Sheriffs have to practice self discipline because of the nature of the job. That is not to say that we don't make mistakes and come up short in that respect at times.

East Los Angeles Assignment

So, on April 3, 1958, I became a California Highway Patrolman and I was ready to return home to my family in Southern California. Each officer gets an opportunity to submit his preference for an Area assignment. It doesn't mean that you will get the Area you want but it's a start. Since my preference was East Los Angeles, I had no problem getting it. Most new officers get either the Los Angeles or San Francisco Areas. And most of them transfer out as soon as they get enough seniority.

Because East Los Angeles borders Montebello, I could continue living in Pico-Rivera and need only add another 5 minutes traveling time to work. When I reported in they already had a motorcycle and helmet waiting. At that time, East Los Angeles had about 20 motor officers. Now, I was one of them.

When you first report into an Area from the Academy, you usually ride with a veteran training officer in a patrol car the first week even though you are a motor officer. You are also on six months probation and receive an evaluation every month. If you fail in any category, you are dismissed.

PART 1: Chapter 2: Entering the California Highway Patrol Academy

My training officer was a very senior officer and didn't have much to say except "let's go." As we walked out to the patrol car I got the impression that he was not happy being assigned as a Training Officer. Most "old timers" aren't. As we drove out of the lot, I only remember him saying, "I've got something I need to take care of before we get started." We then drove a short distance to the unincorporated City of Commerce that borders East LA and was part of our area of responsibility and pulled into the parking lot of a bar. He said, "Come on in." It didn't seem right going into a bar in uniform but I thought maybe it was a follow-up on a traffic accident. When we got inside, the Officer walked over to the bar and said something to the bartender and then I saw him mix him a drink.

He turned around and asked me if I wanted one and I said no. I remember there were a couple of other customers in there, although I really didn't consider us customers. But I did wonder what the real customers might be thinking.

That was the only intoxicating drink I saw the officer consume and he definitely was not under the influence, but so much for public relations. Now, the right thing for me to do would have been to report him to the supervisor on duty because the CHP does not condone that type of behavior. I couldn't help but think of the incident where the cadets were having a beer the night before graduation.

But before you make a decision, you have to think things through. First, I thought, he's my training officer. All he has to do is grade me down in one category. That category could be "He uses poor judgment." Secondly, he could say later that he didn't have an intoxicating drink and I'm sure his bartender friend would back that up. He could claim his stomach was upset and he gave him a glass of water with an Alka Selzer. Could I prove it was alcohol? Needless to say, I let the incident go and passed my probation. The highest rating I got on my first monthly evaluation report was "He uses good judgment."

A couple of weeks later, I was assigned motorcycle duty riding with a veteran motor officer. Officer Meryl DeWitt was an excellent motor rider and dedicated officer. He was also friendly and reliable. I counted him as one of my friends. However, he didn't arrest very many DUIs and he was known to take a few drinks when he got off duty. One night on his way home from work on his CHP motorcycle he struck a car without lights that was sitting sideways in the fast lane of the Santa Anna Freeway as a result of a previous accident. He was killed instantly.

The wrecked car he hit belonged to a DUI.

After I passed probation, I was able to concentrate on doing the job the way I was trained and thought it should be done. After all I was a motor officer for 5 years in the next city over and had more experience than some of my training officers. Nevertheless, you can learn from everyone. I planned on more actively pursuing DUIs. There did not appear to be a shortage of DUIs in the area and some of them were showing up in traffic accidents—some in serious accidents and, occasionally, fatal accidents.

Still Making DUI Arrests in Montebello

Because I still lived in Pico-Rivera, and even later when I moved to Hacienda Heights, I traveled through Montebello city both going to work and returning. And as one would expect, I continued to make DUI arrests in Montebello but the arrests were handled differently than when I worked there.

As a CHP officer, I would radio CHP dispatch and they would notify the Montebello police to dispatch an Officer to the scene where I would turn the DUI over to their officer. The Montebello Police Officer would then handle the arrest in the same manner as if he had made the stop. He would write the reports, inventory and store the car, get a chemical test and then book the arrestee into the local Montebello jail. They would put me on the report as a witness, which would include the DUI's driving and sobriety.

I really appreciated the Montebello Police Department. I worked there for over five years and never once was I questioned about a DUI arrest or any other arrest as far as that goes. If someone was DUI, it made no difference who they were as far as the Police Department was concerned, it was just another DUI off of the road. If there was anything political going on, I wasn't aware of it.

I found out later that was not the case in all cities. Some officers do not want to take DUIs from another officer. They don't want to do the work that goes with the arrest. And there are other reasons. Some officers don't have the confidence or knowledge to make the arrest. Some officers want the DUI to be more than under the influence. They are more comfortable if the DUI is drunk and not just under the influence. And, like some of the legislators in Sacramento, they don't want an enforcement program getting started that may someday include them when they are off duty.

DUI Brags, "I just killed two Okies"

Some DUIs are not remorseful for the damage and grief they cause. One especially cold person was John L. Hoy.

On February 14, 1959, in the unincorporated city of Bell Gardens, Hoy struck Orville Monson, 42, and his wife, Phyllis, 34, shortly after midnight in a crosswalk at Gage and Eastern Aves.

He didn't stop and was reported not only as a hit-and-run driver, but for speeding and being under the influence. Mrs. Monson was hurled 149 feet by the impact, her husband 88 feet. Mrs. Monson was killed and her husband was seriously injured with compound leg and arm fractures, a skull fracture and internal injuries. Another couple with them, Orville Petersen, 43, and his wife Jewel, 36, jumped back just in time to avoid being hit.

Hoy was arrested shortly thereafter for suspicion of manslaughter, felony drunk driving and hit and run and taken to our Area office, where a reporter from the Los Angeles Herald Examiner described his actions this way: "Belligerent Hoy staged a commotion at the California Highway Patrol's East Los Angeles office. He was handcuffed but managed to pick up a telephone book and throw it at a news photographer."

Hoy also "snarled to officers (William Mills and Robert Benton), ' I've just eliminated a few more Okies for you."

Truly one of America's Number One terrorists

Pulling Woman Off of President John F Kennedy

On November 1, 1960, I had the distinction of pulling a female off of John F. Kennedy shortly before he took the oath of office as President of the United States.

Kennedy was campaigning for President in California against Richard Nixon and was scheduled to speak at East Los Angeles College Stadium. I was assigned to escort a black four-door Mercedes with John F. Kennedy, California Governor Edmund "Pat" Brown, Senator Engle and a plain clothes Los Angeles police officer, to the rear entrance of the stadium.

At that time East Los Angeles College was located on Brooklyn Ave. with a rear entrance on Floral Drive. Upon arriving at the rear steel gated fence, even though we had radioed ahead, the Mercedes was forced to stop at the gate where a large number of people had gathered. Security is always a major part of escorting so I was concerned about the need to stop with a large group of spectators surrounding us.

Kennedy was a passenger in the right front seat with the window down as he was waving to the crowd. The plainclothes LAPD officer was in the driver's seat. Governor Brown was in the right rear seat and Senator Engle was seated to his left. I saw a young women running toward the Mercedes so I jumped off of my motorcycle and tried to stop her. She dived halfway through the open window onto Kennedy with only her derriere and legs protruding from the car. I grabbed her around the hips and pulled her from the window.

As I forcefully removed her, I noticed she was holding on to Kennedy's shirt pocket and did not let go until I had removed her completely from the car. She twisted and turned trying to free herself from my grasp while shouting, "Let go of me." After the initial shock, Kennedy had a smile on this face and did not appear to be the least concerned about what was happening.

However, Governor Brown climbed out of the back seat of the Mercedes and while trying to assist in restraining the young woman, accidentally stomped on the toe of my left boot. Brown told me, "Let her go. It'll be alright." I released her and then asked Kennedy what he wanted me to do. She could have been arrested for simple assault.

Kennedy said, "It's OK. All she wanted was my pen," as he handed a black ink pen to me. "Here, give this to her and let her go," he said while laughing. By then the steel gate had been opened and Brown had gotten back in the Mercedes. After they drove through the gate, that part of my assignment was over.

A New Riding Partner from the Past

In East Los Angeles without exception, I always worked the evening shift (1:45 pm until 10:15 pm) but I seldom got off at our regular time because of late arrests and reports that had to be finished before the next day. I rode partners with different officers when I first reported into East Los Angeles, but after I had been there about six months a new CHP motor officer reported into the area and we were assigned as permanent partners on the evening shift.

My new partner was Ace Olguin. When I first met Ace, a few years earlier when I was on patrol for the Montebello Police Department, it was a memorable event.

I had been patrolling with my partner Paul Beard on our police motorcycles in the vicinity of Beverly Blvd and Wilcox Ave. at about 10 pm when we observed a blue Buick with one male occupant speeding about 50 mph in the 35 mph zone. We took off after him and when we got close enough for him to pickup on our red lights, he made a quick turn on to a side street and then another side street and it became obvious that he was attempting to get away. He reduced his speed but he was definitely wanting to lose us. When we turned on to Via Val Verde we observed the blue Buick parked with its lights out and the driver not visible. We cautiously approached the car from both sides and shinned our flashlights into the back and front seats. Lying across the front seat in a prone position was the driver. But as soon as he saw the lights he set up and rolled down the window.

The first thing he said was, "I'm Ace Olguin and I'm going to be one of you next week."

My partner said, "What do you mean you're going to be one of us?"

"I'm going to be a Montebello Policeman. I report to work next week."

My partner, who always got right to the point, said, "Then what the hell are you doing out here having us chase you?"

Ace, always a smooth talker, said, "I was just having a little fun to see what kind of officers I would be working with. I saw you guys back there."

We left Ace in the car and went back to our motors to talk it over. First we called dispatch to check out his story of being hired next week. A couple of minutes later the answer came back "Affirmative." We knew if we wrote him a ticket or submitted a report that he may not be hired. But then there was always a chance he would be hired and we may have to work with him for the next 20 years. Ace got out of the car and asked if he could come back and talk with us. He said he was sorry and that what he did was stupid and to please give him another chance. We decided to give him a strict warning, as opposed to a citation, and then wondered for the rest of the shift if we had done the right thing.

Now, we were partners on the CHP.

I knew Ace wasn't the most ambitious officer but he was willing to do his share. "His share" meaning doing the same volume of work as the average officer in the area, which is the goal of most officers. And Ace didn't mind booking a DUI now and then but he didn't want to over do it either. The biggest complaint the other officers had against Ace was his overriding desire to always have shinny boots.

Normally that kind of an obsession would be OK, but when a traffic stop is made by two officers, it is the responsibility of the second officer to "provide cover" and watch approaching traffic to make sure a careless driver or DUI doesn't "pick you off." Instead of providing cover, Ace carried a shine cloth on his motorcycle and would touch up his "Dainners," as he referred to them.

One night a drunk we had stopped stepped on one of the toes of Ace's shinny boots. I thought it was hilarious, but I had to intervene in behalf of the drunk to avoid an altercation. Olguin thought the drunk did it on purpose. The drunk didn't know it but he had committed the "ultimate crime" and I always thought to this day that he did it on purpose.

There was a slight scuff mark visible only upon close examination, but Olguin wanted the State to buy him a new pair of Dainner boots. The CHP refused—giving the other officers, including myself, the opportunity to make the scuff mark (which we really couldn't see) a standing joke.

Recognizing a DUI Requires Special Training

One night Ace and I had just paired and it was his "up" (when officers work together they take turns on enforcement stops and it was Ace's turn). We stopped a young female who was speeding along with a pattern of DUI. Olguin, who had gained enough experience to know a DUI when he saw one, decided the young female should be given a field sobriety test. He had her walk a straight line, stand with her head back and eyes closed and answer a few questions. Then he got his citation book from his motorcycle and proceeded to write her a citation—which told me he was getting ready to let her drive away.

I called him over, out of her hearing, and asked him what he was doing. He said he was going to write her a ticket for speeding and release her. I told him that it was my opinion that she was under the influence and should be arrested for DUI. He said that it was his "up" and it was his decision and not mine. I told him that the protection of the public overrode his being "up" and as soon as he released her that I was going to arrest her for DUI. This placed Olguin in a very precarious position so he just handed her driver's license to me and said, "You handle it."

If I hadn't been there the young woman would have been able to continue down the street and could have had a serious accident and if that wasn't bad enough, she would have had his ticket in her purse with the date and time of the original stop. During my career I arrested several people for DUI who had just received a citation a few minutes earlier. Letting a DUI go is not "giving him a break."

Unfortunately, DUIs have killed themselves and others after "getting a break" from an officer. Our job is to make sure the public gets the break and not the DUIs.

I arrested the young lady and a "car cop" transported her to the East Los Angeles Sheriff's sub-station where she submitted to a breathalyser test. That test showed she was under the influence (over .15% which was the law at that time.) It's .08% now and .05% in some other countries.

South Gate DUI Incident

A couple of weeks later, when I was passing through South Gate in a cruiser on my way to court to testify, I observed a DUI. I stopped the suspect and gave him a field sobriety test, which he failed. After placing him under arrest, I notified our Dispatch Center and asked them to contact South Gate Police Department and advise them that I needed an officer to take him into custody. The violation occurred in their city and I was en route to court and would not have time to book him.

Shortly, a South Gate Officer arrived and asked me what I had. I told him the details and asked him to book the DUI into the local jail. The officer said that since he had not seen the DUI driving he was not going to accept him. I explained the fact that I had witnessed his driving and that I would testify to that in court. The law permits this and, of course, it's a legal process.

The officer said he wasn't familiar with that procedure and told me to book the DUI myself. To his surprise, I told him if he did not accept the DUI, who was lawfully arrested, I would have no choice but to place him (the officer) under arrest for violating California Penal Code Section 142. That Section basically reads that any peace officer who willfully refuses to receive a lawfully arrested person shall be punished by a fine not exceeding $5,000 or by imprisonment in the state prison or by both. I don't believe the officer was familiar with that section of the law either but he suddenly realized that he was in over his head.

The officer made no comment and just handcuffed the DUI and placed him in his patrol car. He was calling a tow truck when I left. After getting out of court I followed-up on the arrest to make sure the officer did his job. The DUI pled guilty and hopefully the officer learned something from the experience. But more importantly, hopefully the DUI learned something.

DUI Reluctantly Rides Along in Pursuit

I had one situation that is not covered in training and I'm not sure it ever will be. I was alone in a cruiser working one Saturday night in East Los Angeles. It had been raining so all the motor officers were in cruisers. It was still daylight when I observed a DUI on one of the side streets near Eastern Ave. After making the arrest, I handcuffed him and safety belted him in the right front passenger seat. I advised radio dispatch that I was "10-15 (prisoner in custody) with a DUI to ELA booking."

But no sooner had I radioed in than I saw another DUI and he appeared worse than the one I had seated next to me. Plus he was speeding and driving recklessly. I turned on my red lights and siren but instead of stopping he took off. I advised radio dispatch that I was in pursuit, gave the location and described the car I was chasing.

There were no CHP units in the immediate area and I wasn't sure if there were any sheriff's units available either.

It was a wild chase. Speeding, running stop signs, screaming around corners, etc. I looked over at the DUI prisoner who I had strapped in the right-front seat and he appeared frightened but had not said anything. I thought to myself, if it were possible but it isn't, he would be sober by the time I got him to the breathalyzer. But that's not the way alcohol dissipates. It dissipates through elimination (10%) and by oxidation (about 90%).

Finally, the pursuit took us down a narrow alley and the DUI hit a couple of trash cans. The original DUI finally turned to me, with his hands cuffed behind his back, and said, "Look I don't mind going to jail for drunk driving but I didn't think it was going to be anything like this. I've had enough of this chase."

Before I had a chance to answer, the pursued DUI pulled over and gave up. About that time, a sheriff's unit arrived and he cuffed and transported the second DUI to jail for me.

Now, I fully understood how the first DUI felt about being cuffed with his hands behind him, strapped in the right front seat and being involved in a pursuit with red lights and siren blaring. But we also had a DUI driving with total disregard for others who could easily kill an innocent person. It was a decision that had to be made within seconds.

Law of Fresh Pursuit

Some people have the idea that if the police are chasing you that all you have to do is cross a state line or city limits or, in some cases, get home that it's "Kings X" and you can't arrest them. That might work in the movies but not in real life.

There's a law of "fresh pursuit" that basically says if an officer sees an individual commit a crime that he can chase that individual as long as he has him in view or is in immediate pursuit. A good example of the law of fresh pursuit occurred one evening in East Los Angeles.

I saw a suspected DUI and when I turned my red lights and siren on he pushed on the gas instead of the brake and we were off and running. It wasn't much of a chase because it only lasted about six blocks. But this was different than a normal DUI arrest. The suspect pulled into his driveway, jumped out of the car and ran into the house by way of the front door.

I anticipated what he was going to do as soon as he drove in the driveway so I was only a few seconds behind him. As soon as I reached the front room I saw a women, who I assumed to be his wife, standing in the middle of the room with an astonished look.

I said, "Which way did he go?" not really expecting her to answer me.

She pointed toward the bathroom door and said, "He's in there."

I opened the door, which he didn't have time to lock, and he just put his hands up in the air.

His wife said, "What did he do?"

I told her I tried to stop him to check him for driving under the influence. She said, "Oh!" and turned and walked away.

I thought for sure the DUI would use the excuse that he had to get home so he could go to the restroom but he never did. He had a prior DUI and was just trying to get away.

His wife simply said, "Where will he be?"

I told her at the East Los Angeles Sheriff's station on Third Street and she said, "I know where it is."

At least the DUI didn't have to pay a tow and storage bill since his car was in his driveway.

Two Top DUI Enforcers Become Partners

By the late summer of 1962, after Ace and I had been partners for about a year, I met and became fast friends with Jerry Klippness.

Klippness, a former LAPD officer and now CHP motor officer, had a great sense of humor, was dedicated, honest and intelligent. He and I were the two top DUI arresters in the office. We both shared the same philosophy. We believed, and still believe, that one person can make a difference. Likewise, we are both optimist and look for the humorous side of life.

I told Ace that I was going to pair up with Klippness because we shared the same enforcement philosophy. Officer Olguin and I were different in many ways. Even though we associated with each other off of the job at times, we had entirely different personalities and saw the world in a much different way. People that knew us both would comment, "What do you two have in common other than working on the CHP together?" Even on the job we weren't all that compatible.

The next day, before Olguin and I were scheduled to pair up, he asked to meet on the Atlantic on-ramp at the San Bernardino Freeway. This was the northern part of our beat. After I had been there a few minutes and heard several reasons why we should remain partners, he reached in his pocket and pulled out a diamond ring. He said, "I know you and Laura don't have very much money and you probably can't afford to buy her a diamond ring. So, Vi (his wife) bought a new ring and this is her old one. You can give it to Laura and make out like you bought it for her." I thanked him for his thought but told him I could not accept the ring and that if I had I would have told Laura the truth about where I got it. I rode away and that was the last time we ever rode together.

Several years later, after I was promoted and working another area, Ace was sent back to the CHP Academy for retraining. Retraining, not to be confused with In-service Training, is the first step in being fired. When the officer completes the training and returns to his area, he is expected to perform at a higher level than before. If the officer is unable to perform at the higher level and sees the "hand writing on the wall," then he suddenly finds a reason (or more properly a way) to retire. "Forced into retirement" means if you don't retire then we are going to fire you.

Knowing Officer Olguin, I knew he would find a way to retire. Shortly thereafter Olguin was injured on the job and retired on disability.

But this day in 1962, Klippness and I were about to start a partnership that would take us on an adventure neither of us expected.

Chapter 3
CHP Commendations for Record DUI Arrests

Klippness and I paired in August 1962 and almost immediately started receiving commendations from the Department. The first one we got was from Captain W.S. Dahl our Area Commander. It read, "During the month of September, 1962, you and your partner, Gerald R. Klippness made a total of 16 arrests for violation of 23102a VC, driving under the influence of liquor.

"Thirteen of these arrests were completed by you two officers; two were turned over to the Montebello Police Department and one was turned over to a graveyard officer of the East Los Angeles Area.

"You are commended for your keen observation in detecting this type of violation and your diligence in removing these hazardous drivers from the highways."

This was, indeed, ironic. Less than six years later, Captain Dahl, would lead the drive to fire me from the California Highway Patrol as a result of my refusal to stop arresting DUIs.

On January 21, 1963, Klippness and I were again commended for our DUI enforcement by Captain Dahl.

"During the period from September 1, 1962 through January 17, 1963, Officer Mitchell and his partner, Klippness, made 119 arrests for violation of Section 23102a CVC, driving while under the influence of intoxicating liquor. Of the 119 persons arrested, 13 pled "not guilty" and of that 13 there were only 6 cases that went to trial. A jury found 1 person not guilty but the other 5 were convicted.

"The Area Supervisors feel that the heavy enforcement pressure being put on persons driving while under the influence of intoxicants has resulted in this sharp decrease of drunk drivers being involved in accidents.

"Officer Mitchell is again commended for his keen observation in detecting this high accident causing violation and his perseverance in arresting, booking and successfully prosecuting the many intoxicated drivers."

DUI almost got us

Another time when it was not necessary to seek out a DUI was August 8, 1962. And it almost cost my partner and I our lives. Officer Klippness and I were stopped for a pedestrian crossing in the crosswalk on Olympic Blvd between Northside Drive and Hendricks Street. A DUI was approaching from behind and due to his intoxicated condition he was not going to be able to stop without crashing into the back of our motorcycles. An alert citizen, L.J. Serotsky, of West Covina, was standing on the sidewalk and saw what was most likely going to take place. He shouted "Look out" and waved his arms which caused the DUI to swerve over the double line narrowly missing the the pedestrian and us. It was believed that Mr. Serotsky possibly saved our lives so he received a written commendation from Commissioner Bradford Crittenden for "his quick thinking and action."

Protecting Richard Nixon

In 1962, Richard Nixon, ran for Governor of California against the current and very popular Governor Edmund "Pat" Brown. Nixon rode in a parade down Whittier Blvd in East Los Angeles along with his wife, Pat. They sat on the top of the rear seat in the back of a convertible that was being driven by a plainclothes LAPD officer.

It was Klippness and my assignment as motorcycle officers to ride along side their vehicle as security. We traveled at a very low speed and we used our motorcycle to keep the spectators from moving too close to the car.

The parade ended without incident except the limousine that was supposed to pick the Nixons up at the end of the parade didn't show. We left with the Nixons and pulled into an open but secluded location while the LAPD officer radioed the "limo" problem to Los Angeles dispatch.

There was just the five of us there and the LAPD officer was busy on the radio. The Nixons were settled in the back seat of the convertible with the top down and we were on our motorcycles right next to the car with the ignitions off. The LAPD officer advised them the limousine would be there shortly and then there was total silence.

Finally, someone had to say something, so one of us said, "We wish you the best on the run for Governor." Nixon, sounding very official instead of just causal, said, "I'm going to take care of you boys when we get to Sacramento."

During the wait Mrs. Nixon joined into the conversation by asking us about our families. The limousine arrived shortly.

Motherly DUI Hard to Convict

Klippness and I had a very high ratio of convictions in those cases that went to court. However, we knew when we arrested one woman that we were not going to get a conviction if it went to a jury.

We first observed her driving south on Atlanta Blvd near Whittier Blvd in East Los Angeles. She drove in a weaving pattern typical of a DUI and stopped abruptly in the parking lot of a local bar.

We gave her a field sobriety test (FST), which she failed, but her driving was much worse than the FST indicated. She told us that she was out looking for her husband who was suppose to be home. Her breathalyser test supported the fact she was under the influence but at that time the reading was marginal (.14 %) because the presumptive guilt law was .15 %.

We knew from our years of experience that a Blood Alcohol Concentration (BAC) of .15% was far too high for a "presumptive guilt." It took six years, until 1969, to get the BAC presumptive guilt law reduced to .10%.

But this was 1963—and even if she had been over the .15% level, we knew we were going to have big problems getting a conviction. The problem was that our DUI looked like everyone's mother. If you were going to paint a picture and title it "mother," you would paint her. Plus, she was a very sweet person. We knew that when she showed up in court totally sober no jury in the world was going to find her guilty. And that is exactly what happened.

So, why did we arrest her?

First, she was under the influence and could have had a serious accident. Next, her experience that night and expense of going to court, probably prevented her from ever driving drunk again. If we had made other arrangements, she could have been out the next night doing the same thing.

Two Motor Officers Go Down Chasing DUIs

One accident that Klippness and I had that was never recorded occurred one night in the City Terrance area of East Los Angeles. That area is hilly and has winding narrow roads and borders downtown Los Angeles. It's not the safest place to pursue someone but that's the position we found ourselves in one Saturday night. We saw a possible DUI traveling at a high rate of speed and took pursuit with red lights and sirens. Klippness was "up" so he took the lead. The chase took us down a winding hill and as we came around a curve we suddenly observed an oil slick in our path. Klippness went down immediately and, almost at the same time, I went down.

We had to be traveling 40 or 45 miles an hour at the time. The CHP used Harley Davidson motorcycles at the time and they weighed 900 pounds. Of course, we had on helmets, leather jackets and motor boots which is a form of protection. Since our motorcycles weighed more than us they were sliding ahead of us on their sides with sparks flying upward from the pavement. We were rolling over and over as well as sliding behind the motorcycles on the pavement. It seemed like forever but we finally slide to a stop. By coincidence, we came to rest alongside a Deputy Sheriff who was on a traffic stop. He turned in our direction, spread both of his arms out to his side like an umpire and said, "Safe."

Klippness and I got up, looked at each other and then laughed. We had no broken bones or even minor injuries. We each lifted up our motorcycle and

PART 1: *Chapter 3:*   CHP Commendations for Record DUI Arrests   25

checked it for damage. There wasn't much to dust off since we were sliding on the pavement. It was just scrapes and minor bruises. The "Chevy" we were chasing was long gone. Maybe later the driver put a couple of small motorcycle decals on his door.

Klippness and I returned to the Area Office, found a can of black spray paint and did a little touch up on the motorcycles. We both needed side-view mirrors but that would be no problem. After accessing the damage to our boots and uniforms we decided to finish our shift. Later the Office gave us new helmets to replace our scratched ones. Not surprising because we probably slid and rolled over 60 feet. I was surprised that a leather jacket could take that kind of treatment.

On April 2, 1963, we received another commendation from the Department and signed by Captain Dahl. It read, "During the month of March 1963 the enforcement personnel of this Area arrested 177 operators of motor vehicles for driving under the influence of intoxicating liquor. This is contrasted by the fact that only one arrest was made for 23101 CVC, Felony Drunk Driving. These arrests for the month are the highest ever experienced by this Area.

"It was noted that, during this particular month, you and your regular assigned partner accounted for 56 of these arrests or approximately 32% of the total arrests.

"You have been observed in the performance of your duties with particular reference to this violation and you are to be commended for your techniques in observation, interrogation and the processing of these violators.

"It has also been noted that you have previously been commended for your aggressive enforcement of this particular high accident causing violation. Therefore, it gives me great pleasure in again recognizing your continued efforts."

Pro's and Con's of arresting DUIs

The reason so much emphasis was being put on DUI enforcement was the pressure we were exerting on the other officers. In other words, if Klippness and I could arrest so many DUIs then why weren't the other officers doing the same. This caused some real problems. Now, some of the officers were pleased that we were leading the way and in most cases showing them how they could do the same. If they stopped a suspected DUI violator and did not feel competent to arrest him then they would call us to the scene. It was a form of training as well. Another thing encouraging them was the overtime pay for going to court. In some months our salary was more than the Area Commanders. We were told not to worry about the increase in overtime because Headquarters wanted the reduction in accidents and DUI arrests.

At this point, we were drawing statewide attention as well as effecting the court system and other agencies. Especially, the East Los Angeles Sheriff's Department where we were doing most of the booking. Even the LA Times and some of the television stations were getting involved. The East Los Angeles Sheriff reported that there was an almost 50% drop in domestic violence and their armed robberies had reduced drastically. At first we asked what does that have to do with DUI arrests? But they had already figured that out. When a DUI is arrested, he is booked in jail and therefore doesn't have an opportunity to go home and assault his wife. By the time he gets out he's sober. But what about armed robberies? Very simply, our units were all over the place looking for DUIs so the armed robbers were not comfortable with all that enforcement activity going on. The thought was "Go somewhere else where the cops aren't so active."

Most of the publicity was good but some individuals didn't like it. Starting with our own CHP Officers. Jealousy raised it's ugly head. We had so many officers arresting DUIs now that there was a squad of us that was assigned to concentrate exclusively on arresting DUIs. That squad was "getting all of the attention" and making a higher salary than the other officers not involved. Mainly, car cops.

Furthermore, it doesn't take a genius to figure out that when a motor officer arrests a DUI, or anyone as far as that goes, they will need to call a car unit for transportation. That means a car officer will be tied up with transportation and sometimes booking. Some of the car officers complained that they were nothing more than a taxi service. "How can we get out and do our job if all we're doing is transporting drunk drivers?" they would ask. Another common complaint was, "If you want to book drunk drivers then transport them yourself. Get off of that motorcycle and get in a car." We would counter, "If we weren't booking these DUIs then you would be working their accidents."

In an effort to stop the DUI enforcement, some of the opposing officers started saying that we were making bad arrests. "They're arresting people out there that they know are not under the influence just to get the overtime," was a common complaint. Then add, "I know that to be a fact because I'm transporting them and I know I sure wouldn't be arresting them." We would counter, "What you're really saying is that you wouldn't know a DUI unless he was a falling down drunk. So, naturally you wouldn't be arresting them." This type of arguing went on regularly and I have a suspicion it's still going on today. Officers are going to have to be trained to recognize a DUI as opposed to a drunk.

Bar Owners and Booking Officers Complaining

The next big complainers were the bar owners. Even the California Bar Association got involved. They would call CHP Headquarters in Sacramento, CHP Divisions and local area offices. Their biggest complaint was that we were staking out bars. "They're putting us out of business. No one wants to come here and drink because they know they're going to get stopped for DUI when they leave." When asked what evidence they had that their bar was being staked out, they would reply because I see them out there. And my customers tell me they see them." The bartender and/or owners would then be told to write down the license plate of the CHP unit and date and time. To my knowledge no CHP office ever received that information from a bar.

Later, as a Sergeant in Santa Maria, I would be fired and charged with staking out bars but would prove them wrong beyond a shadow of a doubt using their own documents against them.

The next complaints came from some of the East LA Deputy Sheriffs jail personnel. Their work load had more than tripled and their salary was remaining the same. Their jail facility looked like "Grand Central Station" on Friday and Saturday nights. Watching television while waiting on a booking was a thing of the past. I always found the deputies friendly and professional but because of the large increase in bookings some of them became frustrated because they weren't getting any additional help.

Soon there became a backlog where the arresting officer had to wait before he could start the booking. The next change was the arresting officer had to complete all of the booking paper work and then it was suggested that we book downtown in the main jail. That we wouldn't do. Some of the deputies in the East LA area started complaining they thought some of the arrestees should not have been arrested. To me they were just showing their ignorance. The chemical tests alone confirmed their intoxication. If an officer didn't trust a breathalyzer test, then he should have them take a blood or urine test. The arresting officer has absolutely no control over the BAC reading.

Bartenders First Concern is their Customers

Klippness and I were assigned as motorcycle officers the entire time we were in East Los Angeles. One Friday night, as a two man DUI task force, we decided to venture into the City Terrace area and provide some DUI enforcement in an area where officers in cruisers did not frequent at night time. It was a hilly area bordering Los Angeles where gangs and drug dealers hung out. If you were a uniformed officer and you needed assistance for any reason, that's not the place you would want to find yourself. But there were also some very decent people living there and they had the same right to be protected as anyone else.

As we were passing a bar we saw two individuals coming out the front door that opened right next to the sidewalk. An unoccupied old model car was right next to the curb in front of them. It appeared one of them may have been injured because the other one was helping him walk. Klippness and I both looked at each other but just kept going. Neither one of the individuals recognized us as CHP officers, probably because they weren't used to seeing any around there—especially at 1 am. We turned out our lights and made a u-turn and stopped next to the curb.

It soon became apparent what was happening. The individual being halfway carried was drunk and the individual assisting him was either a friend or the bartender. We figured it was the bartender because he went back into the bar and stayed there. The drunk was so intoxicated the bartender had to turn on his lights and start the engine. There were no other cars on the road at the time because this was a neighborhood bar.

The DUI was so drunk that he was just aiming his car as opposed to driving it, but we were able to stop him less than a half block from the bar. We didn't want some of his friends coming out of the bar in a drunken condition and taking the law into their own hands. We knew we were going to have a small wait for a cruiser to transport him and we weren't in friendly territory. Using a "posse comitatus" (summoning assistance from the community) wasn't going to work there.

We got our transporting cruiser and a tow truck and left the scene with the DUI without attracting one spectator during the entire time.

Teaming with Vince Bugliosi

The next complaints came from the courts. They were overloaded with work. Judge Myer B. Marion complained, "We don't have enough judges. And if we did have more judges, we don't have enough court rooms." The Deputy Attorneys had the same complaints. "We just can't handle all these cases. It's impossible." That's when I first met Vince Bugliosi, who prosecuted Charles Manson in 1971.

Bugliosi was a Deputy District Attorney in East Los Angeles Municipal Court where 80% of the DUIs I arrested were adjudicated. We got to know each other quite well because I was the arresting officer and he was the prosecutor. We had the highest respect for one another but we didn't always agree. I was more for prosecution and he was more for clearing the calendar. We had about a 96% conviction rate when we went to trial but because of the volumes of arrests, there had to be deals made. Nevertheless, I have followed his career, read his books (my favorite being "Outrage. The Five Reasons Why O.J. Simpson Got Away with Murder.") As a result of following Vince's career, I think we would be in total agreement now. Out of necessity, East Los Angeles Municipal Court did add another judge.

More Commendations for DUI Arrests

On August 2, 1963, Klippness and I received another commendation from the Department. This commendation documented a record number of arrests that no one will ever come close to breaking.

It reads, "It was noted that on July 12th and 13th, while assigned to the late evening shift, you and your regular partner arrested and processed nineteen 23102a CVC (DUIs) and one 647f P.C. (Drunk in public) suspects.

"These arrests for a two-day period is exceptional and is felt worthy of mention.

"It has also been noted that on previous occasions you have been commended for your enforcement of this particular section of the Vehicle Code.

"You have constantly led this area for 23102a VC (DUI) arrests and as a result it is felt that you have served as an example for other officers of this command to follow.

"It therefore gives me pleasure to again commend you for your efforts."

Besides accomplishing 19 DUI arrests on one weekend, this commendation was even more meaningful because it was initiated by Sergeant Leo Diaz. Diaz was an outstanding supervisor and a strong supporter of our DUI enforcement. He was active in the field and showed up at our DUI arrests scenes regularly. He knew firsthand what we were doing and never hesitated to express his support.

On October 15, 1963, Commissioner Bradford Crittenden sent a letter of congratulations to the East Los Angeles Area.

"My attention has been called to the remarkable increase in drunk driving arrests in the East Los Angeles Area this year.

"Review of the arrests shows each month exceeded the number for the same month a year ago and each month exceeded the preceding month until September of this year. The experience through September is an increase of 318 percent.

"Please convey my pleasure in this remarkable performance to Captain Dahl and the officers of the East Los Angeles Area."

Moving to Hacienda Heights, Joining church

In August 1963 my family and I bought our first home, in Hacienda Heights. I was still able to work in East Los Angeles. It was about 30 miles farther from the office but I still had the CHP motorcycle for transportation. The policy of being able to use the motorcycle for transportation is a win/win situation. First and foremost it's a safety factor (as all motorcycles handle differently and should stay with one rider) and the CHP gets free in-view exposure and enforcement prior to the officer's shift starting. Writing a traffic ticket and making physical arrests while traveling back and forth was not uncommon. However, you did need to notify Dispatch when making an enforcement stop.

In November 1963 Laura and I joined the church and we both decided to give up drinking liquor even socially. Once this information got out (the first time I turned down a drink) the DUI sympathizers started their rumors. I wasn't just a Highway Patrolman doing a job the public hired me to do but suddenly I was a "religious fanatic," a "self-appointed crusader" and that I was even attempting "to bring back prohibition."

I didn't understand then and I don't understand now, why anyone would oppose removing "potential killers" from the highway. Don't they realize that America's #1 terrorists can strike at anytime and that they and their family could be next? It's important to remember the DUI terrorist looks just like anyone else. That's what makes this terrorist so dangerous. He could be behind the wheel of the next car you see coming toward you at 70 mph. With the average car weighing over three thousand pounds, with the possibility of 15 gallons of gasoline ready to explode and only separated by a few feet, you would think that everyone would want that driver to be sober.

Judge Wants to See DUI Arrests FirstHand

Because of the number of DUI arrests flooding the East Los Angeles Municipal court and all kinds of rumors concerning the arrests, the local and senior judge, Myer B. Marion, a small but tough, no-nonsense judge, contacted the area commander, Captain Dahl, and requested to go on a "ride-a-long" with me so he could observe the DUI apprehensions and arrests firsthand. That meant that I had to leave my motorcycle at the office and take a cruiser. I jumped at the opportunity.

I picked up Judge Marion in the Municipal court parking lot on a Friday just after dark. The judge was about 5 ft. 6 inches tall with a slight build, but he looked even smaller that evening. It was probably because he wasn't wearing a black robe and seated behind his elevated courtroom bench. He was dressed casually and, without personal knowledge of his occupation, could easily pass as any well-meaning citizen going on a ride-a-long. I said, "Are you ready to go your honor?" He said, "Yes, I'm anxious to see how you're making all of these arrests." The judge didn't tell me how long he planned on staying on the ride-a-long but I thought to myself, when you're dealing with DUIs you never know what's going to happen. I was kind of hoping we would get into a pursuit or have a combative DUI so he would experience the real world.

In less than an hour, while patrolling eastbound on Olympic Blvd and after crossing Atlantic Blvd., I spotted a DUI about a half a block ahead of us. Back then the presumed guilt law was a BAC of .15%. That's almost double what it is today and a .15% was considered a borderline DUI. So, most of the DUIs we arrested were around .20% which means they were close to being drunk.

With all of our red lights flashing and a spot light shinning into the DUI's car, I asked the driver to walk over to the sidewalk where I could give him a FST (field sobriety test). Once we got over on the sidewalk, Judge Marion got out of the cruiser and walked over near us so he would have a better view of the field tests. After attempting to walk a straight line, heel to toe, and probably out of frustration of not being able to maintain his balance, the DUI glared at Judge Marion and said, "Who's this little guy? He has no business being here." I explained that he was a civilian ride-a-long. The DUI said, "I know one thing he's not a cop." (In the 1960's the minimum height for a highway patrolman was 5 ft. 8 inches) "He's not big enough." I said, "He just wants to see what's going on." The DUI said, "If he's not a cop, he shouldn't be here. This is none of his business."

I arrested the DUI, cuffed him and put him in the right front passenger seat and transported him to the East Los Angeles Sheriff's jail, which is adjacent to the East Los Angeles Municipal Court. All the way to the station the DUI complained about the ride-a-long being in the cruiser. Once I got a chemical test and completed the booking, I advised the DUI, "You'll be appearing in the East Los Angeles Municipal Court in front of the Honorable Judge Myer B. Marion who was my ride-a-long tonight. He's the little guy sitting over there staring at you."

PART 1: Chapter 3: CHP Commendations for Record DUI Arrests   33

Apparently, Judge Marion was convinced after only seeing one DUI arrest. He said, "Since we're right over here near my car, I think I'll call it a night." I jokingly told the judge, "We're just getting started. Most of the DUIs aren't as nice as the last one." The judge laughed because he knew I deliberately didn't tell the DUI who he was until later.

But the judge often joked in court at my expense so we understood each other. On occasion he would comment in open court, "I can't wait for you to get transferred so I can get back to playing golf again," or "I stay home when Mitchell and Klippness are working." It was all in fun and everyone knew it. I didn't follow-up but I'm sure the DUI plead guilty instead of appearing in front of that little guy who had no business being on a ride-a-long.

Drugged Driver Accident

You don't always have to seek out a DUI, sometimes they come to you. A good example occurred one day after I had just left the East LA Area office. I was on duty traveling eastbound on Olympic Blvd approaching Gerhart Avenue with the green light. Just as I started into the intersection a car made a left turn in front of me and I smashed into the right side. The impact threw me over the front handle bars and I landed on the pavement. I really didn't think I was injured too seriously but it soon became apparent that I had extended my left shoulder and was losing the ability to raise my left arm.

But my immediate concern was the driver that turned in front of me. He stopped in the intersection and remained behind the steering wheel. He was under the influence but not of alcohol. He had been taking drugs and was not really sure where he was. He was booked and I returned to work in about six weeks, just in time to pick up my restored motorcycle.

DUI Slams Pregnant Passenger into Dash

One night in East Los Angeles, I spotted a DUI speeding and weaving on Olympic Blvd at Atlantic Blvd. As soon as he saw my red light and heard the siren, he attempted to evade arrest. Olympic is a four-lane street and traffic was moderate with enough space for the DUI to recklessly cut in and out of traffic. But as we got closer to Los Angeles this was not possible so the DUI drove over the double line facing approaching traffic head-on.

Because I was on a motorcycle I was able to stay with him by using the center double line of the roadway. When we reached Duncan Ave. the DUI left Olympic and took a two-lane side street. But when he got to Ford Blvd there was a stop sign and two cars stopped ahead of him. It was a T-intersection and because of his speed, he had nowhere to go and crashed into the back of a passenger car stopped for the stop sign. At a glance, it appeared that there was a male driver and female passenger in the car that was struck. I stopped my motorcycle behind the suspect's car while keeping my eye on the driver. DUIs sometime turn out to be armed and dangerous. I didn't have to worry about turning the siren off because it automatically stops because it works off of the motion of the rear wheel.

I had hardly put the stand down on the motorcycle and finished advising LA Dispatch of the circumstances when I saw the driver of the car that had been struck by the DUI, jump out of his car and run back to the DUI. Without any hesitation the driver jerked the door open and hit the DUI with a solid right to the jaw. As he drew his fist back, the DUIs body followed and he crumbled on the street by the side of his car. The driver walked directly to me and stuck out both of his hands in a position to be cuffed and said, "Go ahead it was worth it. My wife (passenger) is pregnant and she was thrown up against the dash." I replied, "What do you want me to do?" He said, "I thought you would arrest me for what I did." I said, "What did you do?" An expression of appreciation and relief was present on his face as he returned to his car to check on his wife.

But there's one thing I did get a clear view of and that was the DUI smashing into the back of the driver's stopped car. I have no idea what the DUI did when he got to court because unless an officer gets a subpoena and goes to court, you don't always know the disposition of a case. You only know it was adjudicated. I booked him for felony DUI and that should have gotten him some time.

You could not charge a person with evading arrest back then, it was only a bookable offense. In other words, there was no penalty. For example, if a person ran a red light (a misdemeanor) and then attempted to evade arrest, then you could "lock him up" but he would only be subject to the penalty of running a red light. That is not the law now. Evading arrest is a separate charge as it should have always been.

Angry Russian Doesn't Go Easy

DUIs don't always go easy but you usually only get into a physical altercation with them once. But that was not the case with a big strapping Russian DUI that I observed one day at Whittier Blvd and Gasper Way. After I turned on my red lights for him to stop he made a right-hand turn onto Gasper, which was a secondary street. Whittier Blvd is a well traveled four-lane road in the business district. This turned out to be a blessing in disguise because of what followed.

After approaching the vehicle and observing the driver I thought about asking for a back-up. The driver appeared to be about 6' 3", 250 lb, muscular and rugged. (Of course, that would be profiling and the courts say you can't do that) I got him out of the vehicle and gave him a field sobriety test (FST). He was cooperative and friendly enough until I said, "You will need to turn around and put your hands behind you. You're under arrest for driving under the influence."

He jerked his hand back and said, "I'm not going anywhere." When I reached for his wrist again, he grabbed me and we eventually ended up on the pavement, where we continued wrestling. There were two things that came to mind at that moment. One, I wished that I had called for backup and, two, we were wrestling in the street. I don't know exactly why the fighting Russian finally gave up unless it was because I told him very authoritatively, "I hope I don't have to shoot you." We didn't have Tazars at that time.

A car unit arrived, we cuffed him, and he was transported to jail. His case was adjudicated, hopefully, for DUI and resisting arrest, and I had no plans of ever seeing him again. But that was not to be.

A few months later I was outbound on the Santa Ana Freeway east of Atlantic Blvd when I saw a car make an unsafe turn onto the southbound off-ramp. When I turned my red lights on he pulled off the roadway on to the paved shoulder. He got out of the car as I was getting off of the motorcycle, which is what an officer does not want a suspect to do. Officers want you to stay in the car for various reasons, which will remain confidential. Immediately, I recognized the burly Russian as the one I had wrestled with a couple of months before. In a very angry tone he shouted, "What do you want now?" so he obviously recognized me too. I was hoping he wasn't looking for a rematch.

I told the Russian that he made an unsafe lane change when he cut in front of several cars to reach the off-ramp. He said, "So, what are you going to do? Take me to jail again?" I said, "No, I'm going to write you a citation."

As soon as I finished the sentence, he leaned toward me and spit directly into my face. Instinctively, I turned my head and most of the saliva hit my helmet and visor. My second instinct was to punch him right in the mouth. Of course, that's not consistent with our training manual.

But about this same time another CHP unit pulled up in front of us. The officer just happen to be passing by and thought I might need some backup. Very good timing and judgment on his part.

I now informed my Russian "friend" that he was under arrest for "simple assault" and that he was going to jail again and for him to put his hands behind him. We had a slight struggle but there were two of us so it didn't last long. As he was being put in the patrol car he angrily said, "The next time I see you, I'm going to take care of you. And I know where to find you because I know this is the area where you work."

From the time I was a small child, I've always subscribed to the policy that "the best defense is an offense." So, I informed my Russian "friend" that he "had just signed his own death warrant." He looked a little puzzled through his angry glare and muttered "What uh you mean I signed by death warrant?" I tried to speak to him as if I was a doctor telling a patient for the first time that he had a fatal disease.

"You just said you were going to take care of me the next time you saw me. So, the next time I see you I'm going to take care of you first. In other words, you better make sure I never see you again."

I stepped back from the window as the patrol car was driven away. He turned his head around and stared at me until the CHP car was of out of sight. I knew he was dangerous and I couldn't help wondering what our next encounter would be like.

The Russian was so mean and combative that most of the Deputy Sheriff's knew him, especially the jail personnel. About four months later I was at the East LA County Jail booking a DUI when one of the deputies I knew asked me if I was aware of what happened to the Russian. I told him no and that I hadn't seen him since the last booking.

The deputy said, "And you won't either. He was in a bar on Whittier Blvd and got in an argument with the guy setting on the stool next to him. It got pretty heated and the Russian left. He went home and got a loaded revolver and came back and shot the guy on the stool in the head, killing him instantly. The problem is, he shot the wrong person. The guy he was arguing with had left and the guy he killed just happened to take that empty stool. We got him for murder and he has a prior so he'll be gone for awhile."

Commendation for No Accidents

On April 9, 1964, I was commended again by the Department but this time for not having a lost-time occupational injury accident for the year. "By exercising good judgment and taking those actions which enabled you to avoid personal injury accidents, you have contributed substantially to the efforts of the California Highway Patrol to maintain a high level of occupational safety. In so doing, you have also served the interests of the people of the State of California, who in the final analysis pay the costs of occupational injuries."

That last sentence really caught my attention. What better way to serve the interests of the people of the State of California than by arresting DUIs? I think I received this safety commendation because of the high risk of DUI enforcement and the exposure that was sure to lead to a crash now and then, like the drugged driver.

Dynamite Comes in Small Packages

On September 18, 1965, my partner at the time, Larry Blood, and I were at the scene of a DUI traffic accident on Eastern Ave. near the San Bernardino Freeway. It was 3:25 am and we had flares out in the roadway diverting traffic around the damaged vehicles as well as our cruiser. We had a tow truck coming to the scene and the DUI was in custody. The injured had already been removed by ambulance. About 20 neighbors and other sightseers were present at the scene.

We first observed headlights from a speeding vehicle traveling northbound on Eastern Ave. approaching directly toward us. Eastern Ave. is a 35 mph zone and the red flares would be visible for blocks at that time in the morning. The red 1956 Chevrolet sedan speed was estimated at 65-70 mph and only decelerated at the last minute, stopping abruptly in the open lane near where we were signaling with our flash lights for the driver to stop.

The driver was identified as, Yolanda Castillon, 21. Linda Sandoval, 20, was a passenger in the right front seat. Another passenger, Ralph Alcocer, 20, was seated in the back. Castillon was asked for her drivers license and advised she was going to be cited for speeding. In a raised voice, she said, "You don't know who I am. My father will take care of you. Be sure and put your name and ID number on there (citation)." Both passengers began laughing and remarking, "Wait till you find out who her father is. You'll be sorry." When I went around to the front of the vehicle to copy the license plate number, Sandoval, the passenger, leaned over to the drivers side and started sounding the horn.

I asked Sandoval to stop honking the horn but she refused so I walked around to her window and asked her to roll it down. She looked straight ahead with a smirk. I opened the car door and told Sandoval if she continued to sound the horn that she was also going to receive a citation. She laughed and said, "Go ahead and write me. My dad will take care of it." As I was shutting her door and returning to the driver's side, she shouted, "We'll get you for police brutality. You had no business opening my door. Look! I'm going to hit the horn again" while holding her hand about 2 inches above the horn rim. The driver Castillon then told Sandoval to stop "acting that way. I'm the one getting the ticket, not you. I'll take care of him in court."

Everything seemed to be settling down as I was standing near the driver's door. The window was down and the driver was just looking straight ahead. Suddenly, she reached through the window and grabbed her drivers license from the citation book. She then placed her hands, with the drivers license, in her lap. She was asked to give the drivers license back. Castillon said, "Oh! no. I won't" as she laughed. When I asked her a second time, she threw the drivers license on the floorboard and said, "If you want it then get it yourself."

I then informed Castillon that she was under arrest for interfering and to step from the car. She made no comment but held the door and refused to get out. I forced the door open and took her by the arm and she stepped out. I reached down and retrieved her drivers license. I told her to step back to the patrol car and she responded, "You can't do anything to me so keep your dirty hands off of me."

I took Castillon by her left arm to lead her to the police car while reminding her that she was under arrest. She jerked back and again shouted, "I'm not going anywhere. Keep your dirty hands off of me. Do you hear?"

At this point I figured there was only going to be more problems because of her belligerent attitude. She also seemed to be "playing" to the people who had gathered at the scene. So I turned my head and called for Officer Blood to come and assist. As I turned my head back, I saw her fist coming towards my jaw with all of the power she could muster from her small 5' 5", 130 lb frame.

Being 6', 185 lbs, myself, that was the last thing I was suspecting. She hit me so hard that my uniform bow tie flew off. I was momentarily stunned and my jaw was bleeding from a small laceration, possibly caused by a ring she was wearing. I spontaneously, and with force, hit Castillon in the jaw with my fist and she crumbled to the pavement.

She then started crying and shouting, "He hit me. Oh! I'm hurt." She refused to walk to the Patrol car so Sergeant John Tyler, who had responded to the scene, picked her up and carried her. She was taken to Sybil Brand Institute where she was booked for 836.3, 241 PC (Assaulting a police officer during the performance of his duties—a felony), Resisting, delaying or obstructing a public officer in the discharge of their duties—a misdemeanor) and 22350 CVC (Excessive speed—65 mph in a 35 mph zone).

Castillon wasn't injured. And I really did not feel that I was injured although the doctors report read: "Contusion left lower jaw with superficial "V" laceration with musculo-ligamentum sprain. Left side of jaw swollen. Four x-rays were taken of jaw to determine possible fracture. Negative results."

I didn't take any time off but I did learn a lesson. Don't ever assume that a 5'5", 130 lb female won't hit you.

Nine years later, I was a Lieutenant assigned to Headquarters in Sacramento when I received a phone call from the Los Angeles County Sheriffs. The Deputy on the other end said, "Do you remember arresting a young lady by the name of Castillon when you were working East Los Angeles?" I told him that I could not "place the name." He said, "Well, you should be able to remember her. She hit you in the jaw during the arrest." I said, "That I remember."

The Deputy said, "Well, here's the story. She's married now and her husband wants to be a Deputy Sheriff. He's passed all of the tests except his background check. What would you like for us to do? Husbands and wives are package deals when it comes to law enforcement, you know that." I had no hesitation in telling the Deputy that if that's all that's holding him up from being hired, I have no objection to his being hired." It's not like I didn't do some foolish things when I was young but it didn't include assaulting a police officer.

Chapter 4
California Legislators Reject Tougher DUI Law

Klippness and I didn't just arrest DUIs exclusively even though that was our primary concern. For example, we received another commendation on July 17, 1965, that was not related to DUI:

"On June 12, 1965 at 2:15 am, you and your assigned partner demonstrated outstanding abilities as a motor officer in apprehending an auto theft suspect.

"The pursuit which followed the initial observation of a minor traffic violation by the suspect required special attention and skills. You were successful in consummating the arrest without accident or injury to yourself or your partner although the suspect lost control of his vehicle and caused considerable damage to the property of others.

"As your supervisor, I have noticed your enthusiasm and the professional techniques you use in accomplishing your daily duties. Your supervisors appreciate your continuing devotion to duty."

Signed by Captain R.E. Teuber and initiated by Sergeant Emil Heringer. Both were outstanding supervisors.

But there was a bit more to the arrest than the details in the commendation—and it did include an accident.

We were chasing the stolen car when the driver lost control, jumping a curb in a residential neighborhood. The car took out about 30 feet of a white picket fence leading up to the front porch. I stopped my motorcycle and was getting off when the suspect threw the car in reverse, struck my CHP motorcycle, knocked me onto the lawn and dragged the damaged motorcycle about 20 feet.

The suspect took off again with Klippness in pursuit. Other units were responding but hadn't gotten there yet. My motorcycle was laying in the street, but the radio was still blaring. I could hear Klippness radioing his position and suddenly realized that the pursuit was now headed back to my location.

I looked up and at first all I could see were headlights with red lights behind them. Then came the roar of the stolen car and the motorcycle siren. I had a few seconds to make a decision. I drew my 38 revolver and shot three holes in the car as it passed by. I was trying to hit a tire and end the chase. But even though I didn't hit the tires, the bullet holes proved to be significant.

The suspect got away but about two hours later a Sheriff spotted the car with the bullet holes in it and made the arrest. In the meantime, we gave the traffic accident investigators our statements of what happened and left the scene. Officers don't investigate their own accidents for obvious reasons and, after receiving the commendation, I don't think an accident report was ever made. We went back on patrol but our first stop was at the Sheriffs jail to inform the auto thief that he was going to be charged with more than auto theft. He never expressed any concern about the damage he had caused or apologized for deliberately running into the motorcycle with me on it.

California Legislators Reject Tougher DUI Law

While it wasn't surprising that a car thief never apologized for trying to run me over, it was surprising that the state legislative leaders, elected to protect California citizens, ignored the clear and present danger that DUIs presented.

I had always assumed that legislative representatives were doing everything possible to protect the general public; especially, working toward the day when we wouldn't have anymore DUI deaths and injuries. Being

PART 1: *Chapter 4:* California Legislators Reject Tougher DUI Law 43

inexperienced in dealing with the California Legislature in 1965, I believed that all we had to do was to prove to them that a law would correct a problem and it would be passed.

In that spirit, I had sent the following letter to a committee called Action for Responsible Driving in December 1964:

> *Dear Sir:*
>
> *It makes me extremely happy to know that there are some responsible people who are concerned with this slaughter on the highways. It takes this kind of interest and help before we can make any depreciable decrease in accidents statewide.*
>
> *I have been a law enforcement officer for more than 12 years. Seven of those years I have spent with the Highway Patrol. I started arresting drinking drivers from the very start because I soon realized the extreme hazards caused by this particular violation. This does not mean that all the other violations are not dangerous, but they cannot be compared with the drinking driver. More concentration should be exerted for this violation alone.*
>
> *I will do everything within my power to put a stop to this legalized murder. I have actively participated in approximately one thousand "drinking driver" arrests. From my experiences and studies I make the following suggestions:*
>
> *First and most important is the Legislature passing the "Implied Consent" law which the State of Connecticut passed in 1963, and has proven very successful. I'm sure Gov. Dempsey would furnish some excellent material and advise on this matter.*
>
> *Produce modern training films for law enforcement officers on how to detect the driver "under the influence" of intoxicating liquor.*
>
> *Notice I said 'under the influence' and not 'intoxicated' or 'drunk'. Of the few training films I have knowledge that are available today, they are for the apprehension of drunk drivers.*

Anybody can spot a drunk driver. This does not necessitate any special training. Most drinkers fall in the blood range of .10% to .20%. This is the area in which we must concentrate. Ninety percent of your law enforcement officers cannot recognize a driver under the influence.

We need films for schools and television to make the public aware.

The apathy and ignorance by the majority of the public is staggering. Most people and especiallly the jurors take the attitude of "there but for the Grace of God goes I." Although this is true, it is not the proper approach. They must be educated to realize that we must either enforce this crime against everybody or not enforce it at all. Drinking is a universal problem that is socially accepted. The drinking problem strikes every walk of life including police officers, judges, legislators, etc. This is one reason why it is not enforced enough. It seems that many of those arrested know somebody in the judicial system and they are usually their "drinking buddy" when they are not enforcing the law. There is constant pressure from without and sometimes within to "get him off."

Most drinkers overestimate their drinking ability and are not even aware that they are under the influence, especially when their minds become confused after the first drink.

It is my opinion that too many organizations have failed in the past because they attempted to cover too much in their efforts to help the law enforcement agencies in this enormous task of safety on the highways.

It would be more effective if one problem at a time was undertaken. Otherwise, it is too complicated and interest is soon lost. Right now your number one killer anywhere is the drinking driver. If your organization would concentrate on this one problem, maybe something could be done. There would be 15,000 fewer funerals every year and 50,000 less seriously injured victims.

> *In our East Los Angeles area we have reduced accidents over 8% compared with other areas in the state. This was done by the increased enforcement against drinking drivers and the cooperation of the District Attorney's office and judges.*
>
> *I wish you all the success possible and if in any way I can be of assistance, feel free to contact me.*
>
> Bob Mitchell
California Highway Patrol
East Los Angeles Area

In February 1965, a representative from Action For Responsible Driving, based in Menlo Park (in the San Francisco area), contacted me for help in getting two DUI laws passed. The bills were going to be heard before the Assembly Ways and Means Committee in Sacramento a week or so later.

Senator Randolph Collier had authored Senate Bills 41 and 42, that would reduce the presumptive limits and implied consent level of .15% to .10%. It had already passed the Senate and was now before the Assembly, where it faced fierce opposition from Assemblymen Robert Crown, N.C. Petris, of Oakland, and Anthony C. Beilenson, of Beverly Hills.

Klippness and I were working the evening shift in East Los Angeles. We still had the responsibilities of investigating traffic accidents, writing tickets and performing other duties but our primary responsibility was to arrest DUIs. I was a motorcycle officer the entire time I was assigned to East Los Angeles and primarily worked the late evening shift where Klippness and I established a record number of DUI arrests. Even today, no one has come close to the number of arrests we made.

The Action for Responsible Driving, Chaired by A.J. Penico, urged me to meet them in Sacramento and testify on behalf of the bill. I had already qualified in the California courts as an expert witness in DUI enforcement and I knew firsthand from the traffic accidents we were working and arrests we were making that the presumed level of Blood Alcohol Concentration (BAC) of .15% was far too high. Even the .10% that the new law would establish was too high, but at least it was a step in the right direction.

So, on April 20, 1965, at my own expense and using vacation time, my wife and three small children drove 450 miles from Los Angeles to the Capital in Sacramento to testify before the Assembly Ways and Means Committee Hearing. CHP Commissioner Bradford Crittenden, an outstanding administrator, knew the importance of DUI enforcement and was there in case he was given a chance to lend his support to the pending legislation.

There was no doubt in my mind that the bills would pass because it was the right thing to do and I trusted the legislators to make the right decision. Four years earlier, several other states had adopted the .10% level based upon numerous studies and findings from controlled tests over a 15-year period. Why would anyone with an ounce of intelligence vote against it? Well, I was about to find out.

Neither the Commissioner nor I was even given an opportunity to testify and those who were called (primarily committee members) had limited knowledge of DUI. They were soundly intimidated by the Committee members who appeared to have already made up their minds. I got the distinct impression that some of the Assemblymen were not all that enthused about placing any tighter restrictions on driving under the influence and had no intention of passing any legislation that would make it more difficult to avoid prosecution.

In some cases, I think they sincerely thought that it was safe to drive with a BAC of .14% or below. Under the .15% law if a person was arrested for DUI and blew a .14 or below, they would stand a good change of getting it dismissed—especially if that person was a legislator. Passage of Senate Bills 41 and 42 would not have prevented this completely, but it would have made it much more difficult to dismiss cases in which drivers were clearly under the influence of alcohol.

My family and I drove back to Southern California satisfied that we had done our best and realizing that we had learned a valuable lesson about politics.

After the Senate Judiciary Committee Hearing and before the decision had been made to pass or defeat the bill, I sent the following letter to Senator Thomas M. Rees who was on the Committee urging him to pass the bills.

PART 1: Chapter 4: California Legislators Reject Tougher DUI Law

May 10, 1965

Dear Senator,

In regards to SB 42 (Implied Consent) introduced by Senator Randolph Collier.

I made a special trip to Sacramento and attended the Senate Judiciary Committee Hearing on April 20, 1965. I did this at my own expense because I am aware of the importance of the passage of the bill.

My wife and children were impressed, as I was, with the thoroughness with which each bill is discussed to protect our (the public) rights. We left there glad to know that the laws of our state were in such capable hands. This is with the exception of Senator O'Sullivan. We were discussing his tactics and attitude when we got back and it was brought to our attention that he was the one who introduced a bill to give himself a $19,000.00 a year raise while he refuses to come to the aid of more than 18,000 innocent drunk driving victims each year. Those 18,000 that were killed last year can't be present nor will the 18,000 that will be killed this year. However, there are such groups as the Action For Responsible Driving and numerous others that are aware of this problem. Like Mr. Robert Malkin of Vancouver, B.C. Or the East Los Angeles attorney who now refuses to defend drunk drivers because he was crippled by one on vacation two years ago. I know from first-hand knowledge of the danger that exists because I have arrested more drunk drivers than anyone in the state. I believe Senators like O'Sullivan, Miller and Short are judging this on a personal basis and not on the merits of whether it is a good or a bad law.

The two main points that were brought out in your hearing last Thursday were (1) fear of self-incrimination and (2) fear of police indiscriminately demanding blood tests.

(1) For a moment put yourself in the law enforcement officers shoes. Under the present laws of our state you stop a person you suspect of drunk driving. He refuses to make any statements or

take any physical tests. In fact he refuses to get out of his car. He is so obviously drunk that you arrest him anyway. Now without SB 42 he can refuse to take a chemical test and naturally he does. So what do you have as far as evidence to prove your case in court? .... NOTHING.

<u>This is protecting the guilty.</u> On the other hand if a person was innocent he would gladly answer questions or take field sobriety tests. If he was arrested he would <u>demand</u> a chemical test. I ask you, are we not carrying this self-incrimination to such an extreme that we are leaving the innocent people unprotected?

(2) As you gentlemen already know, under our present laws we can demand and forceably take a blood sample (case law) from anyone who is arrested for driving under the influence. Under the able leadership of Commissioner Bradford M. Crittenden we do not exercise this authority as a departmental procedure unless it is an extremely aggravated case such as manslaughter. The point is this! If in the past we have had this authority and we have not abused it then why would we abuse it in the future?

We in law enforcement represent the people the same as you. Our first concern is protecting the innocent person and then prosecuting the guilty if necessary. If you as lawmakers can not trust the departments to enforce the laws fairly and honestly then how can you properly perform your job?

I urge you to pass SB 42 so we will be able to curb this senseless slaughter on the highways. This is a fair and just bill. If you don't pass it, then the men who replace you will. It cannot be defeated, it can only be delayed. In the meantime whose family will be killed by these selfish drunk drivers? Will it be yours or will it be mine?

I am willing to make another trip to your hearing if I can be of any assistance in bringing out the importance of this bill becoming law.

Sincerely,
Bob Mitchell

PART 1: Chapter 4:   California Legislators Reject Tougher DUI Law   49

I sent a similar letter to all of the members of the Committee. On June 24, 1965, I received the following "form" letter from Senator Thomas Rees.

> *Dear Friend:*
>
> *Thank you for your letter concerning drunk driving bills which were pending before the legislature this session.*
>
> *Senator Collier's bills were defeated on the floor of the Senate about a month ago and attempts to revive the legislation failed. I personally favor stronger measures to curb drunk driving, but the Senate agreed that establishing the irrefutable presumption set forth in these bills was a dangerous precedent.*
>
> *Please excuse my replying to your correspondence in this way, but I am sure you understand that because of the tremendous volume of mail on this I am unable to answer each letter individually.*
>
> *Sincerely yours,*
Thomas M. Rees

I don't remember all of the reasons they used for not passing the bill but the main one was the level of .15% was low enough and it was safe to drive at a level below that. Of course, that reasoning was probably based upon their own personal experience at driving at that level as opposed to scientific evidence.

As we know now, the presumptive guilt level went to .10% in 1969 and then to the present .08% in 1989. I will not question their sincerity in "killing" those bills but I do know that they will have to live with the fact that innocent people died and thousands more were crippled because of their decision. Since that time (until the time of writing this book) Candy Lightner's daughter (founder of Mothers Against Drunk Drivers) and over 64,000 other lives have been lost to America's Number 1 Terrorist—the drunk driver. And that is just California. How many of these innocent people would be alive today if a handful of Senators in 1965 had done the right thing?

There are legislators who do the right thing. Assemblyman Mike Feuer, Los Angeles, introduced Assembly Bill 645 that became law January 1, 2008. The bill barely made the news, less than one inch print on a back page of the Sacramento Bee, but it will be very significant in reducing DUIs.

AB 645, "Bars motorists from getting drunken driving, hit-and-run or reckless driving violations dismissed by attending traffic school." This will put more DUIs in jail and help eliminate the "let's make a deal" loopholes that have been flooding our judicial system for decades.

Consider this real-life example.

One early morning hour in the late '60s in the Hollywood area we arrested a well-known singer and TV personality for DUI. He had a BAC of .17% and was booked into the Los Angeles Police jail in Van Nuys. I made an extra copy of his arrest report for my files. He pled guilty and that was it. It never made the news but a lot of celebrity arrests don't make the news. And there's nothing wrong with that as long as there are no deals made behind closed doors. It's hard to play "Let's make a Deal" if the news media is covering the arrest.

A few years later, the singer was stopped for DUI in San Diego and that did make the news. The newspaper reported that he was asked if he had ever been arrested for DUI and he said "No." But, of course, he had been arrested for DUI. Or was his arrest in Van Nuys reduced to "reckless driving" and then later removed by his "attending" a traffic school? Or did his attorneys plead him to DUI with the understanding that he would attend traffic school and have it dismissed?

One thing is clear. With a prior DUI arrest, the singer would have had to spend a few days in jail. This type of maneuvering and deal-making has been going on for years and is a way of circumventing the mandatory jail sentence for prominent individuals who have the money "to swing the deal."

The purpose for arresting and punishing a DUI is to change the DUI's behavior pattern so he or she won't do it again and possibly kill someone. Striking prior arrests, reducing charges and doing public service has not proven effective in reaching this objective.

I would suggest the courts do away with the "public service" and require the DUIs to attend a half dozen funerals where a person has been killed by a DUI.

Even AB 645 did not go far enough. The most prominent and worst deal for the public is when a DUI charge is reduced to "reckless driving." It could be compared to someone being arrested for "armed robbery," but the court letting him plead to "brandishing a weapon."

When it comes to driving under the influence we have a problem with our judiciary system.

Chapter 5
DUI Blamed for Watts Riot

Most people are probably not aware that a DUI arrest was only a pretext for the Watt's Riots in August of 1965. It was not the cause.

In their final report, the Los Angeles County Human Relations Commission concluded that there was "no reliable evidence of outside leadership or pre-established plans for the rioting." But then they later added,

"This is not to say that there was no agitation or promotion of the rioting by local groups or gangs which exist in pockets throughout the south central area. The sudden appearance of Molotov cocktails in quantity and unexplained movement of men in cars through the areas of great destruction support the conclusion that there was organization and planning after the riots commenced."

In other words the Commission was saying it was the DUI arrest that started the Watts Riot.

The perpetrators were actually a militant group that was never officially identified. They had anxiously been waiting for an excuse to provoke a riot. Law enforcement agencies had information that Black Muslims working out of a local mosque were agitating the community and preparing for a major uprising in the area. They were secretly bringing weapons into the area and planning an all out "war" against "the white oppressors." So, when white officers came into their "domain" and attempted to arrest a black man on their soil, the "war" was on.

About a month before the riot, all of the CHP Areas in Southern California were informed that a riot was being planned in Watts. Contingency plans were made and all uniformed officers were advised to carry their riot gear with them so that they would be able to respond without delay when the riot started. Motor officers were the exception because of the need to take their motorcycles to the Area office, pair up and respond in a cruiser. An officer on a motorcycle would not last long in a major riot. We had already received riot training so we were ready to go.

We went on doing our job as usual while waiting for a riot "that wasn't planned" to start in Watts. We were told the riot was inevitable.

On Wednesday, August 11, 1965, CHP Officer Minikus, South Los Angeles Area, was informed by a truck driver, a black man, that a 1955 Buick was being driven erratically northbound on Avalon Blvd near El Segundo. Officer Minikus pursued the speeding car and stopped it at 116th Place. The DUI driver, Marquette Frye, was given a field sobriety test and advised he was being arrested for DUI.

When a crowd started gathering, the driver changed from cooperative to rebellious. The Commission report reveals that less than 30 minutes after Frye was stopped there were more than 1000 persons in the crowd. What a coincidence.

Before it was over CHP Officers Minikus, Bob Lewis, Wayne Wilson, and Veale Fondville, who had responded to Minikus' "11-99" (Officer needs help), made the arrest and fought their way out. They conducted themselves bravely and professionally. If an officer is on an enforcement stop and a hostile crowd starts gathering, then he gets the arrestee into the cruiser and out of the area as quickly as possible. In this case that was not possible. The officers were fortunate to get out with their lives. If you want to read an in-depth story about the Watts Riots an excellent book is "Rivers of Blood, Years of Darkness" by Robert Conot.

As soon as the riot started, all CHP Areas and other law enforcement agencies were alerted to respond. We knew this wasn't just an ordinary riot but that it was going to go "big time."

Klippness and I had just finished our shift when we were notified the "unforeseeable" riot had started.

PART 1: *Chapter 5:* DUI Blamed for Watts Riot 55

We went to the office where we were briefed by Sergeant Tyler, assigned four to a cruiser and headed for 113th St. and Avalon. This was only a few blocks from where the DUI arrest was made.

All units were instructed to take a particular route into the riot area. The riot was spreading and innocent people who were not yet aware of what was going on and just happened to be passing through the area, were being dragged out of their cars and beaten. The rioters would accumulate at an intersection and when a car driven by a white person stopped for a red light, he would be surrounded, dragged out of his car and beaten. Some were beaten almost to death—and they were not all white. If a black person did not support the uprising, he was also attacked. More than 50 cars were set afire, including two fire trucks.

En route southbound on the Harbor Freeway we heard a CHP unit advising Dispatch that a large number of Hells Angels on motorcycles were southbound ahead of us. They asked dispatch to check with Division Headquarters to find out if they wanted the CHP units in the area to take any kind of action. We didn't know exactly what the Hells Angels were doing but we did know they were headed toward the rioting. We didn't want them joining in with the rioters and we didn't want them trying to help us. We had enough concerns already without bringing the Hells Angels into the mix.

Only minutes later, Dispatch advised all units that the large number of motorcycles were actually actors and that one of the movie studios was in the process of making a movie. They further advised that the motorcycles would be leaving the freeway at the next off-ramp and shooting the film at another location. One can only imagine what would have happened if the CHP hadn't notified the filmmakers and they had strayed into Watts.

We arrived at the command post on Avalon Blvd along with other units coming in from surrounding areas. The rioters were now looting businesses and setting buildings on fire. No sirens were being used for very good reasons. There were so many of us it would have been chaotic and served no purpose. Furthermore, we would have alerted the rioters that we were coming and they would be waiting for us with bricks and rocks.

Immediately, upon arriving at the command post, which was also a roadblock, a black gentleman approached us in a pickup truck. He was not permitted to drive any closer than 50 ft. So he got out and walked that distance at the peril of his own life to report rioters looting a surplus store of shot guns. After telling us this valuable information, the brave man ran back to his truck—only to have his truck peppered with stones from rioters as he raced away.

The supervisor-in-charge asked for volunteers to respond to the surplus store. About 20 LAPD officers and 15 CHP officers (including me) volunteered. You would think that I would have known better than to have volunteered, having served in the Navy. They issued each of us a shotgun if we wanted one and we went on foot as a single unit.

It was getting dark and we saw fewer and fewer cars on the roadway, except for LAPD units and they were automatic targets for the rioters who were throwing anything they could get their hands on if they couldn't find a brick or rock.

Occasionally a car other than a police unit would stray onto the roadway. When that happened, police quickly swarmed the car to search it for weapons, which were being transported into the area. If a car ignored their signals to stop, they would open fire in an attempt to stop them.

Our CHP foot unit arrived in front of the hardware store and, as reported, the rioters were jumping out of the front window that they had smashed earlier, carrying all kinds of items. I didn't see any weapons, especially shotguns, in their hands. As soon as we arrived and before I had time to get involved, I heard a car coming in our direction at a high rate of speed. It appeared to slow near some LAPD officers that were just north of us and then suddenly accelerated again. About this time I heard five shots ring out. I know they were being fired at the white, 55-56 Chevrolet because it looked like every window blew out of the car at the same time. The car did not stop and the shooting continued.

Suddenly, I felt a dull pain and burning sensation in my right thigh. I realized that I had been hit but I didn't want to believe it. I said to myself, this can't be, I've got a softball tournament coming up. But when I took a step, my leg gave way and I fell to the pavement. Someone shouted, "He's been shot" and within seconds, an LAPD unit pulled up and two LAPD officers picked me up and pushed me into the police unit. Then we sped off into the night.

The LAPD officer turned on his headlights and pushed down on the gas pedal as rocks and objects hit the side of the patrol car. Fortunately none hit the glass.

By now, I had noticed that there wasn't a hole in my uniform and there wasn't any blood. There was an indentation mark and my leg was still numb so I realized that it was a ricochet. We had now cleared the riot area and were going code three but I told the LAPD officers they could slow down because the injury wasn't serious. They did reduce their speed only slightly and we soon arrived at Los Angeles Central Receiving Hospital around midnight. Dr. Mogge examined the injury and reported "contusion and superficial laceration of the right thigh." He recommended that I go off-duty and I was transferred to a CHP unit and taken home.

Officers' wives are always very concerned when they see their husbands coming home in a police cruiser especially when he normally arrives by motorcycle. That usually means something serious has happened. It was about one o'clock in the morning when the officer was helping me out of the patrol car and to the front door. He rang the doorbell and Laura answered the door half asleep. She said, "What happened?"

And I said, "I got shot while I was at the Watts riot and . . ." She cut me off and said, "Tell me about it in the morning, I want to get back to bed." The CHP officer with a surprised look on his face awkwardly said, "Well, it looks like you're in good hands, so I'm going to take off."

A lot of people would be surprised at Laura's reaction but I wasn't. I thought it was funny and I still laugh thinking about it. In a movie the wife would give her husband a big hug and say something like, "Oh! Honey, are you OK? What happened?" But that's not the real world. The next day, after Laura had had a good nights sleep she said, "I knew you were all right by looking at you so why did I need to know what happened then?" Made sense to me.

I wasn't expected to return to work right away but I knew they needed everyone available. I phoned the office the next day and asked them if they needed me. Captain Dahl said he had a special detail he would like me to work at Division Headquarters near the Hollywood Freeway. The riot was now getting out of control. California Lieutenant Governor Glenn Anderson who was acting Governor in Governor Edmund "Pat" Brown's absence (he was in Greece) finally committed the California National Guard to the rioting. Before it was over 13,900 guardsmen were involved.

Martial Law was eventually declared and the curfew was set at 8 pm in a 46.5 square-mile area. That meant if a person was seen after 8 pm outside of his house in that area he could very easily be shot. In the meantime, I and another CHP officer were stationed on top of the CHP Division Headquarters building with a portable spot light and a shot gun and with orders to make sure that no rioters gained entrance to the building.

After six days of rioting, the most devastating racial disturbance in the United States in decades, was finally ended and peace was restored, but at a tremendous cost. There were 34 persons killed and 1,032 injured, including 90 LAPD officers, 136 firemen, 10 national guardsmen, 773 civilians—and, of course, one CHP officer. Of the 34 killed, one was a fireman, one was a deputy sheriff, and one a Long Beach policeman. Loss of property was estimated at more than $40 million.

Are there really thousands of people who would riot and be responsible for 34 deaths and $40 million in damages just because they were upset over a DUI being arrested? I don't think so.

Nevertheless, there are things to be learned from the Watts Riots:

- (1) You can't rely on a segment of society to always act rational under certain conditions. Riots are one of the most dangerous situations an officer can find himself. Domestic disputes rank a close second. In both cases, they are highly emotional situations (meaning you can get killed).

- (2) Some individuals do not support DUIs being arrested. We're talking about people in all walks of life and at all levels. DUI crashes are just another unfortunate "accident" to them.

- (3) There needs to be an attitude change by the general public toward removing America's # One terrorist from the roadways. Considering all of the deaths and damage done by the Watts rioters, that's only a "beep" on the radar screen compared to the damage the DUI does every year.

Court trial for Seventh-Day Adventist "Tea Totaler"

After the riot concluded, Klippness and I went back to arresting DUIs. Klippness and I had a 96% conviction rate on DUI arrests. And that included cases where a defendant would try anything to be acquitted.

Our arrest of Mr. Anderson was just routine but when we went to court a few weeks later it was anything but routine.

The DUI asked for a trial by jury and his attorney was anxious to put him on the stand. Not only were they going to win the case, they were going to attempt to embarrass and discredit us.

After I had testified concerning the details of Anderson's arrest, which included that he had a "strong odor of alcohol about him as well as a slurred speech" the defendant took the stand.

His attorney asked him, "How much did you have to drink that night?"

He replied, "Nothing. I don't drink. I'm a teetotaler because I don't believe in drinking liquor." "Why's that?" he was asked. Anderson told the court that he was a longstanding Deacon in the Seventh-Day Adventist Church and it was against their church doctrine. He also appeared indignant that anyone would accuse him of DUI. After the subject stepped down from the witness chair, Deputy District Attorney Vince Bugliosi asked Judge Marion for a continuance until after lunch, which was granted.

Bugliosi told us, "I've got to make a phone call, I'll see you after lunch."

When East Los Angeles Municipal Court reconvened and the jury was seated, Bugliosi called his first witness of the afternoon who was the Pastor of the Seventh-Day Adventist Church where Anderson said he was a deacon "of long standing." The Pastor testified that he had been the pastor of the church in question for over 20 years and, to his knowledge he had never seen Anderson before today and that he was not a deacon. The pastor said, "I brought the church records with me, if you would like to see them."

Needless to say, Anderson was found guilty.

DUI and Polio No Joking Matter

Another case that was more personal occurred about a month later. This was also a trial by jury and the subject had refused to take a chemical test, which should have resulted in a 6-month suspension of his driver's license. That suspension would stand even if he was found not guilty. We were wondering what his defense was going to be but it didn't take long to find out.

He took the stand after Kippness and I both had testified. One of the things we testified to was how poorly he performed the field sobriety tests and that included walking a straight line.

He told the jury, "I admit that I had a few drinks that night but I certainly wasn't under the influence." He continued, "The reason they booked me was because I did so poorly on walking a line and trying to stand on one foot. I told them that I had had polio and couldn't do it."

His lawyer asked, "What did the Officers say when you told them that?" The subject looked directly at the jury and said, "They began to make fun of me. They joked about me having polio." The jurors quickly glanced at Klippness and me. The Deputy DA turned to me and said in a very concerned tone of voice, "Did you do that?" I assured him we didn't and asked him to put me back on the stand.

After taking the stand and being seated, the Deputy DA said, "Officer Mitchell you heard the testimony of the defendant whereby he testified that you and your partner made fun of the fact he had polio? Is that true?"

I replied, "No, that never happened and for a very good reason."

The Deputy DA asked, "And what is that reason?"

I said, "When my daughter was two years old, she contracted polio. She's 13 now. I would never joke about that or any other physical impairment a person may have nor would Officer Klippness."

Again, the jury was out for only a very short time before finding the defendant guilty. Without a chemical test all the subject had to do was get sympathy from the jury and he was home free. To me, he was living proof that some people have no conscience.

DUI Defendant Reported Killed in An Accident

One morning, in response to a subpoena, I arrived at the court and went directly to the trial calendar posted outside of the court room to find out when the case was going to be heard. I looked up the defendant, but to my surprise, the disposition read, "Dismissed."

I immediately went to the District Attorney's office and found one of the Deputy DAs. Most cases were not dismissed without first conversing with the arresting officer. Although that is not the case in every District Attorney's office. I asked the Deputy DA why the case had been dismissed.

He said, "We had to dismiss it, Bob. The defendant was killed in an automobile accident in San Jose, California, a couple of nights ago." Smiling, he said, "It would be kind of hard to try the case, don't you think?"

I asked him where he got the information and he said the defendant's attorney had notified the court.

He said, "Unless you have another case, you're free to go home."

I went around to the Court Clerk's office and borrowed her phone. I called the San Jose CHP and asked them if they had had a fatal accident a couple of nights before and gave them the defendant's name. After searching the records, they advised that they had not had a fatal accident recently and no one by that name had been killed in an automobile accident in their area.

I went back to the Deputy DA and told him he had been had. That the defendant was alive and well.

Of course, the Deputy DA wasn't smiling then and he headed straight for the judge's chamber to give him the news. A bench warrant was issued for the defendant's arrest and his lawyer, who was still at the court, was having to do a lot of explaining.

He told Judge Marion that "someone" had called him and given him that information. As I was leaving to go home, I thought to myself that it was probably a relative of the defendant who called him or maybe it was the defendant himself. I hope the DA's office learned a lesson.

Beware of the Smiling Juror

We had another case at about that same time in the East Los Angeles Municipal Court that appeared routine except for one very attractive, smiling juror.

My partner and I were seated next to the Deputy DA at the first table next to the jury. The defendant and his attorney were seated at the other end. During the entire trial, one of the jurist, a fairly attractive female, kept smiling at me. This went on during the entire trial.

I finally turned to Klippness and mentioned what was happening.

He said, "Yeah! I noticed the same thing. Do you know her?"

I told him that I didn't recognize her but that I may have seen her somewhere before. She took one last glance in my direction before she and the rest of the jurors left to deliberate.

We and the prosecution had no doubt about the jury coming in with a guilty verdict because we had a very strong case. And with our friendly juror #7 we knew we would at least have a hung jury.

Well, the jury came back in a couple of hours and the friendly female had even a wider smile on her face when the jury foreman announced the unanimous "Not Guilty" verdict.

The Deputy DA promised that he would talk to the jury and let us know what happened. We wanted to know what we did wrong to make sure we didn't do it again.

Several days later we got in touch with the Deputy DA and asked him if he found out what happened.

He said, "Yes, you remember juror #7 that kept smiling at you? Well, you arrested her husband a couple of months ago for DUI and she was a passenger in the car. She persuaded all the other jurors to vote not guilty."

PART 1: Chapter 5:   DUI Blamed for Watts Riot   63

I asked him if the court was going to charge her with perjury. When she was accepted on the jury she took an oath that she did not know or had she ever had any personal contact with any of the parties involved in the case.

"That's outright perjury. You can't let her get by with that." I told him.

The Deputy DA said, "I agree with you. I understand what you're saying but we'll just keep her off of future juries. We've got too many other cases with higher priority."

And that was the final disposition.

I did remember something I had learned in a college class that proved true in the courtroom: It is impossible to tell whether a smile is one of friendliness or contempt.

CHP Tow Driver Arrested for DUI

One Saturday night about 1:00 am, Klippness and I stopped a DUI southbound on the Long Beach Freeway in the unincorporated city of Bell Gardens. It was a cold night but we were still on motorcycles. Rain is the only excuse for switching to a cruiser. Snow is not a factor because it never snows in Southern California except in the mountains.

We radioed dispatch for a 11-85 (tow truck) and she advised that one was on its way. Tow trucks would usually arrive within 10 to 15 minutes but it seemed like this one was taking an extra long time.

Because of the cold weather we let the DUI sit in the right front seat of his car with the handcuffs on and door open. We called dispatch back and asked if the tow driver had gotten lost.

She replied, "No, but he is responding from his home and that may be the cause of the delay."

About the time the dispatcher had finished, we saw the tow truck approaching. His driving indicated that he was obviously in a hurry. After whipping in front of the DUI's car and stopping, he quickly exited the tow truck and immediately started hooking the DUI's car up to the back of the tow truck. Klippness walked up to where the tow truck driver was working and started talking to him. I stayed where I could watch the "prisoner." Once an arrestee is handcuffed his status changes to prisoner.

Klippness took a few steps back to where I was standing and said, "Bob, this tow truck driver is under the influence too. Why don't you take a look at him and see if you agree?"

As I approached the tow truck driver and before I had an opportunity to say anything, he said, "I'm sorry I was so late getting here but I was at home at the time. I got over here as fast as I could."

I told him it was not how long he took getting there that concerned us, but what kind of condition he was in.

He responded, "I admit that I've had a few drinks . . . ."

I interrupted him and said, "A few?"

"Well, more than a few. Look I normally would not be driving after I've had this much to drink but there was no one else available to answer the call."

I said, "I can appreciate what you're saying but (motioning toward the other DUI) how can we arrest that guy for drunk driving and then let you go for doing the same thing. There's even a possibility that you've had more to drink than him."

Now the tow driver got a little more serious, saying, "You guys are the ones that called me out here. I wouldn't be on the road if it wasn't for you. I'd be at home."

"But we didn't call you out here," I said. "We called for a tow truck. It's true, we didn't request a tow truck with a sober driver. That part can be assumed."

We gave the tow truck driver a FST and advised him we were going to have to arrest him for DUI. He said, "But what are you going to do with the tow truck?"

We told him we would let someone from his garage come out and pick it up. So we got on the radio and advised dispatch, "We need a cruiser for two DUIs, another tow truck and notify the previous tow service that they can come out and pick up the first tow truck. But if they don't have anyone available then call another tow service."

As we were putting the cuffed tow driver in the cruiser he said, "Well, what was I suppose to do when the CHP dispatcher called me and said they needed a tow truck?"

Klippness said, "Tell them you've had too much to drink. We're trying to get drunk drivers off of the road, not call them out on the road."

It was very difficult arresting the tow truck driver because of the circumstances, but DUI is a deadly game we cannot afford to play. I believe a large majority of officers would not have arrested him and that is one of the reasons why the DUI killings continue.

Our first priority in making these kinds of decisions is public safety. Can you imagine letting the tow driver leave the scene and killing himself or a family en route to the tow yard? Where is the fairness of booking the first DUI and letting the second one drive in the same condition with impunity. And what about the deterent factor? Instead of the tow operator laughing and telling everyone he went out and towed a DUI's car while he was drunker than the guy being arrested, he will be soberly telling everyone that you better not drive drunk under any circumstances. That is the message we want out there if we are to win this war.

Prediction Comes True: CHP Motorcycle Officer Killed

Officer Herb Dimon, formerly of the Montebello Police Department, reported into the East Los Angeles office after graduating from the California Highway Patrol Academy. The first thing he did was submit a form requesting to be assigned motorcycle enforcement.

When I arrived at work the next day, Captain Dahl came into our Briefing and asked me to see him in his office before leaving to go on patrol. He asked me to close the door because he wanted to keep the conversation private.

He started out, "Officer Dimon has requested to be assigned a motorcycle. I know that you worked with him in Montebello and that you are familiar with his riding ability. Before I make a decision I wanted to get your opinion. What would be your recommendation?"

I told Captain Dahl, "I don't even have to think about this. The answer would be no. He should not be assigned a motorcycle."

Dahl, "Well, why do you say that?"

I told him, "Because he rides over his head. I'm surprised he didn't kill himself in Montebello."

Dahl said, "Do you really feel that strong about it?"

I replied, "Captain, I'll tell you how strong I feel about it. If he is assigned to motors he will be dead in six months."

Dahl said, "Well, I'm glad I talked with you Bob. Thanks for your opinion."

I left the Captain's office convinced that Dimon would not be assigned a motorcycle and I told Klippness about the meeting. Klippness said, "I hope you're right."

About a week later I rode into the area parking lot and as I was getting off of my motorcycle, Officer Dimon rode his motorcycle in and parked it next to mine. We spoke causally and then walked into briefing together. I actually liked Dimon as a person although we never socialized.

About 3 months later, on a Friday evening, with most of our motor officers working, CHP dispatch broadcast an emergency message to any units in the area, "We have a report of a CHP motor officer down at Third Street and Brooklyn. It sounds like a bad one. We have an ambulance rolling."

Klippness and I were close enough to respond but several motor officers were closer and went "10-97"(arrived at scene) before we got there. The ambulance had already placed Officer Dimon on a gurney and was racing code three to the hospital, where Dimon was pronounced Dead on Arrival (DOA).

Witnesses reported that they first heard a siren westbound on Third Street approaching Ford Blvd.

"The officer also had his red lights on and was traveling at a high speed. When the motor officer got closer I could tell it was a Highway Patrolman but he wasn't slowing for the red light (traffic signal) that had just changed."

The witness said a woman driving southbound on Ford Blvd had the green traffic light when she entered the intersection. As she went through the intersection, the motor officer crashed into the left side of her car. The car windows were rolled up and the woman was listening to her radio and did not hear the siren.

The witness added, "The officer was going very fast when he hit the car. I don't think he's going to make it. He didn't seem to be chasing anyone."

At this intersection there is a small Greek outdoor sandwich shop where Klippness and I stopped from time to time. A person could have a cup of coffee and still be watching traffic. We knew the owner and we were curious if he had seen anything that night.

He said, "Well, I heard the siren and saw the collision but I didn't see anyone he might be chasing."

A couple of days later at briefing, one of the sergeants pulled me aside and asked if I would do him and the Highway Patrol a favor.

"Herb Dimon's wife is coming to the office to pick up all of his possessions." he said. "You worked with him in Montebello and you knew him pretty well. Will you go through everything in his locker before she gets here?" as he handed me the locker key.

I found the locker that was on an upper level and opened the door. The first thing I saw was Dimon's CHP helmet resting upside down on top of some papers and other items. Reaching upward, I picked up the helmet and as I turned it right side up, blood poured all over my hands, shirt sleeves, boots and onto the floor. I could only imagine if that had happened to his wife. After cleaning off as much blood as I could, I finished inventorying the contents of the locker.

Later, Mrs. Dimon picked up her husband's possessions without incident and asked the Captain if he would assign me as one of the pallbearers.

At the funeral a few days later, Officer Dimon was laid to rest in Rosehill's Cemetery in Whittier with full CHP honors. During the funeral I noticed that Captain Dahl did not make eye contact with me and I couldn't help but think that the wrong person got Dimon's blood on his hands.

Murder Suspect Loses Teeth

When it rains motor officers go to the Area office and pickup a cruiser. If one is not available, the motor officer pairs with a car officer. One Saturday night at about 10 pm I found myself in that position. Officer Porter was alone in a cruiser so I paired with him. We were patrolling on Dangler near Gleason, both side-streets, at about 20 mph. Up to that point in time it had been a slow night even though it was lightly raining.

A radio dispatcher broke the silence with "All units. We have a report of a murder that just occurred near Fetterly and 2nd street. Three suspects in a dark older model Chevrolet left the scene just minutes ago." The dispatcher went on to give the license plate number.

Porter and I were in the immediate area so we thought we might have a good chance of finding them. And we did—immediately. Directly in front of us was a dark older model Chevrolet driving the same speed as we were and it looked like there were about three males in the car.

No sooner did she complete her transmission of the license plate than I advised her we were following the murder suspects and to roll some back-up units. Normally, officers will not make a stop until their back-up units are in position but there can be an exception. And we had one.

The suspects were heading for an area in East Los Angeles where law enforcement officers (Los Angeles County Sheriffs, California Highway Patrol, etc.) would not go unless there was an emergency and then they wouldn't respond without extra units going in at the same time.

There was a very good reason for not venturing into that area. If an officer strayed into the district, made up mostly of run-down low-rent housing, in

PART 1: Chapter 5:   DUI Blamed for Watts Riot   69

a "black and white" the officer(s) would be shot at. You couldn't tell where the shots were coming from and no one was going to tell you if you were foolish enough to get out of the patrol car and ask around.

We were only blocks from the area, so we decided to turn on our red lights and spotlight and make the stop right away.

But the driver did not respond and continued driving at about 20 mph. When he got to Brooklyn Ave., he made a slow left turn and a half block later pulled over to the curb and stopped. There was an apartment building with the steps touching the sidewalk and all three of the suspects got out of the car and headed for the steps.

Porter and I jumped out of the cruiser and each one of us grabbed a suspect. All three looked like they were in their 20s and they were smaller than us. Two of their friends came out of the apartment building (which was why they had not stopped earlier) and a scuffle broke out. At this same time, two of our back-up units arrived and we quickly got things under control.

I had one of the suspects over the hood of their car and well under control when suddenly out of nowhere Porter hit the suspect I was restraining in the mouth with a wooden baton. Two or three of his teeth dropped out of his mouth and hit on the hood of the car. I looked at Porter and said, "You didn't need to do that. I had him under control."

Everyone was arrested and taken to jail. I found out later the murder was the result of a knife fight and was suppose to have been self-defense.

The suspect I was holding filed a civil action against the California Highway Patrol for losing his teeth during the struggle.

When his lawyer called me to the stand he asked, "Officer Mitchell do you think it was necessary for Officer Porter to hit my client in the mouth with his baton?"

I said, "No, I do not think it was necessary."

I know the State paid for the young man's dental work and no one ever questioned my testimony in the suspect's behalf including Officer Porter.

I respected Officer Porter for not trying to justify what he did and there is always that chance that, at the time, he thought it was necessary.

Video Would Have Freed Drunkest DUI

While appearing on the Art Linkletter television show, Linkletter asked me, "Who was the drunkest person you ever arrested for DUI?"

That arrest was easy to remember. And the reason it was easy to remember is because the drunkest person I ever arrested for DUI is one of only three or four where the DUI "passed" the physical part of the FST. And that is out of more than 2,000 DUIs that I arrested.

While patrolling in the East LA area, I observed a dark-colored car approaching on Ford Blvd. near Third Street. The car was traveling a little less than the speed limit but weaving slightly as it approached. I got a good look at the driver as we passed and he looked like he was "stoned out of his mind." A phrase Klippness and I often used.

I made a quick u-turn and pulled up alongside him at a stoplight, indicated for him to roll down his window and then asked him to pull over. Everything about his demeanor told me he was "smashed" so I expected to have to hold him up to keep him from falling once he got out of the car. But that wasn't the case. All of his movements were slow and deliberate but his balance was normal. An officer has to take into account that a person is usually nervous when being stopped by a law enforcement officer. But he didn't appear to be the least bit nervous. He was too calm.

I asked him to walk a straight line, which he had no problem doing. Head back and eyes closed with arms extended? No problem. Standing on one leg while holding the other leg out stretched? No serious problem. Finger to nose test? No problem.

Being able to follow directions is part of the test and I did notice he was slow in responding. I then asked the driver how much he had had to drink. He appeared to think for a minute and said, "A couple. Maybe three beers."

I asked him if he had been taking any drugs or medication?

PART 1: *Chapter 5:*   DUI Blamed for Watts Riot   71

He replied, "Not today. I don't take drugs."

"Are you a diabetic?"

He said, "No."

In addition to the odor of alcohol, the pupils of his eyes were dilated and that's not a good sign. His speech was thick and slightly slurred. There was something wrong even if he did "pass" the physical part of the FST.

My next question was, "How did you get into this condition?"

He said, "I passed your tests, didn't I?"

I said, "Well, part of them. But there are other signs that you are intoxicated."

I told him I could not in clear conscience let him drive away. In his condition there were two other tests he would have to take. The first was a breathalyzer and if he passed that then I would want a doctor to examine him.

We were only five minutes from the East LA Sheriffs sub-station, where the breathalyzer was available. I called a cruiser to transport him and I followed on the motorcycle.

Technically he was under arrest but he could have been released if he had overcome those two barriers. It was my opinion that he would show a Blood Alcohol Concentration (BAC) reading of between a .15% and .20%

The subject blew into the machine and in just minutes we got a reading of .37%. Everyone there, including me, said that can't be right. Experts in this field will tell you that a person with a BAC level of .37% is comatose or on the verge of being comatose and, if not, he "will be grossly intoxicated and display unmistakable impairment of all physical activity and mental faculties."

There was only one thing to do and that was to run the test again. The second one came back a .38%.

Somebody joked that we better stop testing him.

When it was pointed out to the DUI that he would have had to consume an equivalent of almost a case of beer to reach that level he changed his original statement from "a couple of beers to I've been drinking all day but I didn't think I drank that much."

I was wrong about his level of intoxication but I was right in not letting him continue driving. It also proves something very important. Some very intoxicated drivers can perform the physical part of the FST. That's why I have mixed emotions on videoing DUI field sobriety tests. The untrained, and that includes most of the general public and half of the law enforcement officers, would have a hard time arresting—or finding someone like that guilty—based upon viewing a video.

Am I Really in San Diego?

One night Klippness and I stopped a DUI on a frontage road of the Santa Ana Freeway in an industrial district in the City of Industry. After administering the FST and advising the DUI of his constitutional rights we started asking him the standard questions.

From where did you start driving?

His answer, "A party."

What is your destination?

He replied, "Los Angeles." Los Angeles was less than two miles from our location, in the opposite direction than he was heading.

While giving him the FST we had noticed a large billboard on the Santa Ana Freeway that was clearly visible and it read, "San Diego. A wonderful place to visit." So instead of asking the next question, Where are you now?, we changed it to "What are you doing in San Diego?" while one of us pointed to the sign.

San Diego was 124 miles south of our location; about 20 miles from the Mexican border.

PART 1: *Chapter 5:*   DUI Blamed for Watts Riot   73

The DUI looked at the sign and calmly replied in a slurred voice, "Am I in San Diego? I don't know how I got here. Am I really in San Diego?"

We both started laughing and on the way to jail, he continued to ask, "Really, am I in San Diego?"

While questioning another DUI we varied from the standard questions and asked, "Would it surprise you if we told you that you were under arrest for drunk driving?" The DUI said, "Yes, that would surprise me." We said, "Well, you're under arrest for drunk driving." The DUI replied, "That surprises me."

Three Different Tests but Same Results

Some DUIs who don't want to be arrested do stupid things, such as trying to evade arrest or fighting with the arresting officer. Actually, it is more common than one would think. That's why there are sections in the Penal Code for resisting arrest and evading arrest. The first thing an officer should remember is the subject is intoxicated so he's going to act like an intoxicated person.

When someone wanted to fight with me I had a standard statement: "Do you have any preference on which hospital you want to be taken to?" I would say it with all sincerity.

Almost without exception the subject would say," Why do you ask me that? I'm not injured."

I would say, "Well, not yet but you will be and we want to know where to take you."

While this didn't work every time, it worked most of the time.

There are other types of DUIs that don't seem to care. It's almost like a game to them. One such person was Daniel Sanchez.

The first time I saw him was one evening driving westbound on Whittier Blvd near Atlantic Blvd., which is part of the business district of East Los Angeles. He was having a little trouble negotiating the lane he was in and following too close to the car in front of him.

After giving him a FST and advising him he was under arrest, I told him that he would be required to take a chemical test or DMV would suspend his drivers license for six months.

Sanchez said, "I don't mind taking a (chemical) test but I don't want no breath test."

I told him if that was the case then he could chose between a blood or urine test. He said, "Then I'll take a blood test."

After Sanchez found out how high his BAC was, he pled guilty. It would be nice if that was the end of the story but it isn't.

A couple of months later, again on Whittier Blvd., I observed a possible DUI ahead of me in traffic. When I pulled up along side of him to motion him to stop, I recognized the driver as Sanchez. As before, he pulled over and stopped and waited for me to ask him out of the car. A FST revealed he was in about the same condition that he was the first time I stopped him.

He offered no excuse for his condition and just said, "This time I want to take a urine (chemical) test."

One of our cruisers transported him to the East Los Angeles Sheriff's sub-station where he gave a sample of his urine to be tested. The CHP officer that transported Sanchez to the jail also took care of the testing and booking so I continued on patrol.

The next time I ran into Sanchez he was on Olympic Blvd almost in the city limits of Los Angeles.

His weaving pattern was becoming more familiar than his car. Olympic Blvd is a wide four-lane roadway so I used my red lights to pull him over. When Sanchez got out of his car and staggered up to the sidewalk it was like filming "Take Three" of a movie.

I called CHP dispatch for a transportation unit and then told Sanchez, "How about a breath test this time? The other two didn't do anything for you."

He didn't say anything but he looked like he was thinking it over. He was handcuffed by the transportation officer and placed in the right front passenger seat. The officer then walked around to the driver side and as he was getting in the cruiser, Sanchez asked the officer, "What do you think of those breath tests? Are they pretty accurate?"

The officer said, "They're just as accurate as the other ones."

Sanchez blew a .18% BAC and pled guilty.

I never saw Sanchez after that either sober or under the influence. Which reminds me of the joke, "I never knew he drank until I saw him sober one day." To put it another way, maybe I saw him and he was sober and I didn't recognize him. Or maybe the court finally did the right thing.

DUI Fire Captain kills LAPD Motor Officer

Just to be able to spot a possible DUI requires special training. For example, while I was working in the East Los Angeles area on March 2, 1966, I got a call concerning a fatal accident on the San Bernardino Freeway at the Marengo on-ramp.

Marengo is an unusual on-ramp because it enters the freeway in the fast lane. Officer John C. Smith, a mortorcycle officer with the Los Angeles Police Department, had been parked at the top of the ramp observing traffic moving inbound. Captain McCrary, Los Angeles County Fire Department, drove onto the Marengo on-ramp and struck Officer Smith, knocking him over the freeway wall where he landed in the fast lane of the San Bernardino Freeway. Several cars struck the prone officer and he was killed almost immediately.

Several CHP officers responded to the scene but I was assigned as the primary investigator. Captain McCrary was seated in his damaged vehicle and I asked him if he was injured. One of the other firemen said McCrary wasn't feeling very well but McCrary said he was all right. He said he was a little shook. I detected an odor of alcohol and noticed other symptoms that aroused my suspicion that he was under the influence. But when a person is involved in an accident, especially a serious accident, you have to be sure he is not in shock. Some of the symptoms are the same.

After obtaining his drivers license, I walked over to Sergeant Heringer to tell him of my suspicions but when I turned back I observed McCrary had been moved to another LA County Fire Dept. vehicle and his friends were attempting to take him from the scene. They used the excuse that they were taking him to a hospital but he had already told me he wasn't injured. I took him from the vehicle, informed him he would need to voluntarily submit to a chemical test or I would have to place him under arrest. The law permits an officer to forcibly take a blood test from a suspected DUI in the case of a felony.

En route to jail after McCrary had submitted to a blood test, he struck up a conversation with me.

"Do you drink?"

I said, "No."

He said, "Did you ever drink?"

I said, "Yes, but I quit about 4 years ago."

McCrary asked, "Did you ever take a drink and drive a car?"

I replied to the affirmative. He said, "You probably took more than one drink and drove. Oh! It doesn't matter anyway. But you see. It could happen to anyone at one time or another."

I told him, "That's true but that's also a good reason for not drinking. That eliminates the problem."

He said, "It could have happened whether I was drinking or not. What happens to me is unimportant. It's the officer I'm concerned about."

I couldn't help but feel sorry for him because he really did feel bad about what he had done. There was no criminal trial because Captain McCrary pled guilty and I never followed up to find out what his sentence was. I did testify at a civil trial in Los Angeles Superior Court, one year and four months later, when the LAPD officer's widow sued McCrary and the Los Angeles County Fire Department.

PART 1: *Chapter 5:*   DUI Blamed for Watts Riot   77

After the civil trial I received a letter from her attorney, Ned Good, wherein he thanked me for my handling of the case and added. "I am pleased to report that the jury returned a verdict for $400,000 to Mrs. Smith. This is the first case that I know of where a law enforcement officer's family has been treated adequately by a jury. Again, many, many thanks."

I also received a commendation from the CHP for a "thorough, unbiased and professional investigation." Signed by Captain R.E. Teuber. A little later, I received my notice that I was going to be promoted to State Traffic Sergeant and would be leaving East Los Angeles where I had spent 8 ½ years plus another 5 ½ years in nearby Montebello.

As I was reflecting back over those 14 years I couldn't help but think about the people that made up the two communities. As a law enforcement officer, you learn to appreciate the public you serve. Yes, there are a lot of bad people out there, but there are many more good ones. And the good ones are the ones that help you put away the bad ones. And, in a sense, if you take your job seriously, you become part of a huge family that is depending upon you to protect them. I left East Los Angeles hoping that I had done my share in fulfilling that obligation.

Chapter 6
Promoted to Sergeant and Transferred

August 2, 1966, my 14 ½ years as a motorcycle officer ended. I was promoted to State Traffic Sergeant and transferred from East LA to the Baldwin Park Area, which is about 14 miles away.

Parking my CHP motorcycle at the area office and knowing that it was the last time I would be riding one, left me with mixed emotions. I had lived on one for the last decade and a half and naturally it had become part of my life. Even switching to regular uniform trousers with a cloth cap instead of a motorcycle uniform, boots and helmet was going to seem strange. But life goes on and there were new challenges to look forward to as situations change.

And I was looking forward to the new position. A sergeant is the first in line of supervision and this would be a real opportunity to teach and motivate others. Removing DUIs from the roadway was still my top priority.

A few months earlier, Klippness had also been promoted to Sergeant and was assigned to the Indio Area. Indio is a small desert city about 150 miles east of Los Angeles and about 40 miles east of Palm Springs. It's a pretty place, but Klippness and his family weren't happy living there.

The one time I visited him in Indio, he said, "These officers here in Indio are a bunch of nice guys but they don't want to arrest DUIs."

Nevertheless, Indio saw DUI arrests balloon from about 30 to 130 a month when Klippness began working the night shift. But there were signs of growing dissatisfaction. This was not the case in large populated areas such as Baldwin Park or East Los Angeles where a large number of officers are assigned. Officers in larger areas are constantly transferring in and out and there is less opportunity for group pressure and conformity.

Small areas are supposed to operate like large areas but not all of them do. In some small areas, there is a subtle but tremendous group pressure upon officers to conform to local policies that have been established over time.

You won't find the local policies written anywhere because they are passed on by word of mouth. Of course, the officers involved will deny that any unwritten rules exist and that they only follow Departmental policy. Most of the time it is the "old timers" in the area that make sure the unwritten rules are followed as well as setting the "tempo" for what level of law enforcement will be conducted in their close-knit community.

This philosophy in small communities is not limited to just the highway patrol but applies to city police and sheriff's departments throughout the nation. It's called the "Good old boys" network. Everyone seems to be related by birth or marriage from the judge to the sheriff to the largest landowners. Now what do you think they're going to do with a local DUI?

As soon as Klippness could, he transferred with his family to Santa Maria, a Santa Barbara sub-station. Santa Maria is about 230 miles northwest of Los Angeles up the Pacific Ocean coastline. I wasn't surprised he left Indio because Jerry has always been a worker. He wasn't looking for a place to retire, which is the goal of a lot of officers who transfer to small areas.

Meanwhile, I had a great start in the Baldwin Park area. In December 1966, after only 3 months, I received a commendation from the California Highway Patrol signed by Lieutenant B.R. Goode.

"This is to commend you for your outstanding contribution in training and directing officers assigned to your supervision, in enforcement against the drinking driver.

"During the period August through December, 1966, you have worked mostly the evening and night shifts with an assortment of very new and inexperienced officers and a few older ones.

PART 1: Chapter 6:   Promoted to Sergeant and Transferred   81

"In July, 1966, officers of this area made 119 arrests for 23102a V.C. (DUIs). Each month since has shown a significant increase to the point that 255 such arrests have been made this month.

"It is sincerely felt that your energy and interest was a significant factor in this record and the guidance and direction given the officers will have a lasting and beneficial effect."

The commendation pointed out that it's possible for one field supervisor to be responsible for an Area having more than a 100 percent increase in DUI arrests.

Baldwin Park, like East Los Angeles, encouraged removing DUIs from the roadway. The more the better. No violation is more important to the California Highway Patrol than DUI. This is what they teach in the Academy and continually stress on the job. So when I reported to Baldwin Park I just kept doing what I was trained to do.

Our immediate success might have been because we had so many new officers. But, one thing is for certain, most of the officers working the evening shift, as they did in East Los Angeles, were out there actively doing their job. I can say with assurance from 32 years of experience that the majority of law enforcement officers are dedicated, hard working individuals serving the public. The large DUI increases in both East Los Angeles and Baldwin Park prove that leadership and motivation can result in a large number of officers working together to make a significant impact.

Can you Find My Arm?

While working the graveyard shift in Baldwin Park, about four o'clock in the morning, Dispatch reported a "11-80" (injury accident) inbound on the San Bernardino Freeway near the San Gabriel River bridge. Dispatch continued, "An ambulance is on its way." The beat units acknowledged they were en route, as did I as the field supervisor.

At that location the San Bernardino Freeway is four lanes wide on each side of the freeway. Because it was early morning and traffic had been light, high speed was possible. Add a drinking driver and a crash can be serious. And that's exactly what we had.

The first priority upon arriving at a traffic accident is to protect the scene. That means setting out flares and controlling traffic. There is always a serious danger that another DUI will crash into the damaged cars and, in some cases, into the injured and dead. Many officers and citizens have been killed by drunk drivers while they were at the scene of an accident.

The second priority is to locate the injured and take care of them. Usually, when there is a serious traffic accident on the freeway, there is no shortage of caring people who stop to help. I'm not talking about people who slow down to see what's happening or those who get in the way. I'm talking about people who sincerely want to help, at least until the officers arrive, and then stay out of the way if they are no longer needed. In this case, a number of people had stopped and were assisting the injured and making sure the DUI didn't wander away. One of those caring citizen's identified himself as a doctor.

Several cars had been inbound at a normal rate of speed when a DUI hit them from the rear traveling at about 90 mph. I don't recall the exact number of cars involved or the number of injuries and it's probably because I was busy with a very unusual request.

The ambulance had arrived and they had placed one of the injured victims on a gurney and were preparing to put him in the ambulance when he asked to speak to a CHP supervisor. As I approached him, it was obvious that he had lost his right arm in the crash.

Before the victim could say anything, one of the ambulance attendants said, "He doesn't want to leave without his arm."

The victim interjected, "That's right. I'm not leaving unless I can take my arm with me."

Another gentleman who was standing there listening to the conversation, said, "I'm a doctor and I believe if you can find his arm it could possibly be reattached. I'm basing this mainly on the fact the weather is cold and they can transport it in ice which they have."

It all made sense and a few more minutes weren't going to make that much difference. So, I said, "Let's look for the arm."

It was still dark and there was wreckage everywhere but everyone who could, started looking. In about five minutes a fireman found the arm under the front seat of the man's car and the ambulance attendants wrapped it in ice and the ambulance sped away.

I didn't find out until over a year later what the results were and that was only by chance.

My family and I were living in Santa Maria and I was in the front room watching the news on television. A television channel from Los Angeles was reporting a public interest story about a man who had lost his arm in a traffic accident and would not leave the scene of the accident without his arm.

Then, who appears on the screen with his arm extended outward and moving his hand and fingers, but the victim from that early morning traffic accident.

I was thrilled for him and extremely pleased that the right decision was made that morning.

Driver Bleeding to Death

Another traffic accident on the San Bernardino freeway that is worth mentioning occurred during a light rain. When I arrived, one of the damaged cars was on its side and the driver was still in the car.

The car was on the shoulder, which had a slight incline. Traffic was moving by the scene because both of the cars involved were on the shoulder and outside lane, so we could keep two lanes open.

By looking through the windshield of the over turned car it appeared the driver was unconscious. An ambulance was on its way and there didn't appear any immediate threat to the unconscious driver. However, drawing on my Highway Patrol training, which teaches that an officer at the scene should always be doing something and not just standing around, I decided to climb upon the car and lower myself down next to the injured driver.

I wasn't concerned the car would burst into flames because we had already disconnected the battery. Something all officers should do if someone is still in a car. Also, I didn't see anyone smoking and it was still lightly raining.

It was a small car and I had trouble moving around but I wanted to see if the injured man was OK. I raised his head slightly and to my surprise blood was dripping from both of my hands from a head wound. What was not apparent was the injured driver was bleeding to death. The reason it was not obvious was the damaged car was on an incline and as the blood flowed from his head wound to underneath the car, the rain was diluting it so that it was not visible by the time it reached the other end of the car.

I took a large compress from the first aid kit that I had brought with me and applied direct pressure to stop the flow of blood. He was later taken to the hospital and fully recovered.

I don't believe this type of situation is that uncommon. The public might be surprised at how many lives are saved by policemen, firemen, ambulance attendants and other public servants even before the victim gets to a hospital.

Fatal Accident—No Median Barrier

Several years earlier near this location and before there were median barriers, I responded to a multi-fatal accident. There were four lifeless bodies laying in the roadway and two extremely damaged cars blocking the lanes. A DUI had jumped the center divider and struck a car carrying a family head-on. The DUI was arrested for four counts of "vehicular manslaughter and felony driving under the influence."

While working the accident and conversing with the DUI suspect, I noticed that he was only interested in his welfare.

"Where are you taking my car? What's going to happen to me next?" and so on.

He also said, "I'm not taking a blood test. I don't have to."

He was then advised that he would either voluntarily submit to a chemical test or we would take it by force if necessary. The law permits force being used to take a chemical test if a suspect has been arrested for felony DUI unless the suspect is a hemophiliac, has a heart condition or is using an anticoagulant.

PART 1: *Chapter 6:*   Promoted to Sergeant and Transferred   85

It's only reasonable the chemical test would be for blood. An officer could not force a suspect to blow into a Breathalyzer and a urine test would be out of the question. The suspect in this case agreed to a blood test but on rare occasions we had to force a suspect to submit to a withdrawal of his blood. That meant physically restraining him. Some doctors will not take a blood sample under those conditions but we were always able to find one that would.

Several months later I was subpoenaed to testify at his trial in Los Angeles Superior Court. After I had finished answering all of the prosecutor's questions and was preparing to step down from the witness chair, the prosecutor had one more question that I had never been asked before in court.

He said, "Officer is there anything that I have not asked you about that you would like to tell the jury?"

I said, "Yes, there is,"

"And what would that be?" was his next question.

I turned toward the jury and replied, "I noticed one thing about the defendant during the entire time he was in my custody and that was he never once showed any concern about the victims or expressed any remorse over what he had done."

The jury did not take long to come back with a" guilty verdict on all charges."

DUI Refused to Get Out of Car

DUIs don't always cooperate when they are stopped. In fact, some won't even get out of their car.

Two CHP officers radioed me one night to meet them on Francisquito Ave about two blocks south of the San Bernardino Freeway. All they said was that they had a DUI stopped. When I arrived several minutes later, they were waiting along side a fairly new Ford with a physically large male sitting in the driver's seat.

He was staring straight ahead. He had his car windows rolled up and all the doors locked.

One of the Officers said, "Here's what we've got. This guy was weaving all over the place going eastbound on the freeway. We came up behind him and turned on our red lights but he just kept going. After a while he turned off onto Francisquito but still didn't stop until he finally stopped here. The problem is he won't roll his window down or get out of the car."

I had run into this before so it wasn't a real serious problem. The CHP officers were fairly new and they wanted to do the right thing. And that was to radio for a supervisor. The three of us walked up to the driver's side of the car and I tapped on the window to get the DUI's attention.

He ignored us, still looking straight ahead. So much for plan A.

Now it was time for plan B. We told the suspect if he didn't unlock the door we were going to have to break the glass window. He totally ignored us. So, we took our batons and slammed them against the glass window but they just bounced off.

The DUI turned and looked at us but then turned and looked straight ahead. So, we stayed with plan B and hit the window harder only this time with the butt of the baton using both hands. This time the window shattered and glass flew all over the DUI.

We reached through the window and opened the driver's door and took the 300 lb DUI to the ground. Two of us took one leg and the other officer took the other one and we started dragging him to the patrol unit behind his car.

After about 10 feet, the subject finally said something, "I can walk. You don't have to drag me."

From that point on it was a normal DUI arrest and he later pled guilty. We gave him a break and didn't charge him with Resisting public officers in the discharge of their duties. We took into consideration that he had to have a window replaced.

DUI OK with Arrest, But Not Religion

As a supervisor I rode in a patrol unit alone. If I stopped a DUI and it was a busy night, I would radio a two-man unit and turn the arrest over to them. But if things were slow I would sometimes book the DUI myself. A supervisor is expected to be available if something "big" goes down.

One night I stopped a DUI and most of the units were busy so I decided to book him myself. As we were traveling to Temple City Sheriffs Sub-station for booking, the subject started telling me that he no longer wanted to live.

"When you stopped me, I was on my way home to kill myself," he said.

He continued, "I have nothing to live for. I lost my wife not too long ago. As soon as I get out of jail, I'm going to end it all. I don't have any friends or anyone."

Going by the book, I probably shouldn't have said anything but he sounded very intent on ending his life. So, as we drove along, I tried to comfort him by saying that getting drunk was only going to make things worse. I told him that there are people out there who would be his friend. I asked him if he had ever gone to church.

He said, "No."

I said, "There are a lot of nice people in church and they will help you and be your friend. You might want to try that."

The subject quieted down and I took that to mean he might be considering taking my advice.

I thought back a few years to a DUI arrest I had made in East LA.

The DUI had told me the night of the arrest, "I'll never go to court." I had no idea that suicide was what he was planning. I thought maybe he was going to leave the country. A check later of his driving record showed three prior DUIs. I guess this incident was still in the back of my mind when I suggested to the DUI sitting in the right front seat of my car that he try attending church.

About two weeks later, I got a subpoena for El Monte Municipal Court where the subject had asked for a jury trial. We had a strong case against him so I was curious to hear his defense.

I soon found out that this DUI's strategy was like that of many other criminal cases—if they don't have a defense, they attack the officer.

He testified, "I didn't mind getting arrested but I don't think it's right that I had to listen to the officer preach to me all the way to the jail. That's not right. I shouldn't have had to listen to that religious stuff."

He didn't mention that he told me he was going to commit suicide or that his wife had died.

When it was my turn to testify, I just told the jury what I had said and why I said it. This included his mental state of wanting to commit suicide and that he said his wife had died recently.

I think he hurt himself by not mentioning that in his testimony. Maybe that was for a reason because we could have checked that out. I made no mention of the East Los Angeles suicide incident.

The jury didn't buy his story and found him guilty. I guess his telling the jury, "I didn't mind getting arrested" could have had something to do with it. I have always been confident that the jury would do the right thing and never had a problem with a jury except Juror #7 in East Los Angeles who perjured herself.

How About Transferring to Santa Maria?

Being promoted to Sergeant and transferred to Baldwin Park was working out very well.

I still lived in Hacienda Heights and, although I didn't have a CHP motorcycle to take back and forth to work, I was only about 15 minutes away. The Area Commander strongly supported DUI enforcement and the officers were doing a great job. I had no thoughts about transferring to another Area.

But I kept getting phone calls from Jerry Klippness who was telling me why I should be transferring to Santa Maria.

"Bob, you and Laura come up here and visit Virginia and I. I want you to see what you're missing," he would say.

So, finally, Laura and I made the 230-mile trip to Santa Maria. It was a pretty drive and our stop in Solvang, a small Danish community, made it even more pleasant.

After showing us his home, Klippness took me to the CHP office on Highway 101 and introduced me to a couple of the officers. The Lieutenant wasn't there because it was a weekend. I found out later that he wouldn't have been there even if it was during the week. I would have had to go out on the golf course to meet him.

The building was on a dead-end road, surrounded by tree less open land dotted with oil rigs. I think most people would have been afraid to stop there at night even if they saw a light on.

The sub-station was not very big, but most sub-stations aren't. At less than 1,000 square feet, it included a small front office and another small room used by the lieutenant, as well as one larger room that was used for the squad room. That was it.

There was no sergeant's office, just a desk and chair in one of the corners. The office had an allocation of one lieutenant (officer-in-charge), two sergeants (field supervisors) and 15 officers. They also had one secretary that had been there for "eternity."

From there, Klippness showed Laura and I around town.

Santa Maria's claim to fame was, and I think still is, their barbecue tri-tip steaks. Once a month all of the law enforcement officers were treated to a barbecue tri-tip dinner at the Santa Maria Club. The tri-tip became so famous, that one year, when all of the governors throughout the nation met in Palm Springs, they ordered the tri-tip from Santa Maria, about 330 miles away.

In the waning days of 1966, the housing market was flat; and that was an understatement. You could buy a home for nothing down and the house payment would be lower than rent in most cities.

After showing us a golf course in Orcutt, a suburb of Santa Maria and where Klippness lived, it was time to get down to business and talk about the job.

Klippness started out, "Bob, this place is like Indio. No one seems to want to arrest DUIs and accidents are way too high for the amount of traffic. And there are DUIs all over the place. But it's almost impossible to get something going."

He went on to say that he was not getting any support from the Lieutenant and it was very frustrating trying to do his job.

Jerry started laughing and said, "You won't believe this but the first day I reported in to the office and Thobe (lieutenant-in-charge) was showing me around, I looked up on the bulletin board and saw a drunk driving arrests chart with a big "36" on it. I commented to the lieutenant that 36 DUIs a month isn't bad for an area this size."

Thobe snapped back, "That's not for a month. That's for the first nine months of the year."

The Santa Maria area was averaging four DUIs a month and had been for years.

But that was going to change. Soon the area was going to be arresting an average of 40 DUIs a month and Lieutenant Thobe (pronounced Toe-bee) was not going to be happy.

Chapter 7
Moving to Santa Maria

Laura and I talked about the transfer to Santa Maria all the way back to Southern California. One of the deciding factors was that our children, Steve, 16, Cheryl, 14, and Bob Jr, 13, were anxious to move to a smaller area. So, after careful consideration, we decided a transfer would be a good move for us all.

The transfer came through effective January 3, 1967. I had mixed emotions about leaving Baldwin Park after being there only six months. Overall the personnel there were great. I felt the same way when I left East Los Angeles. I felt fortunate to be working for such an outstanding law enforcement agency. The California Highway Patrol was everything I had anticipated and, maybe, even more.

Of course, I had never worked in a small area office before but I believed it was still the California Highway Patrol only on a smaller scale. We all got the same training, were governed by the same rules and policies, supported the same Departmental goals and answered to the same bosses at Headquarters in Sacramento.

I mean the CHP is the CHP. We wear the same uniforms and are expected to perform in the same manner regardless of where we are stationed.

I also thought that the experience we had gained in arresting DUIs in Southern California would be of great benefit to the Santa Maria area. It worked in East Los Angeles and Baldwin Park, why wouldn't it work in

Santa Maria? I would be reuniting with my buddy, Jerry, again and hopefully we would be able to do our jobs even more proficiently as sergeants. Ideally, this is the way it's suppose to work.

It was exciting to move into our new home in Santa Maria. We decided to rent rather than buy the home even though we could get it for nothing down. I'm not quite sure why we decided to do that. Maybe it was a premonition. The children were happy because there were open areas to play and it didn't take them long to make friends. Laura was busy fixing the house.

On January 3, 1967, with high expectations, I put on my uniform and drove about 4 miles to the office. Barbara Capitani, the Clerk-Typist in the office with "who knows how many years on the job" was the first one I met and she hardly looked up from her desk. She appeared to be indifferent and withdrawn. Her negative attitude never changed the whole time I was there. Klippness told me beforehand that she was very close with the Lieutenant and wasn't very friendly. My first thought was that she didn't like Klippness and, knowing that he and I were very good friends, had decided she wasn't going to like me. Looking back now, the large increase in DUI arrests may have had something to do with it. It generated a lot of work for her and she was the only permanent civilian clerk in the office. But her attitude had to be more than that.

Welcome to the Area but Let Me Warn You . . .

The Lieutenant was seated only a few feet away in his 10' x 10' office with the door open. I tapped on the door frame and he said "Come on it."

As I walked in, he stood up from behind his desk and said, "I'm Lieutenant Don Thobe. You'll be working for me." Then he added, "Welcome to the area."

I said something like, "Thanks. I'm glad to be here."

My first impression was that he was being a little too formal and that he was sending me a message that he was the boss. Before the morning was over, he made sure I got the message even louder and clearer.

After meeting a couple of the officers in the briefing room, Thobe said, "Since you're a new supervisor in the area, I want to take you around and introduce you to some people in town."

PART 1: *Chapter 7:*   Moving to Santa Maria   93

We went out and got into a patrol cruiser and headed toward the main part of town, which was only about 5 miles away. No sooner had we left the office and with no one else present and no conversation leading up to it, Thobe's first words to me were, "I know you are going to try and get me just like the rest have tried, but it's not going to work. They failed and so will you."

My first thought was "What the hell is this guy talking about?" and then, "What have I got myself into by transferring up here?"

But my response was, "I don't have any idea what you're talking about."

The Lieutenant replied, "Oh! I think you do. But again, I warn you. Better people than you have tried to get me and all of them have failed. I'm still here, aren't I?"

A little while later, we were pulling into the parking lot of the local television station and he told me who we were going to be meeting, so I just concentrated on that for the time being.

After we left the television station I brought the subject up again.

In an irritated tone he said, "One sergeant arresting drunk drivers is enough. I don't know how this is going to work out with both sergeants being drunk driving men."

Later I told Laura and Klippness about it. Klippness was not surprised. He said that's the way he thinks.

"Bob, you are going to find this guy is strange. I haven't been able to figure him out. Apparently he's had trouble with other sergeants going to Fresno (Zone IV, Division Headquarters) about him before we got here. I know Sergeant Sikes complained to Fresno on him and often referred to him as a "psycho."

Having completed my "orientation" into the area, it was time to get settled in and go to work. Even though Thobe's comments were disturbing, I had to put those behind me and move on. Over the next few days I had an opportunity to meet all 15 of the officers. Some of them came into the area office just to introduce themselves. There wasn't a sergeant's office. We just had a desk in the front corner of the briefing room.

Klippness and I had a statewide reputation of arresting DUIs and that reputation always preceded us. Officers who have never worked in a large metropolitan area sometimes feel a little intimidated about not having the experience that goes with working in a high crime area. It is common knowledge that for every year an officer works in Los Angeles it is equivalent to working seven years in a small area and this can lead to resentment by some officers. I had seen this same type of resentment crop up between car officers and motor officers simply because one group has a skill the other one doesn't have.

Even though the officers in Santa Maria were friendly, I could detect some resentment. Another reason for resentment is that officers know that new sergeants, especially when they are the only field supervisors in the area, can have a big effect upon their working conditions. Some of the officers had been living in Santa Maria for many years and they were happy with things the way they were. They didn't want "two hot-shot motor officers from LA" coming in and changing things.

They would never say that but it was apparent by their actions. I was used to holding briefings where the officers laughed and joked and showed some enthusiasm. At briefings in Santa Maria the officers were unusually quiet and as soon as the briefing was over, they just picked up their gear and left by way of the back door where they loaded up their cruisers and left the parking lot. They gave me the impression that they liked things the way they were before Klippness and I got there and this was one of their ways of showing it.

But they had some comfort in knowing that Lieutenant Thobe also liked things just the way they were and had told them "to keep and eye on us." If you want to undermine your supervisors and destroy "the chain of command" that's a good way to do it. Of course, we didn't know that at the time.

The DUI program had already begun before I got there. Klippness transferred there in September of 1966 and one month before I reported in, the Santa Maria Times newspaper ran a story reporting 48 DUIs had been arrested the previous month and traffic accidents had decreased by 46 percent.

PART 1: *Chapter 7:* Moving to Santa Maria

Thobe wasn't holding back in letting us know how he felt. As the DUI arrests increased he became increasingly irritable. He knew he could not put out an order to stop arresting drunk drivers so the next best thing was to let Klippness and me know he was becoming increasingly unhappy with the arrests. One could say he was using the Pavlov's dog theory. I'm sure that some of his "old timers" (officers) were also letting him know how they felt about having to finally go to work.

After only one week on the job, I got the following message from the Lieutenant:

> "Sgt. M., Realizing East L.A. & Baldwin Park were off the beaten path & therefore outpaced and outmoded by more progressive and venturesome areas of the state, henceforth in consideration of the above, your education commences with your recent transfer—USE THE NEW G.D. FORM FOR REPORTING ADDRESS CHANGES."

That was my first written communication from Thobe. Klippness got a similar message but pertaining to something else.

A short time later, we received the next missive from Thobe:

> "With the minimal amount of paper work that you have, there is no reason for Accident Reports or other various reports and forms to remain unfinished or uncorrected past the submission deadlines. Example attached. "PLEASE (underlined three times) TAKE TWO MINUTES TO FINISH THE GD THING. LT"

On January 19, 1967, Lieutenant Thobe got a message from the San Luis Obispo Area just north of Santa Maria. The Area Lieutenant, R.R. Roese, who was our sergeant for a time when we were officers in East Los Angeles, sent the following note:

> "Thobe: The Captain has given me an assignment regarding arresting 23102s (DUIs). Since you have Klip and Mitch, the two best 23102 catchers in the country, in your area, perhaps they could give me some "poop." I know they prepared some

material during their pre-Sergeants training at Sacramento on 23102 catching. Would you have them send me any material they have pertaining to the observation and detection of 23102's and any techniques that they have found that assist in the testing. Make it as soon as possible because I have to get hot on this big program. Sincerely, RR"

Klippness and I both developed a DUI tactical plan and submitted it to Inspector Kridler in the Fresno Zone office. Pressure was being applied to all Areas in Zone IV because of our large increase in arrests and the significant reduction in accidents in Santa Maria. Each area is required to send a monthly report to Zone Headquarters and then Zone Headquarters sends a monthly report to Sacramento headquarters. If one area is showing outstanding progress in reducing accidents and arresting DUIs then Headquarters wants to know why surrounding areas aren't doing the same thing.

Santa Maria Times Newspaper Article

Six weeks after I arrived, on February 16, 1967, the Santa Maria Times published the following story under the heading "The CHP Campaign:"

"The number of highway traffic accidents in the Santa Maria area has dropped 19 per cent in the past three months. At the same time, the California Highway Patrol has carried on an intensive campaign against the drinking driver. Arrests for drunken driving tripled during the last three months of 1966.

"Lt. D.M. Thobe, who heads the local CHP office, said there is a strong indication that the campaign against the drinking driver is a direct cause of the reduction in the number of accidents.

"It could, of course, be a coincidence, but this seems unlikely."

"There is no question that the drinking driver contributes materially to the causing of accidents. The CHP office here said nine per cent of the accidents it investigated in this area in the last quarter of 1966 involved a drunken driver.

"And in fatal accidents, the percentage was even higher. More than half of the fatal mishaps here in 1966 involved drunken drivers.

"There have been some criticisms voiced about the campaign of the CHP. Claims are made that the CHP 'stakes out' bars and catches patrons as they are leaving. This may be true.

"But no matter how the CHP gets on the trail of the drinking driver, so long as it is within legal bounds, we can only urge them to press the campaign even harder.

"Catching drinking drivers is not a 'game' for the CHP or other law enforcement officers. It is deadly serious business. The statistics that show half of the fatalities in a year involved drinking drivers emphasizes just how 'deadly' the issue is.

"Drunken drivers are a menace on our highways. They are a menace to themselves and to others who are on the highway at the same time.

"The CHP campaign is evidently bearing fruit. It should continue with the same intensity in the future."

The article expressed the type of mind set that every one should have and support. It was a great article but what Lieutenant Thobe was telling the Santa Maria Times in public and what he was saying privately were two different things.

Thobe's biggest objection to arresting DUIs was he didn't mind the increase in DUIs as long as the people being arrested were the "general public" who had no political connections or positions of influence. Thobe was telling some of the officers who also opposed the increase in DUI arrests, "I was a fool to ever let this drunk driving thing get started in the first place. I'm getting calls all during the night as a result of this."

Another Attempt to Stop DUI Arrests

The next morning, Lieutenant Thobe issued a directive: "Booking of Drunk Driving Suspects."

In consideration of the adverse 23102 (DUI) jury decisions, and after interviewing jury members, it was decided by Mr. Gourley, with my concurrence, that perhaps our total involvement with individual drunks was too great thereby providing additional sympathy for the defendant."

Thobe was saying that the jurors were finding the defendants not guilty because there were too many officers testifying against the DUI.

The directive concluded: "Our involvement will be limited to one officer or sergeant plus the officer transporting samples to the lab . . . . In the meantime, Mr. Gourley has requested that our members do not contact his staff regarding policy or decisions made by his people. All inquiries should be directed through the Officer-in-Charge of this office.

—Thobe, Lieutenant, Officer-in-Charge."

As it turned out, Thobe had neither talked with Gourley nor interviewed jurors. The memo was his attempt to change some key procedures to make it more difficult to arrest and convict drunk drivers.

Thus Thobe was making no secret about wanting to put a stop to the DUI arrests, and most of the officers agreed with him.

Their method was to take a reactive, rather than a proactive approach. That way they didn't make enemies in the community and didn't have to work as hard. It's a lot easier to let people do what they want to do and then clean up the mess they make. They're happy because you are letting them do what they want to do—and the rest of the people are happy that you're cleaning up the mess. That way everyone is happy except the ones being killed and maimed by DUIs.

An officer gets paid the same whether he is having coffee or booking a DUI. An officer arresting someone is a negative action. An officer working an injury or fatal accident is a positive action. In the first case (in the eyes of many) you're "heartless." In the second case (in the eyes of almost all) you're a "protector." But the truth of the matter is you're neither. You can't be a protector if you're part of the problem. And you can't be heartless if you are saving innocent lives.

There was no doubt that Thobe didn't like the DUI "campaign." we were waging. He had made that clear to us while showing an entirely different face to the public. Most of the officers felt the same way as Thobe. They were reluctantly going along with us, but resistance was building.

Thobe's goal became clear; run these two sergeants out of the Santa Maria area and get some sergeants that fit in. What might have surprised them is that I don't like to work any harder than is necessary. In fact, I'd rather be off duty playing softball or golfing. But when on duty, we're paid to make the highways safe.

Using harassment and forcing us to book all of our DUIs ourselves (both actions directly against Departmental policy) wasn't working. Some of the officers, and I'm sure with the concurrence of Lieutenant Thobe, came up with another idea on how to get rid of Klippness and me. Maybe, just maybe, they could discredit us by making it appear that we were arresting innocent people. That would completely ruin us in the community and possibly lead to punitive action or even dismissal. At least it would put a stop to this DUI "craze."

I have always been one to document everything if I foresee problems coming. Without documentation it is your word against theirs and that could be disastrous. There are too many chances for manipulation and lying. Documents stand alone and speak for themselves.

I started documenting everything when I saw what we were up against and it proved to be invaluable.

DUI visits CHP office

Another DUI arrest that stirred a lot of controversy occurred on June 27, 1967. It started when Clifford Bewley came into the CHP front office to have a mechanical ticket signed off.

Mechanical tickets are issued to violators when their car has defective equipment. The equipment need only be corrected and an officer confirm the correction with his signature.

Bewley was doing everything right except for one thing, he was looking for a CHP officer while driving under the influence of alcohol. Lieutenant Thobe and Officer Cameron were in the front office while Bewley was talking to Clerk-Typist Capitani. All three of them had to be aware of Bewley's condition. Klippness was in the briefing room finishing his shift when I left to go on patrol.

Klippness had just finished his last report and was getting ready to leave for home. As he stood up, he glanced out the window and observed Bewley getting into his car, which was the only car in front of the office. Klippness didn't like what he saw and the manner in which the car was being maneuvered was even more disturbing. Klippness knew I was in the back parking lot getting ready to leave.

He radioed, "You better check out that green, '59 Ford headed toward Hwy 101 northbound. He might be under the influence."

Neither Klippness nor I, trusted either Thobe, Capitani or Cameron to do their job and we were not sure that any of the three would know a DUI "if he walked into the office." Which is what this DUI did.

When I first observed Bewley he was driving on the frontage road that dead ended. Because of his condition, he had missed the on-ramp and had mistaken it for the frontage road. When I asked to see his drivers license and observed his demeanor and other intoxicating symptoms, it was obvious Mr. Bewley was under the influence of alcohol. How could Thobe and Cameron let this drunk get into his car and drive away? Why hadn't Capitani alerted someone?

I called the beat officer to "11-98" (meet at my location). Officer Cochiolo responded and handled the arrest. Officer Cochiolo took Bewley to the Santa Barbara County Sheriffs jail where Bewley submitted to a blood test.

Bewley did not deny being under the influence and admitted that he had drunk "part of a one-half pint of 'Wolfschmidt' vodka and two beers."

When I asked where he was coming from he replied, "Solvang (a small community to the south)"

How many stops had he made? "One"

Where? "Buellton.(another small community to the south)"

Bewley made no mention that he had stopped at the Santa Maria CHP office.

PART 1: *Chapter 7:* Moving to Santa Maria

Officer Cochiolo finished the booking and returned to the office. He told me that the Santa Barbara County Sheriffs jailer had released Bewley before he (Cochiolo) had left the facility. I told Cochiolo that Bewley should have been held there until he sobered up.

In some rare cases a jail will release an arrestee to a sober, responsible person but they do not normally let the drunk walk (or stagger) out of the building on his own. This was another example of how some individuals have accepted this destructive lifestyle as "normal." And we're talking about the "front line," in this case a CHP officer and a Sheriffs jailer.

We decided to go have dinner at one of the local restaurants and Cochiolo climbed into the passenger seat. We were southbound State Route 135 approaching Betteravia Rd. in the City of Santa Maria (there were no decent restaurants in the countys immediate vicinity) when I spotted a green, 59 Ford 2 door, coming in the opposite direction. And sure enough, it was Mr. Bewley and his driving had not changed much from the first time I saw him less than 3 hours earlier. Officer Cochiolo told me he did not feel comfortable arresting Mr. Bewley a second time so I told him I would handle it. That's probably why Cochiolo didn't take any action when the jailer released Bewley while he was still under the influence. Officer Cochiolo was not cutout to be a Highway Patrolman. To his credit, 10 months later he resigned from the Department and went back to his old job of driving a big rig.

Bewley climbed out of his car and said, "I'm just trying to get home." I told him he was in no condition to be driving. He said, "Well, I've got to get home."

Bewley had made only one stop after being released from jail and that was to purchase another one-half pint bottle of Wolfschmidt vodka that he had placed in the right front seat.

He said, "I'm no alcoholic. I bought it for tomorrow maybe."

He also brought up the point that he had been arrested a few hours earlier (he apparently did not remember either of us from the earlier arrest) and he volunteered that the jailer should not have released him until he had "sobered up."

I agreed with him and told him that I was going to try and get the Sheriff's release policy changed. I thought at the time that this incident might be just the catalyst.

Bewley was placed under arrest for a second time but this time was taken to the Santa Maria City jail because we were now in that jurisdiction.

It didn't take long to get a policy change at the Sheriff's jail. When Sheriff James W. Webster, a very competent and progressive law enforcement administrator who headed the Santa Barbara Sheriff's Department, became aware of the situation, he made an immediate policy change: "No prisoner will be released before he is completely sober."

Too Many DUIs being Arrested

In spite of Lieutenant Thobe, and whoever else might be supporting him, we were able to continue our DUI arrests in the Santa Maria area and achieve a noticeable reduction of traffic accidents. The news media and other law enforcement agencies continued taking notice.

In March there were 67 DUI arrests and a 38 per cent reduction in accidents. We were training the officers how to detect DUIs and record details of the arrest to improve their conviction rate. Lieutenant Thobe was still playing golf on duty but was becoming more concerned with the spotlight on the Santa Maria office.

He told Klippness and me, "I want you out there doing other things than arresting drunk drivers."

We asked him what was it that we were not doing?

He said, "That's neither here nor there (A comment he used quite frequently when he didn't have an answer). This whole thing is too political. I was a fool to ever let it get started. And I'm tired of getting these phone calls all night."

One of us asked, "Who are you getting the phone calls from?"

Thobe ignored the question and said, "I want you concentrating on those commercial trucks driving up and down the highway."

PART 1: *Chapter 7:* Moving to Santa Maria   103

A few days later, Thobe came into the Sergeants section and said he wanted to talk to us again.

"You know what they're saying in Buellton (CHP substation bordering the south) about you? How are we going to stop those sergeants in Santa Maria?"

Klippness and I said, "Stop us from what?"

Thobe said, "Arresting drunk drivers. You just don't get it, do you? In San Luis Obispo (CHP substation bordering the north) you're the laughing stock of the office. You're doing a T.O.'s (traffic officer's) work."

Harassment Starts Full Time

Lieutenant Thobe's next move was to have us write a memo on everything we did.

He smirked and said, "I'm going to keep you busy and you won't have time to get out there and play traffic officer." Klippness had already got prior approval to teach a class at college but Thobe changed his days off so that it would be impossible.

He also told the officers that "You don't have to take any orders from the sergeants. And that includes having them book their own DUIs."

Thobe started writing us nasty notes and giving us meaningless assignments. The result was that in May we only had 11 DUI arrests and a 6 percent decrease in accidents.

At the start of each shift officers are briefed about pertinent information they should know and suspects that may be wanted. It was not uncommon for Lieutenant Thobe to wait until we were in the middle of discussing a directive from Headquarters or conducting special training before he would stroll into the briefing room carrying his golf club and interrupt us by saying, "Would you guys like to see my golf swing?" Sometimes he would bounce a golf ball.

The officers would laugh and he would laugh along with them. Then he would say, "Let me show you my back swing—Oh! Am I interrupting anything?" He would look directly at us, smile and then stroll out again without waiting on an answer, which he never expected.

These types of interruptions, which were a form of harassment prohibited by Departmental policy, and Thobe's general conduct concerning DUIs prompted me to refer to Thobe as "stupid" and a "jerk." My comments would prove costly later.

Not long after, CHP Inspector James Bryant came to the Area so I had an opportunity to tell him in person how Thobe had been harassing Klippness and me during the officer's briefing sessions.

Instead of being concerned, he laughed and said, "He set you up and you fell for it."

Bryant meant that Thobe baited me into calling him names so he could file punitive action against me for being insubordinate and discourteous. Apparently it was OK for him to interrupt briefings and harass his subordinates. Inspector Bryant was one of Commissioner Sullivan's cronies and was not known for his intelligence.

We didn't know at the time that Thobe had some of the officers reporting to him everything that Klippness and I did or said. Of course, they were closely protected and given special favors for doing it, such as permitting them to work for a CHP tow service when off-duty. That is strictly prohibited by the Department—but so was Thobe's playing golf on-duty.

Word got back to Klippness and me, through our friend Sergeant Frank Loper, that the Department had spread the word that if we didn't stop arresting DUIs we were going to be fired. It was that simple.

Loper supported us 100 percent in what we were doing and didn't want to see us fired. He was only informing us "for our own good." Some of the DUI arrests we were making were prominent citizens. One was a CHP area Commander's son-in-law, another was a Colonel from Vandenberg Air Force Base, as well as prominent businessmen and anyone else that might be DUI regardless of their status in life.

And it was just as easy to fire a sergeant as it was to transfer him. Showing cause for a transfer is almost impossible—especially if there is no cause.

Lt. Goodwin's Drunken Incident

The Officer-in-Charge of the Buellton substation, George Goodwin, was a close friend of Thobe. They were "two peas in a pod" except Lieutenant Goodwin was known for his heavy drinking. Frank Loper, a Sergeant in the area, said that Goodwin didn't want a DUI program in the area because he (Goodwin) would be the first one arrested. The problem was compounded by the fact Goodwin did all of his traveling in a CHP cruiser and when he got drunk he also used profanity no matter who was present.

During one of our monthly tri-tip barbecues for officers at the Santa Maria Club and in the presence of CHP Inspector Walker, Lieutenant Thobe, Sergeants Dzamba, Klippness and numerous others, Lieutenant Goodwin became extremely intoxicated. There were several prominent Santa Maria community leaders also present.

Everyone was putting up with his loud, boisterous, profane and insulting remarks but when one of the local citizens noticed Goodwin was wearing a 2 inch service revolver, he made an urgent request. He said because of Goodwin's drunken condition and boisterous manner, someone should take his weapon from him before there was a physical altercation.

When he was drunk at a Riding Club three years earlier, Goodwin had fired several shots from his revolver at a citizen's feet. They didn't want a repeat of that in Santa Maria. But no one ever asked Goodwin for his firearm that night and no action was ever taken for his conduct even though a Zone Inspector witnessed it all.

Criticizing Reports for No Reason

After three months of increasing DUI arrests—and phone calls complaining about them—Lieutenant Thobe was determined to get things back to normal in Santa Maria.

The first of March he started criticizing the DUI arrest reports using a black felt pin for emphasis: "The attached arrest will probably be thrown out by the D.A. If it is I can't blame him. A p—poor report that doesn't say a thing." It was an arrest that I had turned over to Officer Pledger and, of course, he had written the report. Thobe thought there should be more in the report about the DUI's driving than "weaving from lane to lane and straddling lanes."

I responded with this memo:

> "Some reports are not as strong as we would like them to be but we can only record what we observe. Our CHP Drinking Driver manual directs us to stop the drinking driver as soon as possible. The deputy district attorney said to let them drive so we can have a better report. This is in direct conflict with our policy and very dangerous for the public. We could write a book every time we arrest someone and there would still be not guilty verdicts and dispositions made. I believe the CHP is being made the "scapegoat" but you tell us what you want and we'll do it."

The next month, in April, we made 37 DUI arrests and accidents were down 10 per cent. In response, Thobe announced to Klippness and me that we were no longer to take a cruiser home.

"If you get an emergency call-out then just get in your car and come to the office and pick one up."

We asked him why he was doing this and he said, "The Buellton sergeants lost theirs so I'm going to take yours."

I called the Buellton office and got this response. "I don't know what Thobe is talking about. One of us takes a cruiser home every night. Someone must be mad at you."

Thobe's next move also came when he ordered Klippness and me to write a memorandum every time we were subpoenaed to court and worked any overtime. This was just another form of harassment because the Overtime slips contained the same information as the memos he was requiring.

His efforts to curb DUI arrests were becoming more extreme. Lieutenant Thobe told Officers Edwards and Hilker that they could go out of service between 1 am and 2:30 am even though he knew they were the only unit available, and that was the time the bars closed and drunk driving was at its height. This was in direct conflict with Departmental policy and would further endanger the public.

Thobe came up with another plan to discourage us from arresting DUIs even though it was also against Departmental policy. Looking back, this should have been the first indication that someone higher up was involved because Lt. Thobe could not operate in this fashion without the knowledge of CHP Headquarters in Sacramento.

The order read: "Sgts. K & M. In order to gather relevant statistical information regarding drunk arrests and to reduce the loss of manpower occasioned by total involvement, in the future please process to conclusion and without assistance all routine drunk drivers that you may observe during your field duty. Thobe"

This order did not slow Klippness and me down one bit. We didn't mind booking our own DUIs.

No Area Coverage for 30 minutes

The next thing that Thobe did was unimaginable. Suddenly and without notice, he changed the monthly graveyard schedule without any input from anyone. He took the 9:30 pm to 6:00 am graveyard shift (also referred to as the drunk driving shift) and changed it to 9:00 pm to 5:30 am. The problem was the day shift didn't start until 6:00 am.

Klippness went to Thobe and said, "Do you realize that you don't have anyone working between 5:30 am and 6:00 am? If we had a major accident or other emergency, there would be no one to respond." Klippness also reminded Thobe that he had also taken our on-call cruiser, which would delay our response even more.

Thobe said, "I know all that. I don't want the graveyard officers getting off at the same time as the early morning officers start. This way they can't get a ride home unless they wait around for 30 minutes."

It was never clear why Thobe did this because if he didn't want the officers giving each other rides home then all he had to do was put out an s.o.p. (standard operation procedure) to that effect. Of course, we didn't have an Area S.O.P manual, which was required in all CHP area offices.

I understand that some one phoned Captain Dahl and told him what Thobe had done and the schedule was changed back as soon as Thobe dropped by the office after playing golf the next day.

Notification Now Required when Arresting Prominent DUIs

Lieutenant Thobe was relentless in his campaign to rein in DUI arrests.

He told the officers verbally, because he couldn't do it in writing, that no more reports would be finished on overtime at the end of the shift. Again, this was in direct conflict with Departmental policy. Thobe added, "I think arresting drunk drivers is just a deliberate attempt to make overtime."

Shortly thereafter, a notice to All Officers, requiring notification of supervisors was posted on the bulletin board. The subject was "Occurrences Requiring Notification of a Supervisor," such as certain fatal accidents, an unusual calamity, etc. It also included arrests of individuals claiming "diplomatic immunity" and "personage whose identity is newsworthy or of personal concern to the Department, i.e., members of the Legislature or political scene, motion picture people, law enforcement members. These are only examples and not all inclusive."

Now this order is consistent with Departmental policy and is required not only by the California Highway Patrol, but almost every law enforcement agency. There's good reason for the policy, but it does depend on the highest ranking officer that is notified and what he decides should be done. If it's for information only then that's one thing but if it's for special favors, then that's another thing.

Requiring the officer to make a notification can be a good check and balance. If there is no notification required, the officer(s) is left to make the decision on his own and on many occasions that can lead to serious problems because of the diverse attitudes officers have toward DUI. There's a chance for abuse but overall I think it's a good policy.

Thobe Ordered to Take Training

Shortly after the Inspector's visit, from June 12-16, 1967, Thobe was called to Sacramento for training. In his absence, Captain Dahl came to the substation for the first time and attended our squad meeting. He told the officers that there was no problem with using overtime to finish reports. Overtime was a motivation for arresting DUIs as it should be. What better way to spend Highway Patrol money than removing drunk drivers from the highways. Unfortunately, overtime doesn't automatically lead to more DUI arrests. Officers get paid the same regardless of their enforcement efforts and some would rather forego the overtime than arrest DUIs.

When Thobe got back from "training" he took a three weeks vacation and Jerry Klippness was, by necessity, assigned as Officer-in-Charge. Lieutenant Goodwin from the Buellton area and Thobe's close friend, showed up in Santa Maria the next day, June 19.

Klippness asked Goodwin, "How about having us come down to Buellton and arresting some of your drunk drivers? It might cut down on some of your accidents."

Goodwin replied, "We don't want to stop accidents in Buellton. The more accidents you have; the more officers you get."

At the time Buellton had 9 officers and we had 15 with a promise that the Santa Maria Office would be increased to 22 officers. Instead Buellton eventually got an additional 6 officers and we stayed at 15, almost exclusively because of the number of increased accidents in Buellton.

Thobe returned from vacation on July 10, 1967, and three days later put out an order that Sergeants would be required to put on a minimum of 100 miles on their cruisers each day.

Sergeant Dzamba was passing through the area and saw the memorandum posted on the bulletin board and commented, "What's that all about?"

Klippness and I both ignored the stupid order and nothing ever came of it.

Decisions Endangering Officers Lives

Lieutenant Thobe didn't restrict his actions toward discouraging DUI enforcement, he also made decisions that endangered the officers' lives.

Even the officers that were secretly supporting his actions against us recognized that his behavior was now jeopardizing their own safety. It's one thing jeopardizing the public's safety by not enforcing DUI but now Thobe was getting "personal" with his outrageous conduct.

In the first incident, Klippness was working the evening shift when Officer Vind returned from the parking lot where he had just loaded his equipment and checked his cruiser in preparation for going on patrol.

Vind told Klippness, "The tires on my assigned patrol vehicle are smooth and unsafe in my opinion."

Thobe overheard the complaint and joined them in going to the rear parking lot to check the tires. After glancing at the tires, Thobe told Vind that "the tires are all right."

Officer Vind said he wouldn't feel safe driving fast on them.

Thobe, raised his voice and, as he turned around and charged into the office, said, "If you don't like our equipment then why don't you get a safe job selling shoes some place."

Eleven days later another officer "flagged" the cruiser, reporting that the tires still were unsafe. Four officers in all reported two different cruisers as having unsafe tires on the rear.

On another occasion, several officers reported they were having problems with a defective battery in one of the cruisers and they went directly to Lieutenant Thobe's office to register their concern.

On the way out from the Lieutenant's office, one of the officers casually mentioned to Klippness that they had just told Thobe about a car battery problem. Klippness knew the officers were "out of line" by going directly to the Lieutenant and not following the chain of command. But this was standard procedure in Santa Maria.

A couple of days later, Thobe, after waiting until all the officers had left the office, told Klippness, "I had the auto mechanic switch the battery to another patrol car, now let's see if we hear anymore complaints."

In law enforcement a dead battery can be disastrous. Just visualize an officer requesting backup in an emergency and the backup officer's cruiser not starting. Even the radio would have been inoperative.

Sergeant Klippness later filed an official grievance against Thobe and included both of these incidents.

The grievance went through Captain Dahl, the Santa Barbara Area Commander, and Supervising Inspector Reinjohn, the Zone 4 Commander. Nothing officially was ever done.

It would not be revealed until the problems in Santa Maria finally became known statewide the role that Captain Dahl, Supervising Inspector Reinjohn, and Assistant Commissioner Kridler played in trying to protect Thobe.

But some of his actions were humorous. One day, after Thobe returned from playing golf, he walked into the squad room during briefing with an angry countenance and wasted no time in remarking, "One of you took my Title 13 (manual)."

Everyone looked puzzled but no one said a word. As he cast an accusatory look from officer to officer, he said, "You might as well bring it back because I've got the inserts (revisions) and it won't do you any good."

Later it was found behind the copy machine after he had ordered another one. Officers would have no use for a Title 13 manual, which only contained regulations used by administrators. Of course, Thobe never apologized.

Performance Report Leads to Another Grievance

It was time for me to receive a Personal Development Checklist (PDC) rating of my performance from Lieutenant Thobe. This is an annual form that all uniformed officers receive but the evaluation is no better than the one preparing it. To put it another way, there is no check or balance unless one files a grievance and provides documented evidence that the rater is bias. That's what I did after receiving the evaluation.

As a result of the grievance, Captain Dahl made Thobe rewrite the PDC evaluation because it didn't comply with Departmental policy. For example, there were no goals.

This is what Thobe put in his rewrite:

> "The productivity of your subordinates reflects your own enforcement interests, i.e., a commendable increase in drunk driving arrests but unsatisfactory effort against commercial vehicles and slow driving violations.

> Goal: While we do not undervalue the importance of a concerted and continuing program directed against drunk drivers, you should make a greater effort to stimulate your subordinates to also satisfactorily discharge other of their enforcement obligations; particularly those which periodically and for valid reasons are given Departmental emphasis."

I filed a second grievance pointing out that I was doing as I had been trained and understood all of my responsibilities.

The comment, "The productivity of your subordinates reflects your own enforcement interest, i.e., a commendable increase in drunk driving arrests . . ." was really very complimentary but that certainly wasn't Thobe's intention. It was suppose to be a negative statement. My goal "of a continuing program directed against drunk drivers" is also the goal of the California Highway Patrol. However, that wasn't Lieutenant Thobe's goal. As far as "stimulating subordinates to satisfactorily discharge other of their enforcement obligations," the following statistics were provided. These accomplishments were a joint effort by both Klippness and me whose performance rating was similar to mine.

The first quarter results before Thobe started his destructive tactics were:

Arrest citations	increase	19% from 1535 to 1831
Drunk Drivers	increase	1,076% from 13 to 153
Mechanical warnings	increase	208 % from 304 to 937
All accidents	decrease	34.5% from 139 to 91
Reportable accidents	decrease	36.5% from 58 to 38
Fatal accidents	decrease	100% from 1 to 0

However, Lieutenant Thobe's tactics and open hostility were beginning to cause turmoil in the office. DUI arrests were slowing and traffic accidents were increasing.

In the month of July there were only 18 DUI arrests with 52 traffic accidents. A 40 percent increase in traffic accidents over the previous year. And it continued to get worse. The next month, August, DUI arrests dropped to 14 and traffic accidents soared to 62, an 82 percent increase over the previous year.

Concentrate More on Slow Moving and Commercial Vehicles

There was nothing in our area statistics to support traffic accidents being caused by violations of slow moving vehicles or commercial vehicles. Fatal and injury accidents were being caused by DUIs and speeders. Occasionally, one would see a slow moving vehicle in the fast lane but how much training does it take to know a car is impeding or driving too slow? I can't imagine a sergeant having to say, "Alright men, I want you to go out there and find a vehicle traveling too slow in the left lane. The violator will be driving slower than the speed limit and cars will be passing him on the right. Do you have any questions?"

Don't get me wrong, I think a vehicle impeding traffic by driving too slow in the left lane, causing other vehicles on the road to suddenly change lanes and pass to the right, is a good ticket. I've written my share even though it's a "hard sell" to the violator. The mentality of the slow mover is "slower is safer" and "you should be out there getting those speeders."

Moving violations committed by commercial vehicles are basically the same as any other vehicle except for their size, which is also a factor. I don't think there was an officer in Santa Maria, including Klippness and me, who would pass up a commercial violation. Our statistics bore that out. We paid special attention to big rigs because we knew that drivers sometime use sleeping pills and other drugs to stay awake. And who hasn't been intimidated by a truck tractor and trailer combination tailgating them?

Lieutenant Thobe concluded the evaluation form with, "Appropriate supervisory training will be conducted for your benefit during the coming months."

I'm glad Thobe said it would be "appropriate" training because I've always thought of "inappropriate" training as a waste of time.

Chapter 8
Harris Grade Fatal Changes my Life

As DUI arrests decreased, traffic accidents increased. Klippness and I would make arrests if we saw a DUI but we weren't actively looking for them. There was no doubt that if we didn't stop arresting DUIs we were going to be fired.

The California Highway Patrol was my livelihood and I did have a wife and three teenage children that I had to consider. Our salary covered our monthly expenses and that was about it. If I was to get fired whose going to take care of the family? I couldn't even afford an attorney. It would be more than "fighting City Hall", I would be fighting the State of California.

It would be Klippness' and my word against one lieutenant, 15 traffic officers, a clerk-typist and other CHP personnel. In addition, Commissioner Sullivan would send investigators into the Area on the pretense they were conducting a fair and impartial investigation when, in fact, their real purpose would be to try to find something that they could use to support what they had already made up their minds they were going to do. And that was to fire us. There was no Officer's Bill of Rights like they have today.

We weren't worried about the evidence they would gather; we could disprove that and we had plenty of our own evidence. All we wanted was an honest investigation but from what we had already experienced, we knew that wasn't going to happen. We knew the group that was in power was not going to play by the rules. We knew they would do some "creative" writing and find some "witnesses." That would include individuals who had been arrested and other officers who could be counted on to be biased.

But my fear of being fired turned to anger one night and a declaration that I had memorized and lived by from my teenage years came to mind. William Penn had said when he was falsely imprisoned: "Prison will be my grave before I budge a jot, for I owe my conscience to no mortal man. Right is right even if everyone is against it; and wrong is wrong even if everyone is for it."

The incident that changed my mind—and my life—occurred on September 9, 1967. I was working the evening shift when a call came in about a possible "11-44" (fatal accident) on Harris Grade near Highway 1.

I acknowledged the call and advised the dispatcher to send two beat units because of the location and the probability of it being a fatal accident. Units responding are suppose to give their location so that the dispatcher will have an idea of their arrival time. Both units with two officers in each car acknowledged the call but did not give their location. I gave my location as southbound US 101 near Betteravia, which was about 12 miles from the accident scene.

While en route to the scene on Highway 1 near State Route 135, I observed the tail lights of a vehicle traveling ahead of me and estimated its speed in excess of 100 mph. I advised dispatch that I was now in pursuit of a vehicle traveling in excess of 100 mph, gave my location and requested backup. Officers Hilker and Edwards, one of the units responding to the "11-44" accident, identified themselves as being the occupants of the car I was pursuing after they heard my broadcast.

I then told them to turn on their emergency lights and siren. They ignored the request and went off the freeway using the Clark off-ramp. I again requested that they turn on their emergency equipment. The second time they complied. Lieutenant Thobe had told all of the officers that they could ignore any directions given by the Sergeants. I couldn't help but think of the liability the State would face if they had crashed at that speed without their emergency equipment activated.

Upon arrival at the scene, I observed an ambulance standing by while Officer Short was attempting to assemble his camera so that he could photograph Lynn Allard, 14, who had been ejected from the seriously damaged car that had apparently hit a ditch and flipped over.

PART 1: *Chapter 8:* Harris Grade Fatal Changes my Life

She was laying near the car with her clothing in disarray. I immediately asked them what they were doing and why the young girl had not been placed in the ambulance and taken to the hospital. Officer Short remarked that he wanted to take a few pictures first and "besides she's dead anyway."

I must admit the young girl appeared to be dead and investigators do like to have photographs to assist them with their investigation but somehow it just didn't seem right. She had just been killed by a DUI and she deserved more respect than just to be left laying there for the sake of a photograph. I had a daughter her age and I would want her in an ambulance being rushed to an emergency hospital. Let a doctor make the final decision.

I told the ambulance attendant to place the young girl on the gurney. She was taken to the Valley Community Hospital where she was pronounced dead upon arrival by Dr. Riehle.

If a person is obviously dead at the scene then a coroner must respond to the scene and "he takes charge of the body." From that point on, no one is allowed to even move the body except the coroner. It can get quite involved and the body may lay there for hours. That's one of the reasons why I told the ambulance driver to take her to the hospital; I felt it was better for all concerned to just testify where the body came to rest and let the coroner respond to the hospital.

An investigation of the circumstances surrounding the accident revealed that four persons were in the car. The driver, Greg Collier, and his male friend and two young 14-year-old girls. One of the girls was Lynn Allard.

Earlier that night the two girls were walking down the street in Lompoc when Collier and his buddy drove by. Both of the males had been drinking and were already under the influence. They were heading to a liquor store to get more beer when they saw the two young girls walking on the sidewalk. They stopped alongside the girls and asked them if they wanted a ride. The girls said they were going to get a malt and the boys said if they would get in the car they would take them to the malt shop. The girls got in the car but instead of buying malts the boys bought more liquor and sped away.

Collier and his friend opened the beer they had just purchased and continued to drink and drive at high speeds. The girls became very frightened and begged Collier to stop and let them out. Collier refused. While continuing at a high rate of speed, Collier, in his drunken condition, missed a curve and crashed the car killing Allard and severely injuring her girl friend.

Seeing Lynn Allard's crumbled little body lying in a dirt field through no fault of her own (other than to believe someone was going to get her a malt) touched my heart to the point of saying enough is enough. I'm not going to stop actively arresting DUIs regardless what happens to me.

At the Valley Hospital, I questioned the driver, Greg Collier, who was in his late teens, concerning the accident and his sobriety. He was upset because he believed the girl to be dead and his intoxicated condition only fueled his emotions. He continually asked if the passenger had died. I finally went to the doctor and explained that the driver was becoming very emotional and angry because no one would tell him the condition of the girl. I asked the doctor if he thought it would be better if he was told. The doctor advised me to tell him.

I explained that one of the young girls, "didn't make it." Collier became extremely upset for a few minutes. He beat his fist on the table and shouted that he had killed a human being.

To make matters worse, the arresting officer, Hilker, turned in a sloppy report. It seemed to me that no one really cared—or understood—that we needed to protect the innocent victims by both arresting drunk drivers and by carefully and professionally reporting the incident so that those responsible would be held to answer.

The accident report submitted by Officer Hilker contained numerous mistakes and omissions. The main problem being that he took the drunk driver's word for the time of the accident as 9:30 pm and ignored an independent witness who notified the police and set the time as 10:10 pm. This caused much confusion the next day and it was necessary to xerox the report three times. The real problem was that this kind of sloppiness could undermine the case against the drunk driver.

This was a distressing symptom of a growing problem in the Santa Maria sub-station. Officer Hilker—heeding Lt. Thobe—had expressed that he did

PART 1: Chapter 8: Harris Grade Fatal Changes my Life

not agree with the drunk driving enforcement policy of the CHP. Like some of the legislators, judges, police officers, CHP officers, community leaders, and the list goes on, he thought the Blood Alcohol Concentration (BAC) of .15% was too low.

It was entirely foreseeable that this basic disagreement with policies for arresting drunk drivers led to incompetent and irresponsible reporting.

The next morning I got Laura's undivided attention and told her about the fatal accident and my decision to follow my conscience and actively pursue DUIs.

"If we don't, more innocent people are going to die," I told her.

Laura agreed and said, "I wouldn't have it any other way."

She continued, "They can't fire you for doing your job."

I said, "Yeah, they can. But if they do, we'll fight them to the end."

She said, "But if you don't arrest drunk drivers, then you become like them and I don't want to see that."

I told her I was going to talk to Klippness and I had no doubt that he would agree. And agreeing meant he would put his job on the line too.

Then there was always the chance that someone at Headquarters would wake up and discover the truth and we wouldn't lose our jobs.

But we weren't kidding ourselves—and the prospects did not look good.

We knew Commissioner Sullivan was not going to back us. We had lost all confidence in him and those he appointed to carry out his will. We knew what his position was on DUI.

But we also knew the real California Highway Patrol had already given us eleven commendations for our DUI enforcement and Dahl had signed four of those commendations.

Klippness Agrees to put Job on the Line

I contacted Klippness that afternoon and told him that I was going to start actively arresting DUIs again. He and his family had just as much to lose as we did but he didn't hesitate in saying, "Bob, I feel the same way you do and so does Virginia. Let's do it." Then he added, "Would you really want to work for an organization that would allow this? I wouldn't."

We also knew that there were some real honorable and respectful CHP officers of all ranks wearing the "blue and gold" and, hopefully, they would not sit idly by and let something like this happen. We figured we could at least count on the California Association of Highway Patrolmen.

At this point, DUI arrests had dropped to 14 a month and traffic accidents had increased 82 per cent. But hopefully that was going to change.

From that point on both Klippness and I became proactive in detecting DUIs as opposed to reactive. But with every DUI arrested came more reprisals.

Some of the reprisals were petty. Three weeks later, Thobe ordered Klippness to be a guest speaker at the Santa Maria Lions Club but would not allow any overtime to be taken. Four months later Officer Hathaway appeared at a similar function and received overtime.

District Attorneys Office Reveals Its Agenda

Unfortunately, we were facing opposition from the DA's Office as well—and not just on DUI cases—because individual Deputy District Attorneys do not always agree with how violations of the law should be handled.

For example, Deputy District Attorney Sprague dismissed a speed ticket involving a passenger vehicle towing a trailer. Officer Vind, who described the violator's passenger as a "beautiful female" was exceeding the 50 mph limit by driving in excess of 65 mph in a fog. The Deputy DA said, "He was just passing through Santa Maria. I don't like to hit everyone."

Officer Vind was under the impression that the passenger was the deciding factor in the dismissal. The Deputy DA just wanted to be the "good guy."

PART 1: Chapter 8: Harris Grade Fatal Changes my Life

That is the same reason some DUIs aren't prosecuted and celebrities are treated differently.

This same Deputy DA had expressed to officers that, "80 mph is proper if the driver is safe." The maximum speed limit was 55 mph at the time. And cars and roadways were not as safe as they are now. This is an example of a court official supplanting his individual enforcement beliefs over the law and, there, lies another major problem with DUI enforcement.

This incident reminded me of when I worked in East Los Angeles and an Alhambra judge had received a citation for following too close. Some officers stopped writing violators for the same offense if the violation occurred within the judge's jurisdiction because, at his directive, all tickets for following too close were to be dismissed. I kept writing the violation. Why let people's lives be jeopardized just because a judge is not doing his job?

Unfortunately, the Santa Maria Court operated like the Alhambra judge and I have no doubt most courts throughout the United States operate in the same manner. My conversations with other officers during my 3-months training at the FBI National Academy bears this out.

It all starts with a liberal judge who has his or her own agenda. They handle their caseloads like the television show, "Let's make a deal."

In one "Deal," the court dropped a second DUI charge against Lynnis McDonald because she had pled guilty to a first DUI charge. That was the official reason given.

That's justice?

And all McDonald had to do was pay a small fine. A DUI with a prior in front of a jury would be a "slam dunk" and should require some jail time. But if you killed someone, the court would take that a little more serious. You might have to spend a couple of days in jail—unless, of course, you were a celebrity.

Another "deal" that just didn't ring right was my arrest of prominent businessman Willard Gallant at 12:45 pm on a Sunday. After observing the car weaving and being corrected in a jerky motion, I stopped him south of Lakeview. He was obviously under the influence and his wife agreed, in his presence, that she should have been driving.

At the jail he blew a .12% but refused to answer any questions.

"I want to call my lawyer first," was his reply.

He did say that he had never been arrested. However, a check of his driving record showed he had been convicted of a prior DUI.

When the arrest report was received by the Santa Maria District Attorney's Office, Deputy DA James Fahres rejected the DUI arrest complaint outright with the following "Reason for Rejection":

> "The combination of minimal driving pattern and low breathalyser reading of .12% and the fact that the defendant answered no questions to indicate how much he had been drinking or if the breathalyser reading might have been higher or lower earlier in the evening does not add up to enough evidence to convict."

Talk about let's make a deal. All of this was done behind closed doors without ever discussing the details with the arresting officer, in this case, me.

The first thing that drew my attention to the dismissal was the fact Gallant worked for Union Oil Company of California, a very influential business in the community. "Lets make a deal" starts with who you are and how much political pressure you can exert. If you have no influence, then there is not going to be any deal. And justifying a deal is not really a problem because courts don't have anyone checking on them.

In this case:

> (1) A driving pattern should have nothing to do with the conviction. The object is to get the DUI stopped as soon as possible before he kills or injures someone. However, Deputy Fahres told several officers that they should wait until they have a good driving pattern before stopping a DUI.

(2) The reading of .12% was more than adequate (it is presently .08%) and the results of his field sobriety tests clearly detailed in the report substantiated that he was under the influence.

(3) How could the defendant not answering any questions on how much he had to drink be considered? Does that mean if a DUI won't tell you how much he's had to drink then you are suppose to him let go?

(4) The justification that "the breathalyzer reading might have been higher or lower earlier in the evening" was nothing more than gobbledygook.

Deals should not be made when people's lives are at stake. You can be assured if a DUI ran into the judge's or deputy district attorney's families, there wouldn't be a deal. I'm only mentioning a few personal DUI cases where a liberal judge or district attorney "let them off." One could fill a volume of books with DUI dismissals and reductions being made across the United States every day.

We could fill a few more books with the number of people the DUIs have killed and maimed since they were released. Courts should be required to publicly report all of their DUI court cases and final dispositions. The public would be shocked—and the public has a right to know.

But prominent businessman Gallant's case was mild compared to the case of Ivan Newberry, who worked at Vandenberg Air Force Base in Lompoc.

Newberry was arrested for DUI and submitted to a breathalyzer test, which revealed his intoxication to be .29%. At a .29% level a person is about to pass out. It's almost four times the recognized level of under the influence. When the case got to court, it was dismissed in the "Interest of Justice" by Deputy D.A. James Fahres.

The reason given was that the defendant pled guilty to a previous drunk driving charge where his blood alcohol level was a .30%. That type of reasoning is like saying we dismissed murder charges against someone because they pled guilty to killing someone a couple of months before. It's a two-for-one deal. Buy one and get the second one free.

If the courts, legislatures and law enforcement took drunk driving more seriously in terms of penalties and enforcement, literally thousands of lives could be saved because the public would be forced to take the issue seriously before a loved one is killed or maimed.

This is the case today, and it was the case in 1967, where the little town of Santa Maria became a perfect example of how court and law enforcement officials refused to protect the public for their own personal reasons. Lt. Thobe was a perfect example.

Thobe's Work Day Included Golf

Thobe played golf on an average of three times a week. Barbara Capitani, the Clerk-Typist, knew how to reach him if she thought he should be disturbed.

One time an Inspector came into Santa Maria unexpectedly and asked Capitani where he could find the Lieutenant. She went into the Lieutenant's office and made a whispering call on the phone. I could just see Thobe, in his golf cart, racing to the clubhouse once he got the news. Only a few minutes later he showed up at the office. He wasn't in uniform but he didn't want to keep the Inspector waiting. There was no doubt in my mind that the Inspector knew Thobe was playing golf by the manner in which he was acting.

I always thought that the reason Capitani never smiled was because of how hard she had to work, especially with the increase in citations and DUIs, and all the time knowing that Thobe's work day consisted of playing golf while making three times her salary. But she also knew that as long as she kept her silence she had real job security. She was Thobe's "eyes and ears" and he was her security blanket. If she ever needed any time off, she had no problem getting it. If she received a citizen's complaint or had a run-in with an officer, the other party was always found at fault. No problem.

Campaign to Discredit DUI Arrests

In November 1967, Officer Edwards and DeLaGuerra made the first step toward discrediting us.

I had stopped Nathan Lewis for DUI and had called them to handle the booking. They arrested him and took him to the Santa Maria jail where he submitted to a breathalyzer test to determine his level of intoxication. They reported over the radio that he had a reading of .08%. A .08% was considered low back then even though today the driver would be legally drunk—and they were just as dangerous then as they are now.

I knew immediately that that was not a true reading for Mr. Lewis. So when Officer Edwards asked me what he should do with him, I said "Just stay put and I will meet you at the jail."

When I got there, I gave Mr. Lewis a second breath test. Giving the test properly, he registered .15% almost double the reading they had reported. If an officer wants, he can get a lower reading by having the arrestee only "puff" into the machine. I knew after that night that Klippness and I had better watch "our back side."

One month and one day later, on March 17, I turned over another DUI but this time to Officer Cameron. Shortly thereafter, he radioed me from the jail that Mr. J.O. Young only registered a .04% on the breathalyzer. Of course, I didn't believe him for one minute and told him to standby at the jail, I was en route.

Mr. Young was told that it would be necessary for him to submit to another breath test since the first test was not administered properly and we had gotten a false reading.

With Mr. Young giving a fair sample of his breath, he showed a level of intoxication of .20% which was five times his first reading and consistent with his intoxicated condition. Cameron had no explanation for the low reading.

"I guess I did something wrong," he remarked.

I noticed that he had put me down as a witness to the .04% test even though I wasn't there.

The Phantom Foggy Weather

One DUI arrest that became part of my punitive action dismissal a year and three months later occurred on March 29, 1967. The arrest, which occurred on a clear night, turned foggy at my hearing later.

At 2 am on that date, I saw a dark green, 55 Chev. 4 door, station wagon, eastbound on the frontage road approaching Winter Road traveling at a moderate rate of speed run off of the roadway and spin out in the dirt. As I was approaching the car, I saw the driver, James Ramos, climb out of the driver's side and noticed that he was possibly under the influence.

When I asked why he ran off of the road, he replied, "I've had too much to drink and just lost control of my car."

I asked how much he had had to drink. Ramos said he had consumed "16 glasses of beer at Teresas" between 11:30 pm and 2 am.

Beat officers, William Pledger and Art DeLaGuerra, were called to the scene and arrived about five minutes later. They arrested Ramos, stored his car and booked him in jail.

On April 3, Deputy D.A. James Fahres, Santa Barbara County, who was assigned to prosecute Ramos, reduced the charge to reckless driving, giving this reason:

> "After discussion with Assistant D.A. Bruce Gourley, it was decided that the evidence is insufficient to convict, in that at this time the jurors are not prepared to accept a .12 as being sufficiently under the influence except in unusual cases."

One would think that running off of the road is a little unusual.

Harassment and Intimidation Weren't Working

By this time, Captain Dahl and Lieutenant Thobe had made up their minds that the only way they were going to get rid of Klippness and me was by firing us. It was very clear that we were going to continue arresting DUIs and insist the officers do the same. All the threats and devious tactics had failed so it was time to play "hard ball."

Klippness and I were both a little naïve. We thought we had to do something wrong before we could be fired. But we weren't so naïve that we didn't know Commissioner Sullivan's reputation, which had preceded him from his time

PART 1: *Chapter 8:*   Harris Grade Fatal Changes my Life   127

with the Los Angeles Police Department, and we were also aware of the officers whom he had surrounded himself through promotions.

In fact, LAPD officers told us they were happy we got Sullivan (he was an LAPD Deputy Chief before becoming CHP Commissioner). They said he was known for his lack of ambition, his incompetence, and for just putting in his time.

I think the Santa Maria officers could also see the "hand writing on the wall" and they had no desire to lose their jobs, especially over a few drunk drivers. They were already talking about the party they were going to throw as soon as we were gone. Of course, Klippness and I knew who most of the officers were. We also knew there might be a couple of officers in the Santa Maria area office that wanted to do their job and arrest DUIs but they weren't willing to be fired over it.

Chapter 9
Choice of Coffee or Arresting DUI

It's important to remember that Klippness and I knew that the fact we were only doing our job as we were trained to do it by the CHP would not protect us from being fired. But we also knew it wouldn't be the CHP prosecuting us. The CHP is a great organization. These were a few individuals who should never have been permitted to put on a CHP uniform. We never thought of them as highway patrolmen. We looked at them as a band of renegades using their authority while hiding behind the uniform.

In essence, they were saying, "We don't care what the Highway Patrol wants, you'll do as ordered. We don't want you arresting DUIs in our community unless you are more selective." We knew this wasn't the California Highway Patrol's policy but we also knew this corruption led all the way to the Commissioner's office and it was going to be a difficult and long battle.

A DUI arrest that led to one of the punitive action charges against me took place in Denny's Restaurant in Santa Maria. Here is the way the charge read: "On October 16, 1967, at 3 a.m., while having coffee with Officer Hilker in Denny's Restaurant in Santa Maria, you observed Reginald Berve in an intoxicated condition. Nevertheless, you permitted Berve to leave the restaurant, enter his vehicle and drive from the parking lot onto a public highway before you pursued him and arrested him for a violation of Vehicle Code section 23102(a), misdemeanor drunk driving."

If that were true, then I would have been wrong. But that's not what happened and Deputy Attorney General Richard Turner, Captain Dahl, Lieutenant

Thobe and Officer Hilker all knew that that wasn't what happened. And in the long run they made fools of themselves at the hearing.

Here's what really happened. While in the restaurant, in the early morning hours, I observed Reginald Berve under the influence of alcohol. Officer Hilker and I were having coffee at the time. By Berve's actions it appeared he was also a friend of the waitress, Vantrice Burke, and that he was getting ready to leave the restaurant. I knew her only as Van but I felt comfortable talking to her about the situation.

She confirmed that Berve was a friend of hers and that he was preparing to leave. I asked her if she would tell him not to drive because he appeared to be under the influence. "Tell him if he drives I will have to arrest him." She assured me that she would relay this information to him and I observed her conversing with him in front of the restaurant. I went back to where Officer Hilker was drinking coffee. The waitress came back into the restaurant and informed me that she had told Berve not to drive and he had agreed that he wouldn't.

However, when I turned around a minute or so later, I saw that he was slowly driving his vehicle from the parking lot. I told Officer Hilker, "Let's go," and then hurried to our cruiser. Officer Hilker did not get up but just continued drinking his coffee. I had no choice but to leave Hilker behind.

Breve's vehicle was overtaken and stopped about one block from Denny's Restaurant. A series of field sobriety tests confirmed my original belief. I asked Berve why he had driven after being told not to drive.

He replied, "Maybe you're right. I thought I was all right."

I arrested Berve for DUI. On the way to the Santa Barbara County Hospital for a blood test, I stopped at Denny's and picked up Hilker. Actually, Officer Hilker should have been censored or received punitive action for his conduct that night but he knew he was protected by Thobe all the way up to the Commissioner's office.

After Berve took a blood test, we took him to the Santa Maria Police Department for booking. An alcohol level reading of .17% was recorded on the breathalyser machine. This level would substantiate that Berve was under the influence but not necessarily "in an intoxicated condition." For sure, he shouldn't have been driving.

A few weeks later, CHP Sergeant Dwight Bell, from the Zone 4 Fresno office, came to Santa Maria and reported that he was conducting an investigation for Inspector Bryant, Office of Inspection. Sergeant Bell inquired about this particular arrest. After I explained the details, I asked him what he would have done. He replied, "No problem here. I would have done the same thing." Several months later Bell would testify at my hearing that the conversation never took place.

Thobe's Misrepresentation of Judge Backfires

About that same time, Lieutenant Thobe and Captain Dahl thought they finally had the opportunity they had been waiting for. Something happened that night that they could exploit. At 7:40 pm I arrested a Mr. Eder for DUI on US 101 at Betteravia Road. I requested Officer Schuermann to handle the storage of the vehicle. After Schuermann arrived on the scene, I placed Eder in the patrol cruiser and left for the jail. Eder agreed that he would take a breathalyzer test.

While en route to the jail with Eder I observed another DUI, later determined to be Mr. Cota, near Main and Miller Street at 8:10 pm. Although I already had one DUI in the cruiser, I was not going to let Cota continue driving in his apparent intoxicated condition. Even the first DUI, Eder, commented, "There's the guy you ought to get," after Cota had made a left turn in front of us.

A request was made for the nearest officer to my location who could handle a DUI. Officer Pledger acknowledged the call and upon his arrival I left for the police department with the first DUI, Eder. I still had to finish the intoxication questions, handle the booking and complete the reports.

While I was completing the booking and testing of Eder, I got a phone call from Klippness. He told me that there wasn't a cruiser available for him to start his shift. He asked me to come to the office and pick him up. It was my intention to pick up Klippness and return to the police department to finish the booking and let Sergeant Klippness have my cruiser.

While en route from the Santa Maria Police Department to the CHP office at 8:50 pm, I encountered another DUI on Main Street near Concepcion. I informed Klippness of the situation and that I would pick him up as soon as I processed Chavarria for DUI.

It should be noted that four DUI arrestees were being processed at this time. Officer Pledger was booking Cota and Officer Roberts was booking a DUI (name unknown). Officer Kuhbander was assisting with the booking of Eder. Chavarria refused to take a chemical test so I asked Officer Kuhbander to also take custody of Chavarria until I could return from picking up Sergeant Klippness.

I was able to pick up Klippness at the office at about 9:15 pm. We started back to the Santa Maria Police Department, which was located almost in the center of the city, and whose location accounted for some of our DUI arrests. DUI arrests that ultimately resulted in punitive action accusing us of deliberately patrolling in the city. En route we decided that it would be just as practical for Officer Kuhbander to finish the bookings because Kuhbander could not leave the jail until his partner was through with his booking. This would allow for a minimum amount of officers in the jail and give Officer Kuhbander additional experience, which he needed.

Klippness and I remained paired because I only had one hour left of my shift. At about 10:00 pm a maroon station wagon was observed traveling westbound on SSR 166 approaching Blosser Road. The maroon station wagon was casually drifting from one lane partially into another. Klippness, being the passenger, radioed the information to "any unit in the vicinity." A graveyard car, occupied by Officers Hilker and Cameron, were right behind us and were able to make the stop. Officer Hilker approached the driver and Officer Cameron covered the right side. We stopped behind them.

No sooner had we stopped than a DUI, Ralph Robbins, driving a 66 Chevrolet pickup truck, stopped behind our cruiser. Robbins probably stopped behind us because he saw our flashing red lights and thought it was a roadblock.

Officer Hilker left the station wagon and walked back to where we were standing with Robbins. The station wagon drove away going west on SSR 166. Officers Hilker and Cameron were then detailed to handle the DUI arrest of Robbins.

PART 1: *Chapter 9:*   Choice of Coffee or Arresting DUI   133

Klippness and I left the scene going west on SSR 166. Shortly thereafter, we again observed the same maroon station wagon ahead of us drift to the center line. Knowing Hilker and Cameron's attitude toward the Department's DUI policy, we decided to stop the station wagon again to satisfy ourselves as to why the vehicle was drifting.

Upon approaching the vehicle, I recognized the driver to be Judge Stewart of Guadalupe. He was very friendly and asked me where I had been lately. He introduced his wife and commented that he wished we would work closer to Guadalupe so we would be in his jurisdiction. He said, "I thought maybe you stopped me because I just made the light back at the intersection of Blosser Road." He did not appear to be under the influence and his drifting could have been a result of talking to his wife who was seated in the right front seat. The entire stop was handled in a friendly and courteous manner.

The next day Hilker and Cameron made a visit to Thobe's home and told him about the Judge Stewart incident. If either officer had considered the incident more than routine, they should have discussed it with their immediate supervisor but they had a different agenda and they knew Thobe was waiting for any incident or action that he could exploit.

Most sergeants would have received a commendation for that one nights accomplishment, but instead, I received a censurable incident report from Lieutenant Thobe. It read, "As a result of information brought to my attention by Judge Stewart of the Guadalupe Court, [this being a lie] your supervisory performance during the evening of October 28 was investigated and found to be unsatisfactory.

"During the last hour of your shift you rode with the other on-duty supervisor. [No mention is made that no cruiser was available] During this same hour, 3 or 4 drunk drivers were being processed at the Santa Maria jail. [No mention was made that I was the one that had arrested the DUIs] Instead of providing supervisory guidance at the jail to expedite the testing procedures and to limit officer involvement [My presence there would not have accomplished either] you elected to ride on patrol with Sgt. Klippness. [All units were tied up at the jail booking except for one other unit so we were needed on the road].

"Additionally, while you were on patrol in company with Sergeant Klippness, he directed another unit to check out a car which seemed to be, as you describe, 'drifting.' The officers, one with 13 years experience and the other with six years [Who did not agree with the Department's DUI policy] released the driver after establishing to their satisfaction that the driver was sober. You then fell in behind the driver after his release and again stopped him for 'drifting.' As you later related, you recognized the driver as being the Judge of the Guadalupe Court [The fact that Judge Stewart and I were friends was purposely omitted] and after satisfying yourself as to his sobriety, you also released him.

"Several days later I learned indirectly through the Court [How about that night through Officers Hilker and Cameron?] that the Judge was quite upset over the incident. [Later revelation will reveal the Judge was not upset at all]. During a subsequent interview with the Judge [In an attempt by Thobe to get him to file a complaint against us] he related that he had not had anything to drink [Possibly, but he may have had one or two] and that he was not 'drifting' or weaving, nor was he committing any driver error which could be interpreted as cause of the second inspection. [I guess one can assume that there was probable cause for the first "inspection."] He also stated that the supervisor [Sergeant Mitchell] had directed the other officers to check him out for drunk driving and then had subjected him to a second inspection because of the sergeant's apparent lack of belief in the first officers' competence. [This was obviously another fabrication. How would Judge Stewart know this detail without being told?] The Judge said he was most upset by being stopped twice under these circumstances."

Upon receiving this censurable incident report two and one-half months after the incident, I told Lieutenant Thobe that it was not possible for Judge Stewart to be upset over being stopped because I know him personally and I'm the one that spoke to him that night. I said, "I have personal knowledge that he's not the least bit upset and he will tell you that himself." In an angry response, Thobe shouted, "I'm ordering you right now to never speak, phone or contact Judge Stewart in any manner. If you do, I'll recommend dismissal immediately. Do you understand?" "What if I get a subpoena to testify in his court?" I asked. Still shouting, he said,"You won't. I'll see to that."

Later Thobe tried to make this a part of my dismissal package but they couldn't persuade Judge Stewart to go along with it. Judge Stewart was an honorable man and he wanted no part of this punitive action being concocted by Thobe and Dahl. Thobe went on to write Klippness and me three more censurable incident reports as a result of this one incident. Two Sergeants riding in one vehicle, use of overtime at end of shift, allowing three officers to be involved in one arrest (I had made the original stop so I was the third officer) and the Judge Stewart incident. Of course, Klippness and I knew they were building a dismissal package and the package would look more impressive with four separate incident reports than one with several charges. The Government Code was changed later so that this type of chicanery can no longer be used.

Officer Loren Scruggs was very close with the Lieutenant. He started asking me for a ride to the office as soon as he was assigned to the evening shift that we were both working. Most of the time his conversation was about our problems with Thobe. It didn't take long to figure out why he wanted a lift to the office. So Klippness and I made up a story that Zone IV was sending someone to check on Thobe playing golf on duty and that it was important that he not find out about it in advance. Sure enough, the next day Thobe called us in and wanted to know what we knew about it. When neither of us could hold back a smile, Thobe knew he and Scruggs had been setup. Scruggs never called for another ride.

Officer Scruggs would arrest a DUI now and then, but he mainly wrote speed tickets on Highway 101, mechanical tickets and gave out twice as many verbal warnings as any one in the office. When an officer makes a DUI arrest he submits his report to the sergeant for review and approval. One day Scruggs turned in a DUI arrest report and it was almost void of answers to any of the intoxication questions. A line had been drawn through the questions and "diabetic" written above the line. I asked Officer Scruggs if he had taken the arrestee to the hospital to be examined by a doctor. His answer was, "No." I told him that was Departmental procedure and he said, "You can't expect me to know everything."

A diabetic suffering an insulin reaction can display the same symptoms as a person under the influence of alcohol. However, it is not unheard of to have a suspect say he is a diabetic to avoid being arrested, which is another reason for having the suspect examined by a doctor. The doctor can then tell the officer whether the suspect is a diabetic or not. If he is a diabetic, then he's not a DUI, and if he isn't a diabetic, then the doctor can testify as an expert if the case goes to trial.

It's Thobe's Word Against Your's

A Statistical Report from Zone IV reported the following: "Santa Maria CHP arrests decreased considerably in May and June. Whereas in January-April they accounted for 64% of all CHP arrests in the county; in May-July they accounted for only 23%." These figures are an example of what effect an administrator can have on a DUI program.

But we knew the next report covering September would show a change. Now that Klippness and I had decided that we were going to actively pursue DUIs and remove them from the roadway before they killed and maimed other innocent drivers, our arrests had gone up and our serious accidents had gone down. But we also knew without some support from Sacramento Headquarters our days were numbered.

We had to get someone in power to listen to us.

Since it was necessary to go through the chain of command, the first step was to contact Captain Dahl who was Area Commander in Santa Barbara and who had responsibility for Santa Maria. Lieutenant Thobe answered directly to him. We worked for Captain Dahl in East Los Angeles and received commendation after commendation for arresting DUIs and reducing felony hit and runs, felony drunk driving and regular accidents. He had always appeared to be fair and that was all I was asking. I was sure he would listen to me if I only had a chance to talk to him face to face. A couple of months earlier, I had phoned him and told him what Lieutenant Thobe was doing but Dahl more or less told me it was his (Thobe's) word against mine. Dahl said, "Bob, you've got to have proof this is going on before I can do something about it."

Secretly Taping Thobe

So I placed a tape recorder in the sergeant's desk drawer and waited for Thobe to make his next move. It didn't take long.

The next evening he stormed into the squad room, totally ignoring that I was doing some paper work, and said, "I've got some things I want to talk to you about."

PART 1: *Chapter 9:* Choice of Coffee or Arresting DUI 137

I stopped what I was doing, put some papers in the desk drawer and turned on the tape recorder. I didn't close the drawer all of the way in the hope of getting better reception.

I said, "What do you want to talk about?"

Thobe always stood, even though an empty chair was available, so that he could look down on the person he was talking to.

Very officially he said, "About your performance. It's unacceptable." He also said, "Your past record isn't all that good either."

I asked him what he meant by that statement.

He said, "You know what I mean."

I said, "No, I don't. So why don't you tell me."

Thobe gave his standard answer, "That's neither here nor there."

I told him I would put my record up against his any day and added, "I hope you can stand on your record as well as I can stand on mine."

He said that I was only interested in arresting drunk drivers and I was deficient in training the officers in their other duties.

I pointed out to him that that was simply not true. That I trained the officers in all aspects of their job and the quarter we had just completed would confirm that. We had a 19% increase in traffic tickets, 208% increase in mechanical warnings, 34.5% decrease in all accidents, 36.5% decrease in reportable accidents (injuries) and 100% decrease in fataliities. And a 1,076% increase in DUIs (13 vs 153).

Lieutenant Thobe gave it the old, "That's neither here nor there. I want you to concentrate more on other CHP violations and less on drunk driving. You just don't get it, do you?"

I thought to myself, yeah, I got it. Now I had him on tape, so I was ready to meet face to face with Captain Dahl.

I set up an appointment with Captain Dahl and drove 120 miles round trip on my day off, hoping that I could finally get someone to listen and we would be able to stop the madness in Santa Maria.

First, I told Dahl what Thobe had said and implied. Dahl indicated that Thobe was wrong, but told me there wasn't anything he could do about it: "You don't have any proof."

I said, "Yes, I do. I've got it all on tape."

Dahl, looking very surprised, said, "You do? Can I hear it?"

I said, "Sure" and I played it for him. After hearing the tape, he said, "Sounds like you got him."

Captain Dahl said he was going to have to talk to the Zone Commander first "and I'll want to play him this tape."

Dahl was very friendly and assured me that with the tape I had given him, he had the evidence he needed now to correct the situation in Santa Maria. I left Santa Barbara with high hopes. I was confident that something was going to be done now that Captain Dahl had the independent evidence he said he needed. Klippness shared my enthusiasm.

The next day Lieutenant Thobe called me into his office and said, "Sit down. I know you went down to see Captain Dahl yesterday and took him a tape of one of our conversations. He called me before you left the city limits of Santa Barbara." He continued, "What the hell are you doing tape recording me? That's a felony to tape someone without their knowledge so you're the one who's in trouble, not me. So, your little tape recorder is only going to get you into more trouble."

I told Thobe: "We'll see what happens."

I didn't want Thobe to know how disappointed I was that Captain Dahl had betrayed me.

About two weeks later, Lieutenant Thobe came into the sergeants' area with a smile on his face and told me that I needed to make myself available the following Friday.

PART 1: *Chapter 9:*   Choice of Coffee or Arresting DUI   139

"Division (Zone IV, Fresno) wants Santa Barbara to prepare a punitive action package against you for illegally taping me," he said. "It's a felony and they're looking for dismissal. Captain Dahl will be doing the investigation and he wants to interview you here at the Santa Maria office."

It was hard to believe the turn-around Captain Dahl had made after talking with Supervising Inspector Reinjohn in Zone IV.

On Friday, at 1:30 pm, I went to the office. Captain Dahl was seated behind the Lieutenant's desk and Thobe was sitting in a chair in front of him. Thobe got up, without saying a word, closed the door behind him and left the room.

Dahl was not the same person I had left in Santa Barbara two weeks before. He started out, "This is an official investigation into your use of a recorder to tape Lieutenant Thobe without his knowledge. You have already admitted to me that you did tape him and that he had no knowledge of it at the time. Taping a person without their knowledge is a felony, did you know that?"

I looked Captain Dahl straight in the eyes and said, "You should know that I haven't committed any violation of any type; misdemeanor, felony or anything else. Captain, have you read the section of the code that covers taping? There is an exception. A police officer can secretly tape a person without their knowledge if it's an investigation. I am a police officer by definition and I was conducting an investigation."

He said, "That's not what the legislators meant when they passed that law. They meant a criminal investigation."

I said, "The law reads 'an investigation' and says nothing about a criminal investigation."

Captain Dahl hesitated for a few seconds as if he was in deep thought, then he said, "OK. You're free to leave. I don't have any further questions."

I got up and left the room and on the way home I came to the conclusion that Klippness and I were not going to get any justice locally. It wasn't going to do any good to go to Division or to follow the chain of command because their intentions were clear. We were going to have to go to Plan B and start filing grievances in hopes we could get to someone in Sacramento Headquarters with some sanity.

Thobe immediately posted a notice on the bulletin board reading, "Effective this date, Sergeant Mitchell is prohibited from tape recording any personnel in the office for any reason."

It was interesting to note that he only singled me out and no one else. However, they now would have grounds for dismissal if I did violate the order. Ironically, in their eagerness to get me, they made another mistake, which became obvious in less than a month.

Even with all of this turmoil going on, Klippness and I continued to do our job and that meant arresting DUIs. Of course, anytime a person is working and his boss is trying to find a way to fire him, there's always something that person can be criticized for doing. It wasn't long after the taping that Lieutenant Thobe got that opportunity.

DUI Ignores Red Light and Siren

At 10:10 pm one Saturday, I observed a blue Ford northbound on Blosser Road at Morrison. It was necessary to make a u-turn and overtake the vehicle. South of Main Street, a distance of a mile, I sounded the horn and used the red spot light to illuminate the interior of the car. This area is a well-lit business district so there was no reason for the female driver not to stop. Instead, the vehicle continued north from Main Street without yielding. The siren was also activated but to no avail. Radio dispatch was notified that I had a possible DUI that was refusing to stop.

The blue Ford was traveling about 25 mph as the driver ignored the red lights and siren. At the intersection of Donovan Road, a distance of over a mile, the driver appeared to be stopping for the posted stop sign. But instead, she continued through the stop sign in front of a car approaching from the east. I believe there would have been a collision if the approaching car had not seen the red lights and heard the siren on the cruiser.

Now the suspect vehicle was approaching a residential district where the street was narrower with parked cars on both sides. The suspect slowed to 10 mph to make her turn into the residential area and continued at

PART 1: *Chapter 9:* Choice of Coffee or Arresting DUI

that speed while still failing to stop. At this point I nudged the rear of the vehicle with the rubber padded push bumper of the cruiser as we were both traveling 10 mph. The contact was very slight and could be compared with matching bumpers when preparing to push a disabled vehicle. The vehicle slowed to a stop east of Blosser Road on Cox Lane.

After determining that the driver, Marjorie Clapper, was driving under the influence, I asked her why she hadn't stopped for the red light and siren.

She replied, "I didn't know you wanted me. Besides I thought you were an ambulance."

I arrested Mrs. Clapper for DUI but not for failure to yield because of her intoxication and low speeds. The entire distance covered about 2 miles. No other CHP units responded.

The next day when I got to work I found a memo written in bold large letters and black felt ink laying on the desk for all the officers to see:

> "Sgt. Mitchell, in reading the Intox. Report wherein the procedures used in apprehending a Mrs. Marjorie M. Clapper were described it is noted that you found it necessary <u>to run into the rear</u> of her car before being able to affect the stop. (Write a) memo please describing <u>damage if any</u> and at what point you feel <u>deadly force</u> is necessary in stopping a drunk woman driver.
>
> LT."

Lieutenant Thobe wanted to file punitive action against me right away for this incident, but Captain Dahl was a little "gun shy" after the taping fiasco. He wanted to make sure they were on solid ground before getting Zone IV involved again. So they requested a memo; they wanted to have in writing what authority I was acting under when I used the push bumper to stop Mrs. Clapper.

They didn't want a repeat of the taping incident whereby they came out looking like Moe and Curly. Since Klippness and I had not stopped arresting DUIs, in spite of all the tactics and harassment, there was only one thing to do and that was to get rid of us. The sooner the better. Commissioner Sullivan was probably getting a little impatient with them and their failure to take care of us.

So, having no other choice, I answered Thobe's memorandum and concluded with: "I relied upon my experience and evaluation of the circumstances that existed at the time. After researching our manuals, I will state that I was unable to locate any material that covers this situation."

I waited several days until Thobe had almost completed his punitive action package before telling him I had found the authority for the method I used in stopping Mrs. Clapper. He just stared at me without saying a word, waiting on me to continue. I told him I just happened to be looking in the CHP manual under "The Use of Roadblocks" and noticed that it read:

> "A particularly difficult problem is presented by the operator who refuses to stop after having been given ample opportunity to see and understand a signal to stop. The degree of hazard to which other users of highways are exposed must be the dominant factor in determining subsequent action by the officer. In very extreme cases 'bumping or ditching' may be used to force a stop."

Thobe looked at me like Laurel use to look at Hardy and said, "Let me see that."

I told him, "That's yours. I made you a copy."

Although that particular guideline referred to roadblocks, it fit this occasion. Even Thobe's "creative writing" wasn't going to be enough to convince a Hearing Officer that I did something wrong. After I left, he tore up his punitive action request in small pieces and threw it in his waste paper basket. He later accused me of scotch taping the pieces together so I could read what he wrote. This was one of the few times he was right.

Grim Reminder of the Havoc DUIs Cause

As Klippness was reading through the current California Highway Patrol magazine he came upon three horrendous photographs of a young mother and four children who had been killed in a traffic accident.

PART 1: *Chapter 9:*   Choice of Coffee or Arresting DUI   143

It was described as the most tragic accident that had ever occurred in Antelope Valley. At 7:30 pm, just west of Pearblossom on Highway 138, a local resident, in a hurry to get home and with a BAC of .21%, failed to negotiate a familiar curve in the road and struck another car head-on. In the other car was a young mother with her four children and stepfather. The stepfather was critically injured—the rest of his family was killed. The DUI driver died the next day from injuries. At the time of the accident, his drivers license had been denied temporarily for a Failure to Appear in a previous DUI case.

Klippness posted this heart-wrenching article with photographs of the victims still in the wreckage with a message typed in capital red letters:

> "THIS COULD HAPPEN TO ANY ONE OF US . . . THIS IS WHY WE CANNOT AFFORD TO BE SITTING BACK ON OUR HANDS. PLEASE TAKE A GOOOOOOOD LONG LOOK. IF WE SIT BACK AND BE SELECTIVE IN OUR DRUNK DRIVING EFFORTS THESE PICTURES MIGHT BE TAKEN IN OUR AREA."

Klippness returned to the squad room about 30 minutes later and found it in the trash basket.

We never found out who threw it there.

It would be impossible to calculate the amount of taxpayer money and man-hours being wasted in the Santa Maria area by Supervising Inspector Reinjohn, Captain Dahl, Lieutenant Thobe and Commissioner Sullivan in their effort to get Klippness and me, two lowly sergeants. What we looked at as "aggressively arresting DUIs," they saw as "insubordination."

In this case, insubordination was being defined as, "You can't just go out and arrest everybody that's DUI. There are some people who should get a free pass and you don't seem to know who they are or you don't care."

It didn't take long for the rest of the state to get the word that there were problems in Santa Maria. It was a big embarrassment to the Department because everyone knew the conflict was over DUI arrests. And it didn't make sense to the average officer, or the public, as to how that could be a conflict.

Thobe's Controversial Hypertension

Thobe was reported to be suffering from hypertension. He said, "Oh! I go to the doctor now and then but I've had hypertension for years. This is nothing new. I've also got a loss of hearing"

A few years later Thobe would file for disability. The Los Angeles Times reported on August 29, 1969: "Thobe was involved in a controversy with Sgts. Bob L. Mitchell and Gerald R. Klippness in 1967-68, when Thobe commanded the CHP substation there."

The article went on to say, "Both officers were accused of willful disobedience and other charges." No mention was made that the "willful disobedience" was our refusal to stop arresting DUIs.

Referee Charles Sorrow of the State Workmen's Compensation Appeals Board awarded Thobe $5,880 dollars with a finding of 28% disability from the hypertension. The California Highway Patrol filed an appeal and asked me if I would testify that he had hypertension before the problems started in Santa Maria. I agreed to testify but was notified a few weeks later that my testimony would not be necessary as Thobe had withdrawn his alleged injury claim.

Meanwhile in Santa Maria in 1967, Thobe continued to write Klippness and me censurable incident reports for almost everything imaginable as a form of harassment. One was for being 5 minutes late for work because I was in the front parking lot writing my wife a check, another was for asking two officers to write a memo about an arrest they made, and so forth.

But on December 12, Thobe thought he had hit the "mother lode."

Another Secret Taping in the Office

On that night Officers Scruggs and Cameron were in the squad room talking as they wrote their reports at the end of their 10:15 pm shift. No one else was in the building at the time. All of a sudden, Scruggs and Cameron heard a "flipping" noise coming from the closet behind them. When they investigated they found it was a tape recorder with the loose tape spinning around. Scruggs had just picked up the tape recorder as Sergeant Klippness and I walked in the back door from the back parking lot.

PART 1: *Chapter 9:* Choice of Coffee or Arresting DUI　　　　　　145

Officer Scruggs said, "Look what I found" and as he held out the tape recorder added, "Who does this belong to?"

Klippness said, "Me" and took it from him.

Cameron said, "What's the deal?"

Klippness told them that he was tired of lies being told about him and he was going to find out who was responsible. Scruggs said it wasn't him. Cameron said, "What are you going to do with that tape?"

Just 30 minutes before, while patrolling in a cruiser, Klippness had confided in me that he had placed a tape recorder in the closet. I had nothing to do with it being placed there and, in fact, I was quite surprised. After a short discussion, he decided to go back to the office so he could remove it, not knowing that it had already been discovered.

Scruggs and Cameron weren't satisfied with Klippness' answer but they were more concerned about what Klippness was going to do with the tape. To calm things down and to help resolve the matter, I said, "Look, he didn't mean anything by this," and as I turned to Klippness I said, "To show your good faith why don't you destroy the tape."

They agreed but everybody knew that this taping incident wasn't going to end there.

As soon as we left the office, Klippness said, "Bob, I wanted to find out who's been going to the Lieutenant and telling him all those lies."

He said, "You saw me bring it into the office earlier."

I said, "Yeah. But I didn't know what you were going to do with it."

It is not uncommon for an officer to have a tape recorder while working. They are used to tape DUIs and other criminals while they are cuffed and sitting in a cruiser, where they are likely to be discussing their crime. This is especially true of felonies. Taping suspects during an arrest is approved by the CHP.

The next day, Lieutenant Thobe called both of us into his office and said, "What in the hell is going on? I understand you both were taping a couple of the officers and they caught you. I want a memo explaining exactly what happened."

I told Thobe that I wasn't involved in the taping and had nothing to do with it.

Thobe, with a Cheshire the Cat smile, said, "Oh! Yes you are. We'll just see about that. I ordered you by memo to never tape anyone in this office and now you've disregarded that order."

Thobe said he wanted the memos on his desk no later than the following day. As we all left the Lieutenant's office, Thobe gave a hand gesture to Officer Scruggs, who was waiting outside, indicating that "we finally got him."

In Klippness' memo to Lieutenant Thobe he wrote, "My purpose of using the recorder was an attempt to discover if someone was telling false information to the Lieutenant or if information was being misconstrued. I see nothing illegal about it. It is an accepted police practice and administrative tool. I know of no law or order prohibiting its use. If information had been gained, it possibly could have been used to prove my purpose."

In my memo to Thobe, I told him I had nothing to do with the taping and had no prior knowledge of the tape recorder being placed there.

A week later, on Dec. 12, Lieutenant Thobe told me to be at the office that Friday to meet with Captain Dahl, who would be conducting a final interview with me before recommending punitive action because of the taping.

I told Thobe that he and Dahl were wasting their time because I had nothing to do with the taping.

Thobe said, "What do you mean we're wasting our time. I issued you a written order on November 29 prohibiting you from using a tape recorder and I have two officers who will testify that you said 'we' didn't mean anything by taping. Here's their memo right here," shaking two pieces of paper in his extended hand.

PART 1: Chapter 9:   Choice of Coffee or Arresting DUI   147

I was waiting at the sergeant's desk when Captain Dahl arrived from Santa Barbara, a 120 mile round trip.

He said, "Come on in to the Lieutenant's office and let's get this over with."

I followed him in and he turned around and closed the door. He sat down behind Thobe's desk and took some papers from his attache case and placed them in front of him. Captain Dahl started out by saying, "You're not denying that you received a memo from Lieutenant Thobe on November 19 prohibiting you from using a tape recorder or similar device to record someone without their knowledge, are you?"

I said, "No, Sir, I'm not."

"Then why did you disobey that order the other night? December the 12th?"

"I didn't," I responded.

Dahl, with a look of determination, said, "We've got two officers who heard you admit that you were involved. I have their memos right here," pointing to the papers in front of him.

I said, "They're mistaken."

He said, "Here, I'll read their statement right off of the memos. Sergeant Mitchell said, 'Look we didn't mean anything by this."

I responded, "Like I said, Captain, they are mistaken. I didn't say we, I said he."

Captain Dahl didn't say a word, picked up his papers and put them in his attache case, got up and walked out. I went out and got in my car and left. The subject was never mentioned again. If Captain Dahl had called me on the phone earlier I could have saved him that long drive.

Officer Hiding in the Office

One night, a few weeks later, I decided to go to the office to do some paper work even though the place took on an eerie appearance late at night. The Santa Maria area office was very small, less that 1000 square feet in size, and it sat alone off of Highway 101. It was surrounded by a few oil derricks and sand. It was not open to the public at night, and if it had been, it would have been too spooky for most people to venture over there.

There was only one light near the sergeant's desk and a person would have had to stand on their toes to look in. It reminded me a little bit of the movie Psycho. The only person you would expect to see there would be a sergeant doing paper work. However, if an officer had some rare reason for going there he would park his cruiser in the front and go through the front door. The gate to the rear parking lot was always locked and closed.

That was one advantage about the building. No one could drive up in front without you hearing them approaching because it was totally silent inside and the parking lot was covered with gravel.

I had been working at my desk for about 10 minutes when I decided to go into the Lieutenant's office to get a manual. I saw no need to turn the light on because there was some light shinning through the window from the front parking lot. I was kneeling down, in the dark, in front of the book shelve, looking for the manual when I suddenly got the feeling that someone was watching me.

I turned around slowly and saw Officer Scruggs standing in a darkened corner in a military position of "attention." He was in his CHP uniform and staring straight at me. If he had made a quick move, I believe I would have drawn my weapon and fired.

I turned on the light and said, "What are you doing in here?"

Calmly he said, "I was looking for something."

I said, "What were you looking for?"

"Oh! The Lieutenant wanted me to pick up some papers but they're not here." He then left by the back door.

There were a few things that bothered me about the encounter. Why hadn't he parked his cruiser in the front? He stood motionless for at least 10 minutes while I was writing a report, thinking I was alone. What was he really doing there? There was no way I could have pursued the matter further though because he was one of Thobe's untouchables.

Less than four years after this incident, Officer Scruggs was shot to death while on duty after stopping a car for a registration violation. While he was talking to a passenger in the car he had stopped, a driver of another car, walked across the freeway to ask him a question. During an exchange of words, the driver suddenly pulled a gun and shot Scruggs in the head. The shooter fled the scene and after crashing his vehicle, walked into a field and shot and killed himself.

I knew I couldn't report the incident that happened that night. Thobe had already written me a censurable incident report for asking two officers to explain why they had taken a subject home and left his car locked at the scene. It was quite obvious why they did it. He was a DUI and they took him home instead of arresting him. Let's hope the DUI they took home didn't kill anyone later while DUI. The officers were never required to explain their actions. It is totally proper for a sergeant to have an officer explain his actions and/or write a memo. However, in Santa Maria, it would have meant another censurable incident report to the supervisor.

Things were only getting worse. We knew we couldn't afford an attorney, and if we didn't do something quick, it was going to be too late. It was obvious that Commissioner Sullivan was in full support of our dismissal.

And frankly, we did not trust the California Association of Highway Patrolmen to come to our aid. It's not that they didn't do some good and defend some officers who were "under fire" but this wasn't just a routine matter. Not every CHP officer or member of the CAHP agreed with our plight and a defense would run into hundreds of thousands of dollars.

We would definitely get opposition from some of the voting Area Reps who wouldn't want aggressive DUI enforcement in their area and there were those who thought the .15% presumptive guilt limit was too low. More than one officer had told us, "Don't ask me to make those kinds of arrests." In a lot of cases it wasn't so much they were opposed to the .15% as it was they lacked the confidence or competence to detect a DUI unless he was almost falling down drunk. This is one of the big problems today with DUI enforcement and it crucial that it be addressed. There has got to be specialized and extensive training in the area of DUI enforcement. It can't be just one of many responsibilities.

Rumors

A common tactic used to destroy individuals and gather support for a cause is to start rumors. And there was no shortage of those in Santa Maria. One of the first rumors was that Klippness and I had had someone in our family killed by a drunk driver. There was no truth to that. The next big rumor was that it was my religious belief that no one should drink intoxicating liquor. Again, no truth to that. Some of the officers knew that I was a deacon in one of the churches and had stopped drinking several years before so that gave them more rumor material.

I believe—like most everyone else—that a person has a right to drink what he wants, but for the protection of others he shouldn't drive if he has been drinking. Rumors go with the turf so we just ignored them. Anytime you do something different from the norm or out of the ordinary, there will be jealousy and rumors.

Request for Legal Defense

Not only did we think we would have a problem getting the support of the CAHP, we decided that we thought it would be best to go outside of the Department. We were members of the California State Employees Association (CSEA) and they had a reputation of independence and strongly defending someone they thought was innocent. They also had the funds to back them.

So, Klippness and I contacted the CSEA, headquartered in Sacramento, and they made arrangements for one of their attorney's, Bob Zech, to meet us in San Luis Obispo on December 21, 1967.

It would be Zech's responsibility to find out what was going on and to recommend whether the CSEA should represent us. Zech patiently listened to us explain what was happening. He also asked several questions to make sure he understood the situation.

After a couple of hours of conversation, Zech said, "I think you guys have a very strong case against the Highway Patrol. I'm going to level with both of you. This kind of garbage has been going on for sometime now and we have been looking for a case just like this to take on. These guys have got to be stopped."

We didn't have to ask him who "these guys" were. We knew it was Commissioner Sullivan and the people he surrounded himself with. He went on to say that he was going to need all of the documentation we could furnish him.

We told Zech that that would be no problem.

Zech said, "Now, I'll work with you at first but then it will be turned over to some other attorneys. You'll like them though. They know what they're doing."

Klippness and I both left there feeling like we had finally got the support we were looking for. And we weren't disappointed. CSEA made a complete commitment from the beginning and that included spending hundreds of thousands of dollars before it was over.

Chapter 10
Battle Continues Over DUI Arrests

Lieutenant Thobe continued his harassment unabated. Among his numerous tactics was to make unmerited and meaningless comments on my monthly Activity Report in December 1967, which led to me filing a formal grievance against him.

Thobe accused me of the following:

> "Ineffective supervisory guidance was demonstrated by what appeared to be excessive use of directed manpower in accomplishing singular arrests for drunk driving.

> "Become more proficient in effective and legal drunk driving arrest procedures. A DMV Form DL-367 was submitted wherein the information subjecting the arrested party to a possible loss of license was not within the current framework of the law."

I responded in writing and for the record, "Please indicate what arrests you are questioning. Your statement did not clearly indicate if there was anything improper. Please be more specific."

Thobe refused to answer my questions, so I filed a formal grievance against him and also included that he had failed to discuss the items with me, which is required by CHP regulations.

That same month, Sergeant Klippness made one more attempt to resolve his differences with Thobe by meeting with Captain Dahl in Santa Barbara.

Klippness had purchased a new home and was settled in with his wife, Virginia, and five small children. Klippness just wanted to do his job and eventually get promoted, but he was finding it impossible to work under Thobe's constant harassment. Both he and I had worked for Captain Dahl in East Los Angeles so Klippness thought that he could trust Dahl to resolve the problems. Of course, I no longer entertained such a thought because I felt we were not dealing with a rational person. This was just another version of The Caine Mutiny and we had a Captain Queeg on our hands.

A few days after his meeting, Klippness wrote the following letter to Captain Dahl:

> "Thanks for hearing me out on Thursday. I gave your advice serious consideration the rest of the night and had a good sleep on it. I didn't feel it was a matter of loyalty to Bob necessarily, but a matter of what was right and what was wrong from my own personal viewpoint. What occurs between the Lieutenant and others is not my concern. I am concerned when it affects me or the people around me. I know you are too busy to be pestered with what perhaps appears to be petty disputes and I dislike bothering you with them so I will come immediately to the point.
>
> "Two or three months ago I spoke to the Lieutenant about his shouting at people and me in hopes to avert this precise situation that now exists. He agreed that it was wrong and I'm sure was sincere when he told me that it would stop. He said he wasn't sleeping at night because of the turmoil that existed and I felt that this perhaps was the answer. Things here began to function smoothly, everyone was satisfied, however, an uneasy calm prevailed. At least things were at a pleasant state. This unfortunately did not last long. I'm not going to indulge in details because you have heard most of them anyway.
>
> "Now to the point. Friday morning I had intended to again talk to the Lieutenant and clarify my position to Bob's

grievance, using your advice as my guidelines. I was going to use the advice that I had given the men, remain neutral, also as you and I had suggested to each other. He asked me what happened in Santa Barbara and I said not much. I then told him that I would appreciate a little notification of my schedule change rather than come to work and see that I had to double right back in the morning.

"This apparently was the wrong thing to say, because he answered by saying that he would change the schedule a lot more and that it would be changed for court and 'if you guys want to play f—around with the overtime, you can sleep in your own s—.' He then spoke of numerous other changes that were in the offing, however, I was so upset I don't even know that I heard him correctly so I will make no effort to repeat them. I must admit that he did not shout, but the tone was such as to imply that he'd fix us.

"As far as Mitchell's grievance I'm neutral. My question is how in the world can anything be solved when I am greeted with this type of conversation? I ask myself what I would do if an officer spoke that way to a citizen, and the obvious answer is probably an incident report at the very least. Yet, I'm supposed to grit my teeth and say 'don't spoil your promotional chances.'

"You and I spoke of an obvious lack of communication that led to the current situation. You're right, but when one is subjected to this treatment, it's no wonder there is a breakdown. I have no intention of going back into the Lieutenant's office again unless called. Life is too short. I had to go out and park the patrol car for forty minutes after my last conversation to avoid possible unfortunate happenings. I suppose all our communication will be by memo now also.

"Skipper, I'm not trying to play the 'cry baby', but what am I supposed to do? My family loves Santa Maria and our new home. Sure I want to climb the ladder of success, but I've had it. I've tried.

"Let me close now by telling you that I have a pet gripe about people who come to work late. Bob will verify this. I was late this morning twenty minutes and I can only offer the excuse of lack of sleep last night after all the mental gymastics I went through after going to bed."

War of Grievances Begins

In the middle of December, I decided it was time to go on the offense. I had already decided that appealing to their sense of fairness was not going to work. It was now an all out war. I felt these individuals (Thobe, Dahl, Reinjohn) who represented the California Highway Patrol must not be permitted to obstruct the enforcement of DUI. Too many lives were at stake. I had to expose them for what they were and that meant taking my case to the public.

One thing was certain, I was not going to stop arresting DUIs. That decision had already been made.

I filed a Formal Grievance against Lieutenant Thobe that read:

"As a direct result of certain acts and/or omissions on the part of Lt. Thobe, it has progressively become more difficult for me to perform my job as a sergeant on the California Highway Patrol in an efficient manner. These acts and/or omissions have been of an abusive and discourteous nature and are reflected in the following incidents and /or situations."

The charges included being unavailable during working hours (playing golf), discourteous acts, discourteous treatment (3 counts), incompetent leadership, harassment and injudicious use of State time, failure to explain unmerited criticism, nonfactual departmental reporting, dishonesty, approving unauthorized overtime contrary to departmental policy and making a false and slanderous statement.

Fifteen days later, January 2, 1968, Thobe acknowledged receipt of the grievance but refused to respond to any of the allegations. Departmental policy requires a supervisor to respond to a grievance in writing and

PART 1: *Chapter 10:* Battle Continues Over DUI Arrests

resolve, or at least attempt to resolve, the grievances at the local level. All Thobe did was sign that he had received the grievance and attach these comments:

> "I have reviewed the contents of the written grievance report that you submitted on December 18, 1967. You alleged that I committed 10 acts ranging from dishonesty to infactual reporting, acts which I have to assume caused your implied distress."

Thobe went on to say that "it would be impossible for (him) to provide a satisfactory written explanation of each and every act that (I) cite(d)."

That was for sure. Especially when I had documented evidence to prove each allegation. He was in a "catch 22." If he truthfully answered the grievances in writing as required (and that was never going to happen) then his answers would amount to a confession. If he lied in his answers in writing then I would be able to prove he was lying because it would be in print. So that's why he closed his memorandum with "With respect to your allegations, I am willing to discuss them with you. If this is not satisfactory then it would appear that your solution would include using the next step in the prescribed grievance procedure."

There was no way he was going to put anything in writing.

The Department requires that a grievance be advanced to the next level if the grievance is not resolved. Captain Dahl was the next level. He responded:

> "In total, our findings give us no cause for serious censure of Lieutenant Thobe. Separately, most of your complaints strike us as having provocative, disputatious overtones which border on insolence; if not outright insubordination.

> "Those of your charges which appear to have some substance will receive our immediate attention and corrections will be effected. To wit: prohibiting the lieutenant's further use of profane abbreviations, more expeditious processing of Sergeants' Monthly Activity Reports and cancellation of the erroneously approved overtime.

> "If you are dissatisfied with our treatment of your other complaints, you may, if you so desire, present your grievance to the Zone Commander for his consideration and any further action he may deem appropriate."

Department Continues Protecting Thobe

Of course, I pursued the grievances to the next step, which was Supervising Inspector G.R. Reinjohn, Commander of Zone IV, in Fresno. I emphasized the "Infactual Departmental Reporting" grievance because I wanted Zone to know the real cause of the problems in Santa Maria was DUI enforcement. Under this section I wrote:

> "The enforcement of drunk drivers last year (1967) had a definite effect upon reportable traffic accidents in this area. When we *actively* enforced drunk driving arrests, we showed a *decrease* of 26% in reportable accidents. During the months we (through necessity) *routinely* enforced drunk driving arrests, we had an *increase* of 12.5% in reportable accidents.

"Just for the short period of time this year (January 1—22), we show an increase of 22 reportable accidents compared to 5 for the same period of time last year or a 340% increase. We have had 2 fatal accidents, which represent one-fourth of last year's total fatal accidents of 8. There have been only 8 arrests for drunk driving (compared to the same period last year), which produced 29. (That is a) decrease of 262% DUI arrests.

"There appears to be a conflict between the enforcement policy as expressed by the Department and the permitted application in the field. This is one of the causes for the present discord in the Santa Maria Sub-station."

"On October 4, 1967, Lt. Thobe submitted an infactual monthly_report to Headquarters. He stated in the report, "Enforcement remained rather consistent," when in fact he was aware that there was a 142% increase in drunk driving arrests over the previous month. There were 14 arrests for August compared to an increase of 34 arrests for September. This was common knowledge amongst the personnel of the Santa Maria sub-station.

PART 1: *Chapter 10:* Battle Continues Over DUI Arrests

"I believe his statement was a deliberate attempt to conceal the real reason for the 30% reduction in total accidents because of such comments by him that he was a fool to ever let the drunk driving arrests get started in the first place and that he would never let it get started again. There's too much politics involved."

How could any Zone Commander ignore this information?

Supervising Inspector G.R. Reinjohn responded to the third step of the grievance, and like Captain Dahl, justified the most serious grievances by rationalization.

The actual investigation was done by Deputy Zone Commander, Inspector R.M. Walker, who was the Inspector present at the dinner when Lieutenant Goodwin was in such a drunken boisterous condition and Walker stood by and did nothing.

Zone IV's answer read:

> "The investigation indicated that the Sub-station Operational Report is accurate. The enforcement was rather consistent. It is true that drunk driving arrests were up, but there is no infactual reporting. You express concern that there appears to have been a conflict between enforcement policy as expressed by the Department and the permitted application in the field. Again to assure full investigation, the Area commander (Dahl), an adjacent Area Commander (probably Captain Pugh of San Luis Obispo), an adjacent Sub-station Commander (Goodwin) and Lieutenant Thobe have been contacted and each stated that he affirmatively pursues and will continue to pursue Departmental policy on the apprehension of drinking drivers."

Naturally, they would all say they "affirmatively (whatever that means) pursue and will continue to pursue Departmental policy." What else could they say? Did Reinjohn expect them to say, "No, we don't pursue drunk drivers. We don't follow Departmental policy." If they were to say that, they would be either fired or transferred to Winterhaven or Needles. Commanders of Areas and sub-stations can be transferred at the will of the Department.

I had based one of the charges that Thobe was dishonest on his adamant denial that he told me: "Your statement carries no more veracity than a traffic officers." I told Zone IV to listen to the tape I made of him and turned over to Captain Dahl.

Zone IV's response in this "unbiased" investigation was:

> "The documentation of the tape recording taken by you does confirm his remark but this <u>does not</u> indicate dishonesty. If the individual taped would have known that his every word was being recorded and was not normal conversation the Lieutenant's utilization of words may have been expressed differently."

This answer was so stupid that it embarrassed me to think that I worked for the same organization. Our grievances were apparently never forwarded to CHP Headquarters, although, as it turned out, it probably wouldn't have made any difference.

We File More Grievances

Thobe hardly had breathing room until he received a grievance from Sergeant Klippness four days later.

Klippness' grievance read:

> "Within recent months, as a direct result of certain acts and/or omissions on the part of Lieutenant Donald M. Thobe, it has become difficult for me to perform my job as a sergeant on the California Highway Patrol. These acts and/or omissions have been of an abusive and discourteous nature and are reflected in the following incidents and/or situations.
>
> "I respectfully request that action be taken which will prevent me from being subjected in the future to similar kinds of harassing, unjustified and unwarranted treatment."

Thobe's written response to Klippness' grievances was exactly the same as his response to mine except for our names.

PART 1: *Chapter 10:* Battle Continues Over DUI Arrests 161

Klippness asked for it to go to the next level by responding:

> "Lieutenant Thobe chooses not to answer the grievance, but offers information that I am inaccurate, that I have taken quotations out of context, and that quotations are erroneous. It would seem appropriate that he either confirm or deny my grievance and stop trying to cast aspersions on my character.
>
> "Lieutenant Thobe states he is now willing to discuss the allegations. This is a reversal of the grievance procedure. We have passed this stage. The fourth item under "Discourteous Treatment" would indicate that I have attempted to discuss specifics with him before, and the first item under "Unfair Treatment" would disclose the results of a past discussion.
>
> "Therefore, I respectfully request that Lieutenant Thobe comply with this stage of the grievance procedure and explain his actions."

Sergeant Klippness' grievances were treated almost identically to mine. Even getting the same verbal rationalization. However, there were two different answers that Klippness received from Zone IV that are worth mentioning.

One answer was in response to officers not wishing to drive cruisers because the tires were too worn and unsafe.

Their finding was, "Your accusation that Lieutenant Thobe showed intentional disregard for the safety of his subordinates is a serious allegation. This is not only an offensive suggestion, it is completely indefensible.

"The tires on sub-station vehicles are regularly inspected by the Maintenance Man. They are removed when thread is reduced to near 1/32" in summer months and somewhat sooner during inclement seasons. Please note: Santa Maria Sub-station personnel have not experienced a worn tire blow-out since Lieutenant Thobe's assignment to that office."

In regards to Klippness' grievance of "Harassment," Zone IV provided the following response:

"Lieutenant Thobe categorically denies making the latter remarks you attribute to him. Since his version of the conversation contradicts yours and there is no evidence of an independent nature, we must treat your charge as unproven."

Klippness and I were now convinced that we could not count on Zone IV to be fair and impartial. The next step for justice would have to be the Commissioner's office and we already knew that was out of the question. Thobe was going to be "rubber stamped" all the way to the top.

That didn't mean we were going to stop filing grievances. At least I wasn't going to stop filing. I've found, from experience, that ruthless individuals are not loyal to anyone. I believed in due time—if I put enough pressure on Dahl and Reinjohn by bringing Thobe's misconduct to them—that they would turn on Thobe once they didn't need him any more.

Right now their number one priority was to make an example out of me by firing me. They wanted Klippness too but not as bad as they wanted me.

A Tempest over Rubber Boots

On January 10, 1968, there was heavy rain in Santa Maria as I reported to work at 2:00 pm. When I left home I was dressed for the occasion. A light plastic cover for the cap, a yellow heavy-duty rain coat and black rubber boots. They were the same raincoat and boots I had been wearing for the past 10 years.

Lieutenant Thobe was at the office (normally he would be playing golf on state time) with his two favorite officers, Hilker and Cameron, from whom I had requested memorandums concerning the Judge Stewart DUI stop.

As soon as I entered the briefing room and sat down at the Sergeant's desk, Lieutenant Thobe, followed by Officers Hilker and Cameron, walked over to the desk.

Thobe said, "I want the original memos that you forced Hilker and Cameron to write. And I'm ordering you to never ask them to write you another memo."

PART 1: *Chapter 10:* Battle Continues Over DUI Arrests 163

I told Thobe that it was totally proper, as a supervisor, to have an officer write a memorandum concerning an incident that occurred during their shift.

Thobe said, "I don't care what you think. Now, where are those memos?"

While I was searching through my attache case for the memos, Thobe said, "Those rubber boots you have on are not regulation."

I stopped searching for the memos and said, "I've been wearing these rubber boots since I came on the Highway Patrol."

He said, "I don't care how long you've been wearing them. Take them off and get some regulation boots."

"The boots are regulation" I told him. "The Department specifies black rubber boots and that's what I have on. The soles are cream colored but they can't be seen in the rain and mud."

Thobe became very angry and shouted, "I said take those boots off now."

I replied, "If I took them off now I would be in my socks. Then I really would be out of uniform."

He shouted, "Then get out of the office and go get your shoes."

I told him I would go home and put on a pair of dress shoes as soon as I finished the coffee I had been drinking.

Thobe said that he was going to write me a censurable incident report for my "lack of knowledge of uniform requirements."

Both Hilker and Camerno appeared to be enjoying Thobe's display of knowledge and authority even though Thobe's actions were opposed to all supervisory principles.

But now it was my turn. I said, "Lieutenant, while you're writing me a censurable incident report for my lack of knowledge of uniform requirements, you will need to write yourself one."

This got the attention of all three of them.

Thobe, "What are you talking about?"

I said, "That tie clasp you have on is not regulation."

Thobe, looking down at his tie clasp and obviously embarrassed, said, "There's nothing wrong with this tie clasp."

I told him he should familiarize himself with Departmental policy and he would know that he is "out of uniform" if his tie clasp is "illegal."

Thobe said in a demanding tone, while trying to avoid Hilker's and Cameron's stares, "What's wrong with my tie clasp?"

I told him, "You are wearing a chain type tie clasp and that type of clasp is not approved and you should know that."

Thobe became very emotional and charged me in a threatening manner with his arms waving. I had to retreat backwards to avoid physical contact with him. I knew if there was physical contact that he would have claimed that I assaulted him. He also knew his "two stooges" would have testified to whatever he wanted them to say. I would have surely been fired and probably arrested.

For a couple of days Thobe didn't wear a tie clasp and, of course, his tie waved back and forth. It looked terrible. But on the third day he showed up at the office wearing a departmental approved snake type tie clasp and told me that he had decided to continue wearing the same tie clasp he had on the other evening because it was regulation. Of course, he was lying.

I told him that was not the same tie clasp he was wearing that night and it was obvious that he had bought a regulation one.

Thobe followed through with his threat to write me a censurable incident report:

> "On January the 10th, 1968, in the presence of Officers C.V. Cameron and T.N. Hilker you were insubordinate

and/or insolent in response to your immediate supervisor's questioning of your actions of January 9, 1968.

"1. At the demand of the Officer in Charge you refused to surrender the original written statements that you acquired from the officers as the result of your unauthorized conduct of January 9, 1968. [Thobe purposely did not mention what the unauthorized conduct was because what I did was proper. Any reviewing supervisor with an ounce of sense would require Thobe to list what the unauthorized conduct was.]

"2. When told by the Officer in Charge to remove your yellow and black rain boots and to report for duty in proper and regulation uniform you obtained a cup of coffee, leaned against the door frame and insolently announced that you would comply after you finished your coffee. In addition, you challenged the Officer in Charge about wearing an improper tie clase (MS), a chain type. When asked what was improper about the chain type clasp, you stated it had to be a bar type to be regulation. [Of course that was a lie. I didn't say that because a bar type was not regulation.]

"Your defiant attitude and refusal to comply with Department regulations was inexcusable. Your demonstrated lack of knowledge of uniform requirements, especially in front of your subordinates, reflects adversely on your supervisory leadership."

And Captain Dahl approved the censurable incident with his blessings.

As long as Thobe and Dahl kept us busy, at least we wouldn't be out arresting DUIs.

Thobe's Record of Arresting DUIs

One evening when Thobe was complaining to Klippness that too much overtime was being spent on DUIs, he told Klippness, "I've arrested over 600 drunk drivers and I have never gone to court on any of them."

Later, Thobe, with a smirk on his face, asked Klippness if he believed what he had said about arresting 600 DUIs and having never had to go to court? Klippness said, "No, because you told me a few months ago that you had only arrested 2 drunk drivers in 20 years." Thobe smiled and said, "I did?"

Checking Thobe's Golf Course Records

On January 18, 1968, I was fed up with Thobe's lying and I wanted proof to support one of the charges in my grievances against him. That was the charge of playing golf on state time and reporting it as worked. I knew that his Attendance (work) sheet had to be forwarded to Personnel Section at CHP headquarters. That, he could not change. So, all I needed was to prove he played golf on those days when he reported he had been working.

On my day off and in civilian clothes, on a day that I knew Thobe would be out of the area, I went to the Santa Maria Golf Course where he spent most of his time because it was close to the office. There were other golf courses in the area but he wanted to be able to get to the office as quickly as possible in case a CHP Inspector just happen to be passing through.

I couldn't think of any other way to do it but by the direct approach. There was a risk involved in case they refused to cooperate and then called the CHP area office and complained. But some things are worth the risk and this was one.

I walked up to the club house and asked to speak with someone in the office.

A gentleman dressed in a suit and seated behind a desk, asked, "How can I help you?"

I showed him my badge and I.D. Card and told him I was conducting an investigation on a party that claimed he did not play golf at this golf course but I have reason to believe that he did. I thought for sure he was going to ask who the party was, so I quickly added, "I just want to keep this low key. The golf course is not involved in any way and I only have to look at a few records."

He said, "Oh! There's only one problem. The records are down in the basement and haven't been filed yet. But you're more than welcome to go through them. There's one thing that will be of help though. At our golf course, everyone who plays must sign their name on the starting time before they can tee off." He added, "Just take your time and I apologize for the records not being in better order."

The records were just pitched on a table but they were in order of dates and it didn't take me long to find "Don Thobe" signed on sheet after sheet. When I got enough sheets to prove Thobe was lying about playing golf on state time, I went up stairs and asked if I could pay them to make copies of the documents I had. They said there would be no problem and ran the copies for me.

Handing the copies, they said, "No charge and I hope you found what you wanted."

I thanked them and assured them that I had.

I now had the undeniable evidence that I needed. But I had another lesson to learn. Evidence is only of value if a district attorney or the Office of Internal Affairs will charge the individual with a crime or punitive action. No action was ever taken against Thobe.

Thobe was relentless in his harassment against Klippness and me especially because we had filed grievances against him. He wrote us censurable incident reports for almost every imaginable thing.

On January 10, I filed a grievance against Thobe for writing incident reports that contained "distorted and misleading" information. Thobe's tactics were obvious: The more censurable incident reports I received, the better it would look in my package for dismissal.

That was why, on January 18, I filed a grievance against Thobe for "charging me in a threatening manner." I did this mainly to protect myself in case he did accuse me of physically assaulting him.

Suddenly Transferred to Santa Barbara

Finally, someone decided that the situation in Santa Maria could not continue. Suddenly and without any prior notice, I was transferred to the Santa Barbara area February 6, 1968. The transfer was suppose to be temporary but that's all the information they would provide. They said they needed me to replace a sergeant who was on vacation.

Santa Barbara is an Area as opposed to a sub-station. They had about 50 officers assigned plus about 6 sergeants.

I did have to drive more than 120 miles to and from work because I still lived in the Santa Maria area. I was furnished a cruiser and when I came home at night I had to always watch for deer. Governor Ronald Reagan's ranch and Michael Jackson's Neverland were located right off of Highway 151 which I always took.

I knew a large number of the officers and sergeants in Santa Barbara and got along fine with them. It was a pleasure getting away from Santa Maria and Thobe. I told one of the sergeants in Santa Barbara I was glad that I was working down there, even temporarily. And that I had worked for Captain Dahl in East Los Angeles. The sergeant looked me straight in the eye and in a monotone voice said, "He's an asshole." There were a few personnel present including a female. All of them laughed.

Get those Cuffs Off of That Kid

There were a couple of DUI arrests that I made while working in Santa Barbara that stand out. One involved a DUI teenager. CHP radio dispatched us to an "11-80" (accident—major injuries). There were three people seriously injured, one critically.

The teenage DUI that ran the red light was uncooperative and combative. We told him that he was going to have to take a blood alcohol test, that he was being arrested for a felony.

He was swearing and saying, "I'm not taking any tests and you can't make me."

The DUI was arrested and handcuffed and taken to a local hospital for a blood test. Normally, if a DUI is cooperative, we take the handcuffs off while he is getting a blood test. But in this case the teenage DUI was actually swearing and wanting to fight. When we walked into the emergency room with the DUI and the doctor saw that the teenager was still handcuffed, he angrily said, "Get those handcuffs off of that young man and don't ever bring a prisoner in here in handcuffs again."

I told the doctor that the DUI was uncooperative and combative but before I could finish he said, "I said get those handcuffs off him right now."

The DUI appeared to have calmed as we took the handcuffs off. The doctor got a new syringe and then directed the DUI to extend his arm with his palm upward. As the teenager extended his left arm and the doctor leaned toward him, the DUI suddenly and without warning, doubled his right fist and struck the doctor in the stomach with all the force he could muster. The doctor doubled up and staggered backwards.

Having had the air knocked out of him, the doctor gasped, "Get those cuffs on him."

We immediately restrained the DUI and forceably got him handcuffed. After recovering from the blow to the solar plexus, the doctor cautiously obtained a blood sample. A DUI can be unpredictable.

Get the Gun and Shoot Him

One evening, while still assigned to the Santa Barbara area, I observed a late model car being driven by a middle-aged female weaving on a residential street. There was no centerline, but the pattern in which she was driving indicated she was possibly DUI.

I turned on the cruiser's red lights and sounded the horn. I saw her look in the rear view mirror but she continued on at about 20 mph. It is not unusual for a DUI to try and make it home or to their destination when signaled to stop by a law enforcement officer. For some reason they think they can't be touched if they make it to the sanctity of their home.

Sometimes though, it is for a more sinister reason. Some want to make it to a location where they can get friends or family members to help them resist the police.

The woman pulled into her driveway and stopped the car. I parked the cruiser in the driveway a few feet behind her, walked up to the driver's side and asked her to roll her window down. I could smell an odor of alcohol and she had other physical symptoms of being under the influence.

She said, "What did you stop me for?"

I told her, "Suspicion of being under the influence of alcohol."

I asked her to get out of her car so I could give her a field sobriety test (FST).

As she was climbing out from behind the steering wheel she stated with authority, "I'm not taking any of your tests. I want you off of my property."

While this discussion was going on, the DUI's young son, about 15 years old but smaller than average in height, came out on the front steps of the house.

I told the DUI that she was going to have to take the FST or I would have to arrest her without her taking it. She became very loud and emotional, screaming, "I'm not going to jail. I'm going in the house," and she started in that direction.

I took a hold of her arm and said, "You're not free to leave."

She jerked her arm away and said, "Leave me alone." Her son, showing great concern, said something like, "What's the matter mom?"

The DUI, in an obvious intoxicated condition, looked at her son and shouted, "He's wanting to take your mother away. Get the gun and shoot him."

The youngster stood there momentarily looking at us with a confused expression.

The DUI screamed again, "Go get the gun and shoot him."

The youngster turned and started running for the front door and I took off running after him. I picked up a few steps because he had to open the front door but there was still some distance between us.

He entered the kitchen as I was coming through the front door. My greatest concern was that I would have to shoot him.

In the kitchen there was a loaded rifle above the kitchen door with two supports underneath it. All a person needed to do was lift the rifle. Because of the young boy's height, he needed a chair to stand on to reach it. He slide the chair underneath the door frame, stood on it and put both hands on the rifle just as I grabbed him and pulled him down off of the chair and took the rifle from him. I felt very sorry for the young boy who was crying the entire time.

I arrested the DUI and placed her in the cruiser. Then I explained to the young boy why it was necessary to take his mother to jail. The youngster was taken to a next-door neighbor who volunteered to look after him until his mother sobered up and came home.

The DUI was also charged with Penal Code Section 272, contributing to the delinquency of a minor. Alcohol was obviously not her only problem.

Chapter 11
Firing Conspiracy Leads to Headquarters

On February 25, 1968, I was notified I was being transferred to the West Los Angeles Area effective March 1. This was not at my request and in violation of Departmental policy. Santa Barbara was about 60 miles from where I lived. Now, I would be about 145 miles from home. They said I could go to West Los Angeles and pick up a motorcycle in a couple of days. At this point it was apparent that the CHP was trying to get me to resign. They tried harassment and that didn't work. Then they transferred me to Santa Barbara, figuring I'd either have to move or quit.

Two days later, I left Santa Maria in my private car and without any travel reimbursement en route to West Los Angeles, 145 miles away. I was told to stop at the CHP office in Santa Barbara and pick up some papers I would need in WLA. About an hour and one half later, I stopped in the Santa Barbara office and was told to see Captain Dahl in his office. He greeted me with, "Your transfer to West Los Angeles has been rescinded. You can return to Santa Maria."

It was becoming very clear what was taking place. On March 1, a good friend, Sergeant Frank Loper, was transferred to the Santa Maria Area from Bulleton, where he continued to live. The CHP did not know that we were good friends. I doubt that they even knew we knew each other. Loper had already told me that Captain Dahl had announced to those present at a drunken party at the VFW Hall, in Santa Maria on January 26, that "as soon as possible, we are going to get rid of two sergeants here in Santa Maria."

He continued among the laughter and applause: "We are going to promote Officer Short to sergeant and hopefully we will be able to keep him here."

This was the man who was conducting a "fair and impartial" investigation on Klippness and me.

Two weeks later, on March 14, Inspector John Bryant, Internal Affairs, and Deputy Attorney General Richard Turner came to the Santa Maria sub-station and interviewed Klippness and me at 10:00 am. It was obvious they were there to gather information or find something they could exploit in their effort to build a dismissal case against us. They were just "sizing us up" and hoping we would say something they could use. I never believed either one of them for one minute and time proved that to be true.

Who Slashed Tire on the Cruiser

A few days after Bryant and Turner left, I was assigned to figure out who deliberately slashed a tire on Officer Cameron's cruiser. Cameron said it appeared to be deliberate.

I didn't try to second guess why I was assigned the investigation. After getting DUIs off of the road, investigation was my favorite assignment. I liked the challenge of solving a problem.

I was told they had no suspects. First, I examined the tire to see if it was a deliberate cut or could have been accidental. The location of the cut and angle indicated that it was deliberate. I asked the CHP maintenance man if he had any thoughts on how it could have occurred. I mainly wanted to see his reaction. He said it looked like someone deliberately cut the tire with a box knife.

I agreed. I then asked him how he got along with Officer Cameron. The maintenance man's reaction and comments convinced me that he had not had anything to do with the incident.

I then asked the maintenance man the name of the tire facility and if he knew who may have installed the tires. He gave me the name of the person who installed the tires and I ran him through the National Crime Information Center (NCIC) to see if he had been arrested. A further check revealed that

PART 1: Chapter 11: Firing Conspiracy Leads to Headquarters

he had received a citation a month earlier for reckless driving out of our office and the citation was issued by Officer Cameron.

My next move was to visit the tire man at the service facility. I asked to speak with him alone, and we walked out into the back of the business. First, I asked him if he thought the ticket he received was fair. He said he may have deserved it but he thought he should have gotten a break since he did the service on the cruisers.

"What do you think of the Officer who issued you the ticket?" I asked.

He said, "He was a real jerk. He's been here in Santa Maria for as long as I can remember and I don't know anyone who likes him."

I wanted to say that he could add me to that list but instead I asked, "Do you dislike him enough to slash one of the tires on his cruiser?"

He said, "No. I wouldn't do anything like that."

I said, "Do you know anyone who would?"

He said, "No."

The continuance on his face, the tone of his voice and maybe just a gut feeling told me he was the guilty party. I tried every way I knew to get him to confess including "Would you be willing to take a polygraph test?"

I knew there was no way in the world that he was going to confess to slashing the tire and we had no evidence of any kind to prove he did it. So, I tried something I had never done before or since.

I told him, "Look I've been assigned to investigate this case and all I want to do is close it out. It's a very serious matter and I just want to make sure it never happens again. I know you're not going to admit to doing it but would you do me a favor? If you did do it then nod your head up and down. I promise you that I will not arrest you. Then I can close the case and not have to spend anymore time on the investigation."

The tire man slightly nodded his head up and down.

I closed the case with the comment," I believe the tire man slashed the tire but there is no evidence to prove it. Recommend the case be closed."

There were no more incidents of tire slashing. Captain Dahl returned the investigation report with the comment, "Excellent job."

Officers Give DUI a Ride Home

On March 28, Barbara Capitani left Officer Cameron the following note:

> "A Mrs. McCallister, 350 Silver Lane, called and said some Highway Patrolmen brought her son home about 2 am yesterday morning. He had been sleeping in a vehicle. She wants one of them to call her at the above number, as she has a question she wants to ask.
>
> B.C. (good luck—I had two sessions with her.)"

If this had been properly handled, the note would have gone to a sergeant. Then the sergeant would discuss it with the officers. Then the sergeant could do an investigation. But it's not always done that way in every area, city, county or state.

It is obvious that Barbara Capitani was covering for Cliff Cameron who no doubt was one of the officers that took a DUI home instead of booking him. "Sleeping" in the vehicle means he was passed out drunk, otherwise, he could have been awakened and drove himself home. The mother probably wanted to know where the car was left.

And to think, this young man may have driven drunk again and killed a family.

If the only thing that is going to happen when you are caught DUI is a free trip home in a cruiser then why not drive under the influence? The public must realize that there are a lot of Officer Camerons working throughout the nation. And then there are other officers that will lock your car keys in the trunk and let you walk out into traffic and get killed. Then there are others that will just turn you loose and let you crash on your own. And this is going to continue unless the public rises up and says enough is enough.

PART 1: *Chapter 11:* Firing Conspiracy Leads to Headquarters

'We Can Hold It Over His Head'

On April 2, I made a formal recommendation that punitive action be taken against Officer Edwards for (1) Outside employment incompatible with State job, (2) Negligence in performing official duties, and (3) Discourteous treatment of a supervisor.

Not only does the California Highway Patrol not want officers bidding on state vehicles, even more so, they prohibit officers from working part time jobs that could compromise their law enforcement position. That especially applies to tow truck businesses that are Official tow services for the CHP.

One of Santa Maria's Official CHP Tow Services was Cox Garage in Orcutt, a city that is served by Santa Maria. I discovered that Officer Edwards was working there with Thobe's knowledge.

Thobe made this known to Sergeant Klippness a year before. He told Klippness to forget it and "we can hold it over his head if we ever need to use it."

It was common knowledge that Edwards was working for the owner, Ed Cox, and had at times been seen towing a vehicle. On February 23, Klippness and I both saw Edwards working on a ¾ ton truck tractor in Cox Garage. We just happened to be driving by and Klippness said, "Hey. Look. That's Edwards working on that truck." We went around the block just to make sure it was him.

Personally, I liked Ed Cox. He was a gentleman and a nice guy. I never saw or heard of him doing anything dishonest until he testified at my hearing. Edwards' hobby was restoring old cars, but even if that was his only purpose for working at Cox Garage, it would be incompatible to be using the facility.

The purpose for this policy is to prevent an officer from favoring one tow service. When an officer calls for an "11-85" (tow car request) the dispatch center is to call the next tow service in rotation. There are two exceptions. The first is if the tow service cannot respond, in which case the dispatcher goes to the next garage in rotation. The second exception is "owner's request." That's how an officer can favor a tow service and that's what happened on March 23 at US 101 near Cat Canyon.

Edwards requested an "11-85, owner's request, Cox Garage."

I contacted the owner of the disabled car and he said he was just passing through on his way to San Francisco. He said he had no knowledge of any tow businesses in the area.

Before I made the recommendation for punitive action, I spoke with Captain Dahl and he said, "Yes, I know. He (Thobe) told me that he (Edwards) was welding part time or something."

I sent a copy of the request for punitive action against Officer Edwards to the Commissioner's office "return receipt requested." Captain Dahl denied ever having the conversation with me. Lieutenant Thobe denied ever having the conversation with Klippness.

And instead of filing punitive action against Edwards, the Department used this incident as a charge to support my firing. I was getting sick and tired of all the lying that was going on so I sent the following message to the Commissioner's office:

> "An investigation based upon lies is of no value to the Department. I, therefore, urgently and respectfully request that all parties involved (especially Lieutenant Thobe) submit to a Polygraph test. It is available in Santa Barbara and the expense is approximately $75 per person. I am willing to pay the expense of the tests for all the personnel involved and will post the money in advance."

Inspector Bryant of Internal Affairs denied ever receiving the request at the Commissioner's office.

Thobe Slips Up and Then Covers Up

Lieutenant Thobe finally put something in writing that Klippness and I could document. And it was something the CHP takes very serious. One of the CHP cruisers blew an engine and Thobe wrote the following message to the officers, with a grease pen, on the equipment locker in the automotive service room.

PART 1: *Chapter 11:* Firing Conspiracy Leads to Headquarters 179

"Engine Blown . . . . Will probably be sold. If interested think about bids. At Home Motors."

At briefing, a few of the officers inquired about the message and asked Klippness how they could bid on it. Klippness said he would inquire into it and let them know. After the officers left on patrol, Klippness took his personal camera and photographed the message. That evening he told me about it.

The CHP strictly prohibits all CHP employees from bidding on state vehicles because it could easily lead to abuse of the system, and would give state employees an unfair advantage over the public. The Motor Transport Manual (MTM), section 1.19.1 reads, "All vehicles are sold by sealed bid in accordance with instructions issued by Accounting Section when the sale is authorized. All bids shall be forwarded to Accounting Section for opening and awarding. California Highway Patrol employees may not bid for vehicles."

I wanted to see how Thobe was going to lie his way out of this one and how the CHP Gang would cover up for him. The Gang included Deputy Attorney General Richard Turner.

On April 4, I sent a memo to Captain Dahl in Santa Barbara: "On or prior to April 1, 1968, Lieutenant D.M. Thobe wrote a message on the equipment board soliciting bids from the officers for a disabled Department of California Highway Patrol vehicle. He also specified the location of the vehicle as Home Motors. The message was printed on the equipment locker reserved for patrol unit #1424.

"Several officers have made known to the sergeants that they would like to bid on the car and, if possible, purchase it. We have informed the officers that this is improper and illegal whenever they have approached us. One officer replied, "How about getting someone else to bid for us?"

"If the public was to become aware of this type of conduct it would surely cast discredit and doubt upon our Department.

"I, as a supervisor at this substation, have been forbidden by the Officer-in-Charge, Lieutenant Thobe, to conduct investigations or even require a subordinate to write a memorandum. Therefore, I urge that steps be taken to correct this situation."

Captain Dahl contacted Thobe as soon as he received the "return receipt requested" letter. (I sent all communication "return receipt requested" otherwise they would deny ever getting the communication).

I'm sure Thobe's first thought was to erase the message but word had also gotten to him that Klippness had already photographed it. So, the next best thing he could do was add or remove a word to try and change its meaning. He chose the word, "obtaining." That's the best he could do under the circumstances but it was obvious that it had been added. By adding the word "obtaining" he could argue that he just wanted the officers to assist the Department in getting bids from the public.

I took a photograph of the message with the word he had added so we could show from Klippness' photograph that the word had been added.

That night, I got some bad news from Klippness. He took the role of film to the Santa Maria Police Department to have it developed and Sergeant George Squires phoned him that "the picture did not take." By now the message had been changed by Thobe but I still had my photograph and I had no intentions of taking it to the Santa Maria Police Department to have it developed.

At roll call a couple of days later, Thobe interrupted the briefing by asking one of the officers to photograph the message on the equipment board.

I said, "That's not necessary I've already taken one and a registered letter is already on the Commissioner's desk."

Hearing this, Thobe demanded that I give him a copy.

I told him, "No. I don't have a copy."

And I didn't have a copy. I had sent that to the Commissioner's office. I only had the original. Instead of disciplining Thobe for soliciting bids for a CHP cruiser, they chose instead to make it a part of the package they put together to fire me five months later. And they did the same thing on the next misconduct I reported.

Just Sign these Blank Papers

On April 9, 1968, Lieutenant Thobe brought some papers to the sergeant's desk where I was working and asked me to initial each page and sign the last one. I told him that I would have to read them first.

He said, "We don't have time for that. Just initial and sign and I'll give you a copy."

I told him that I wouldn't initial or sign anything until I had read it thoroughly.

He called Barbara Capitani over to the desk and told her to initial and sign the documents for me. I never did know what he wanted me to sign. I actually thought it was amusing.

I told Laura about it when I got home that night and added, "If you wanted to look up the meaning of 'stupid' in the dictionary, you would look it up under 'Thobe." I knew that was a trite remark but it seemed so appropriate.

About this time, Thobe stopped using "Sgt. M" when addressing his messages to me. He now used my initials "Sgt. BM" and told the officers that it stood for "bowel movement." They all had a good laugh.

The Case of the Green Ledger book

Klippness and I had been keeping a ledger on all of the officers' performances to help us with our annual evaluations, which were forwarded to CHP Headquarters in Sacramento. This is a common practice and recommended by the Department. However, some of the officers, Scruggs and Cameron in particular, were "beginning to lose sleep" thinking about what some of those entries might be.

Quite often they went through our desks and file cabinets looking for whatever they could find to read or take. Klippness and I assumed that Thobe had given them a key so anything of value had to be taken home. We both had file cabinets at home just for that reason and we carried everything else in our attaché cases.

On several occasions, over a number of months, officers saw us writing in a green ledger book but none of them could find it no matter how hard they looked. And they all took their turns trying.

On occasions, Klippness and I would leave each other a note and "hide" it in the desk where we knew they would find it. It might say, "Don't forget to make that entry on Scruggs." or "I've got the information I need now."

Thobe kept everything in his office under lock and key but he left his door open.

He told me on several occasions, "I know you go through my waste paper basket at night."

I asked him why he thought that I did.

Thobe said, "Because I have torn up some papers and thrown them in there and they're not there the next morning."

I told him, "I'm not the only one working here, you know."

He said, "But no one would want them but you."

I said," How would the other employees know that the papers would only be of interest to me if you tore them up?"

Thobe just glared at me and said, "Go to work."

But the case of the green ledger was far from over. Officers Scruggs and Cameron went to Lieutenant Thobe and said they wanted to know what we were writing in the ledger. They probably told him that he was more than likely a part of the ledger and he should be just as concerned as them. Sergeant Loper told us that the officers were worried that we were "keeping book" on them and they wanted to see what we had.

It didn't take long to convince Thobe. He marched to the Sergeant's desk where Klippness and I were seated and demanded to see the green ledger with all the entries.

Thobe said, "I understand you guys are keeping book on everyone."

PART 1: *Chapter 11:* Firing Conspiracy Leads to Headquarters

We said we're just jotting down notes to assist us with evaluating the officers on their annual performance report. There was no way Thobe or anyone else, short of our lawyers, was going to get their hands on the green ledger.

Thobe said, "I want that ledger now, and if I don't get it, I'm going to file punitive action against both of you. Now where's the ledger? You made those entries during your working hours so I have every right to see what you wrote."

I told him the green ledger was at home and we would get it and bring it to him tomorrow.

He said, "That ledger better be on my desk when I come to work in the morning."

Later that evening Klippness and I got together and discussed what would be the best way to handle this. We decided that we would give Thobe the green ledger but there's nothing in Departmental orders that prohibits a supervisor from purging pages that have already been used to assist in the evaluation of the officers. So, we removed every written page in the green ledger except for the blank pages. We made enough new entries to cover a couple of pages but those entries would be of no real value to Thobe or anyone else.

I didn't want to just take the green ledger and lay it on the Lieutenant's desk for him to find. I wanted to see his face when he opened it.

As soon as I walked into the office, Thobe shouted, "Where's that green ledger that you were suppose to have on my desk?"

I said, "Here it is," as I handed him the book.

He immediately opened it and then rapidly thumbed through it.

"Where the hell are the entries? There's nothing in here," he yelled. "Where are the pages you cut out?"

Holding the ledger in an out-stretched hand he said, "This is worthless. I want to know what you did with the pages."

I said, "We purged them. The entries were to be used for the officers evaluation . . ."

Thobe cut me off, "I know that but you're not fooling anyone. I know what you both are up to. I want the pages you cut out of here."

I assured Thobe that that would be impossible. "There is nothing that requires us to keep purged notes once evaluations have been completed."

Department's Investigator Visits a Second Time

May 20, 1968, Klippness was assigned to Santa Barbara, supposedly as a relief sergeant for 10 days. It was really to get him out of the area while the Department was gathering all the information they could locally to support our dismissal. They couldn't very well justify sending us both out of the area at the same time.

Sergeant Bell, who I had talked with several months earlier, came to the Santa Maria area to investigate further and when I asked him if I was going to have another opportunity to give my side of the story, he replied, "I'm working for (Inspector) Bryant (Internal Affairs) and I have no intentions of talking with you."

About this time, Klippness and I were contacted by the California Association of Highway Patrolmen, of which we were members, and told that the Board (made up of officers representing CHP Areas throughout the state) had decided not to become involved. They said they would monitor the situation. In other words, you're not getting any support from us. You're on your own.

We were still in contact with the California State Employees Association and they made it very clear they were 100% behind us. They had two lawyers and one investigator ready to go in case we were fired. By now there was no question in our minds that we were going to be fired. It was inevitable. As we went on doing our job, which included arresting DUIs, we didn't know that Internal Affairs was interviewing the DUIs we were arresting in an effort to get them to testify against us at our hearing.

On June 18, 1968, we received a memorandum from Zone IV announcing that the Santa Maria sub-station would become an Area effective July 31,

1968. That meant we would have our own Captain and no longer be administered by the Santa Barbara Area.

Thobe Transferred to Fresno

Six days later, Lieutenant Thobe received the news he had been fearing for the last 18 months. Effective one week later, July 1, he would no longer be an Officer-in-Charge of the Santa Maria Area. He was being transferred to Zone IV, Fresno, where he would be just another Lieutenant and they could keep their eyes on him. They had known all along that he was a "loose canon" and he couldn't be ignored any longer. To Thobe it was devastating because he had a nice home in Santa Maria and he and his wife were planning on retiring there.

Now, his commute to work would be about 280 miles round trip. And his golf games on state time were over. The very ones who had been protecting him were now "throwing him under the bus."

This action didn't mean that Klippness and I were home free. All it meant, as far as I was concerned, was that Thobe got what was coming to him.

The temporary Officer-in-Charge was Lieutenant George Goodwin from the Buellton sub-station and Thobe's "bosom buddy." I knew he was going to do everything he could to help Inspector Bryant build a case for my dismissal. But, I must be honest, I never thought that Goodwin was very bright and nothing ever happened to change my mind.

Goodwin's First Move is a Setup

A few days later, Lieutenant Goodwin made his first move. I was working the evening shift and was closing out paper work at around 11:00 pm. Goodwin and I were the only ones in the office. (This is significant because, like Thobe, he wanted no witnesses).

As he handed me a traffic accident report, he said, "Here's an accident report I want you to complete tonight. The driver took off and I want you to contact the passenger, Donna Martin, and get her statements of what happened. She's about 16 years old and lives with her mother in Lompoc. Get her statements and then transfer the information from the non-injury form to the injury form. I want this report with her statements on my desk in the morning. Do you understand?"

I said, "How old did you say this young girl is?"

Goodwin, "I think they said she was 16."

I said, "First, it's pretty late and Lompoc is quite aways from here (25 miles)."

Goodwin snapped, "I know how far Lompoc is. I want that report finished tonight."

I said, "My shift is over and that would mean overtime."

"I don't care about any of that, just go get her statements and change the forms," he said, as he turned to go into the Lieutenant's office.

I couldn't believe that Lieutenant Goodwin was so stupid that he thought I would fall for such an obvious setup, but apparently he was. The traffic accident occurred May 11, which would make it 22 days old. It was only a "complained of pain" injury accident. The location of the accident was recorded as Highway 1 and Los Alamos. There was no such connecting highway as Los Alamos.

Officer Cameron who had done the initial "investigation" had coded the driver's sobriety as "HBD-ability impaired" and then wrote in his report, "Driver had a slight odor of alcoholic beverage on his breath when he was interviewed at the scene but did not appear to be intoxicated nor under the influence of alcohol." The wording and coding were in direct conflict with each other. But Cameron turning in a messed up report was no surprise.

The setup was sending me to a 16-year-old girl's house; a girl who lived with only her mother. With an arrival time of after midnight, she would almost certainly be in her nightgown to answer a few questions about a minor accident that occurred 22 days earlier.

In my defense, I could argue that I was ordered to do this by my superior, Lieutenant Goodwin.

But there lies the problem. All Lieutenant Goodwin had to say was "I don't know what Sergeant Mitchell is talking about. I never told him to go over there at that hour of the night to talk to a 16-year-old girl."

And that's exactly what he did. But it didn't matter. Thinking that I had followed his directions, he committed himself to saying that he had not ordered me to interview the girl late at night. I then informed Captain Dahl that I had contacted the passenger, Donna Martin, the next morning and questioned her in the presence of her mother. After discussing the details of the accident with her, I changed the driver's sobriety coding to a "4" (HBD—not known if ability impaired).

Goodwin's scheme didn't work but they filed punitive action against me anyway.

Temporary Transfer to Santa Barbara

I was notified that I was again being temporarily transferred to the Santa Barbara area effective June 21 until July 22. I actually enjoyed working in an area where I could do my job. I continued to arrest DUIs and at times turned them over to beat officers when I was busy. Even though Dahl was the Area Commander he never said a word and just let me do my job the same as when I worked for him in East Los Angeles.

While at the Santa Barbara Area, I was assigned to direct traffic for the Rancheros Visitadores, a group of horsemen that take an annual 60-mile ride in the hills off of Highway 154 in the vicinity of San Marcos Ranch. Ronald Reagan was a member and his ranch was nearby.

After the event, Horace Rupp, General Manager, sent a letter to Commissioner Sullivan commending me for "the outstanding manner in which (I) controlled the traffic on Highway 154. His actions and complete control of the situation were highly commendable . . . . you have no idea what satisfaction and gratitude I express to you for the conduct of this officer."

Commissioner Sullivan acknowledged his letter:

> "Thank you for your letter regarding the help of Sergeant Bob Mitchell during your recent ride. I am sorry I had to

miss meeting with you this year, but am hopeful that next year I possibly can. I will inform Sergeant Mitchell of your very kind comments and do appreciate your writing."

What Commissioner Sullivan didn't tell Mr. Rupp was he was in the process of firing me at the time on premeditated false charges.

Request to Train Officers Denied

On July 9, 1968, Santa Barbara Sheriff James Webster sent the following letter to Captain Dahl in the Santa Barbara Area office:

> "The Santa Maria sub-station, Santa Barbara Sheriff's Office is currently engaged in an In-Service program, a portion of which will cover Drunk Driving Arrest Procedures and Breathalyzers Use and Operation. I would like to request that Sergeant Mitchell of your Santa Maria office, instruct this class as it has come to our attention that he is eminently qualified to instruct in the field of Drunk Driving. I have had occasion to discuss this with Sergeant Mitchell and he has agreed to instruct this class with your permission.
>
> "Due to my being sent out of town to school, starting on the 15th of this month, we would like to hold this class prior to that date. If it is convenient for you and Sergeant Mitchell can be spared on the 11th of July, 1968, we would appreciate his giving this class at 2000 hours on that date. In reply, please refer to Sergeant D.R.Hersman, Santa Maria Sheriff's substation, Santa Maria.

Captain Dahl forwarded the letter to Lieutenant Goodwin and he, in turn, advised Sergeant Hersman, Santa Maria Sheriff's sub-station, that he "couldn't spare me."

Cameron's Sarcastic Tale: The Fate of Sarge Bob-Bee

Officer Cameron knew, like everyone else in the office, that I was going to be fired within just days so he took the opportunity of having a little fun at my expense. He knew he was "untouchable" at this point so he could be very brazen. The first memorandum he posted on the bulletin board for all to see and enjoy was:

The Fate of Sarge Bob-Bee

"The rain drop arced toward the ground from its home in the umbrella cloud where it had ridden since its birthplace over the North Pacific. It fell past the metal sign that read, California Highway Patrol, Santa Maria Sub-Station, and impacted against the office window.

"Inside, seated behind his littered desk, sat kindly old Lt. Don Toe-Bee. His eyes roved sadly across the room. They brushed past the hat tree that stood in the corner and to the wall behind it. There, secured to the wall by a myriad of spider webs, stood a mallet type putter with the shaft bent exactly ten degrees. On the table to his rear were piled hundreds of Employees Grievances, some of them yellowing with age. A fine film of dust had settled over the entire stack.

"Suddenly a wild look of frustration crossed his face. He tilted his back and roared, "Bob-o, come in here."

"A CHP Sergeant shuffled into the room from the adjoining hall, and with downcast eyes cautiously approached the Lieutenant's desk.

"Don't put your hands on me," he muttered.

"Listen Bob-o, I've been attempting to answer your last grievance, number 143 for calendar year 1968 I believe it is, but I hit a snag. So I called the Captain for some clarification, but when I asked him if you spelled bastard with one S or two, he generously offered to answer this one himself. So that is one that will not be handled by me, do you understand?

Eyes still downcast the sergeant replied, "Don't put your hands on me."

"And another thing, get out of them Gosh-dang Portagee cow milking boots. We ain't running no slip-shod dairy here, Get it Bob-o, slip-shod. I know, you're thinking it's wet outside and you got nothing else to wear. Well you just get out of those boots and go back into the Squad Room and daub some black shoe polish on the tops of your feet. Do you hear me?

"The Sergeant, thoroly (ms) alarmed now, snapped his gaze from the floor to the Lieutenant.

"What's the matter Sergeant, something about my shirt you don't like? No? My tie? No? Ha, my tie clasp. You're thinking it's not regulation. Right?

"The Sergeant, relaxing slightly now began to the opening bars of 'Jesus wants me for a Sunbeam.'

"O.K., Bob-o, if my tie clasp displeases you then I guess you know how to correct the situation. So you just hop it out of here and have at it."

As the Sergeant backed toward the open door he murmured in a firmer voice, "Don't put your hands on me."

"The happy clatter of his typewriter was soon heard from the Squad Room and as the keys imprinted the words-Employees Grievance No. 144, his newly shined bare feet tapped cadence to the song he hummed, "I am Jesus Little Man, Yes by Jesus Christ I Am."

"The raindrop, now joined by some of his brothers, rolled down the window pane, across the sill and fell to the ground to become the problem of the Santa Barbara County Flood Control Engineer and the Santa Maria Valley Water Conservation District.

"Conclusion: Sometimes it rains in Santa Maria."

PART 1: *Chapter 11:* Firing Conspiracy Leads to Headquarters

A few days later, either Scruggs or Cameron filled out a phony Employee Grievance and posted it on the bulletin board.

Called to Internal Affairs at Commissioner's Office

Sergeant Klippness was recalled from his vacation and told that he and I were to be at the Commissioner's office at CHP Headquarters in Sacramento on July 24 at 1:00 pm. We were directed to take one of our private cars and told we would receive mileage reimbursement for the 450 miles round trip. We were also told to bring all the documents or material that we had that was pertinent to the problems in Santa Maria.

Actually, both of us being optimist, were very encouraged by the order believing that Headquarters was finally going to give us an opportunity to tell them our side of the dispute. This optimism was even fueled more by the fact that Thobe had been removed as the Officer in-Charge in Santa Maria and transferred to Fresno three weeks earlier.

But while we were driving there, reality started to set in. There was nothing that had occurred up to that date that would lead anyone to believe they cared about finding out the truth. Could it just be possible that they were bringing us to Sacramento to get all the information they could while we were still employed?

After we were fired, we could just tell them to "go pound sand." But if we did that now, they could charge us with "insubordination." We knew the entire interview would be on tape and/or court recorder. We also knew that they would interview us separately, hoping to get conflicting answers. But we knew they weren't going to get conflicting answers. Both of us were telling the truth so they could forget the conflicting answers.

We both came to the same conclusion before arriving at CHP Headquarters. We had been called to Sacramento for one purpose and one purpose only. This was their last chance to find out what our defense would be to their phony charges. We both agreed that when they advised us of our rights, it should go like this. "You don't have the right to remain silent and anything you say will be misquoted and used against you."

We walked up the steps and through the glass doors to the front counter. We identified ourselves and told the desk clerk we had an appointment to meet with Internal Affairs at 1:00 pm. The clerk looked at us like we were Butch Cassidy and the Sundance Kid.

After making a phone call she said, "Someone will be right down."

The elevator opened just minutes later and a uniformed Captain said, "We're going to meet upstairs."

They told me I could wait in the cafeteria until they got through "talking" to Klippness. About 45 minutes later, Klippness and the Captain walked into the cafeteria.

The Captain said, "We're ready to talk to you now."

I got up and as Klippness walked by me he nodded, which told me that we were right in our prognosis—they were only "head hunting."

The actual location of the interrogation was a conference room directly across from Internal Affairs. The Commissioner's office was on the other side. As I walked into the room I recognized Inspector John Bryant, Lieutenant Lloyd Sellers, Deputy Attorney General Richard Turner and a female Court Recorder. There was also a tape recorder setting on the table.

Tape recorders have at least two purposes. To record and to intimidate the person being interviewed. The Court Recorder and the tape recorder didn't have the slightest effect on me. I only wished that the interview was on live television for all of the world to see.

They started out with the usual, "This is an official interview and you are expected to tell the truth and . . . . the date is and the time is . . . and we're at CHP Headquarters and the following people are present . . . ."

They questioned me for over an hour and tried every way possible they knew to trip me up. It was a game. I answered all of their questions but they didn't know anymore what our defense was going to be when I left than they did before I sat down.

PART 1: *Chapter 11:* Firing Conspiracy Leads to Headquarters   193

I made it very clear that they failed terribly in handling the whole Santa Maria fiasco. In fact, with the tape recorder turning and the Court Clerk typing, I put them on defense every time they asked me a question. My answer would be something like this, "No, that's not true but if you and Inspector Bryant had followed up on the documents we provided you and talked to Judge Stewart . . . ."

One of the most embarrassing moments for Inspector Bryant was when Turner said, "You keep mentioning you sent us supporting documents to prove your allegations but you know that's not true."

I said, "Yes, it is true and you know it. I sent Inspector Bryant a package of documents to the Commissioner's office on March 24 supporting all of our allegations."

Inspector Bryant said, "Well, we never got it."

I said, "Yes, you did. I have a return receipt requested with your signature on it."

Bryant got up and left the room. When he returned he said, "Yes, he's right. We did get a package from him."

Then I directed this next statement to Turner, "You and Inspector Bryant interviewed Klippness and me at the Santa Maria sub-station and I provided you with most of that information and you apparently ignored it."

Most people know that when you are testifying in court you are required to answer a question. You have no choice. But what many people don't know is that you have a right to explain your answer. The lawyer questioning you is hoping, and in some cases, depending upon you not to explain your answer. A very good example is the old question, "Do you still beat your wife? Yes or no?" Either answer, without an explanation, means you're a wife beater. Lawyers are very clever in phrasing a question that cannot be answered by a simple yes or no. Always clarify your answer.

This wasn't the type of information Bryant and Turner wanted on tape so they decided that it was time to end the interview.

I said, "Don't I get to tell my side of the story?"

They looked at each other as if to say, "What else is there to tell."

I knew one thing for sure, Bryant and Turner would not be transcribing the tape or court recorder's notes. The last thing they would want is for someone to hear or read them.

Later, when CSEA attorneys asked for a copy of the interview, Turner lied and said there were no notes or recordings made of the interview.

My Attorney, Dan Dodge, asked, "Bob, are you sure they recorded the interview because Turner said they didn't. And so did Bryant."

Dan was not questioning my integrity but my memory.

I said, "Dan, they are both liars. I saw the court recorder and even talked to her and the tape recorder was setting on the table. You've got to believe me that these two guys give no thought to lying."

Dan said, "O.K, we'll get a subpoena duces tecum and see what they do."

A couple of weeks later, Turner mailed Dan Dodge one sheet of paper with one paragraph on it that read that there was an interview on that day at that place and time and that was it. There was nothing else.

Dan said, "Maybe they didn't think anything worthwhile came out of the interview."

Dan added, "I'll put this worthless piece of paper in as evidence and the Hearing Officer will realize what they did."

As soon as our interview in Sacramento was over Klippness and I got in the car and headed for Santa Maria. All the way home he and I went over the interviews. We would tell each other what question they asked and then what answer we gave. Pretty soon we both began laughing.

He would tell me some stupid question they would ask and then tell me his answer and I would do the same thing. We weren't laughing so much at our answers as we were their ineptness. They had no idea what was going on in Santa Maria because they never bothered to investigate and were believing what Thobe and Dahl were telling them. On the serious side, we both agreed that we were days away from being fired.

But the "powers that be" got their heads together, after what amounted to "final" interviews, and decided that they had one more "brilliant strategy" that would assure them of victory.

It was obvious that phony charges and lies weren't going to work. They decided not to fire Klippness but to suspend him for 30 days. For some reason they thought Klippness would go for the "old divide and conquer" tactic. They knew it wouldn't work with me, and besides, they wanted me much worse than they wanted him.

Chapter 12
The Day I Had Been Dreading

On Monday, July 29, 1968, five days after returning from Internal Affairs in Sacramento, I was having breakfast with Laura before getting ready to go to work. It was a beautiful summer day and I was working the day shift. It was just an every day type conversation until I brought up the possibility that this might be my last day on the job.

Laura said, "Why would you say that?"

I told her it was rumored that we were going to have some visitors from Internal Affairs and that could only mean one thing. "So, don't be surprised when I come home this evening not wearing a badge," I added.

The first thing I noticed when I got to the Santa Maria office was everyone's demeanor. Hardly anyone was talking and when they did it was more of a whisper. None of the officers said anything and they appeared to be avoiding eye contact.

I got the keys to the sergeant's cruiser, took my attache case and headed for the back door. Lieutenant Goode, who worked for Captain Dahl in Santa Barbara, was now the interim officer-in-charge until July 31, when Santa Maria would become a new Area and would be commanded by Captain Robert Roese. Even though Goode was only temporary, he had already canceled all of Lieutenant Thobe's local orders that conflicted with Departmental orders.

As I was leaving he said, "Bob, be sure and make yourself available for a 10-19 (Return to office)."

I knew what that meant.

It was real strange driving around. I didn't feel like writing tickets or doing anything else. We had a large area to patrol from Highway 166 north into the mountains to Vandenberg Air Force Base near Lompoc next to the Pacific Ocean. But I hadn't forgotten the words "be sure and make yourself available." That meant don't get too far away from the office.

Thoughts kept racing through my mind. I thought about my career on the Highway Patrol, whether I should have stayed with the Montebello Police Department, that this craziness all started because Thobe didn't want us arresting DUIs, that my family and I were going to be without finances, I had no job lined up, what would our friends and the community think, and so on. The very supervisors, Captain Dahl and Lieutenant Goode, who had given Klippness and me so many commendations for arresting DUIs were firing us now for doing the same thing. It didn't make sense.

Things were beginning to look pretty gloomy.

Then all of a sudden I thought to myself, What am I worried about. I haven't done anything wrong. If I look at this predicament from a worldly point of view, of course, I can't win. But if I look at it from the position of my Christian faith, then they can't win. A verse from the Bible came to mind, Samuel 17:47. David was surrounded and out numbered by the Philistines but he informed them he had no fear that, "The battle is the Lord's." And with this thought, I put my trust in the Lord that He would see us through this battle and I would eventually be exonerated. I had no more anxiety and was completely at peace concerning the future.

While traveling northbound on US 101 near Palmer Road at about 2 pm, the "S-9 10-19" call came. I had been dreading it earlier, but now it was just another call.

As I approached the office, I noticed two CHP cruisers and one unmarked car parked in front of the office. This was very unusual. I parked in the back and walked to the front of the squad room.

PART 1: *Chapter 12:* The Day I Had Been Dreading

Captain Dahl walked in and said, "Take your 'Sam Brown' off and come into the Lieutenant's office. We want to talk to you."

Take your "Sam Brown" off means leave your gun belt, cuffs, holster and especially gun in the sergeant's area. You never know how a person is going to react to being fired and they didn't want this to be another "O.K. Corral."

Captain Dahl walked in ahead of me and sat down between Lieutenants Goode and Goodwin.

They were all three seated behind a small desk in this very small room. I must say it looked strange to see all three of them crowded together when there was only room for one comfortably. I would not have been surprised if one of them had access to a service revolver. I'm saying this from personal experience as a supervisor.

Captain Dahl said, "We called you in here to inform you that the Department has decided to dismiss you from the California Highway Patrol effective right now. Lieutenant Goodwin has a copy of the punitive action packet and you will need to sign that you have received it."

I was still standing as Goodwin handed me the packet. As I was signing the form, Captain Dahl said, "We'll also need your badge and I.D. Card."

I took off my badge and then reached in my wallet and took out my I.D. Card and laid them on the desk.

Captain Dahl said, "Is there anything you want to say?"

I said, "No. I've already said everything I wanted to say and no one seemed to listen."

Captain Dahl then said, "Well, I'm glad it's finally over."

To which I replied, "Oh! It's not over. It's just beginning" while making it a point to look all three of them in the eye.

Dahl said, "Then you plan on appealing?"

I said, "That's just a small part of what I plan on doing. You don't really think that I'm going to let you get by with this, do you?"

Lieutenant Goodwin sarcastically chimed in, "You're scaring us now."

I commented, "You don't have enough sense to be scared."

Dahl didn't want things to get out of hand so he quickly changed the subject, "Well, I'm sorry it ended this way."

I replied, "Captain, like I said, it's not the end, it's only the beginning."

After I left the Lieutenant's office, I completed all the papers that needed to be closed out and I pointed out that I had only worked 6 hours of the 8-hour shift.

Barbara Capitani said, "Oh! You have to take those last two hours as vacation." Forcing an employee to take vacation hours is in direct conflict with the State Personal Board rules but, then again, maybe they could force me to take vacation since I was no longer an employee.

After I left the office and headed home, Klippness, who was also working, got a call to "10-19 to the office." It was time for them to serve him with his punitive action, a 30 day suspension. There was a problem, however. Klippness had just stopped a drunk driver near Righetti High School. He advised the office of the situation and said he would be busy booking the subject.

He was advised by Lieutenant Goodwin to call a beat officer and turn the DUI over to him. There was nothing wrong with handling the situation this way except that was one of the very reasons they used to fire me 15 minutes earlier—and it was one of the charges they were using to justifying giving Klippness 30 days off. I came to the conclusion that they were so arrogant that they thought they could get by with anything.

When I got home I asked Laura if she noticed any difference in the uniform. "Yeah, you don't have a badge."

Then she said, "But you don't seem to be bothered too much by it."

I told her, "There's not a whole lot I can do about it right now but, be assured, the battle has only begun."

Then I told her, "They didn't fire Klippness. They only gave him 30 days off. But that's just a maneuver to get him to testify against me."

Laura said, "He could only testify that you did your job?"

I said, "You don't have to worry about Klippness, He's a loyal friend. Something those rats know nothing about."

Laura and I explained to Steve (18), Bob Jr.(15) and Cheryl (16) what had happened, but it was no big surprise, they knew what had been going on for the last 18 months and were prepared for this to happen. Both Bob Jr. and Cheryl said, "Don't worry Dad. They can't fire you for doing your job." Steve wasn't so sure.

We File an Appeal

I called Dan Dodge, CSEA, and told him of the situation.

"Yeah, we expected as much. Don't worry, we're already filing an appeal. The hearing probably won't take place for a couple of months. Now, be sure and let us know about anything you think is important and send us any documents you think we should have."

I told Dan that I was already working on the answers to all 26 charges and there wasn't a one of them with any merit except "I did at times say that Thobe was 'sick' and referred to him as a 'jerk.'"

Dan said, "They can't fire you for that. From what I hear they wouldn't chance putting him on the stand because others would come to the same conclusion."

Another priority was to find a job. The owner of a Union Oil 76 gas station in Orcutt was a good friend of mine and he made no secret about who he thought was right even though his station was one of the Official stations where the officers gassed-up their cruisers.

He said, "You can come to work for me tomorrow and I'll get you all the hours you need."

I told him I really appreciated his support but I didn't think it would work out if one of the Officers came in and said, "Check my oil and clean my windshield." He understood.

Santa Maria Times Publishes Article on Firing

On Wednesday, August 7, the Santa Maria Times came out with a large article about the punitive action with the heading, "CHP FIRES ONE SERGEANT, SUSPENDS ANOTHER HERE."

Karen White, Times Staff Writer, wrote:

> "Bob Mitchell, a Santa Maria-based sergeant of the California Highway Patrol, has been discharged from the force and a second local sergeant, Jerry Klippness, has been given a 30 day suspension.
>
> "Action against both men was taken on July 29 and both were charged with general incompetency, insubordination and inefficiency following a several months investigation, according to R. A. Kridler of Sacramento, Deputy CHP Commissioner. Both men have appealed the charges.
>
> "Mitchell and Klippness said today that in reality their disciplinary action came because of their refusal to cease action against drunken driving in the Santa Maria area and because they had brought misconduct to the attention of the CHP department. Mitchell also said that he had been charged untruthfully with 'staking out bars' to catch drunken drivers. Kridler neither confirmed nor denied the claims."

The article went on to say that a public hearing would be held on the appeal and that no date had been set but it would probably be held in Santa Maria. It mentioned the California State Employees Association would be representing us. The article mentioned our experience as law enforcement officers and that

PART 1: *Chapter 12:* The Day I Had Been Dreading   203

we had filed 22 grievances against Lt. Don Thobe, officer-in-charge of the local office until July 21 when he was transferred to Visalia (Fresno area).

But the paragraph that jumped out was the one where the deputy commissioner said that he knew nothing of any official grievances made against Lt. Thobe. "We have a regular procedure for this and have received no grievances in this formal manner," he told the newspaper.

Of course, I had sent a packet to Kridler myself (return receipt requested) so he was being dishonest. But by using the wording "in this formal manner" he could "worm" his way out if he got caught. My packet was sent to him in an informal manner.

First Los Angeles Times article

The next day, the Los Angeles Times came out with a large article, "TWO IN CHP BLAME FIRING, SUSPENSION ON DRUNK DRIVING ARRESTS."

The article read:

> "Two veteran Highway patrol officers charged Wednesday that they were dropped from the force—one of them permanently—for arresting too many drunk drivers.
>
> "Sgt. Bob Mitchell, 38, a highway partolman for more than 10 years, was discharged July 29. On the same date, Sgt. Jerry Klippness, 36, an 11 year veteran was given a 30-day suspension." The article went on to quote Klippness, "But what it was really about," said Klippness, "was that we arrested too many drunk drivers. We had been told to be on the alert, and in April, 1967, we set a record for drunk driving arrests. Mitchell and I arrested more than anyone else in the state."
>
> "Then our former officer-in-charge, Lt. Don Thobe, called the whole thing off, and said he had been a fool to let it get started.
>
> "I gathered that some people were putting pressure on him. I ultimately discovered that some of those arrested were

prominent people around Santa Maria. One was a local Lawyer, and others were big shot businessmen.

"The arrests slackened, Klippness said, and in a short time the accident rate had climbed to a new high.

"We couldn't just sit back and ignore it," he said. "Mitchell and I went back and started seeking out drunk drivers again. We felt it was our duty.

"The lieutenant indicated displeasure with the increased arrests, Klippness said, but the two sergeants continued their efforts.

"Last September, the lieutenant started making out incident reports, making minor complaints about us. We started writing our grievances against him.

"Charges were eventually filed against himself and Mitchell, Klippness said, and early last week, CHP commissioner Harold Sullivan ordered the dismissal and suspension."

The article continued, "They were harder on me because I filed 17 of the 22 grievances against the lieutenant," Mitchell said. "But I still feel we were right in making those arrests. After all, drunk drivers kill more people than all other crimes combined."

"CHP Dep. Commissioner R.A,. Kridler denied that enforcement of drunk driving laws led to the action against the two officers. The action was taken against them on the basis of the charges listed," Kridler said. "Their charges are without basis.

"We wouldn't criticize anyone for enforcing drunk driving laws. We might criticize methods employed, but enforcement per se, no."

"Klippness said the charges against Mitchell and himself included allegations that the pair improperly patrolled

PART 1: *Chapter 12:* The Day I Had Been Dreading 205

within the city limits of Santa Maria, looking for drunk drivers. "We didn't patrol there," he said. "Any time we happened to pass through it was routine and lawful. They said I staked out bars in the city. That isn't true either."

"Klippness said he and Mitchell also were accused of breaking departmental rules by asking junior officers to fill out arrest reports after the two senior officers had apprehended violators. This is done all over the state."

"As for the extra charges of 'incompetence, insubordination and inefficiency' filed against him, Mitchell said: "I can't tie them in with anything specific, I don't know where they came from."

"Both officers said they were proud of their service histories. Both had had good records with other police agencies before joining the highway patrol—Klippness with the Los Angeles Police Department and Mitchell with the Montebello Police Department. ' And since I joined the highway patrol, I've had many commendations, and Mitchell, too,' said Klippness. 'Now—no matter how it comes out—it looks like our careers could be ruined."

Well, this article in the Los Angeles Times was the last thing the department wanted. They probably thought they could handle a local newspaper like the Santa Maria Times but they definitely did not want a major national newspaper picking up the story. And that wasn't the only thing that they weren't happy about.

Through the Los Angles Times article, Klippness had made it very clear where he stood. And I'm sure, if they had it to do over again, they would have fired him too. They misread him completely. And they knew they couldn't trump charges up against him and fire him then. I knew I would have at least one highway patrolman at the hearing who would be telling the truth.

Commissioner Sullivan and his cronies were now realizing that this truly was just the beginning. I doubt that Captain Dahl and Lieutenants Goode and Goodwin had taken me too serious when I told them, on July 29, that it was "not finally over" but "only the beginning."

Southern California TV Talk Show Appearance

The day after this major article came out in the Los Angeles Times Klippness and I were invited as guests on KHJ-TV Channel 9 in Los Angeles. It was the Maria Cole (Nat King Cole's wife) and Stan Bohrman daily talk show. Channel 9 covers Southern California and has several million viewers. This was a golden opportunity to tell our side of the story to a very large audience.

As we drove to Los Angeles we had an opportunity to talk over what we wanted to stress but we didn't need to review anything because we had been living this for 18 months. After arriving at the television station, they told us we would be on in about 30 minutes and to wait in the special room for guests. The room was comfortable and had a television monitor so we would know when to leave for the production room.

Congressman Robert K. Dornan was scheduled for the first half hour and us for the second half hour. Cole and Bohrman were interviewing Congressman Robert K. Dornan at the time. As soon as their segment finished, Maria Cole said, "After the commercial break we are going to be talking to two California Highway Patrol Sergeants who claimed they were disciplined for arresting drunk drivers. One of them was fired."

That was our clue to leave the waiting room and walk a very short distance to the production room. As we got up from our chairs, Congressman Dornan came into the waiting room and said, "Are you the two CHP Sergeants they are going to interview?"

We said, "Yes."

Dornan said, "I just want to warn you that you are being setup."

We didn't have a chance to ask him how we were being setup because we only had 2 or 3 minutes before air time.

We said, "Thank you very much for the warning."

PART 1: *Chapter 12:* The Day I Had Been Dreading   207

As we continued walking, he warned us a second time, "Be careful. It's a setup."

The few seconds it took to walk to the production room, Klippness and I only had time to agree that we were used to being setup so we should be able to handle one more.

Both Maria Cole and Stan Bohrman were very nice and asked what we considered very pertinent questions, giving us every opportunity to explain our responses. Of course, Klippness and I didn't withhold anything. We made it very clear we were disciplined because we wouldn't stop arresting DUIs. We told the television audience that we received numerous commendations for arresting DUIs in Los Angeles but everything changed in Santa Maria. We said it wasn't just the local CHP administrators but it went all the way to the Commissioner's office.

For a fleeting moment I thought to myself, how can this be a setup? This interview couldn't be going better if we had scripted it ourself.

There was only about 10 minutes left of the program when a red phone started ringing while I was answering a question. The ring was so loud all of the attention went to the phone including the television cameras.

Bohrman announced to the television audience that it was Deputy Commissioner Kridler on the phone and that he had been listening to the entire show and the Sergeants were "just simply not telling the truth."

So Maria Cole asked Deputy Commissioner Kridler to tell the television audience what the real story was. The television audience could not see Kridler but only hear his voice on the phone and the camera was kept on Klippness and me to show our expression as Kridler was talking.

Kridler said the punitive action didn't have anything to do with arresting DUIs but he was not in position to discuss the real reason for the punitive action because of our present appeal. If he had been honest, he would have said, "I'm too embarrassed to tell you what the charges are."

All the time Kridler was talking, I was telling Stan Bohrman I wanted to reply to Kridler because he was lying to the audience.

Bohrman said, "I promised him if he would call in that he would not have to talk to you."

I said, "You know why he doesn't want to talk to me—because I'll expose him and his cronies as liars."

For whatever reason, Bohrman suddenly changed his mind and told Kridler that he was going to put me on the phone with him.

My first words were, "Commissioner you know you are telling one lie after another. We were commended in Los Angeles for doing the same thing we are being fired for in Santa Maria and you know it." I continued, "Just tell the audience one thing that we did wrong"

Kridler said, "I'm not going to get into the details on television."

I said, "You're not going to get into the details because you don't have any details."

He said, "Well, I don't know everything that went on there."

I said, "That's the problem. If you had done your job, you would know."

At this point, Deputy Commissioner Kridler started shouting, "Get me off of the line. Get me off of the line right now."

All of this was being heard on live television. Maria Cole said, "That will end the phone conversation." Then Maria turned to Bohrman and said, "The Commissioner is very upset and wants to talk to you now."

She thanked Klippness and me for being guests and said she wished us the best with our appeal. Even after the show went to a commercial, you could still hear Bohrman telling Kridler, "I know Commissioner. It wasn't planned this way. I know I promised you . . . ."

On the way back to Santa Maria it was easy to figure out what Congressman Dornan was talking about when he said we were being setup. Maria Cole and Stan Bohrman were supposed to get us to tell our version of what happened in Santa Maria and hopefully it would be something that could easily be disproved. They made a deal with Kridler in advance that neither sergeant would be permitted to talk with him on live television while he was on the phone. Kridler would then be able to refute anything we said and then give his phony version of what supposedly happened. And we wouldn't have an opportunity to respond.

The setup didn't work for the Highway Patrol for two reasons. The television station had decided in advance that Klippness and I were guilty. After interviewing us for 20 minutes, they came to the conclusion that we were innocent and being railroaded.

Secondly, the setup would only have worked if I had not been allowed to talk to Kridler so Bohrman, wanting to right a wrong, let me debate Kridler for all of Southern California to see and hear. It was a bad day for Commissioner Kridler and the Highway Patrol. It reminded me of a passage in the Bible that says "Your enemy will set a trap for you and fall in it himself."

Public Not Buying CHP's Reason for Firing

The Los Angeles Times had already told us that they would be covering the story from start to finish. Also, other newspapers throughout California were picking up the story. It was nearly impossible for the department to convince anyone our punitive action wasn't a result of DUI enforcement because 10 of the charges against us involved DUI enforcement. Then it became known we both had received nine commendations from the CHP over a period of eight years for our diligence in removing DUIs from the highways and teaching other officers in East Los Angeles and Baldwin Park to do the same thing. It didn't make sense that as soon as we got to Santa Maria we were suddenly incompetent and inefficient.

The public was starting to wonder if the CHP had an "unwritten" policy toward DUI enforcement based more on a person's standing in the community than his blood alcohol level. And maybe these two CHP sergeants were refusing to go along with the "unwritten" policy of "making other arrangements" instead of "arresting" certain people for DUI in Santa Maria. Maybe the special order by the officer-in-charge that he shall be notified when certain individuals were stopped could be a subtle way of saying these are the individuals we don't want you arresting.

But the prosecution against Klippness and me can't all be blamed on Lieutenant Thobe and the Officers in Santa Maria. Commissioner Harold Sullivan and his cronies, with the help of Deputy Attorney General Turner, are the ones that put together the contrived charges that resulted in our punitive action. Thobe had no authority to fire anyone. He could only make recommendations. This is what happens when two individuals, in this case sergeants, refuse to play by the "unwritten" rules and are willing to stand up and fight for what they know is right.

Hired as High School Teacher

Now that the newspapers and radio stations were covering the firing, I wondered what the publics reaction was going to be and if it might affect my getting a job. While all this turmoil was going on in Santa Maria over the past year, I still found time to graduate from Hancock College and earn a teaching degree. I also completed a year of Law from La Salle University, a correspondence course, in Chicago. My first choice was to be a substitute teacher in Orcutt, a suburb of Santa Maria. So, I made a visit to the Orcutt Unified School District shortly after I was fired and filled out an application.

I was pleasantly surprised that the staff at the school placed no credence in the charges against me and openly expressed their support.

"Sure, we've got a job for you here teaching at the high school. We'll keep you busy until you get your job back." They went on to comment that the "public knows what's going on." and I didn't asked them to explain.

There was only one occasion where my dismissal became an issue at Orcutt High School. I was teaching a class of eighth graders and while I was explaining their assignment, one of the boys spoke up and said, "I hear you're one of those officers that got fired, is that right?"

I said, "Yes, that's right."

Then one of the girls said in an accusatory tone, "Yeah, you were a bad cop, that's why they fired you."

Others in the classroom wanted to know what they were talking about.

PART 1: *Chapter 12:* The Day I Had Been Dreading 211

One of the other students said, "Are you really a cop?"

Another student said, "No, he was a highway patrolman."

I said, "O.K., I'm going to take a minute to explain this. I was a highway patrol sergeant and I was fired. I wasn't fired for being a bad cop, I was fired because I was a good cop. But I'm not asking you to believe that. I'm asking you to have an open mind and wait until I've had my day in court. The truth will come out at the hearing."

Everyone accepted the explanation and it was never brought up again. I was told later that it was Officer Scruggs' daughter that made the accusatory remark but I never bothered to find out. It didn't matter.

Sergeant Klippness didn't fare as well as I did. His daughter Becky, 14, was frequently razzed by her classmates as she walked home from school. One day she came home to tell her father how she was taunted by one of the bullies, "Why don't you get in the gutter where your dad is?" His other children, Kirsten, Kelly, George and Ronnie got the same treatment.

Preparing Answers to Charges

I went to work immediately answering the 26 charges against me. It's a violation of an individual's rights for the department to fire someone today in the manner in which they fired me. It's called "piling on."

Back then, if an agency or department wanted to get rid of an employee and they didn't have any grounds for doing it, they charged the employee with a series of omissions and commissions of minor infractions and alleged "incompetency and inefficiency." But in our case, they didn't have any minor infractions so they just made up a bunch of accusations, twenty-six, knowing they weren't true, but hoping we would not appeal and, if we did, it could be handled "behind closed doors."

But there was no way that we were going to let that ever happen. Even back then we could have filed a major civil suit against them and won. But that wasn't our goal but we didn't totally eliminate it as an option.

A good example of their dishonesty was the following allegation:

> "On June 3, 1968, during a discussion on the monthly evaluation for May 1968, you brought several incidents to the attention of Officer Loren Scruggs relative to said officer's attitude which you indicated needed improvement. (1) The said incidents had happened one or two months prior to June 3, 1968 but had never promptly been brought to the attention of Officer Scruggs. (2) Your evaluation of Officer Scruggs' attitude was based on alleged complaints which said officer was never permitted the opportunity to refute or offer any explanation."

The very thing they were charging me with, they were doing themselves. For example, they said the incidents occurred one to two months earlier and some of the charges they fabricated against me were suppose to have occurred over a year earlier. But they had good reason for not discussing the incidents with me at the time because there were no such incidents.

As I testified in court, Officer Scruggs' attitude was based upon (1) Discourteous treatment of a California Highway Patrolman's wife (Jayne Shannon) on a traffic stop. (2) Being discourteous to Tony Dias, Orcutt Chevron Station. (3) Swearing at a tow truck driver that works at Barrett's Union Station. (the owner complained to Lieutenant Thobe) (4) Discourteous and insulting statements to a juvenile traffic violator. (5) Discourteous over the telephone to a Santa Maria Police Officer. (6) Failure to stop for a citizen who was waving his hand. Forcing him to turn around and drive back a block. (7) Discourteous attitude toward immediate supervisors at the Santa Maria sub-station.

On June 3, 1968, when Officer Scruggs was presented with the evaluation, he was given an opportunity to refute or offer any explanation. His response to swearing at the Barrett's Union Station tow driver was, "So what? I swore at a tow truck driver just yesterday." This remark and others did not change my opinion that Officer Scruggs' attitude needed improvement.

The state offered nothing to support this allegation and no rebuttal to my testimony.

As mentioned earlier, it is ironic that three years later, a person approached Officer Scruggs to ask him a question and during their exchange the individual suddenly pulled a gun and shot Scruggs, who died three days later. No information was ever provided as to what, if anything, provoked the shooting.

Another charge was:

> "On or about June 24, 1967, you made the following notation on a CHP Form 180 (storage of vehicle) filled out by Officer Edwards: 'In the future do not store a vehicle without looking in the trunk. Even if you must force the deck lid open.' It would be improper for an officer to force open the trunk of a vehicle which is being stored without his supervisor's authority in each and every instance."

I testified that Headquarters General Order (81.15 D, 5, d) reads that a vehicle shall not be intentionally damaged in order to complete the inventory unless unusual circumstances are present. In this case the vehicle had been abandoned for at least 4 days. There was an unusually large inventory which necessitated the use of an attached inventory sheet. The registered owner was unknown and Officer_Edwards did not follow policy and check whether it was stolen. Officer Edwards made no attempt to contact the shift supervisor (Klippness) when he was confronted with this problem.

My testimony continued, "The reason for forced entry under these circumstances goes back to the time when an LAPD officer stored a vehicle without first checking the trunk and a dead body was found there a few days later. Furthermore, entry can sometimes be made through the rear seat lean back."

Later at the hearing, Hearing Officer Hill will rule that Officer Edwards should have contacted his shift supervisor and I was correct in the directions I provided him.

Like all of the allegations, this next charge was so absurd Dan Dodge said, "These guys must have been drunk when they were putting these charges together."

RUARY 14, 1959   PART I   1★   MA 5-2311 — 145 S. Spring, Los Angeles 53 — TEN CENTS

.S WOMAN,
TE

Car Runs
sband and
rosswalk

 an was killed and her
ured last night by a
r who later snarled to
nated a few more Okies

to take his own life.
. Phyllis Monson, 34, of 6207
-year-old child, Patricia.
 Her husband, Orville, 42,
suffered compound leg and
arm fractures, a skull fracture and internal injuries.
He is at General Hospital.
 The Monsons were struck
shortly before midnight in a
crosswalk at Gage and Eastern Aves., Bell Gardens, after emerging from a drugstore.

Thrown 149 Feet
 Mrs. Monson was hurled
149 feet by the impact, her
husband 88 feet.
 Another couple with them,
Orville Petersen, 43, and his
wife Jewel, 36, jumped back
just in time to avoid being
hit.
 The driver, John Loren
Hoy, 24, jobless machinist of
8134 Otis St., South Gate,
was picked up early today on
suspicion of manslaughter,
felony drunk driving and hit-
run.

—MIRROR NEWS Photos
CARRIED OFF TO HOSPITAL FOR BLOOD TEST
Dragging suspect Hoy are CHP officers William Mills (l), R. J. Benton.

DUI Brags, "I just killed two Okies."

I was a motor officer in East Los Angeles

Department of
CALIFORNIA HIGHWAY PATROL

INCIDENT REPORT

Name	Rank
BOB L. MITCHELL	Traffic Officer

Area and Location	I.D. #
East Los Angeles	2556

Incident: ARRESTS MADE FOR VIOLATION OF SECTION 23102a C.V.C.

Date and Time March 1963

Location East Los Angeles Area

Details: During the month of March 1963 the enforcement personnel of this Area arrested 177 operators of motor vehicles for driving while under the influence of intoxicating liquor (23102a C.V.C.). This is contrasted by the fact that only one arrest was made for 23101 V.C., Felony Drunk Driving. These arrests for the month are the highest ever experienced by this Area.

It was noted that, during this particular month, you and your regular assigned partner accounted for 56 of these arrests or approximately 32% of the total arrests.

You have been observed in the performance of your duties with particular reference to this violation and you are to be commended for your techniques in observation, interrogation and the processing of these violators.

It has also been noted that you have previously been commended for your aggressive enforcement of this particular high accident causing violation Therefore, it gives me great pleasure in again recognizing your continued efforts.

Signature below acknowledges only that the recipient has read and has knowledge of the content of this report.

| Name: Bob L. Mitchell | I.D. No: 2556 |
| Date: 4/3/63 | Approved: W. S. Dahl, Captain |

| Commander or Supervisor | |
| Date: April 2, 1963 | Time: 1000 hours |

CHP 2 (Rev. 3-62)　　　　　　　　　　　　　　　PTM. Sec. 15

One of nine commendations for DUI arrests

Department of
CALIFORNIA HIGHWAY PATROL

INCIDENT REPORT

Name	BOB L. MITCHELL	Rank	Traffic Officer
Area and Location	East Los Angeles		I.D. # 2556

Incident: ARRESTS MADE FOR VIOLATION OF SECTION 23102a C.V.C.

Date and Time: July 12 and 13, 1963

Location: East Los Angeles Area

Details:

It was noted that on July 12th and 13th, while assigned to the late evening shift, you and your regular assigned partner arrested and processed 19 23102a V.C. and 1 647f P.C. suspects.

These arrests for a two-day period is exceptional and is felt worthy of mention.

It has also been noted that on previous occasions you have been commended for your enforcement of this particular section of the Vehicle Code.

You have constantly led this area for 23102a V.C. arrests and as a result it is felt that you have served as an example for other officers of this command to follow.

It therefore gives me pleasure to again commend you for your efforts.

Signature below acknowledges only that the recipient has read and has knowledge of the content of this report.

Name: Bob R. Mitchell 2556
Date: 8/5/63

Approved: W. S. DAHL, Captain

Commander of Supervisor
Date: August 2, 1963   Time: 1000

CHP 2 (Rev. 3-62)   PTM. Sec. 15

A DUI arrest record that stands today

Department of
CALIFORNIA HIGHWAY PATROL
COMMENDATORY
INCIDENT REPORT

Name BOB L. MITCHELL	Rank State Traffic Officer
Area and Location East Los Angeles Area - 535	I.D. # 2556

Incident: OUTSTANDING ENFORCEMENT EFFORTS

Date and Time July and August 1963

Location East Los Angeles Area

Details:

In reviewing the statistics kept by this area reference to the "Drinking Driver", this area has shown a continuous increase in arrests for Vehicle Code Sections 23101 and 23102.

During the months of July and August, this area made 595 arrests for the above violations, which have exceeded any two month experience for this area.

These arrests have been reflected in Departmental statistical reports showing an increase in arrests of this nature. Percentage wise, there has been an increase of 43% statewide. It should also be noted that this area alone has accounted for 15.4% of the statewide total arrests.

While assigned to the late shift on Fridays and Saturdays, it has been noted by your supervisor that you and your co-workers have done more than your share to attain this remarkable record.

You are to be commended for your perseverance in attempting to eliminate this hazardous violation.

Signature below acknowledges only that the recipient has read and has knowledge of the content of this report.

Name Bob L. Mitchell I.D. No. 2556	Commander or Supervisor Sgt
Date 10/12/63 Approved	Date 10-8-63 Time 1500 hours

CHP 2 (Rev. 3-62)

PTM. Sec. 15

This commendation received statewide attention

CALIFORNIA HIGHWAY PATROL
INCIDENT REPORT

Name: Bob L. Mitchell
Rank: Sergeant
Area and Location: Baldwin Park Area
Ident. No.: 2556

INCIDENT:

Date and Time: August - December, 1966

Location: Baldwin Park Area

Details:

This is to commend you for your outstanding contribution in training and directing officers assigned to your supervision, in enforcement against the drinking driver.

During the period August through December, 1966, you have worked mostly the evening and night shifts with an assortment of very new and inexperienced officers and a few older ones.

In July, 1966, officers of this area made 119 arrests for 23102a V.C. Each month since has shown a significant increase to the point that 255 such arrests have been made this month to December 30, 1966.

It is sincerely felt that your energy and interest was a significant factor in this record and the guidance and direction given the officers will have a lasting and beneficial effect.

Signature below acknowledges only that the recipient has read and has knowledge of the content of this report.

Name: Bob L. Mitchell #2556   Commander or Supervisor
Date: 12/30/66   Date: 12/30/66   Time: 1600

CHP 2 (Rev 12-64)

Baldwin Park CHP commendation after only 5 months

Santa Maria CHP office today hasn't changed much

January 19, 1967

Thobe:

The Captain has given me an assignment regarding arresting 23102's. Since you have Klip and Mitch, the two best 23102 catchers in the country, in your area, perhaps they could give me some "poop." I know they prepared some material during their pre-Sergeants training at Sacramento on 23102 catching. Would you have them send me any material they have pertaining to the observation and detection of 23102's and any techniques that they have found that assist in the testing. Make it as soon as possible because I have to get hot on this big program.

Also attached is a list of a few of the scores for the last Captains examination.

The best to Lorena and the kids.

Sincerely,

Klippness and I had a statewide reputation

ALL VEHICLE ACCIDENTS 1967
DRUNK DRIVING ARRESTS 1967

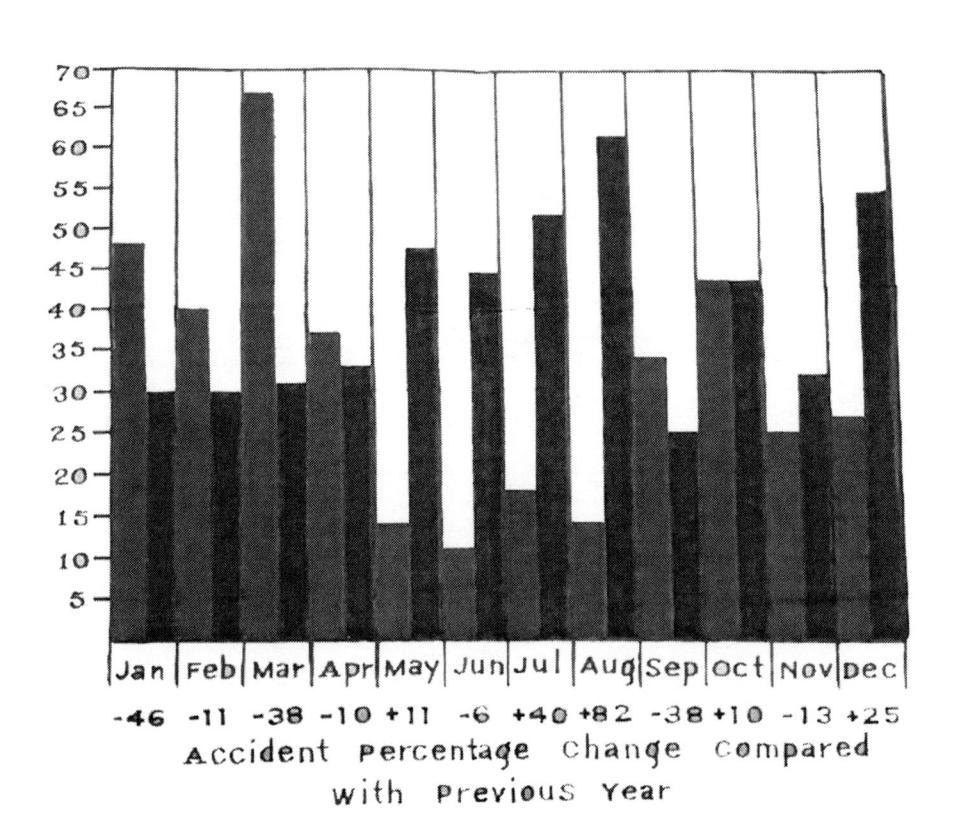

Jan	Feb	Mar	Apr	May	Jun	Jul	Aug	Sep	Oct	Nov	Dec
-46	-11	-38	-10	+11	-6	+40	+82	-38	+10	-13	+25

Accident percentage change compared with previous year

This Accident/DUI Arrest chart couldn't be refuted

DRINKING DRIVER
KILLS MOTHER AND 5 CHILDREN

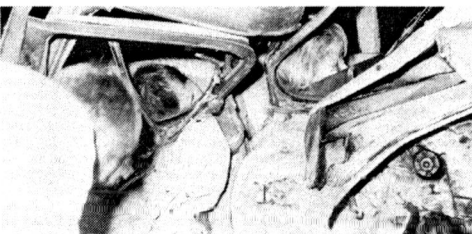

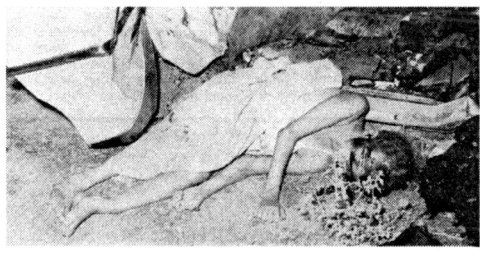

THIS COULD HAPPEN TO ANY ONE OF US.. THIS IS WHY WE CAN NOT AFFORD TO BE SITTING BACK ON OUR HANDS.

PLEASE TAKE A GOOOOOOOOD LONG LOOK. IF WE SIT BACK AND BE SELECTIVE' IN OUR DRUNK DRIBING EFFORTS THESE PICTURES MIGHT BE TAKEN IN OUR AREA.

Found in trash can
10-30-67

One of the most tragic accidents ever to occur in the Antelope Valley Area took place at 7:30 p.m. August 20, 1967, just west of Pearblossom on Highway 138.
A local resident, in a hurry to get home, left Pearblossom enroute to Littlerock, 4 miles away, at high speed. An autopsy report later indicated his B/A was .21.
From the other direction, eastbound on Highway 138, a family of seven were on their way home to Pomona, after spending the weekend in the Valley with grandparents.
The lone driver, <u>because of high speed and drinking</u> was unable to negotiate a familiar curve in the road and struck the other car head-on. The stepfather and 4 children were thrown out of their car on impact. The mother and one boy remained in their car. The stepfather was critically injured—the rest of his family killed! The other driver, too, died the next day from injuries he received in the collision.
The investigation revealed two sets of license plates on the lone driver's car. Interviews later revealed that the subject had been hiding from patrol officers earlier in the day, so that they wouldn't see the two sets of plates. His car had not been registered for 1967. A status and record check with DDL also revealed that his driver's license had been denied temporarily for a Failure to Appear dated August 11, 1965.   CHP Photos, Lancaster Area

OCTOBER, 1967

This was removed from the bulletin board immediately

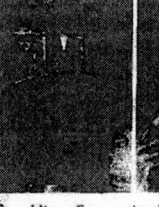

Santa Maria newspaper reporting firing

MRS. RONALD REAGAN
EXECUTIVE RESIDENCE
SACRAMENTO, CALIFORNIA

September 5, 1968

Dear Mr. Mitchell:

    Thank you so much for writing and for telling me about your problem.

    I am forwarding your letter and a copy of mine to Mr. Ed Meese, the Governor's Legal Affairs Secretary, and I'm sure you will be hearing from him soon. I do hope that, as you say, justice will prevail, and I'm sure it will.

    Thank you also for the kind words of support for my husband. We both appreciate it.

Sincerely,

Mrs Ronald Reagan

Mrs. Ronald Reagan

Mr. Bob L. Mitchell
1431 Rosalie Drive
Santa Maria, California 93454

Mrs. Ronald Reagan made sure we got a fair hearing

Bob L. Mitchell

Testimony at Punitive CHP Probe Clashes

BY KEN OVERAKER
Times Staff Writer

Two entirely different versions of what went on at the Santa Maria substation of the Highway Patrol through about 18 months of 1967 and 1968 are emerging in the hearing on the appeal of two veteran CHP sergeants from punitive action taken against them last summer by the patrol.

The testimony shows that someone must be lying.

The officers, Bob L. Mitchell, 38, and Gerald R. Klippness, 36, charge they were disciplined because they made too many arrests for drunk driving.

But that's not the story at all, according to CHP witnesses.

Mitchell, fired after 10 years with the CHP, contends also that he was punished because he filed 22 grievances against Lt. Don M. Thobe, then Santa Maria substation commander.

Written Arguments

One conflict after another has marked testimony taken by Robert L. Hill, State Personnel Board hearing officer, in the Mitchell case, now completed except for written arguments by attorneys.

And more conflicting testimony is expected when the Klippness case resumes Tuesday at 9 a.m. in the Santa Maria City Hall.

Klippness, suspended for 30 days without pay, now works at the Buellton CHP substation.

Mitchell spent three days on the stand recently answering some 25 charges the CHP has leveled against him.

He contends the CHP "trumped up" these charges to obscure the real issues, the "misconduct of officers" and the "inadequate drunk driving policy."

Both Commended

Testimony showed that he and Klippness were commended by superiors, including a former CHP commissioner, for sharply increasing drunk driving arrests at posts in East Los Angeles, Baldwin Park and Indio.

But after they had been at Santa Maria a few months, Lt. Thobe told them to stop such arrests because they were becoming "too political," Mitchell testified.

He said Thobe told him that other CHP commanders and "influential citizens" were complaining.

However, Thoe denied giving any such orders and testified he had never had any such complaints and that "the pressure was really the other way", calling for more such arrests.

Thobe said his orders against patrolling in the city of Santa Maria implemented departmental orders to "stay out of other jurisdictions."

Two maps of Santa Maria, one prepared by the CHP and one by Mitchell, showing locations of 26 drunk driving arrests made by Mitchell, were introduced.

The CHP map also showed locations of bars to support its allegation that Mitchell "staked out" bars, contrary to CHP policy, to make drunk driving arrests.

But Mitchell denied such stakeouts and showed on his map places where suspects said they had had

Please Turn to Pg. 2, Col. 1

2 *Los Angeles Times*
Sec. E—Sun., Jan. 5, 1969

Gerald R. Klippness

PATROL

Continued from First Page

their last drinks before he arrested them.

Both sides agreed that stakeouts are permitted.

Mitchell denied he patrolled in the city contrary to Thobe's orders.

Arrests he made in the city occurred after booking suspects at the city jail in the heart of the city or while he was on his way from one CHP beat to another "in my capacity as a supervisor," he said.

He said several of the 26 arrests were made in the county and that pursuit of several others started in the county.

On one incident where he said he had been called by two officers to help in booking a suspect at the jail, one officer testified he was not called.

Arrests Elsewhere

Mitchell said only 17% of his arrests were in the city, not 50% as Thobe indicated earlier. He pointed out he made many other arrests elsewhere in the county which were not considered at the hearing.

Mitchell, who is accused of calling Lt. Thobe a wide variety of derogatory names, said he usually called him "sick" because Lt. Thobe "suffered from hypertension, and took medication for it most of the time he was at the Santa Maria office."

Mitchell said he sometimes made the comment to other officers "in defense of Lt. Thobe," and sometimes "when I get upset."

A dozen CHP officers testified they heard Mitchell call Thobe derogatory names or make such claims as "We've got him on the run now."

However, Thobe denied he took any medication other than aspirin and said he did not know he had hypertension "until six weeks ago"—long after he was transferred from Santa Maria to Visalia.

Charges Denied

Thobe and Mrs. Barbara Capitani, acting office secretary, denied Mitchell's charge that Thobe screamed and swore in the office.

Such conflicting testimony has marked almost all phases of the proceedings to date.

Probably the most perplexing testimony concerns the twice-in-one-day arrests of Clifford C. Bewley for drunk driving by Mitchell on June 27, 1967.

The CHP charges Mitchell saw Bewley at the CHP office, noted he was drunk but permitted him to drive before he arrested him.

Bewley testified he went to the CHP office late in the afternoon to have a mechanical warning checked off for his car.

It was cleared by an officer he did not know, he said.

"But it was not Mitchell," he testified.

He said Mitchell arrested him at a stop sign about a block from the station.

Gave Warning

Klippness said he was the one who cleared Bewley's warning in front of the CHP office shortly before 5 p.m., thought that he was drunk and warned him not to drive.

Klippness said he thought Bewley would call a cab but that when he saw Bewley's car leaving the parking lot he went to another parking lot behind the station to alert Mitchell about him.

Both Mitchell and Klippness said Mitchell was loading a car with gear for patrol duty starting at 5 p.m. Neither recalled that other officer was in the station at the time.

However, Mrs. Capitani

Please Turn to Pg. 3, Col. 3

LA Times article never reported Officer's prejury

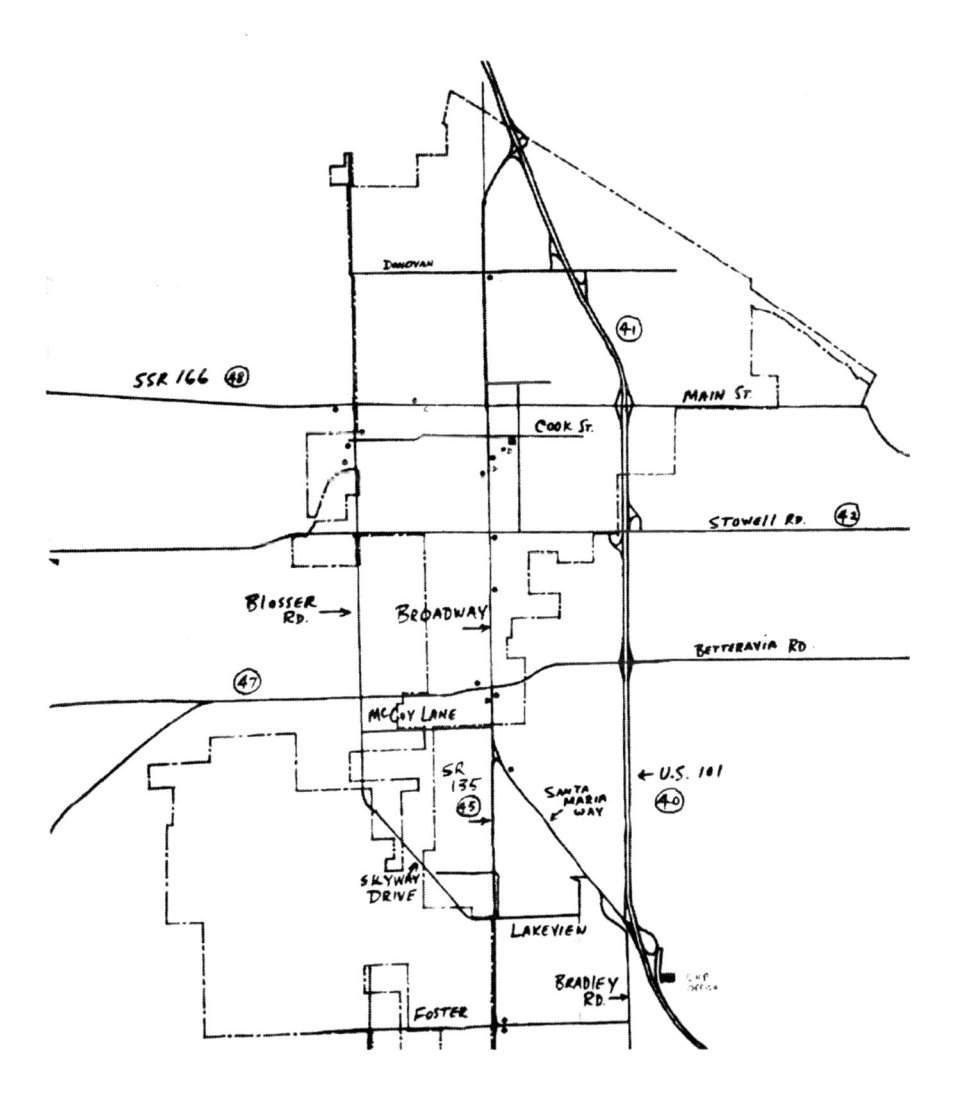

Prosecutors were ordered to use map I prepared

SECTION E ★   **Los Angeles**

Bob L. Mitchell

Views Clash in Testimony at CHP Probe

BY KEN OVERAKER
Times Staff Writer

Two entirely different versions of what went on at the Santa Maria substation of the Highway Patrol through about 18 months of 1967 and 1968 are emerging in the hearing on the appeal of two veteran CHP sergeants from punitive action taken against them last summer by the patrol.

The testimony shows that someone must be lying.

The officers, Bob L. Mitchell, 38, and Gerald R. Klippness, 36, charge they were disciplined because they made too many arrests for drunk driving.

But that's not the story at all, according to CHP witnesses.

Mitchell, fired after 10 years with the CHP, contends also that he was punished because he filed 22 grievances against Lt. Don M. Thobe, then Santa Maria substation commander.

Written Arguments

One conflict after another has marked testimony taken by Robert L. Hill, State Personnel Board hearing officer, in the Mitchell case, now completed except for written arguments by attorneys.

One of many LA Times articles on the firing

Los Angeles Times

CC PART II
LETTERS—TV
SATURDAY, FEBRUARY 8, 1969

CHP Sergeant Rehired; Loses $6,300 in Pay

BY KEN OVERAKER
Times Staff Writer

A veteran Highway Patrol officer who was fired at Santa Maria last summer won his job back but will not be paid for the more than six months he was off the job, the State Personnel Board ruled Friday in Sacramento.

The board upheld a recommendation by its hearing officer, Robert L. Hill, that Sgt. Bob L. Mitchell, 38, is "too able and dedicated" an officer to be fired.

It ruled that he may return to his job Feb. 15 as a sergeant.

In effect the ruling amounts to a suspension without pay for six months and 17 days, costing Mitchell more than $6,300.

'Very Pleased'

At Orcutt School, near Santa Maria, where he has been teaching part-time, Mitchell told The Times by telephone that he understands the ruling exonerates him in every respect except for calling his commanding officer derogatory names.

"If that is true, then I'm very pleased with the decision," he said.

He added that he will resume his CHP job and plans to continue following CHP directives to "actively seek out and arrest drunk drivers."

He and fellow Sgt. Gerald R. Klippness, 36, charged publicly when they were disciplined last July 29 that the action was taken because they were arresting too many drunk drivers.

Klippness was suspended for 30 days without pay.

The personnel board Friday sustained this suspension.

The rulings were made after Hill took testimony over several months in Santa Maria.

NEAR MISS AT TRAGEDY—Mrs. Hampton Hawes, fourth grade teacher at Purche Elementary School in Gardena, entered her classroom Friday to find this hole. Car driven by William Perry, 30, of 16808

Court OKs Delay in Scheduling New Trial for Shepard

The setting of a new trial date for City Councilman Thomas D. Shepard was postponed Friday for one week to give prosecutors time to reevaluate the evidence in the case.

Superior Judge George M. Dell continued the case until Friday at the request of Dep. Dist. Atty. Michael J. Montagna and Dep. Atty. Gen. Robert P. Samoian.

Montagna told the court he and Samoian want to study the evidence in the first trial—which ended two

Argument on P(Closes State Wa

Recommendations by Study F Form for Submission to State

BY KEN
Times Staf

SACRAMENTO—Argument over fines for pollution violations and hints of bureaucratic in-fighting Friday marked the final day of hearings into recommendations for a new state water-pollution control law.

The recommendations by a study panel now will be put into final form and submitted to the Legislature about April 1.

Friday's hearings also saw an unusual exchange in which the

LA Times article reporting reinstatement

THE CALIFORNIA STATE EMPLOYEE, FEBRUARY 28, 1969

CSEA staff members confer with the two CHP sergeants in Mitchell hearing during ten-minute recess. Left to right: Dan Dodge and George Pavlick of CSEA's legal division; Sgt. Bob L. Mitchell; Sgt. Jerry Klippness; and Walter Lowrey, CSEA area representative.

Major Legal Victory for CSEA Puts CHP Sergeant Back on Job

A major CSEA legal victory has made it possible for a California Highway Patrol sergeant to return to work after being fired six months earlier.

The State Personnel Board in February upheld a recommendation by its hearing officer that Sgt. Bob L. Mitchell, 38, a 10-year CHP veteran, was "too able and dedicated" to be fired.

Mitchell and Sgt. Gerald R. Klippness, 36, were represented by Dan Dodge and George Pavlick of CSEA's legal division in Santa Maria before SPB hearing officer Robert L. Hill. Klippness lost an appeal from a 30-day suspension.

"The case demonstrates the value of CSEA legal services to members," Pavlick said.

Since October, Dodge and Pavlick, with assistance from other CSEA staff members, spent more than 150 days — at a cost of more than $12,000 — in behalf of the two sergeants.

CSEA successfully refuted 26 of 27 serious charges filed against Mitchell. The only charge upheld against both officers was discourteousness to Santa Maria substation commander Lt. Don M. Thorpe.

The sergeants had been charged with inexcusable neglect of duty, discourteous treatment of the public or other employees, willful disobedience and other charges. Additional charges against Mitchell included incompetency, inefficiency and insubordination.

As a result of the hearings Mitchell won his job back, although he was not paid for the six months and 17 days he was off the job. Klippness' 30-day suspension was upheld by Hill, on the charge of calling his commanding officer derogatory names. But, as with Mitchell, Klippness' record was cleared of all other serious charges.

Both Mitchell and Klippness charged publicly when they were disciplined last July 29 that the action was taken because they were arresting too many drunk drivers.

In the decision, Hill found that CHP failed to establish its charges that Mitchell staked out Santa Maria bars to make drunk-driving arrests, and that a number of charges against him were either not established or were "too trivial" to warrant dismissal.

The hearings began in November and resumed in December. In this time, Mitchell answered all 27 allegations with Klippness serving as his main witness. The Klippness hearing was completed in January.

"The two sergeants successfully made point-by-point refutations of the numerous allegations," Pavlick said.

Pavlick explained that charge after charge against Mitchell was dismissed by the hearing officer in his written findings.

Hill ruled, Pavlick said, that "it was not established by the evidence that:"

Mitchell made a certain drunk driving arrest without probable cause, that Mitchell falsely reported seeing the driver run off the roadway, that Mitchell had no probable cause to arrest an individual for being drunk in a public place, or that Mitchell violated his supervisor's orders by requesting other officers to leave their assigned beats to complete normal, routine drunk driving arrests.

"This allegation is not true," the hearing officer said of a charge that Mitchell improperly advised a subordinate not to store a certain vehicle, and that Mitchell later falsely told the lieutenant that friends of the accident victim would be responsible for the wrecked vehicle.

CSEA spent hundreds of thousands in our defense

CHP Commissioner Walter Pudinski, Senator Randolph Collier and Patrol Lieutenant B. L. Mitchell examine the statute which authorized the abandoned vehicle program.

lems — removal of derelicts from both public and private property," says Senator Collier. "Although cities and counties will give priority to removals from public lands and parks, beaches, rivers and wild life areas, we want them to have the tools for abating the nuisance of these vehicles sitting for long periods on private property as well."

It is expected that, like Monterey County, many jurisdictions will employ abandoned vehicle investigators whose duties will include locating cars, trucks, and other vehicles that should be removed, and assisting property owners in overcoming legal obstacles.

For example, frequently a landowner desires to rid his property of a vehicle abandoned there by someone else but is unfamiliar with lien sale procedures, giving the property owner clear title to dispose of the vehicle. If the property owner himself owns the derelict vehicle but refuses to cooperate in having it removed, the law offers a means of having the vehicle hauled away, with costs added to the individual's tax bill.

The Highway Patrol presently removes more than 15,000 abandoned vehicles annually from highway rights of way, and will continue to do so.

"But w governm sibility wi said Pud as state cities anc set up, tractual burseme

Senato portant fa gram" as wreckers the equ vehicles the cost received

He poi "vary wic different counties, many vel or stream cult. It c remove stances rain. Bec is imposs cost for

"Of coi well. Ofte the mos Highway signed tc and make mulate a statewide

The fu necessai must be may be s mantled.

One t will not program tioned. vehicles tions for rigid stru for resis dinarily t covered automati from the

"I belii to the tir donied v substai eliminate

September-October, 1973

Commissioner Pudinski, Senator Collier and I review AVA bill

The allegation was:

> "On 6-11-68 you advised Officer Pledger at the scene of an accident that it was not necessary to file a CHP Form 180 (storage of vehicle) although it was clearly necessary. Lt. Goode discussed this with you, you stated that you did not feel the Form 180 was necessary because the victim of said accident had two subjects with him who would be responsible for the vehicle. The victim was alone in his vehicle when the accident occurred and there were no other persons at the scene who indicated that they would be responsible for the wrecked vehicle."

In response to this allegation, I told the court that Lieutenant Goode did discuss this with me and I stated to him that I did not feel the Form 180 was necessary because the victim of the accident had two subjects with him at the scene who would be responsible for the vehicle. The driver was alone in his vehicle when the accident occurred. However, his friends were following him in a separate vehicle and witnessed the accident. One of the friends stated that he would accept the responsibility of the vehicle. Officer Pledger was advised to identify the friend and put the necessary information on the Form 110 accident report. Lieutenant Goode concurred with my decision when I discussed it with him. This is standard procedure on the California Highway Patrol.

The Attorney General's Office and the Highway Patrol knew I had followed departmental procedures, they were just trying to discredit me with the public. They knew this allegation was false at the time they filed it. They had no defense in court and looked like fools.

After answering these and 23 other allegations and enclosing the supporting documents, I sent them to Dan Dodge, CSEA, in Sacramento. I also had several file cabinets with other supporting documents that I was prepared to take to court every day in case I needed them.

I had been advised that the Appeal Hearings would start October 15. But I wasn't going to be waiting around idly for the Hearing.

Letter Writing to Legislature and News Media

My next step was to write a letter to every Assemblyman and Senator in California, the California Traffic Safety Foundation, major national magazines, television stations, newspapers, the Governor and Lieutenant Governor's offices, Governor Ronald Reagan's wife Nancy, Mr. Robert Malkin, a prominent and influential official in Vancouver, Canada, whose son was killed by a DUI in Palo Alto and who I had been working with to change DUI laws here as well as Canada, Paul Harvey News, and the Attorney General's Office. The purpose was to let them know what was happening and ask for their assistance in the battle.

Mother's Against Drunk Drivers (MADD) did not yet exist. Candy Lightner, who founded MADD, had not yet lost her daughter to a DUI. And if the legislators had passed Senate Bills 41 and 42 in 1962 maybe her daughter would be alive today.

Almost everyone I sent a letter to responded. Only a few were "form" or "standard" letters.

An article appeared in the Santa Maria Times, which reported our hearing to be slated for October 15. The new Santa Maria area Commander, Captain Robert Roese, explained that the appeal would be a "semi-legal" hearing, with rules of evidence enforced. However, he said that it would be much more informal than a regular court hearing presided over by a judge.

"Following the presentations from both sides the hearing officer will rule on the case," he reported.

Captain Roese was our Sergeant in East Los Angeles and commended us for arresting DUIs. He knew firsthand that we were getting railroaded yet he went along with it. I lost all respect for him.

Word Spreads Throughout the State

A news article appeared in the Sacramento Union newspaper on Aug. 12 so I knew the word was spreading throughout the State. The heading was, "Citing of Drunks Led to Firing, Officers Say."

The article had basically the same information that appeared in the Los Angeles Times. The part in the article that the Department would not be pleased with was Klippness' statement, "after he and Mitchell made more drunk driving arrests than any other state patrolmen in April 1967, their officer-in-charge told them to slack off. I gathered that some people were putting pressure on him," Klippness said. "I ultimately discovered that some of those arrested were prominent people around Santa Maria."

Letter to the Editor Calls for Probe

In the August 19, 1968 edition of the Santa Maria newspaper appeared a letter to the editor titled, "CHP Suspensions Need Probe."

The letter was written by a very wealthy and prominent person in the Santa Ynez area, Thomas Storke, Editor and Publisher Emeritus of the Santa Barbara News-Press. He started out by relating the risks he had to take driving to his ranch near Cachuma Lake because of DUIs. His ranch was near Governor Ronald Reagan's ranch where I had made several arrests for DUI while I was traveling from Santa Barbara back to Santa Maria.

In part of his letter he wrote, "The purpose of my writing this letter is that County newspapers have been running stories stating that two highway patrolmen have been relieved from duty because they have been making 'too many arrests for drunk driving.'

"Personally, I have no knowledge of their conduct in such problems, but as a citizen I cannot understand why any highway patrolman should be relieved from duty because he has arrested drunken drivers. I believe that such patrolmen should be rewarded and those who do not help in making the highways safe for drivers should be relieved.

"As to the patrolmen involved, Bob Mitchell and Jerry Klippness, I know them only slightly. From inquiries I have made among their neighbors, I learned that they are highly respected citizens and, as far as the public knows, they are men of honor and good officers."

Storkes closed by writing, "I ask for a thorough and honest investigation."

I sent a letter of thanks to Mr. Storke and informed him that some of the arrests that I had made near his ranch were part of the punitive action

PART 1: *Chapter 12:* The Day I Had Been Dreading   235

brought against me. "We want you to know that before we were fired and suspended, we made arrests for drunk driving near your ranch. Two of the general charges against me include those arrests.

"On March 20, 1968, Jerry Klippness and I arrested John Leo Kieran. He was very intoxicated while driving at a high rate of speed. He was stopped southbound on Highway 154 at the Cachuma Lake entrance. On June 21, 1968, I observed another drunk driver who was traveling northbound on Highway 154 in the same area. He was finally stopped north of that location. This was about 9:30 pm while returning from Santa Barbara where I had been temporarily assigned.

I also sent Storke a copy of a subpoena that I had received on the DUI arrest I made of John Kieran. The case was dismissed because Kieran was suppose to have been killed in an automobile accident. I told Storke, "I was unable to verify the validity of the dismissal but several years ago in East Los Angeles I had a dismissal for the same reason. When I checked, it was discovered that the DUI was very much alive. A bail bondsman had reported his death to the court so that the bail would be returned. I'm not saying that is the case here. I don't know."

CAHP Response to Dismissal

I had been a member of the California Association of Highway Patrolmen (CAHP), Sacramento, for over 10 years and when an officer needs legal assistance they are supposed to come to his aid. So when I received the following letter and saw on the envelope where it was from I couldn't hardly wait to open it.

> Dear Mr. Mitchell:
>
> We regret to inform you that under the by-laws of the California Association of Highway Patrolmen, your *resignation* (emphasis added) from the California Highway Patrol precludes your membership in the Association. Also, your Blue Cross insurance will be discontinued.
>
> Sincerely,
> W. Howard Jackson
> Executive Manager

The following day a response to this letter was mailed to W. Howard Jackson.

> Dear Mr. Jackson:
>
> In reference to your recent letter: As you know, I did not resign from the California Highway Patrol. I was dismissed and am waiting a hearing set for October 15, 1968.
>
> I paid dues to the CAHP for over 10 years and in a time of need—I am not guilty of the charges—your organization steps out. While I was seeking aid through the Personnel and Welfare Committee (of the CAHP) one of your members, Dave Larson, reportedly made unkind and untrue statements about both Jerry Klippness and me.
>
> "Now, on August 20, I get a 'form' letter advising that I'm being dropped. Has your organization forgotten that I still have a right to a hearing, and if need be, appeals to higher courts? Or do you plan on sending me a nice letter of "welcome back" after I'm reinstated?
>
> "I believe the CAHP has an obligation to see each member through and stand <u>solidly</u> behind him until he has been proven guilty. You should be interested in correcting injustices against your members and, at least, wait until they have had a chance to be heard. This is supposedly the American way.
>
> "We are going to win—with or without your help—but it would be so much better and easier if we had it.
>
> "The California State Employees Association is sending one legal advisor and two lawyers to conduct an investigation in this area. At our request the Lieutenant Governor's office is investigating certain misconduct on the California Highway Patrol.

PART 1: *Chapter 12:* The Day I Had Been Dreading

> "This letter is written in an effort to point out just how unfair and indifferent a group can become. You should re-evaluate your actions and then decide if you are really being fair in this matter."
>
> Sincerely,
Bob Mitchell

A couple of days later W. Howard Jackson replied.

> "I want you to know the letter advising you that you had been dropped from membership in the Association because of your dismissal from the CHP, was in line with the policy long established by our Board of Directors according to the by-laws.
>
> "It comes as a shock to me to find you have petitioned for a hearing to prove your innocence of the charges preferred by the Department, because this office was never advised that you filed such a petition. Now that you have established this point, I feel it is only fair that we continue your membership until a decision has been made in your case.
>
> "However, until you have been placed back on the official payroll of the CHP, your dues to the Association must be paid by you directly to this office.
>
> "Wishing you the best of luck with your forthcoming hearing on October 15, we are
>
> Very truly yours,"
W. Howard Jackson

Correspondence with Nancy Reagan

On August 23, 1968, I wrote the following letter to Governor Ronald Reagan's wife, Nancy, who preferred to be addressed as Mrs. Ronald Reagan.

"Dear Mrs. Reagan:

"My wife met you at a tea gathering hosted by Mrs. Manning in Hacienda Heights prior to your husband being elected. Before she left home that day, I asked her to find out if Governor Reagan was a strong advocate of drunk driving enforcement. She spoke with you briefly but never asked you the question. However, she feels that you're a Christian so that is one reason for writing to you.

"On July 29, 1968, I was fired and my partner, Gerald Klippness, was suspended for 30 working days from our positions as State Traffic Sergeants on the California Highway Patrol in Santa Maria.

"During our 16 years as law enforcement officers we discovered a method of detecting drunk drivers. We have arrested more than anyone else. One night alone, we arrested 17 during our shift. Every area where we have worked, accidents have noticeably decreased as the drunk driving arrests continued.

"We transferred to Santa Maria and continued our enforcement. Fatal accidents were reduced 150% in 1967 (1966-20 to 1967-8) due to our efforts. The latter part of 1967 we were pressured to stop the arrests. Our superior told us that it was too political.

"When we didn't stop, we were disciplined on July 29, 1968. They charged us with patrolling the city (the California Highway Patrol is primarily responsible for the unincorporated area) and staking out bars. We have documented proof that the charges are not true and are willing to take a lie detector test to prove it.

"This is going to be the worst scandal that has ever hit the California Highway Patrol.

"We voted for and support Governor Reagan and was thrilled when he won office. We thought that the appointment of Mr. Sullivan as Commissioner was a wise one.

"Now it seems like a bad dream. I lost a good job because I wanted to make the highways safer. The charges against us are based on lies and the Attorney General's office knows this. Had they conducted a fair investigation, they would have uncovered drunk driving in patrol vehicles, drunken and profane parties, as well as other acts of misconduct.

"I know that Commissioner Sullivan is going to be shocked when he finds out the truth of this matter. But it will probably be irreparable by then.

"We pray that justice will prevail at our hearing."

Yours very truly,
Bob Mitchell

September 5, 1968, Mrs. Ronald Reagan sent me a personal letter.

"Dear Mr. Mitchell:

"Thank you so much for writing and for telling me about your problem.

"I am forwarding your letter and a copy of mine to Mr. Ed Meese, the Governor's Legal Affairs Secretary, and I'm sure you will be hearing from him soon. I do hope that, as you say, justice will prevail, and I'm sure it will.

"Thank you also for the kind words of support for my husband. We both appreciate it.

Sincerely,"
Mrs. Ronald Reagan

This letter was tremendously encouraging but what Mrs. Reagan did behind the scene was of far more importance. In fact, Nancy Reagan did more to assist Klippness and me in our struggle for justice than any one individual.

Of course, the California State Employees Association did the most and at a cost of several hundred thousands of dollars. But to ensure us of a fair trial, Mrs. Reagan wanted her husband, Governor Ronald Reagan, to assign someone from the governor's office to attend our appeal hearing in Santa Maria and monitor the proceedings. She put her words into action and we will be eternally grateful.

However, it was decided that to have someone from the governor's office to ensure we got a fair trial was not a good idea because of what it implied. The right to appeal and the procedure for handling the appeal was established by the State of California and it must be assumed the procedure is trustworthy.

So, no one was assigned to attend from the governor's office. However, Mrs. Ronald Reagan's concern in wanting to ensure that we got a fair hearing reverberated throughout state government. There's no doubt the State Personnel Board discussed this with Hearing Officer Robert Hill before he headed for Santa Maria.

Hill was one of their most experienced Hearing Officers and they could rely on him not to do anything foolish.

Letter From Lieutenant Governor Robert Finch

The letter I received from Lieutenant Governor Robert Finch was also encouraging. He said he had required the Department of Transportation to submit a report concerning our case. He said it would be improper for him to intervene in the situation at this time. But most significantly he wrote.

"If, after the hearing, you feel that you have not received a fair hearing, we would appreciate it if you would contact this office for a personal appointment."

PART 1: *Chapter 12:* The Day I Had Been Dreading

No Justice in Felony DUI Killing

In the middle of the fight for my job, the mother of three small children was killed by a drunk driver. It crystallized why it was so important to win the hearing and fight to effectively get drunk drivers off the road.

On Monday, September 2, a story in the Santa Maria newspaper reported that Mrs. Lela Clark, 36, Santa Maria, was killed at 2:05 am when her car was struck head-on by a car driven by Nicholas Matrullo, 24, Tanglewood.

The story reported:

> "Matrullo, a truck driver, was jailed by the California Highway Patrol following the crash on charges of manslaughter. The CHP reported Matrullo's car crossed a double yellow line, crashing head-on into the Clark car.
>
> "The report also indicated Matrullo was under the influence of alcohol. He received cuts on the knee in the crash and was treated at a local hospital before being jailed.
>
> "The accident occurred on the Lompoc-Casmalia Rd. (Black Rd.) at NTU Canyon Rd. The Clark vehicle was northbound as Mrs. Clark was returning from work as a cocktail waitress in Casmalia. The Matrullo auto was southbound.
>
> "She was taken from the crash scene in critical condition with massive injuries and died shortly after arriving at Valley Community Hospital.
>
> "Mrs. Clark was born May 3, 1932 in Oklahoma. She is survived by three children."
>
> The accident was tragic enough but what followed was also a tragedy. Several months later the newspaper reported, "Motorist Sentenced For Misdemeanor Manslaughter."

> "A motorist who pleaded no-contest to misdemeanor manslaughter in the death of another driver in a two-car crash on Black Rd., Sept. 2 was fined $623, given a one-year suspended jail sentence and placed on three years probation Wednesday by Municipal Court Judge Morris J. Stephan.
>
> "The motorist, Nickolas Matrullo, 24, Tanglewood, lost control of his car and drove head-on into a car driven by Mrs. Lela Clark, 36, who died a short time later in Valley Community Hospital.
>
> "Matrullo was slightly injured in the early morning crash. He was originally charged with felony manslaughter but charges were reduced to a misdemeanor, a lesser degree of negligence."

It doesn't take much reading between the lines to know what may have happened. The original report "indicated Matrullo was under the influence of alcohol." Why wasn't he given a chemical test, and if he was, then what was the reading? This is part of an investigation and should have been explained. Secondly, why was a felony manslaughter reduced to a misdemeanor? A person driving over a center line and hitting someone head-on who is under the influence of alcohol should be charged with a felony. The reason they weren't charged should be explained.

There were a lot of questions that needed to be answered but since the woman was dead and she had only three small children to pick up the pieces; I guess it shows courts can do whatever they want. And then we have one more problem. The driver got off with only a $623 fine. (An amount that would probably not cover the cost of the flowers for the funeral.) The one-year suspended jail sentence and three years probation was an insult to a person's intelligence. How about the "motorist" at least paying for the cost of the funeral?

I recognized it as a typical Santa Maria deal and it just motivated me to fight harder. But at the time I was a civilian fighting for my job back.

PART 1: *Chapter 12:* The Day I Had Been Dreading   243

Assemblyman Winfield Shoemaker Becomes Involved

In my letter to Assemblyman Shoemaker I pointed out an article that I had recently read in a national magazine which I wholeheartedly agreed with. "In spite of the clear evidence that the drunk driver is a guilty driver, American people seem to be lost in a hodgepodge of conflicting plans and campaigns that leave the comical drunk, as usual, at the wheel."

That a study of 1,147 California drivers who killed people with their cars while drunk showed that only 270 were convicted of drunken driving, and only 47 went to jail.

Five days later I received the following response.

"I have forwarded copies of your communication with my office to the State Attorney General and have requested that he look into this matter and report his findings to me.

"I will contact you as soon as I have a report. Best wishes."

About one month later, Assemblyman Shoemaker kept his word and sent me a copy of Deputy Attorney General Richard Turner's letter of response. The letter was cleverly written so as to hide what he and Inspector James Bryant were really doing; placing Assemblyman Shoemaker in such a position that it would appear improper if the Assemblyman did anything. But I don't believe it was a complete waste of time because now Turner and Bryant knew that they were being watched.

First, Turner reported there had been a "lengthy investigation," which was not true.

He justified not giving any details to Assemblyman Shoemaker by commenting "since the case is pending before the State Personnel Board and the substantiation of the charges will be subject to the rules of evidence, it would be inappropriate for us to comment at length in this matter." Turner went on to write: "The sergeants were not disciplined simply (emphasis added) because they were arresting drunk drivers or because they were bringing acts of misconduct of other members of the Patrol to the Department's attention.

"The reasons for the disciplinary action are set forth in detail in the notices of punitive action, which were served on the sergeants and filed with the Personnel Board."

When Turner added the word "simply" in his letter, he was admitting that we were being disciplined for arresting drunk drivers and reporting misconduct of other members of the Department, thus substantiating the accusations we had made against him and the Highway Patrol, which they consistently denied.

Press Conference in Los Angeles

The appearance on the Maria Cole/Stan Bohrman television show, newspaper coverage and letters to the legislators were generating a lot of publicity. The general public was calling radio talk shows and expressing their support for us. All of the letters to the editors were in support of us. A women wrote from Huntington Park in the Los Angeles area, "If they don't want you in Santa Maria, we sure would like to have you here catching our drunk drivers."

CHP Officer Keith Davis wrote me a letter from the CHP Visalia area where Lieutenant Thobe had been transferred, "Just a line to let you know I would be willing to testify on your behalf, or if you desire, I could prepare an affidavit. Good Luck."

Truck drivers were upset and calling into radio talk shows in response to my comment on the television show that Thobe wanted us to spend more time citing truck drivers and less time arresting drunk drivers.

So, we decided now would be a good time to hold a press conference in Los Angeles. We choose the Greater Los Angeles Press Club, 600 No. Vermont Ave. and it just happened to be located one block from the California Highway Patrol Zone V Headquarters. The time was set for 10 am but when we arrived there at 9 am, we had to work our way through the crowd.

Every television station in Los Angeles was represented except Channel 5. I don't know how many radio stations were represented but all of them were trying to put their microphones on the podium and there wasn't enough room without taping the microphones on the sides. All of the major

PART 1: *Chapter 12:* The Day I Had Been Dreading 245

newspaper reporters were also there. The Greater Los Angeles Press Club recorded more than 40 media personnel.

As Klippness and I were getting ready to start the press conference, I couldn't help but reflect back on what Captain Dahl said when I was fired, "Well, I'm glad it's finally over." And I told him," Oh! It's not over. It's just beginning."

Klippness and I spent about an hour and a half answering the media and telling them what took place in Santa Maria and the CHP cover-up that was going on. As reported on television and the newspapers the next day, we stressed "a legislative probe of the inner workings of the patrol would reveal inconsistencies with the Department's stated rules and policies."

We also brought a copy of the punitive action and our answers with us. After the conference we handed out previously prepared information sheets for them to take with them. Including the arrests and accident statistics supporting our accomplishments and which the Highway Patrol could not deny since they were their figures. We were satisfied that we had covered the bases. And that night it was one of the major stories on most television channels.

Before the press conference Klippness and I both scanned the audience for any familiar face. We knew, although we could not prove it, the CHP would have a "plant" there to report back to the Department.

There were a couple of questions asked during the conference that could have been orchestrated from Sacramento but it didn't really matter. We were use to testifying in court. We had many years of experience handling "loaded" questions.

As soon as the press conference ended, a middle aged stranger approached me and asked to speak with me alone.

After we moved to a spot where we could talk in private, the man said, "From what I gathered here, it sounds like the Highway Patrol is really doing you guys wrong. You know they'll do whatever it takes to get you. And they have unlimited funds. If you're going to get your job back, you're going to need some help."

I said, "I agree with everything you said but where do we get that help?"

The stranger said, "I'm with the ACLU (American Civil Liberties Union) and your case is the type of case we are looking for. If you and your partner want us to get involved then we will handle your appeal."

I thanked the stranger but told him I could not in clear conscience let the ACLU represent me even if it meant losing the Appeal. He didn't ask me why but, if he had, I would have told him that I disagree with almost everything the ACLU stands for and that they are a destructive force when it comes to America.

Klippness and I were very pleased with the way the press conference went.

Assemblyman Walter Karabian 'Can't Do Much'

One of the Deputy District Attorneys that Klippness and I worked with in East Los Angeles and that handled the prosecution of some of the DUIs we arrested was Walter Karabian, who was now an Assemblyman. We wanted him to be aware of what was happening and had hoped he would be able to assist us in some way.

He responded in a personal letter, as opposed to a "form" letter, which I appreciated.

> Dear Bob:
>
> "Thank you for your letter of August 16, 1968. I do remember you and Jerry Klippness very well and the days we worked together in East Los Angeles where you were both traffic officers and I was a Deputy District Attorney for Los Angeles County.
>
> "I knew you and Jerry to be honest, reliable and trustworthy officers as well as excellent witnesses, but I must admit, in all candor, that I have little knowledge or information about the matter you discussed in your letter pertaining to the hearing involving your conduct or that of Lieutenant D. Thobe.

"I think you have done the proper thing by bringing any grievance you have to the attention of Senator Collier. He is, of course, considered one of the 'fathers' of the California Highway Patrol. When we go into session on September 9, I will ask around about this matter, but I don't want you to get your hopes up because, in all honesty and sincerity, I am fairly certain there is little I can do. I could easily say something you would want to hear, but I think, in the spirit of our friendship, honesty at this point is more important."

Sincerely,

I sent a letter thanking Karabian for his "kind and sincere" letter and that I understood his position. I also told him "we are satisfied to exercise our judicial privileges" and recognized "it would not be proper for him to intervene in departmental disputes." I did add, "However, we do feel that it is of concern to all that we have honest efficient law enforcement. It is of utmost concern that all of our legislators be alerted when there is a breakdown in this area."

The main purpose of my letters was to get the "word out" so the public would know what was going on, and believe me, the California Highway Patrol listens to the legislators.

The Governor, with the approval of the Legislature, appoints the CHP Commissioner. Therefore the Commissioner does not want the Governor and legislators getting feedback that he is not doing his job.

In fact, the blow-out in Santa Maria may have been responsible for the change in State policy for appointing CHP Commissioners. Word was circulating that all future Commissioners would come from the CHP ranks. Harold Sullivan was a former Deputy Chief in charge of traffic from the Los Angeles Police Department and it was the opinion of many, including Klippness and me, that he did not know what he was doing. He was "in over his head." The next Commissioner was appointed from the CHP ranks.

Letter: 'Penalized for Doing Job'

Another letter to the editor appeared in the Santa Maria Times from Eugene Santos, Nipomo, with the heading "Penalized for Doing Job."

> To the Editor:
>
> "The firing of that highway patrol officer is a shame. It's the sign of the times to get fired because you do your job too well and step on toes. At 2 in the morning you can see all the potential accidents leaving the bars in the area, but I guess to be sporting you have to let the drunks get in the wrong lane before you arrest them.
>
> "How many murders did you have last month by drunks in cars? That's what they should be sent up for, instead of three years probation like the last fellow did."

My letter to the editor

The radio talk shows in the area were asking people to call in and give their opinion on the dismissal and suspension of the two sergeants in Santa Maria. Ninety per cent of the calls coming in were in support of us but some of the callers seemed to be a little confused over what was really happening.

So, one day when the line was open to the program, I phoned in. I started explaining what had happened and I identified myself.

Immediately the talk show host said, "Oh! Don't give us your name. We don't want callers to identify themselves."

I said, "OK, I'll just hang up and call you back and when I call you back I won't identify myself."

He said, "No, you don't have to do that. We'll make an exception this time."

I continued and was able to explain a portion of what was going on. As a result of this experience and the growing strong interest of the public, I decided to write a letter to the editor. It appeared in it's entirety in the Santa Maria Times newspaper the next day:

> Dismissed CHP Sergeant Explains Reasons Why.
>
> "To the Editor:
>
> "On July 29, 1968, we, as State Traffic Sergeants on the California Highway Patrol, were disciplined by suspension and dismissal. This was a direct result of charges we had brought against our supervisors through the departmental grievance procedure. The charges against us were trumped up in an effort to divert attention away from the real issues of misconduct of officers and the inadequate drunk driving policy.
>
> "By placing us on the defensive the CHP has guaranteed our silence regarding the original issues because we will only be permitted to answer the charges against us at the State Personnel Board hearing on October 15-17, 1968. We feel that this was the intended purpose.
>
> "Before being assigned to the Santa Maria area both Sergeant Klippness and I were regarded as above average supervisors. Every area where we worked, drunk driving arrests increased and accidents dropped. In East Los Angeles drunk driving arrests increased 318 percent or about 200 arrests more per month. We showed a decrease in traffic accidents for the first time in contrast to an 8 percent increase statewide. We were commended for our enforcement efforts by Bradford Crittenden, then Commissioner of the California Highway Patrol.
>
> "Klippness was promoted to Sergeant and assigned to the Indio area. Drunk driving arrests jumped from 30 to 130 a month when he was working the night shift. I was promoted to Sergeant and assigned to the Baldwin Park office on July 1, 1966. I was scheduled the night shift and by December 30 of the same year drunk driving arrests increased from 119 to 255 per month. I was commended for the enforcement effort by my superior, Lieutenant Bob Goode.

"In 1966 the figures in Santa Maria indicated an average of 4 drunken driving arrests per month prior to our assignment to the area. This was increased to an average of 40 a month, which resulted in a consistent decrease of 35 percent of traffic accidents. According to national figures this represents a saving of $61,800 per month.

"In the Santa Maria area in 1967 we reduced fatalities 150 percent (1966-20 to 1967-8). Drunken driving arrests increased 101 percent for the year (1966-176 to 1967-376). All accidents were reduced 2 percent (1966-500 to 1967-487). Injury accidents were reduced 7 percent (1966-228 to 1967-212). All arrests were up 43 percent (1966-6,262 to 1967-9,046). This was all accomplished in spite of the fact that we were prevented from actively arresting drunken drivers during the months of May, June, July and August.

"During those four months traffic accidents increased 27 percent (1966-162 to 1967-207) or a loss of $185,400. This occurred even though more citations were issued than any other time in Santa Maria history-an increase of 56 percent in all arrests (1966-2,232 to 1967-3,493). We believe this occurred because drunken driving arrests were down 236 percent in comparison to the first four months when we were permitted to make the arrests.

"It is felt that the drunk driving enforcement is inadequate when one or two officers can increase the arrests two and three hundred percent. Something is drastically wrong with our enforcement throughout the state and we are convinced that it cannot be solved through regular departmental procedures because that's what led to my dismissal and Klippness being suspended.

"Over half of all the fatal accidents are being caused by drunken drivers. This represents 26,500 lives a year in the United States. California accounted for 4,883 traffic accident victims in 1967. We can give credit to the drinking drivers for killing 2,442 of those. An increase of 53 over the previous year. This means that in California we lose a person every 30 minutes and your chances of becoming a statistic is greater between the hours of midnight and 3 am because 83 percent of the drivers involved in accidents are drunk. Adequate drunk driving enforcement could reduce this at least by one-third or by 1,627 lives each year in California alone.

"The CHP added 730 more traffic officers last year and issued 321,613 more tickets than the year before but no meaningful emphasis was placed on the number one killer—the drunk driver. To the contrary, in Santa Maria and other areas throughout the state, officers were hindered and discouraged from making "excessive" arrests for drunk driving.

"As explained recently in a national magazine, "In spite of the clear evidence that the drunk driver is a guilty driver, those responsible for drivers' safety seem to be lost in a hodgepodge of conflicting plans and campaigns that leave the comical drunk, as usual, at the wheel." A study of 1,147 California drivers who killed people with their cars while drunk showed that only 270 were convicted of drunken driving, and only 47 went to jail.

"We are willing to sacrifice our jobs and, if necessary, face public derision to bring about a stop to this senseless slaughter.

"As a citizen and potential victim, you have a right to know how the present statistics in your area compare to last years. Contact the local CHP office. We also urge you to write, telegram or telephone Governor Reagan and request an investigation of the California Highway Patrol's drunk driving program today—now."

Bob L. Mitchell

Thobe Files for Disability in Fresno

Lieutenant Thobe was now assigned to the CHP Visalia office near Zone IV, in Fresno. On September 22, 1968, he filed a disability claim against the department. An employee does not usually file a disability claim until he is getting ready to retire unless he thinks he is going to be fired.

Thobe claimed he had, "Loss of equilibrium and hypertension, believed caused by extreme job stress."

He further claimed, "Partial deafness in both ears believed incurred while performing range-master duties." But the significant part was when he reported that the hypertension was caused by recent events.

It was common knowledge in the office that Thobe had hypertension and had been seeing a doctor for the past three years. All the officers knew it but they had suddenly contracted "selective" memory. Thobe testified at my appeal November 14th, seven weeks later, that he did not suffer from any illness and the only medication he took was "an aspirin" now and then.

Another lie but who was counting?

Offer to Take Polygraph Test

I also sent a letter to Edwin Messe III, Governor Ronald Reagan's Legal Affairs Secretary, with basically the same information I had sent to the Attorney General but with some additional information concerning our interview at CHP Headquarters on July 24th. I pointed out that Deputy Attorney General Turner "was not adequately aware of Departmental procedures and confused about certain points of law."

I cited as an example, "he did not make a distinction between drunk and under the influence of liquor. And when it comes to enforcement it is imperative that this distinction be made. Turner said he did not think that consuming a couple of beers would constitute "had been drinking." I had pointed out during the hearing that Lieutenant Goodwin, of the Buellton CHP area office, had been observed driving a CHP cruiser under the influence on several occasions, but Turner refused to let me continue and replied that he did not want to hear about it.

PART 1: *Chapter 12:* The Day I Had Been Dreading

I reported to Mr. Messe that in preparation for my defense my lawyer had requested the recorded interviews and Turner refused to surrender the records as required by Government Code Section 19574.1. Turner was, in fact, withholding evidence and should be forced to surrender the interview records without further delay.

I also offered to take a polygraph test and challenged Turner to do the same.

Letter to Attorney General Stirs Trouble

The next letter I wrote to Attorney General Thomas Lynch got me in trouble with one of my attorneys, James M. Bordenkircher.

> Dear Mr. Lynch:
>
> "Enclosed is a copy of correspondence that I have mailed to Mr. Edwin Meese III. This is in response to a letter that I received October 14, 1968.
>
> "It is only fair that you should be made aware of your subordinate's conduct. During one of our conversations on March 14, 1968, he boasted of swearing at physicians when he interrogated them at disciplinary hearings. Mr. Richard Turner also told me that his boss was an alcoholic. He appears to be immature and reflects adversely on his position with the Attorney General's Office. It has been the general feeling of the employee's throughout the state that the AG's office was fair and impartial and was only interested in the facts so that justice could prevail. Mr. Turner is quickly changing that opinion.
>
> "I am sure you would be surprised to learn how he has represented the Attorney General's Office in this matter and I would volunteer a confrontation with Mr. Turner in your presence if you desire it.
>
> "I have documented evidence that Mr. Richard Turner has maliciously and with intent, omitted and distorted the charges against me in an attempt to falsely reflect an unfavorable case.

"Mr. Lynch, you have a reputation of being an honest and just man. I respectfully request that you conduct an investigation into Mr. Turner's conduct and association with the California Highway Patrol's Office of Inspection. Mr. Turner has "(refused to give) my lawyer and me the recorded interview of July 24, 1968, that we are entitled under Section 19574.1 of the Government Code.

"Your immediate action on this matter will be greatly appreciated."

One Defense Attorney Threatens to Quit

I didn't get a response from the Attorney General but I did get one from one of my attorneys and he wasn't happy.

Dear Mr. Mitchell:

"I recently learned of your letters to the Attorney General and the Governor's Legal Secretary wherein you make personal accusations against Deputy Attorney General Turner.

"You have been advised in the past by both Mr. Walt Taylor and by myself to not make any public statements, write any letters or other communication concerning your case. The effects of such communications can only detract from your best interests.

"This letter is to advise you that any further actions of the kind set out in the first paragraph hereof will leave me no alternative but to withdraw as your attorney. In short, keep your lip buttoned and your pen in your pocket.

"Very truly yours,"
James M. Bordenkircher
Attorney

I certainly didn't want to lose my legal counsel but more importantly I wasn't going quietly. I'm sure Bordenkircher had his reasons for not wanting me to "stir the pot" but I wasn't about to button my lip and put my pen away. I had my strategy and he had his. It was my neck in the noose and not his, so I went with my strategy.

I never personally heard from him again but the Santa Maria Times ran an article that "Illness in the family of Sacramento defense attorney Jim Bordenkircher has caused at least a month's postponement of Tuesday's (October 15) scheduled appeal hearing here for two disciplined California Highway Patrol sergeants."

The hearing was rescheduled for November 13-15, 1968, and another article in the paper reported that attorney Jim Bordenkircher's "wife underwent emergency surgery a few days before the first scheduled hearing."

Dan Dodge assured me that he would be handling our appeal. Later I was informed that Bordenkircher would be handling Klippness' appeal and it was requested and granted by Hearing Officer Hill that Klippness would have a separate hearing from mine. His hearing would start after mine ended.

Attorney George Pavlick replaced Bordenkircher as my second attorney. For the record, Neither Dan Dodge or George Pavlick ever said one thing to me about writing letters or making statements. At the appeal hearing I sat between both of them and actively participated in my defense.

Dan was the lead attorney and did all of the talking. From time to time he would discuss strategy with both Pavlick and me. I had two large file cabinets sitting on the floor where I could retrieve a document within seconds. When one of the CHP officers lied on the stand, I would confer with Dan and then hand him a document to support the officer was lying. The system worked very well. From time to time someone would joke about the need for two file cabinets of documents as we rolled them into the hearing but I would usually comment that we had a lot of liars testifying.

Which we did.

Foot in Hornet's Nest

The letter of response from Robert Malkin, Vancouver, Canada, was very interesting because of two comments.

First, he reported that he had written to various sources he had in California. "You will hardly believe this, but they clammed up and/or told me to keep out—the door is closed. I could do little or nothing. I have to be frank and I won't go into details as I don't want to involve you."

I never did find out what he meant by his last comment.

The second comment in his letter was, "The bar owners' association—a strong lobby is against you, and you can't lick it. And please don't try."

I knew exactly what he was talking about and this is a major problem with DUI enforcement today. He also sent me a copy of the letter from the Minister of Justice and Attorney General of Canada, John N. Turner, assuring Malkin that the House of Commons would be passing the presumptive guilt law "to deal with the problem of impaired and intoxicated drivers."

Malkin then offered some friendly advice: "You put your foot in a hornets nest and you should accept that you can't beat city hall."

He closed with, "Courage my friend, it's not the end of the world, but I know how you feel and I'm sorry."

I appreciated his letter but I didn't accept his advise that you can't beat City Hall.

Chapter 13
A Search for the Truth Begins

On November 13, 1968, the hearing started at 10 am in the Santa Maria City Council Chambers before Hearing Officer Robert Hill.

Finally, I was going to get my day in court. Something I had been looking forward to for months. I told Laura, Steve, Cheryl and Bob Jr. I wanted them to attend every hearing even if it meant missing school.

"I want you to know firsthand what happened," I told them.

I also wanted them to help me keep a close eye on the two file cabinets of documents I took to the hearing each day.

The Los Angeles Times assigned Staff Writer Ken Overaker to Santa Maria to cover the story each day. The Santa Barbara News-Press had Ken Lewis and the Santa Maria Times Staff Writer was Joe Graziano.

There was plenty of media coverage and that meant the two deputies from the AG's office, Richard K. Turner and Robert J. Sullivan (I have no idea whether he was related to CHP Commissioner Harold Sullivan) were going to be desperate because they were going to have to operate in the open now as opposed to behind closed doors.

They knew they had a loser and all the 26 charges were based upon lies except for the one charge that I said Thobe was "sick" and a "jerk."

11 Charges Dismissed Immediately

The prosecution itself asked for dismissal of nine charges immediately due to lack of evidence.

Then Hill ruled that 11 charges—including the nine the prosecution asked to drop—were so petty that he would not even rule on them other than to say they were not established by the evidence and not cause for punitive action.

In fact, as many of these petty allegations were brought up, Hill had to caution the audience to stop laughing. A couple of examples were "calling a tow truck out of rotation" and my testimony "that the tow agency had been removed from our official tow service list."

Another example was: "Requesting an officer to look in the trunk when storing a vehicle." I testified that the car had been abandoned, there was a large inventory and the officer did not run a check to see if it was stolen—and I wanted to make sure there was no body in the trunk.

Still another incident drawing laughter from the audience occurred during the testimony concerning the allegation that I was deliberately patrolling in the city for DUIs. In an effort to show where the DUI arrests were made, Turner had Sergeant Dwight Bell from Zone IV, Fresno Area, prepare a map of the Santa Maria area which he pinned on the bulletin board. And he brought a wooden pointer to trace on the map during the testimony.

There were some problems, however. The map 12" x 18" was too small, it was not to scale and it didn't show the city limits of Santa Maria.

The Hearing Officer complained to Turner that he couldn't see the map well enough to know what he was talking about.

"Is that map the only thing you brought with you?" the Hearing Officer asked, then he turned to Dan Dodge and asked, "Would your client be willing to let us use the map he prepared?"

Dan turned to me and without him saying anything, I said, "Sure" and retrieved a map I had made especially for the appeal. It was 3 ft x 3 ½ ft on white packing paper, drawn to scale, color coded, showing the city limits

PART 1: *Chapter 13:* A Search for the Truth Begins 259

(green broken lines), city area (yellow), each major street, line beats, every bar in the city (green dots) and the CHP office and Santa Maria jail (red).

The map covered the entire bulletin board and could be seen by the public attending the hearing in the first two rows. The Hearing Officer said, "Thank you" and turned to Turner and said, "Now, maybe I'll be able to tell what you've been talking about." The map was indicative of how unprepared and disorganized Turner and Sullivan were.

Of the 15 charges that were addressed at the Hearing, officers were continually perjuring themselves and it was never printed in the newspaper or addressed by the Hearing Officer. This was very disappointing.

The Phantom Fog Exposed as Perjury

One of the most obvious examples of perjury came in the case of the Phantom Fog.

The charge read, "You had no probable cause to . . . arrest James Ramos. This (arrest) report was false in that you did not see the vehicle run off the roadway and spin out in the dirt. Further, you did not at any time see Ramos driving the vehicle."

I simply could not believe the charge when I first read it.

But I was in for a bigger shock when I heard the officers testify in court. Both Officers Pledger and DeLaGuerra testified under oath that it would have been impossible for me to see the car spin out or Ramos driving because on that particular night it was so foggy you couldn't see 25 feet in front of you. They testified that they had a hard time finding their way on the road because of the thick fog. Ramos followed them to the stand and testified that he ran off the road and spun out because of the fog.

I turned to my attorneys, Dan Dodge and George Pavlick, and said, "These officers are telling blatant lies. There was no fog."

Dan Dodge, with a smile on his face, leaned over and speaking in a low voice so as not to disrupt the court, said, "I know they are but don't worry about it. We'll take care of them."

When it came time for our defense, Dan said to the Hearing Officer, Robert Hill, "We would like to call Richard Carter to the stand."

Mr. Carter took the stand and identified himself as the local Meteorologist for the United States Weather Bureau. He went on to testify that on both March 28th and 29th at the location of the arrest "the weather was clear and no fog existed."

The prosecutor, Deputy Attorney General Richard Turner, having been caught "red handed" could only make a feeble request that the Weather Bureau document not be placed into evidence. Hill, naturally, denied his request while glaring at Officers Pledger and DeLaGuerra who had just been exposed as dishonest cops in front of a packed courtroom.

When DeLaGuerra testified on rebuttal, he changed his testimony concerning the weather. One of the obvious reasons why he was forced to change it was because he coded the weather correctly on his original arrest report as "clear."

It was disappointing that the weather bureau testimony was never reported in any of the newspapers.

The Perjury Continues

I had previously submitted a request for punitive action against Officer Edwards for working for an official CHP tow service on his days off.

Instead of filing punitive action against Edwards, the Department used this incident as a charge to support my firing:

> "On 4-2-68 you filed a memorandum with the Santa Maria substation Officer in Charge requesting that formal punitive action be brought against Officer Edwards. You alleged that Officer Edwards was engaged in outside employment incompatible with his state job in that Edwards allegedly worked for Cox's Garage. This serious allegation was made with no proof whatsoever as to its validity. In fact, the allegation is false."

PART 1: *Chapter 13:* A Search for the Truth Begins 261

As Officer Edwards finished testifying that he didn't work at the garage and stepped down from the witness stand, I turned to Dan Dodge, my attorney, and told him, "Edwards was lying, too."

Dan smiled and said, "Don't worry about it. In a minute, we'll prove beyond any doubt that he's lying."

Dan didn't always tell me in advance what supporting evidence that he had but maybe that's because he had to wait and see what lies they were going to tell on the stand.

After I testified that Klippness and I had seen Edwards working on a truck and about my conversation with Dahl (where he admitted that he knew Edwards worked there), Dan called his next witness which was an investigator hired by CSEA. Not only did the Investigator testify that Edwards worked for Cox Garage, he produced Edward's income tax returns for the previous three years showing how much Edwards had reported he earned during his employment with Cox Garage.

Hearing Officer Hill, obviously disgusted with Deputy DAs Turner and Sullivan, snapped, "I've heard enough on this. Let's move on."

Chalk up another CHP Officer who should have been charged with perjury.

I told Dan, "If they're going to get up there on the stand and perjure themselves, the least they could do is not wear their uniform."

Unfortunately, this testimony was never reported by the news media. They were too busy reporting me calling Thobe a jerk.

DUI Arrested Twice in Three Hours

The next charge was so ludicrous, it left the hearing officer shaking his head. It was based on an incident a year earlier in which a DUI came into the Santa Maria CHP Office to sign off on a mechanical ticket. Thobe allowed the DUI to leave the station and I arrested him a short time later.

The first part of the charge read:

> "You permitted Mr. Bewley to enter his vehicle and drive off California Highway patrol property before you stopped and arrested him for a violation of Vehicle Code Section 23102(a)."

This part of the charge was easily dismissed because it was Lieutenant Thobe who had permitted Bewley to leave the office and drive off. I wasn't even in the office. I was loading my equipment in the rear parking lot when Klippness—who just happened to be looking out the front window—radioed me to say he thought there was a possible DUI leaving the office.

I ended up arresting Bewley twice in 3 hours, the first time, shortly after he left the office. I turned Bewley over to Officer Cochiolo for booking. Later Bewley was released from jail while still drunk and I ended up arresting him a second time.

The second part of their charge against me in this incident was:

> "You failed to advise Mr. Bewley of his constitutional rights."

This charge revealed the ignorance of those prosecuting me. I advised Bewley of his rights the second time I arrested him, although it was probably not necessary because Cochiolo should have advised him of those same rights only 3 hours earlier.

But, if in doubt, I always advised an arrestee of his rights. But with Cochiolo there were always doubts. If you were to inform the arrested party of his rights a half dozen times, it's not going to hurt anything. But if you don't tell or read him his rights, after he is arrested and before you start questioning him then it weakens the prosecution and the case may even be dismissed.

But it wasn't my responsibility to advise Bewley of his constitutional rights on the first arrest. That was Officer Cochiolo's responsibility. The three stooges prosecuting me—DAs Turner and Sullivan and Inspector Bryant—knew that. The officer doing the questioning is required to read or advise a suspect of his rights. It would have been illogical for me to advise him of his rights and then leave.

PART 1: *Chapter 13:* A Search for the Truth Begins

Hearing Officer Hill shook his head in disbelieve at the charge.

The companion charge against me (based on the same incident) was:

> "You stated to Mr. Bewley: 'You're an alcoholic. You're going to be out here drinking and driving again. If you ever run into a friend or my family, I'll take my 38 and blow your head off.'"

Of course, I never said that, but I did tell Bewley that I thought he was an alcoholic and that if he continued to drive in that condition that he was going to kill someone. Other people's loved ones are just as important as mine. We all hurt alike. I don't want anyone to lose a loved one especially in such a tragic manner. And the part about the 38 and blowing his head off was a figment of Prosecutor Richard Turner's imagination. Nevertheless, he asked Bewley to testify at my hearing about the threatening statements.

When asked in court, Bewley testified, "I don't remember Sergeant Mitchell saying that."

This told me that Bewley was more honest than Officer Cochiolo, who followed him to the stand and chose to perjure himself. In fact, Turner, who was beginning to look more and more like "Moe" of the Three Stooges, also tried to get Bewley to say he wasn't under the influence when he was arrested.

Instead, Bewley testified, "The officers would have been in a better position to make that decision."

I thought for a minute the Hearing Officer was going to excuse Bewley by saying "the witness for the *defense* may step down."

The next charge in relation to this incident was even more ludicrous but Turner had no choice but to proceed. The charge was,"On June 27, 1967, the same day as above, at about 8:10 pm you stopped and arrested Mr. Bewley once again for a violation of Vehicle Code Section 23102 (a), a misdemeanor drunk driving, with no probable cause for said arrest whatsoever."

Besides the testimony of Bewley that we were in a better position to make that decision, I had two chemical tests (one blood and one breathalyzer) independently supporting the validity of both of the arrests.

Nevertheless, in support of the State's charge against me, Officer Cochiolo, knowing that he had already committed himself to testify falsely, said he saw no irregular driving and that Clifford Bewley was not under the influence the last time we stopped him.

Of course, I had the results of a Santa Barbara County Breathalyzer test conducted in front of and witnessed by Santa Maria Officer Biggs supporting an intoxication level of .18 % conclusively proving Mr. Bewley was under the influence. Likewise, Bewley pled guilty to both charges of DUI in a deal where one charge was dismissed.

I hope as a result of this experience Bewley got his life together. He may have had a problem with drinking but he was honest on the stand. That was more than I could say for the CHP Officers that were openly committing perjury with impunity. They knew they wouldn't be prosecuted because the very person who would be prosecuting them was the one encouraging the false testimony.

No Evidence to Support Charge

The next charge also had no basis in fact:

> "On December 24, 1967, you arrested, charged, and jailed one Manuel Lopez for an alleged violation of Penal Code section 647(f), drunk in a public place, with no probable cause for said arrest whatsoever."

> "On the Intoxication Report, you stated that Mr. Lopez was 'staggering and swaying,' and that his speech was 'slurred and thick,' and you described his walking ability as 'staggering from side to side' and 'swaying in a circular motion.' You made these statements on this official California Highway Patrol report with full knowledge that said statements were false and untrue."

I testified in court that all of the statements on the Intoxication Report (CHP 218) were true and accurate. Both Lopez and his brother, Richard, who was arrested for DUI, had been drinking together. In fact, Manuel Lopez stated at the jail, "I'm not a drinker. I can't hold my liquor."

Manuel and Richard Lopez both pled guilty and paid their fines.

No evidence of any kind was ever presented in court to substantiate the charge against me. Only the allegation was made. Hearing Officer Hill promptly dismissed it and began to show signs of irritation toward Turner's unethical tactics. Later on in the hearing, Hill began to question Turner as to what his motive was for bringing these charges and not providing any evidence to support them.

Tactics Used to Get Us to Stop Arresting DUIs Emerge

The CHP strives to limit the number of officers involved in DUI arrests. This reduces overtime by avoiding the need for officers being subpoenaed to court. I understood this and did everything I could to comply with the policy.

So this charge actually came as a surprise:

> "In making arrests for drunk driving you have consistently requested other officers to proceed to the scene and complete the arrest procedure. You have further required other officers to fill in and sign intoxication reports wherein facts were reported which you, not the officers, had observed. This conduct violated the direct orders of your immediate supervisor Lt. Thobe of 12-8-67."

They failed to mention that Thobe's order was in direct conflict with CHP policy.

Thobe used his personal order to concoct this charge against me. It worked this way. I made three DUI arrests April 2 & 3, 1967, and turned them over to beat officers for booking. Eight months later, Thobe issued an order that Klippness and I could not turn over DUIs to beat officers; that we had to book them ourselves.

By ordering me to explain the April 1967 occurrences in a memorandum on March of 1968, it would appear that I had disregarded the order, when in fact, the events occurred before Thobe even issued the order.

But there was one thing they didn't count on. I copied everything. When we went to court I knew they would tell their dirty little lies but it was hard for them to convince the court when I produced a document they signed that contradicted their testimony.

When I testified in court, I pointed out the discrepancy to the Hearing Officer and the fact the order was issued to discourage Klippness and me from arresting DUIs. Thobe thought if we had to book them ourselves, we would not arrest them.

Secondly, I testified, "The practice of a supervisor requesting officers to come to the scene and complete the arrest of drunk drivers is the normal practice of the CHP throughout the State. This includes writing the events as related by the supervisor making the stop."

Ironically, at the time I was testifying, the Santa Maria CHP office had returned to the very policies I was being prosecuted for following. Lieutenant Goode, who was the interim Officer-in-Charge, reestablished these Departmental policies upon replacing Lt. Thobe in the Santa Maria area.

Even more damaging to the prosecution, we also had a document dated September 25, 1967, that read, "In the event a supervisor encounters a 23102a VC (DUI) suspect and releases the suspect to a two man unit . . . ."

The prosecution was surprised when I produced the document because Thobe, not knowing that I had already made a copy, removed it from the bulletin board.

It became apparent to the packed courtroom that I was being fired for following departmental policy.

Again, Hill had to admonish the court spectators to stop laughing.

Deputy Attorney General Turner and Inspector Bryant had nothing to counter the testimony. Hearing Officer Hill was given a copy of all of our documents with a request that they be placed into evidence.

PART 1: *Chapter 13:* A Search for the Truth Begins 267

Green Ledger Re-emerges

As expected the green ledger incident was part of the package to support my dismissal. The charge read: "On May 10,1968, Lieutenant Thobe demanded that you produce the ledger book in which you recorded the traffic officers' conduct. Your answers to proper questions, seeking to ascertain the whereabouts of the book, were purposely evasive and at one point sarcastic. You failed to cooperate with your superior officer in this inquiry."

I testified that the ledger book was given to Lieutenant Thobe as he demanded. I answered his questions although they might not have been what he wanted to hear. I also testified that Lieutenant Thobe should not have expected pages, covering the previous year, to still be in the ledger 3 to 4 months into the new year.

The prosecution did not have any rebuttal and, for all practical purposes, we were wasting the court's time. I could just see the people in the courtroom looking at each other and saying, "What was that all about?"

Setup Exposed in Court

The next charge was the result of Lt. Goodwin's attempt to set me up by ordering me to interview a 16-year-old girl inappropriately.

Here was the charge:

> "On or about June 3, 1968, you were directed by Lt. Goodwin to transfer information from a non-injury accident form (CHP Form 109) to an injury accident form (CHP form 110). On the latter form you indicated that the driver "had been drinking, not known if ability impaired," although there was no evidence whatsoever that the driver of the vehicle or any passenger in the vehicle had been drinking."

At the trial I testified that Lieutenant Goodwin ordered me to contact Donna Martin, a 16-year-old girl, who lived alone with her mother, after midnight, concerning a minor accident that had occurred 22 days earlier. I recognized it as a setup from the very beginning, knowing Lieutenant Goodwin would lie and say he didn't. I, therefore, went over the next morning, knowing that that was the proper way to handle it and got the information in the presence of her mother.

I testified that I based the sobriety coding of "HBD (Had Been Drinking)-not known if ability impaired" upon the following: Donna Martin said she and the driver had been drinking at a party following a wedding. The tow operator, Bob Gates, said he had talked with the driver and he may have been drinking. Officer Cameron, who wrote the initial report, coded the driver's sobriety as "HBD-ability impaired" and wrote in the accident report, "Driver had a slight odor of alcoholic beverage on his breath when he was interviewed." So I coded the driver as "HBD-not known if ability impaired."

Turner and Bryant had no rebuttal and, as with all of the other charges, had no justification for alleging them. And I noticed they couldn't look me in the eye as I walked by their table.

Hearing Officer Hill said, "I don't know what else Sergeant Mitchell could have done. Let's move on."

Fired for Arresting Kidnapper/Rapist

The charge that drew the most laughter from the courtroom was an arrest I made in the city. I had just left the Santa Maria jail where I had booked Robert Daigneault who I had arrested for DUI in the county. I had turned off of Cook Street where the jail is located and was southbound on Broadway. Broadway has four lanes divided by a double line and is a business district at that location. I was driving in the outside lane at about 25 mph when I heard a woman screaming. I turned to my left and saw a woman with her body half way out of the right front passenger window of a car that was passing me at a high speed. She was waving her arms and screaming at the top of her lungs, "Help. Police. Help" as the car passed.

I immediately took off after the speeding car using my red lights and siren. The driver, Mario Balderas, was making every effort to evade arrest as he was being pursued. Just before we got to Lakeview, he made a right-hand turn and suddenly realized he was on a dead end street. At this point, Balderas gave up.

PART 1: *Chapter 13:* A Search for the Truth Begins 269

The young women jumped out of the right front seat and ran back to the cruiser, screaming hysterically, "He kidnapped me. He was going to rape me."

I arrested Balderas for kidnapping, attempted rape and DUI. For arresting Balderas and saving the young lady from being raped and, who knows, possibly being murdered, the arrest was used as one of the charges to justify firing me.

This testimony and arrest never got in the newspapers or the findings of the court. And you can be assured the legislators were never told about it either. But the fact I called Lieutenant Thobe "sick" and a "jerk" was all over the news. I always thought that "freedom of the press" meant freedom to report corruption when it's uncovered but I guess it means "freedom to be selective on what you report."

If the news media had been doing their job the headlines of their newspaper would have read:

> "*CHP Sergeant Fired for Arresting Kidnapper and Rapist."* with a secondary headlines, *"He wasn't on a county line beat at the time."* And why didn't Hearing Officer Hill say to Dep. Atty. Gen. Richard Turner, "What's going on here? This is insanity. How could you bring this charge into my courtroom?"

It was obvious from the beginning that the punitive action was "malicious prosecution" and it should have been exposed.

Why didn't one of the reporters ask Turner, "Did you really expect the sergeant to ignore the kidnapped woman's screams?" and then ask Hill, "Do you think the California Attorney General's office should have used this charge as a reason for firing the sergeant?"

And then both answers should have been reported in the next day's newspaper and I would have made sure the legislators got a copy.

But one must remember Santa Maria was where Michael Jackson had his trial so maybe it's just something in the water that makes them different.

The Appeal Hearing was scheduled for three days and after that they wanted to start Klippness' appeal which was now separated from mine.

The State used all three days parading 31 witnesses to the stand, including one CHP inspector, two captains, two lieutenants, one sergeant, one clerk-typist, eight civilians, one garage owner, one waitress and fourteen officers.

Newspaper headlines over the next few days read, "*Improper Arrests Charged At Hearing,*" "*Threat By Officer Charged At Hearing,*" "*Three More Officers Testify At Hearing,*" "*CHP Firing Case Drags,*" And on the final day of testimony for the prosecution, "*Parade Of Officers Testify Against Fired CHP Sergeant Mitchell*" and "*CHP's Charges Backed.*" The Santa Barbara News-Press printed, "*Mitchell's Degrading Remarks Are Related.*"

There was one paragraph that appeared in the November 15 issue of the Santa Maria Times concerning the appeal about Dep. Attorney General Richard Turner's underhanded conduct. It read, "A sidelight to the hearing is Dodge's (my attorney) continuing requests and Turner's reluctance to produce many CHP reports on investigations into the list of 26 charges against Mitchell. Turner has vigorously objected saying the reports were 'privileged' but was continually overruled by Hill."

Turner did not want us to get our hands on the "many CHP reports" because they proved my innocence and he knew it. Once he was forced to turn them over we used them as our evidence against the charges. Can you imagine someone bringing charges against someone and then refusing to show the supposed "documented evidence" by claiming it was privileged? Turner had also assured all of the legislators earlier that he had provided us with all the documents, which is required by law.

On November 16, 1968, The Santa Maria Times devoted about a one-third page reporting the testimony against me and the heading, "*Appeal Hearing For CHP Officer Continues Dec. 10.*" That meant I had to wait almost a month to answer the additional phony charges. In the meantime I could only hope the public was not going to draw any conclusions until I had a chance to answer the allegations.

Evidence Against Patrolmen Flimsy

At least one citizen wasn't buying the phony charges. On November 22, 1968, in his second letter to the editor, the following appeared:

"Evidence Against Patrolman Flimsy.

"I write again about the C.H.P. Officer in trouble with his superiors.

"I hope he can ride trains because it looks like he's getting a railroad job.

"I can sympathize with him because I've seen this type of thing before. Look at the testimony of the people against him. With evidence like that he shouldn't even been reprimanded.

"His fellow officers testified he calls his superiors names. Which one of you can cast the first stone on that? It just sounds terrible when you get them all together.

"He claims a fellow officer was moonlighting. The officer claims that it was work for a friend. He got the W-2 return for money invested. Come on now, who believes a story like that. There's no way in the world to pay back money and receive a W-2 for it.

"He gave a man (apparently drunk) a ticket for driving his car after, get this, after he had warned the man not to drive. How much fairer can you get. He couldn't have given him a ticket until he drove, now could he?

"Another complaint is that he continually puts down on the tickets he issues "apparently drinking." This is quite legal insofar as the C.H.P. is qualified to state conditions regarding the issuance of violations such as rainy, dry, heavy traffic, etc. They are trained in such matters so it would follow that the insertion of the words (apparently been drinking) is quite within the framework of his training.

"Let's have better relations between civilians and law enforcement."

Eugene Santos
Nipomo

I really appreciated Mr. Santos' letter. It increased my confidence in the general public.

LA Times Makes No Mention of CHP Perjury

On December 8, 1968, two days before resuming the appeals hearing, when I would have had an opportunity to answer the allegations, the Los Angeles Times came out with an article, covering two-thirds of a full page, in their Sunday edition. The main heading was, "CHP Substation a Nest of Dissension" and a secondary heading of "Santa Maria Hearings Disclosure." The article started out: "Testimony in hearings being conducted in Santa Maria indicates that disciplinary action taken last summer against two veteran Highway Patrol sergeants stemmed from their enthusiasm in making drunken driving arrests."

The article mainly covered the allegations of calling Lieutenant Thobe a "psycho," "sick," "lying jerk'"and "stupe." I have never used the word "stupe" in my life and I looked it up in Webster's New World Dictionary to see if there was such a word. Webster reports it as a slang meaning, "a stupid person." I'm accused of using a word that I didn't know existed. But there were a lot of things I was accused of doing that I never knew existed.

Thobe admitted the following and it appeared in this article, "Thobe admitted that he made an uncomplimentary remark about Mitchell and said he should not have said it. But he never apologized for it. He testified he never called Mitchell a derogatory name in front of other officers." There was no testimony as to whom he made the derogatory remark or what the remark actually was. How strange.

Some of the other charges reported in the Times article were patrolling the city, staking out bars, arresting DUIs in the city limits, and a tape recording incident involving Klippness which the Times article reported, "The recorder incident is not involved in the current case against the officers, but . . . ." then it goes on to relate the incident. If the incident is not "involved in the current case" then why were they reporting it? This is something you might expect to happen in a movie but not in real life.

No mention was made of the CHP officers committing perjury.

PART 1: *Chapter 13:* A Search for the Truth Begins

Appeal Starts Second Time

On Tuesday, December 10, 1968, the appeal hearing resumed in Room 107 of the Applied Art Building of Allan Hancock College at 9 am. The Santa Maria Times reported the hearing "will last at least through Tuesday and probably Wednesday." They, along with the accusers, must have thought I was just going to take the witness stand, testify I didn't do what they were accusing me of doing and then just step down. Well, if that was their thinking, they were in for a big surprise.

By now, Sergeant Klippness had served his 30 days suspension and returned to duty in a non-patrol staff position at the Buellton sub-station. The prosecutors, in my opinion, had given him a 30-day suspension in place of dismissal, using the old tactic of "divide and conquer." If their strategy worked as planned then Klippness would not testify in my behalf and it may even be possible they could turn him into a Cameron, Scruggs, Hilker or Edwards.

They couldn't have been more wrong. Klippness was a loyal friend that could be counted on to tell the truth and that was exactly the stand he took.

The appeals hearing started by Deputy Attorney General Turner recalling Captain Dahl, Officer Loren Scruggs and two more officers to testify in support of the following charges:

> "On October 16, 1967, at 3 am, while having coffee with Officer Hilker in Denny's Restaurant in Santa Maria, you observed Reginald Berve in an intoxicated condition. Nevertheless, you permitted Mr. Berve to leave the restaurant, enter his vehicle and drive from the parking lot onto a public highway before you pursued him and arrested him for violation of Vehicle Code Section 23102 (a), misdemeanor drunk driving."

No mention was made that I had asked the waitress Vantrice Burke, who was a friend of Berves, to warn him not to drive because he was under the influence. In fact, they persuaded Vantrice Burke to testify that I never talked to her. But for them to prove their case against me, it was necessary to prove Berve was intoxicated as opposed to being under the influence—and there is a definite difference.

We introduced the original official breathalizer showing Berve had a BAC of .17 percent. To make matters worse for the prosecution, Vantrice Burke apparently became confused on the stand and on cross-examination testified she thought it would be safe for her friend to drive, so it was not necessary to warn him. This discredited her original testimony that she had not talked with me and it did nothing to prove Berve was intoxicated.

I had gone after the DUI when I saw him get into his car and Officer Hilker, who was with me in the restaurant, stayed inside, which amounted to dereliction of duty. Thirteen days after the arrest, I had a discussion with Hilker about his failure to take action that night. He told me that he did not completely agree with the Department's policy and would not follow it because he sometimes drove around on his days off "in that condition."

I appreciated his honesty, but his answer emphasizes another major reason DUIs are not being arrested throughout the nation. It should be pointed out that Hilker did arrest DUIs and even worked the DUI shift but like many officers he believed the DUI level established by the Department was too low and established his own level, which was higher. Back then, the BAC was .15%. Today, it's almost half that amount at .08%.

Officer Hilker's refusal to follow DUI Departmental policy was brought to the attention of the CHP—but instead of taking corrective action against him, they charged me with permitting Berve to drive and ignored Hilker's action of not even getting up from drinking his coffee.

In answer to the charge, I pointed out at the hearing that under the law, no violation occurs until a person under the influence drives his vehicle upon the roadway. That's the reason that Deputy A.G. Turner used the wording "intoxicated condition" when referring to Berve inside the restaurant. It's against the law to be intoxicated in public so Turner was trying to set the stage to show that Berve should have been arrested for being intoxicated.

Of course, with a BAC of .17%, his devious tactic backfired. He tried to cover up by saying there was no difference between being under the influence and being intoxicated. Unfortunately, for Turner, the law does see a definite difference.

Hearing Officer Hill made an interesting finding on this charge. "It is plain that the motorist (Berve) referred to in this Finding VII (charge) should not have been driving and if appellant's (Mitchell) efforts to protect the public were improper, the exact nature of his fault is at least not sufficiently clear to warrant punitive action."

"Not sufficiently clear?" Hill should have had the guts to rule that my actions were proper. But if a Hearing Officer rules in your favor even if it's balderdash, you take what you can get.

Chance to Answer Charges

The morning newspaper article recounted another major part of the testimony in that first day of my rebuttal under the headline: "Fired CHP Sergeant On Stand; Tells His Side."

The article read:

> "Sgt. Bob Mitchell, fired by the California Highway Patrol, took the stand in his own behalf this morning as the hearing on his appeal from the firing resumed at Hancock College.
>
> "Mitchell's testimony this morning centered on the derogatory remarks reportedly used by him about Lt. Donald Thobe, commander of the CHP office here at the time of the incidents that led to Mitchell's firing.
>
> "The 10 year CHP veteran said he had referred to Thobe as "sick" because the lieutenant was extremely nervous, suffered from hypertension and took medication for his condition.
>
> "He also said Thobe screamed and used profanity, sometimes in the presence of citizens visiting the CHP office here.
>
> "Mitchell denied that he had ever termed Thobe a "psycho" as was testified to by other CHP officers last month when the hearing first opened. Mitchell said other officers used this term to describe Thobe when he first was assigned to the Santa Maria office in early 1967.

"The fired sergeant also produced a poem that was circulated in the substation containing derogatory remarks about himself."

Another newspaper, The Santa Maria Times reported after the first day of rebuttal: "Fired CHP Sgt. Mitchell Denies Charges At Appeal Hearing" with a secondary heading, "Didn't Violate Orders To Catch Drunken Drivers."

In the article it was pointed out, "Mitchell's direct testimony, which consumed most of Tuesday as he began a point-by-point refutation of the many allegations against him, continued in today's fifth day of the hearing before Hearing Officer Robert Hill of the State Personnel Board."

"Sgt. Jerry Klippness, whose appeal from a 30-day suspension without pay will follow the Mitchell hearing, took the stand in Mitchell's behalf Tuesday. His testimony was sandwiched in between Mitchell's testimony. Cross-examination of Klippness was reserved until he testifies again later in the hearing."

Charge of Patrolling in the City for DUIs

As my rebuttal continued in the following days, another very embarrassing time for the prosecution occurred during my testimony on the 25 DUIs I had arrested in the Santa Maria city limits. First, they could not produce any witnesses to testify that I had been patrolling the city as they alleged.

The reason? I never did patrol the city for DUIs. That was the city's responsibility and we had enough DUIs in the county to keep us more than busy.

Now, if I was in the city en route to the Santa Maria jail which was centrally located in the city, or if I chased a DUI from the county into the city, then of course, I would arrest the DUI regardless of the location of the stop.

Not having any witnesses did not prevent the prosecution from making the unfounded charges. Allegations, though false, can still serve a purpose if it is the goal of the perpetrators to smear a person's reputation.

Most people believe "where there's smoke, there's fire." I use to believe that but I can assure you that I don't anymore. That "smoke" is sometimes a

PART 1: *Chapter 13:* A Search for the Truth Begins 277

"smoke screen" and it was in this case. Knowingly filing false charges against anyone is a serious criminal act. As outrageous as it may sound, justice would have been served by placing Turner, Sullivan, Dahl, Thobe and the whole lot, in handcuffs and booking them into the Santa Maria jail for conspiracy to file false charges and perjury. Actually, their crimes were more serious than some people presently in prison because my opponent's crimes were being done "under the color of authority." There's got to be some check and balance within our judiciary system to bring these types of individuals to justice.

Because they had no witnesses, they placed into evidence the 25 DUI arrest reports. I wrote most of the reports myself, but some were written by the officers who I had turned the DUI over to for booking. The arrest reports were the only thing they had to prove their allegation—and they thought the reports would be enough.

What they didn't know was we were going to use the very reports they entered into evidence to prove my innocence. The following questions appear on every arrest report:

> Have you been drinking? Where? From where did you start driving? Time? And Destination? There are other questions but these were the only questions and answers we needed.

It's important to remember I had my 3 ft. x 3 ½ ft. map to show were every arrest was made and the fact that every beat in the CHP Santa Maria Area passed through the city limits of Santa Maria. That's correct. It was impossible to travel on a CHP beat without going through some portion of the city limits. So whether an officer was making the arrest in the county or the city depended upon when the DUI stopped. In some places it amounted to less than a block in distance.

Secondly, in regards to the 16 arrests reports submitted by the prosecution, this was the Hearing Officer's finding, "This charge is based on 16 drunk driving arrests allegedly made by appellant within the city during this period. In fact with respect to 4 of the arrests the suspect was first observed by appellant in county territory and arrested close to the city but still in the county. (Talk about incompetency) An analysis of the remaining 12 intoxication reports and of the circumstances surrounding these arrests establishes that in 13 months appellant:

- 4 times – made an arrest in the city after first observing and pursuing the suspect in the county.

- 4 times – made an arrest in the city on his way to or from booking suspects at the Santa Maria City jail.

- 1 time – made an arrest in the city while traveling from one beat to another

- 1 time – made an arrrest after the suspect backed down a freeway off ramp onto a city street.

- 1 time – interrupted a break at an authorized coffee stop in the city to arrest a suspect. (This was the Berve case at Denny's Restaurant)

- 1 time – observed and arrested an individual a short distance inside the city limits.

The finding continued, "It was necessary as a practical matter for appellant to travel through the city to properly supervise officers on beats to the west of the California Highway Patrol office and all suspects were booked at the Santa Maria City Jail virtually in the center of town. Also, appellant had no choice but to take enforcement action with respect to violations he observed while traveling through the city. To the extent that appellant pursued violators from the county into the city the evidence offered against appellant not only does not support but even tends to refute the allegation to the effect that he neglected his county responsibilities to patrol in the city.

"Also the fact that appellant was taking a coffee break in the city at a CHP authorized stop near the freeway hardly tends to establish that he was patrolling in the city. The remaining 7 arrests over the 13 month period in question do nothing more than establish that appellant remained normally alert and reasonably diligent when his duties took him into or through Santa Maria and the 7 arrests fall far short of establishing on a statistical basis that appellant was patrolling within the Santa Maria city limits."

Only five DUIs said they had left bars and the bars were so far from the location of arrest they were not considered. The other 20 said they had been drinking at home, with girlfriends, at restaurants, etc. So that took care of the "staking out bars" allegation.

More "Confusion" by the Prosecution

Advising a person of his constitutional rights was another thing they were "confused" about. That allegation was so stupid the Hearing Officer did not even mention it in his decision summary. But I want to mention it here just for the record.

The exact allegation was: "You have continually failed to advise persons arrested for drunk driving of their constitutional rights as required by law."

The prosecution did not provide one piece of evidence to support this allegation. They charged me with this just to mislead the public, knowing I would beat them in court. It was like scattering feathers in the wind, knowing I wouldn't be able to find or pick them all up.

Besides testifying there was no truth to the allegation and it was without justification, we also submitted two documents into evidence to support how important I thought it was for an officer to advise a suspect of his rights.

The first document was an arrest report submitted to me for approval on September 9, 1967, wherein Officer Scruggs reported he did not advise a Louise Weathermon, arrested for DUI, of her constitutional rights because "Subject would not have been able to understand because she was too drunk." I advised him in the future to advise the arrestee of her constitutional rights regardless and then record, "No response, etc." He also did not ask Weathermon if she was a diabetic. Scruggs' response was, "You can't expect me to remember everything."

The second document was an arrest report submitted to me for approval on January 7, 1968, wherein Officer Vind reported that he made an arrest for DUI at 5:45 pm and gave a breathalyzer test at the Santa Maria jail at 6:00 pm. He was asked in the note how he could arrest someone, question them, advise them of their constitutional rights, search and handcuff them, drive to the jail and then give them a breath test in 15 minutes. He responded that the 15 minutes was "correct" and that he did advise the arrestee of his constitutional rights.

Both documents confirmed how important I thought it was to advise an arrestee of his rights. No evidence was ever provided to support this phony allegation. It was obvious it was a smear tactic.

Vind also testified that I had made derogatory comments about Thobe, and that I "compared the Santa Maria CHP operation with the Third Reich of Nazi Germany."

And he was right. But he didn't tell the Hearing Officer in what way I was comparing the two. It had nothing to do with the brutality and inhumanity of the Nazis. At the time I explained to the officers that I was referring to the mentality of "I was only following orders" to justify one's actions.

This completed the final day of the hearings and Hearing Officer Hill declared the appeal closed. He said he would take it under submission and provide a decision "possibly sometime in February."

Gov. Reagan Asks for Tighter Drunk Driving Laws

The same day as my hearing ended, a significant article appeared in the Santa Barbara News-Press. I don't think it was a coincidence, but instead it was the result of all the publicity we were getting and the letters we wrote to the legislators.

The article heading was, *"Drinking Driver Problem Studied"*

"Sacramento—The drinking driver will be the single most important problem under attack at this year's Governor's Traffic Safety Conference in Sacramento, starting today.

"State Secretary of Business and Transportation Gordon C. Luce, pointed to alcohol as the most deadly menace on California Highways today.

"Drinking drivers account for more than half the 5,500 deaths on the streets and highways in California and a way must be found to stop this senseless slaughter. [This sentence was almost exactly the same as the wording I had used to the legislators].

"Stronger enforcement by an expanded California Highway Patrol has resulted in almost a 20 percent increase in drunk driving arrests over last

PART 1: Chapter 13: A Search for the Truth Begins

year, Luce said. ***But still we estimate the Patrol and local police officers are arresting less than 10 percent of the drinking drivers—the potential killers—in California.***" (emphasis mine)

"Luce pointed out that while fatal accidents this year to date are about 10 under the same period last year, total injury accidents have gone up by almost 1,000.

"This in spite of the fact that there has been an increase in total arrests of almost 70,000 by the California Highway patrol. And of the total increase in arrests, more than 5,000 were for drunk driving."

Was it a coincidence that on Friday, December 13th, the last day of my testimony in Santa Maria, the Los Angeles Herald-Examiner ran this story.

"Reagan Asks Tighter Drunk Driving Laws"

"Sacramento—Gov. Ronald Reagan hit out at members of the state legislature who failed to vote for passage of a "presumptive limits law" which, he said, would help in the prosecution of drunk drivers.

"The Governor addressed the opening session yesterday of the 2nd annual Governor's Traffic Safety Conference attended by 1,200 adult and teenage delegates.

"He told delegates he would seek passage of the presumptive limits law again at the next legislative session, and said he believes "the situation will be different" this coming year because Republicans control the State Assembly.

"I'm sorry to report that not all my suggested legislation became law," Reagan said. ***"Instead, some legislators decided to play politics with the lives of their fellow Californians and blocked passage of this legislation."*** (emphasis mine)

"The new measure, to be introduced in the next session, would establish a limit of .10 parts of alcohol in the blood-stream for a person to be presumed drunk. The current limit is .15 parts of alcohol.

"Reagan told the meeting, many of whom were young drivers, that the "presumptive limits bill would streamline procedures in the prosecution of drunk drivers."

"Yesterday the California Highway patrol issued a report indicating the state's death total for 1968 was nearly 2 per cent higher than last year. In the first 11 months 4420 persons died on streets and highways compared to 4349 in 1967."

The next day the Santa Maria Times reported, *"Testimony Completed In Hearing For Fired CHP Sgt. Bob Mitchell"* and then just rehashed the charges and testimony. On Sunday, January 5, 1969, the Los Angeles Times had a full page story with photographs, *"Testimony at Punitive CHP Probe Clashes."* The article covered the entire appeal and testimony given on each allegation.

Sgt. Klippness Appeal Begins

Sergeant Klippness' appeal from his 30-day suspension started the next day, Monday, January 6, in Santa Maria. As reported in the Santa Maria Times, "The allegations against Klippness, in support of his suspension, are the same type as some of those lodged against Mitchell."

One of the major differences in Klippness' hearing, from mine, was Deputy Attorney General Turner, who was prosecuting the case, took the stand and testified against Klippness.

As reported in the Santa Maria Times, "In what seemed unusual, Deputy Atty. Gen. Turner, chief counsel for the CHP in the two hearings, took the stand to testify about Klippness altering a drunken driving arrest report that Officer Roberts had filled out". Turner testified that Klippness admitted to him during an investigation conference in late 1967 that, "You have got me on this one."

Not surprisingly, Klippness testified that the incident never occurred.

First, I didn't believe a word that Richard Turner said and I don't think anyone else did. Turner was referring to the final interview held in Sacramento where he interviewed both Klippness and me prior to our punitive action.

Turner denied that a clerk-typist had been present and recorded the entire interview. Turner is also the person who refused to provide Dan Dodge, our lead attorney, with documents from the recorded interview which he was required by law to provide. He claimed they were "privileged" documents.

Of course, Hill wasn't buying that "garbage" and ordered him to surrender copies of the documents.

Turner finally surrendered a one page document with one paragraph. There should have been several pages from two hours of solid testimony. He probably destroyed the originals, which he knew would have exonerated us and also exposed his illegal conduct.

Klippness had 10 witnesses testifying against him including a Santa Maria police sergeant, a CHP captain, a sergeant and six officers and Deputy Atty. Gen. Richard Turner. Their testimony was basically the same testimony as the testimony they gave at my appeal—orchestrated and malicious.

Santa Maria PD Sgt. Hicks testimony

One testimony against Klippness stood out because the officer should have been physically arrested for interfering with an arrest. Instead, the prosecutor called him as a witness.

Sergeant James Hicks, of the Santa Maria Police Department, testified in reference to charges that Klippness staked out bars. Hicks testified, that during one grave-yard shift, he drove an unmarked police car to the area of the Beacon Outpost and Ranch House bars at Betteravia Road and South Broadway where he saw a CHP cruiser parked in the service station at McCoy Lane.

Hicks said he found a convenient spot nearby and waited until a man came out of the Beacon Outpost and started to drive away in his car with the lights off. The CHP car started to follow, Hicks said, but he drove his unmarked car in between them. The CHP cruiser passed both of them and continued heading north. Hicks then stopped the man to tell him about the lights, he said.

Returning to his observation post, Hicks said he saw the CHP car again. A second man emerged from the bar and drove off with the CHP unit following. Again, Sgt. Hicks drove his car in between the two. The CHP car then passed both of them and continued northbound.

Hicks said he stopped the man to warn him about a burned out tail light. Then he headed for the police station to resume his routine duties when a speeding auto came southbound on Broadway in front of the Santa Maria High School. Hicks gave chase with the aid of another police car. After the speeder was stopped south of the Vandenberg Inn, a CHP car pulled alongside to offer aid. Inside was Sgt. Klippness.

Here's my analysis of Sgt. Hicks' testimony. The only reliable part was when he testified that Sgt. Klippness pulled alongside to offer aid. Everything else was worthless and prejudicial. Number one, he testified he did not know who was in the CHP cruiser at the intersection of Betteravia Road and McCoy Lane. But, if it was Sgt. Klippness, he had every reason to be parked there.

It was not against Departmental policy and it was a logical location for a supervisor because Betteravia Road was our line beat 47 in both east and west directions. McCoy Lane also separates the county and city at that point and was our line beat 45.

Klippness and I never staked out bars. However, if we drove by a bar and saw a car driving out of the parking lot, we took a close look at it. I know of no Departmental order that prohibits an officer from staking out bars. The Department would be foolish to issue such an order. There may be some private unwritten rules floating around out there "discouraging" officers from staking out bars. As long as it's unwritten the Commander can always lie and say he didn't know anything about it. It reminds me of the guy who accused someone of something and the accused said, "Can you prove it?" and the accuser said, "No." Then the accused said, "Well, if you can't prove it, I deny everything."

The biggest question of all is, what was Sgt. Hicks doing there in the first place? What right did he have to interfere with a CHP officer pulling over a possible DUI? And then, on his own testimony, he did it a second time. What if Hicks was attempting to arrest a person in a stolen car in the county and an unmarked CHP car cut between them to prevent the arrest—twice?

PART 1: *Chapter 13:* A Search for the Truth Begins   285

I don't know who was the biggest "pinhead," Sgt. Hicks or Dep. Dist. Atty. Turner who called him as a witness. The CHP officer that Sgt. Hicks deliberately cut off should have arrested Sgt. Hicks and booked him into his own jail. Hicks was, on his own admission, guilty of violating Penal Code section 148 (a) (1) (Delaying or obstructing a public officer in the performance of his duty), which is punishable by a fine of $1,000, or by imprisonment in a county jail not to exceed one year or both.

But I asked myself, how does an individual who doesn't know any more about the law than Turner get a job with the California Attorney General's office?

The appeal hearing for Klippness lasted for one full day. Hearing Officer Robert Hill, of the State Personnel Board, took Klippness' appeal under advisement after hearing all of the testimony. He said he would present it to the State Personnel Board along with his recommended decision on my appeal. But still to be entered in the record was written closing arguments from both sides. So, we knew it would be another month before we would receive the results.

Finally a Decision

On Friday, February 7, 1967, I was teaching an eighth-grade class at Orcutt High School when I got a call to come to the office. It was unusual to get called out of a class in session so I knew it was important. One of the school officials said a reporter from the Los Angeles Times "wants to talk to you. You can take the call in my office."

Ken Overaker identified himself and said, "I called you up for your comment on winning your job back."

I said, "This is the first I've heard about it. What was the ruling?"

He said, "You were cleared of everything except calling Thobe "sick." You're scheduled to return to work on February 16th, in nine days."

"What about Klippness?," I asked.

Overaker said, "Same as you. He was cleared of everything but saying the Lieutenant was 'sick'." He went on to tell me that I was not going to be reimbursed for the time I was off. Our conversation appeared in the next day's edition.

Saturday, February 8, The Los Angeles Times read:

> "CHP Sergeant Rehired; Loses $6,300 in Pay."

"A veteran Highway Patrol officer who was fired at Santa Maria last summer won his job back but will not be paid for the more than six months he was off the job, the State Personnel Board ruled Friday in Sacramento.

"The board upheld a recommendation by its hearing officer, Robert Hill, that Sgt. Bob L. Mitchell, 38, is "too able and dedicated" an officer to be fired.

"It ruled that he may return to his job Feb. 16 as a sergeant.

"In effect the ruling amounts to a suspension without pay for six months and 17 days, costing Mitchell more than $6,300.

> *"Very Pleased"*

"At Orcutt School, near Santa Maria, where he has been teaching part-time, Mitchell told the Times by telephone that he understands the ruling exonerates him in every respect except for calling his commanding officer derogatory names.

"If that is true, then I'm very pleased with the decision," he said.

"He added that he will resume his CHP job and plans to continue following CHP directives to 'actively seek out and arrest drunk drivers.'"

"He and fellow Sgt.Gerald Klippness, 36, charged publicly when they were disciplined last July 29 that the action was taken because they were arresting too many drunk drivers.

PART 1: *Chapter 13:* A Search for the Truth Begins

> "Klippness was suspended for 30 days without pay. The personnel board Friday sustained this suspension.
>
> "The rulings were made after Hill took testimony over several months in Santa Maria.
>
> *Charges "Trivial"*
>
> "Hill found that the CHP failed to establish its charges that Mitchell 'staked out bars' to make drunk driving arrests contrary to CHP policy, and that a number of other charges against him were either not established or were 'too trivial' to warrant dismissal. (Hill said some charges were even too trivial to comment on).
>
> "He said the evidence failed to support a CHP charge that Mitchell patrolled in the city of Santa Maria against orders of the Santa Maria substation commander, Lt. Don Thobe.
>
> "But he found that, Mitchell and Klippness carried on a "war" against Lt. Thobe in conduct which sergeants should avoid.
>
> "They engaged in a 'personality conflict of heroic proportions' where the smallest incidents were blown out of all proportion, Hill said.
>
> "Much of the testimony related to the turmoil and dissension that rocked the substation for about 15 months in 1967 and 1968."

I was looking forward to Captain Dahl, Lieutenant's Goodwin and Goode calling me into the Santa Maria office and giving back my badge and ID card. After accepting it and pinning it on, I was going to tell them, "Well, I'm glad it's finally over." Not only was this not ever going to happen, I never saw any of the three again. As far as I know, Lieutenant Goode is retired and healthy and both Dahl and Goodwin have passed on. All three have long been forgiven.

Chapter 14
Big Win in Santa Maria

The California State Employees Association (CSEA) had two large stories in their newspapers:

> "Major Legal Victory for CSEA Puts CHP Sergeant back on Job" and "Big Win in Santa Maria"

They pointed out in the stories that:

> "Dan Dodge and George Pavlick of the CSEA legal staff were assigned to the cases last October. They devoted many hundreds of man-hours to on-the-spot investigation of the charges in Santa Maria, where the appellants were employed by the California Highway Patrol. But the effort and expense paid off handsomely in the widely publicized hearings, which started in December and ended last month. A dedicated CHP member was restored to his job.
>
> "Few cases in CSEA's legal representation history have presented so many ill founded charges against employees, or so well illuminated the principle that punitive actions are supposed to be based on evidence of wrong-doing. The measure of success achieved was enough to serve notice on any agency that unsubstantiated charges against any employee will be fought as long and as hard as necessary by CSEA.

Commissioner Sullivan was caught flat-footed when I was reinstated. I'm sure Inspector Bryant and Dep. Atty. Gen. Turner had assured him the dismissal would be upheld. How could they lose with 26 allegations and 31 witnesses testifying? Never mind that the charges were ill-founded and the witnesses were not telling the truth. It looked like a slam-dunk to them. They only had the one allegation that had merit and that was I said Thobe was "sick." I also said he suffered from hypertension. The CHP contended he did not suffer from any illness and Thobe also alleged that in his testimony.

Six months and two weeks after my reinstatement, the Los Angeles Times reported Lieutenant Thobe had sued the California Highway Patrol and was awarded $5,880 for hypertension which Thobe claimed was a result of his "controversy with Sgts. Bob L. Mitchell and Gerald R. Klippness in 1967-68 when Thobe commanded the CHP substation."

The CHP appealed the award and asked me if I would be willing to testify Thobe was "sick" prior to our "controversy" in Santa Maria. In other words, they were asking me if I would testify to the only allegation sustained against me and that had cost me $6,300 in lost salary. The very allegation they accused me of being dishonest about, they now wanted me to testify was true.

Well, it might come as a surprise but I didn't hesitate to tell them, "Sure, I'll be glad to testify." About two weeks later, I got a phone call telling me that my testimony would not be necessary because Lieutenant Thobe had dropped his suit against the Department.

Unauthorized Transfers to Los Angeles

Now, that I had been reinstated and Klippness had served his 30 days suspension, the Commissioner's office had less than a week to figure out what they were going to do with both of us. It was not surprising there was mass confusion.

On February 13, 1969, Klippness and I were notified by Captain Robert Roese, new Commander of the Santa Maria Area, that, "Effective February 17, 1969, you are administratively transferred to Zone V, Message and Dispatch Center in Los Angeles. You shall report at 0800 hours on that date."

PART 1: *Chapter 14:* Big Win in Santa Maria

Almost immediately, we were contacted by the Santa Maria Times and asked what we thought about being transferred to Los Angeles in place of remaining in Santa Maria.

Captain Roese had already given the Times a statement. The next day the Times read:

> *"CHP Sergeants Protest Shift To Los Angeles"*
>
> "California Highway Patrol Sgts. Bob Mitchell and Gerald Klippness objects of disciplinary hearings here in late 1968, told the Times today, they are appealing their transfer to Los Angeles.
>
> "Calling the transfer 'further harassment' by the CHP, the two sergeants said they will reluctantly report for duty on Monday at the Los Angeles Message and Dispatch Center but are filing an appeal with the State Personnel Board, requiring a hearing probably within three months.
>
> "Both had been assigned to Santa Maria prior to the disciplinary action.
>
> "Capt. Robert Roese, local CHP commander, in announcing the transfers today said, 'The new assignments will afford the sergeants a fresh start. They are career officers. The CHP has a big investment in them and we want to put them in a new environment.'
>
> "At the Los Angeles Message & Dispatch Center, Mitchell and Klippness will act as operations and watch officers supervising radio dispatchers. The center is the hub of all CHP activities in Los Angeles, Capt. Roese said.
>
> "The sergeants would supervise from 10 to 15 men each shift. There are 68 CHP personnel in the center at Vermont Ave. and the Hollywood Freeway.

"Capt. Roese said the new duty assignments are administrative transfers and the CHP will pay all moving costs.

"However, Mitchell and Klippness said they want to stay in Santa Maria and considered that they had 'won' in terms of the decision in their prior appeal.

"When asked about the possible problems of working with men here who testified against them at the hearings, Mitchell said, 'If the officers don't want to work for us, they can transfer.'

"Klippness expanded this by saying he and Mitchell were proven right in all of the instances except for the derogatory remarks. So they should be allowed to remain in Santa Maria, he said.

"Lt. Thobe has since been transferred to Visalia.

"Klippness said the transfer would be a 'big hardship' on his family because his children are in school presently and he has not sold his house.

"Both sergeants said they were informed of the transfers on Thursday.

"Since then, the sergeants said they asked to see CHP Commissioner H.W. Sullivan and have communicated with the office of Lt. Gov. Ed Reinecke, in an effort to have the transfers stopped."

On this same date, February 14th, I sent a personal letter to Commissioner Sullivan requesting he provide in writing the reason for my transfer to Zone V, Los Angeles, pursuant to section 19360 of the Government Code and advised him the transfer was placing an insurmountable hardship on my family and me. I never received an answer even though an answer is required by the Government Code.

PART 1: *Chapter 14:* Big Win in Santa Maria 293

Two days later, I received notification that effective March 1, 1969, I was transferred from the Santa Barbara Area to West Los Angeles and to report at 0800 hours on that date. I ignored this transfer and chalked it up to further incompetency.

Klippness and I drove down to Los Angeles together and stayed all night in a cheap hotel in North Hollywood. We got there late that night and when we got up early the next morning and put on our uniforms, I think some of the occupants thought it was a raid. The hotel hadn't looked that bad when we checked in, but it was late at night. It was quite a contrast to being home with the family.

We reported in to Zone V a little before 8:00 am and the Inspector asked us if we wanted a cup of coffee. He introduced us to the radio dispatchers and officers and told them we would be the new watch officers.

We knew some of the dispatchers from when we worked East Los Angeles and Baldwin Park. Everyone appeared friendly but reserved; even the dispatchers we had known earlier. We both came to the same conclusion: the Department thought we might get tired of working at Zone V, Message & Dispatch, being away from our families and just quit.

They would soon find out that there was no way that was ever going to happen.

I decided to stay with my mother, who lived in Bellflower by herself. Klippness did a lot of commuting to Santa Maria.

After about 10 days, Supervising Inspector Walt Pudinski, called me into his office. I didn't know at the time but Klippness had been in there ahead of me.

A Lawsuit or a Highway Patrol Career?

Pudinski was just a regular guy and I trusted him. He had a reputation as a "straight shooter" so I was interested in what he had to say. After a short friendly conversation he said, "What are your future plans? Are you planning on suing the Highway Patrol? Or are you planning on making the Highway Patrol your career?"

I thought to myself, there's a chance I'll do both, but it's common sense before you make a decision, you get all of the facts and I felt Pudinski was getting ready to make some type of offer. Also, I trusted Pudinski so I said," I'm interested in a Highway Patrol career."

Pudinski said, "I'm glad to hear that. We need officers like you on the Highway Patrol and I've worked out a real opportunity for you."

Pudinski went on to say that a new Area was opening in Los Angeles. That it would be named, "West Valley" and located in Van Nuys. "Here's your chance to get a fresh start. Captain Clemons is going to be the Commander. You'll like him, he's a great guy. Also, it will be a new office for everyone reporting in. What do you think?"

I told Pudinski I would take it as long as he would guarantee I would be treated like any other sergeant.

He said, "You have my word. You'll report in March 1st and the Highway Patrol will pay your moving expenses."

I thanked Pudinski and left there with the confidence I was back working for the real California Highway Patrol.

After I left the office I ran into Klippness in the coffee room. He said he had accepted a transfer to San Luis Obispo (the area bordering San Maria on the north.)

He said, "That way I won't have to move and I'm only a short distance from home." I told him I had chosen West Valley, a new area office in Van Nuys. Both of our transfers were to take effect March 1st, two days later. That was the last time Klippness and I would work together. But we have stayed friends over the years and are still close friends today.

About six months after reporting into San Luis Obispo, Klippness resigned from the California Highway Patrol.

He said San Luis Obispo had a good area commander, Captain Tripki, but he was "tired of being a second class citizen there. They wouldn't even recognize my seniority as a sergeant." Frankly, it was too close to Santa Maria, not only in distance but in similarity.

"I should have transferred to the Los Angeles area like you did," he said.

After a couple of years out of law enforcement, Klippness joined the Immigration and Naturalization Service (INS) where he was a Special Agent and served as Acting District Manager of Southern California before he retired in 1992. He presently works part time for the Los Angeles Police Department doing background investigations.

West Valley Office: Eating on the Embalming Table

West Valley was a newly created CHP Area office and all the officers reporting in on March 1, 1969, would be new to the area, transferring in from different parts of the state. Theoretically, no one would know each other. West Valley was located in the unincorporated city of Van Nuys in the San Fernando Valley. Hollywood and Beverly Hills were to our south and Universal city and Burbank were to our east. Celebrities were part of our clientele.

The West Valley CHP office was a converted funeral home. On the surface it looked like any other CHP facility. The briefing room where the sergeants held roll call was the old "mourning" room. Not only was it the right size room, we thought it was appropriately named. The sergeants' podium was where a body would normally be on display.

The only problem was the new kitchen. The table where everyone ate lunch was located where the embalming platform was previously located. Everyone tried to ignore the large pipe that was capped underneath the table.

The West Valley office consisted of one captain, two lieutenants, seven sergeants and about 50 officers. I was one of the Field Sergeants and worked the evening shift. I continued to actively arrest DUIs and most of the time I turned them over to the beat officers. Every once and a while I would book one myself just to stay in practice. It didn't matter if I arrested them in a city or the county or on the freeway or a surface street. Nor did it matter what standing the person had in the community or the world, as far as that goes. The officers gladly took the DUI into custody and most of the time I didn't even have to call them to the scene. They would hear the stop on the radio and come to the scene and volunteer. The Captain and Lieutenants would commend us for the number of arrests we were making and tell us to keep up the good work.

In fact, Captain Clemens even went a step further. He knew I was staying with my mother in Bellflower until I could move the family from Santa Maria so he provided me with a CHP cruiser as transportation until I could move to Van Nuys. The city of Bellflower is 34 miles from the West Valley office and I had just suffered a $6,300 loss of salary so his thoughtfulness was appreciated.

And as you might expect, because I was driving almost directly from one side of Los Angeles to the other, I encountered DUIs along the way, which I turned over to the officers having jurisdiction. One of the officers I turned a DUI over to was Officer Jim Smith, South Los Angeles Area, who later was appointed Commissioner of the California Highway Patrol by the Governor. He had a distinguished career and we still remain friends today.

Motorist Crashes Twice at Same Location

We had a very strange traffic accident happen in West Valley and it had us all puzzled. A young man was driving his car northbound on the Ventura Freeway between Van Nuys Blvd and Sepulveda Blvd when he suddenly drove off of the roadway, across the apron and crashed into an embankment. He was not seriously injured and no other cars were involved. The officers called me to the scene because they thought the driver might be DUI.

I checked him out and he was definitely not under the influence of anything. He just appeared normal but he could not give us a reason for running off of the freeway and crashing his car. "I don't know what happened," he said. The report read, "Ran off roadway for unknown reason."

That might have been the end of the story except for another accident a couple of weeks later. We received a call of a traffic accident northbound Ventura Freeway between Van Nuys Blvd and Sepulveda Blvd. The dispatcher reported, "It's a single car into the embankment." When we arrived we could hardly believe our eyes. The accident involved the same driver, in the same car, at almost exactly the same location. The driver was not seriously injured and there was only moderate damage to the car. Again, the driver said he didn't know what happened. "Maybe I blacked out," he said. The driver had not been drinking and insisted he was not a diabetic.

The officers and I knew there was something wrong and we finally came up with what we thought was a probable cause. It was just possible the driver had an epileptic seizure causing the first accident and then approaching the same location triggered another seizure. We suspected the driver wasn't telling us because he knew a seizure would result in his driver's license being revoked.

Having compassion for anyone who suffers from seizures, we presented our deduction to the driver. He said that it was possible that that was what happened. We made arrangements for him to get home, confiscated his driver's license and submitted a request for reexamination and forwarded a copy of the two accident reports to the Department of Motor Vehicles (DMV).

About two months after reporting into West Valley, I was able to buy an old home in Van Nuys for nothing down from my friend Sergeant Frank Loper, who I worked with for several months in Santa Maria and who also supported our cause behind the scene. It was only a small two-bedroom home but our oldest son, Steve, had married and was in the Army so there were only four of us.

Charles Manson Murders

On August 9, 1969, the newspaper headlines reported the brutal murders of Sharon Tate, Jay Sebring, Wojciech Frykowski and Abigail Folger in their home off of Benedict Canyon Drive. LAPD had the responsibility of investigating the murders because they took place at 10050 Cielo Drive in Los Angeles, less than a mile from Beverly Hills. The house where they were murdered has since been torn down and the land bulldozed.

We patrolled the Ventura and Hollywood Freeways that surrounded the area so we were concerned who the suspects might be.

The next night the equally horrendous murders of Leno and Rosemary LaBianca in the Los Feliz area were reported. I did not know the LaBiancas personally but they owned a grocery market in Montebello at Beverly Blvd and Hay St when I worked for the Montebello Police Department. One night we had cornered a burglar inside their market and we had to wait for LaBianca to respond from the Los Feliz area to let us into the market.

A few days after the Tate murders, Jim Cole, the administrative sergeant in West Valley said he had something interesting to tell me.

He said, "I live in the Simi Valley area and when I go home after work (he worked day shift) I pass that old Spahn Ranch on Santa Susana Pass Road. It's an old ranch where they used to film western movies. I keep seeing hippies driving around there in dune buggies and those dune buggies look new. I think they are probably stolen because it looks like they're hiding them under trees and covering them with tree limbs." He continued, "I think I'll call (CHP) Auto Theft and tell them."

I encouraged Jim to call Auto Theft and, of course, we had no idea there was a tie-in with the Manson murders.

The LA Times reported on August 16, 1969, one week after the Tate murders, that sheriff officers raided Spahn Movie ranch and arrested Manson and twenty-five others as "suspects in a major auto theft ring."

The suspects had been stealing Volkswagens and converting them into dune buggies. At 4 am, officers surrounded the east, west, and south sides of the ranch. The police filmed the raid with the intentions of making a training video. Everyone arrested was eventually released when it was discovered that the warrant was mis-dated. Little did police know that in the weeks prior to the raid the Manson family had committed 8 murders.

Manson and his group fled to two unused desert ranches, Myers and Barker, near Death Valley. Authorities there, not knowing the Manson group, were concerned that someone had set fire to a piece of earthmoving equipment in the area. They raided the Myers and Barker ranches and found stolen dune buggies and other vehicles and arrested two dozen persons including Manson who was found hiding in a cabinet beneath a bathroom sink at Baker ranch.

Manson and his family were later convicted of the murders in the Los Angeles area. My friend, Vincent Bugliosi, who used to prosecute our DUIs in East Los Angeles, was the lead prosecutor.

Four CHP Officers Killed Within Minutes

I was assigned to the West Valley Area for three years and two months and during that time we had five CHP officers killed. Four of the five were killed within 4-1/2 minutes on April 6, 1970. It is known as the Newhall Incident

PART 1: *Chapter 14:* Big Win in Santa Maria 299

because that's where it occurred, but the four officers worked in the West Valley Area.

I had talked to Officers Walt Fargo and Roger Gore about their annual evaluations about 2 hours before they were killed. They always rode partners on the graveyard shift, as did Officers George Alleyn and James Pence. All four of them were close friends. I had roughed out Fargo's and Gore's evaluations and was going to have it typed the next day. Although all four officers were young, they conducted themselves professionally. I had them rated as outstanding in performance, attitude and reliability.

The next day when I came to work, I got the bad news. I was stunned and, like everyone else, wanted to know how it could have happened.

Officers Fargo and Gore received a radio dispatch that someone in a vehicle had brandished a weapon. After requesting an "11-99" (officer needs help) they made a stop on the vehicle in the parking lot of a restaurant in Newhall near Magic Mountain, a recreational park now known as Six Flags. Both of the officers were shot and killed instantly by the passenger, Jack Twinning, and the driver, Bobby Davis.

When Pence and Alleyn drove in moments later, they could see neither the suspects nor the downed officers, but immediately came under fire. Although the officers took cover and drew their weapons, both were mortally wounded. One of the suspects was hit but not seriously.

Both suspects, Twinning and Davis, escaped, later abandoning their car and separating. During a nine-hour search, they discovered Twinning had broken into a house and had taken the owner hostage. The officers stormed the house using tear gas but before they could get to him, he killed himself with the shotgun he had stolen from Officer Fargo. At least that was the way it was reported and, frankly, I don't think anyone cared. Davis was captured, stood trial and convicted on four counts of murder.

On the day of Bobby Davis' trial in Van Nuys Superior Court, every CHP uniformed officer who could make themselves available was asked to go to Davis' arraignment for the officer's murders and fill the jury box. During an arraignment there are no jurors so we were able to take all twelve of the seats in the juror's box. The rest of the CHP officers set on the front rows in the spectators' seats. The court cooperated by making sure Davis was not brought into the courtroom until we were all seated.

The judge ordered the bailiffs to bring the prisoner into the courtroom. A few minutes later the door opened and the cuffed and shackled Davis took about two steps into the court room but upon seeing all of the CHP officers staring at him, he stopped and stepped back into the bailiffs who nudged him forward. They had to actually take him by both arms and lead him forward. And while the judge was reading the charges to him, Davis continually glanced toward the jury box (containing twelve uniformed CHP officers) and behind him at the other CHP officers as if he was afraid we were going to harm him. He was very nervous and did not appear to be listening to anything the judge said.

The reason for all of us attending the arraignment was psychological. We were delivering a message, and apparently Davis got it, that you may kill four of us but there will be four times that many more you'll have to deal with.

Bobby Davis was sentenced to die in the gas chamber, but in 1972 the California Supreme Court declared the death penalty to be cruel and unusual punishment and his sentence was modified to life in prison. He is presently housed in Pelican Bay State Prison, the home of California's most notorious criminals.

As a result of this tragedy, a completely revamped set of procedures was adopted for high-risk and felony stops. It can truly be said that these brave officers did not die in vain.

The fifth CHP officer and his wife were visiting her parents in northern California and while returning to Van Nuys they were both killed by a DUI in the Bakersfield area. They were driving in the lane next to the center divider on Interstate 5. The center divider at that location has high shrubbery with no center barriers. A DUI came through an opening in the shrubbery into the fast lane directly in front of the officer. He and his wife were killed instantly and the DUI was seriously injured. The DUI was probably intending on making a u-turn but who knows the mind of a drunk.

Bad Timing for Obscene Phone Call

One night I was on routine patrol southbound on the Hollywood Freeway approaching Mulholland Drive when radio dispatch broadcast, "Attention. Anyone in the area. We have an obscene phone call to one of our dispatchers and the suspect is still on the phone. He is using an emergency freeway phone on the Hollywood Freeway at Mulholland."

I acknowledged the call and told the operator that I was "10-97 (arrived at scene)."

I observed a male, about 40 years old, dressed in a suit, hanging up the phone as soon as he saw my cruiser approaching.

The dispatcher said, "He just hung up the phone."

I replied, "I know. That's because he saw me drive up."

Immediately, the suspect started denying that he had done anything wrong.

I asked him, "Who said you did?"

He said, "Isn't that why you stopped?"

I told him, "Let's stop playing games. You know what you were doing and I know what you were doing."

He was arrested for making an obscene phone call and pled guilty. I told him on the way to the jail—as if he needed to be reminded—that his "timing was terrible."

Major Earthquake

At 47 seconds after 6:00 am on Tuesday February 9, 1971, a major earthquake struck the northern San Fernando Valley where the CHP West Valley and Newhall Areas are located. The first initial shock recorded a 6.6 on the Richter Scale and resulted in two different sections of the Golden State Freeway collapsing at the Foothill Freeway and San Diego Freeway. Two other over-crossings were destroyed over the Golden State Freeway between Highway 14 and Weldon Canyon.

Both structures were under construction, the highest falling 150 feet to the freeway below. Other portions of the roadways were buckled or separated in these areas.

I was home asleep when the earthquake hit. The doors started banging back and forth. Dishes fell from the cabinets and some cracks appeared in the walls. It was almost impossible to stand during the initial tremor.

But in emergency situations like this, an officer knows to get in uniform and report to the office without waiting on a phone call. Most of the time phone lines are down or the lines are tied up.

The only highway fatalities occurred on the Golden State Freeway when the SSR 210 over-crossing collapsed on a 60 Chevrolet pickup truck, killing Arthur Mikkelsen, 46, and Milton Gonne, 45. The overall height of the truck was reduced in size to 15 inches. The drivers left arm was extended from the elbow outside of the crushed steel and the wrist watch was stopped at one minute past 6:00 am.

Another huge problem arose. The earthquake had damaged the Van Norman Lake dam that supplies water to the Los Angeles basin above Granada Hills. Early reports indicated the dam was damaged so severely it was inevitable that it would give way and cause massive flooding. It was estimated that water would be 10 feet above the top of the CHP office building.

The only thing we had going for us was that the freeways would act as barriers and divert the rushing water, allowing us about 20 minutes advance notice of the deluge. Evacuation boundaries were established and notification was being made to everyone in the path to leave immediately.

I was able to reach Laura by phone and she, Cheryl and Bob Jr. left within minutes for Bellflower.

She said, "What are you going to do?"

I told her we may have to seek "higher ground" which would probably be a freeway. There were no immediate plans for us to evacuate the Area office unless, or until, the dam broke.

To help prevent the Van Norman Lakes dam from breaking, the water was pumped from the lake by the Department of Water and Power at 1000 cubic feet per second which lowered it about one foot per hour. One of our officers was assigned there to keep us informed of the progress.

Gradually the water was reduced to a safe level and the area evacuation alert was removed.

Porno Films Next Door

Sometimes you can live for years and never get to know your next-door neighbor. West Valley was living proof of that. Our West Valley CHP office, a former funeral home, was in a business district surrounded by large metal buildings, each protected by sturdy 6-foot fences. Cars were parked on the streets and in the lots. There was ordinary foot traffic but overall it looked like any other manufacturing district.

But the building to our left—one with which we shared a common fence—was not your usual neighbor. A police raid revealed it to be a highly productive porno movie studio. I could only imagine what might of happened if the dam had broken and everyone had had to run for their lives.

Officer Scruggs Murdered

A little more than a month after the earthquake, on April 24, 1971, one of the sergeants asked me if I had heard that Officer Loren Scruggs, of the Santa Maria Area, had been shot and killed.

I mentioned that I had not heard, but asked them if they had any details about it.

One of the officers said he thought I might have some details, then he said: "Where were *you* four days ago?"

I knew the officer was only being light-hearted, but I wanted them to know that I had forgiven everyone who testified against me in the Santa Maria ordeal. And that included Officer Scruggs.

I told them, "Hate or revenge only destroys the individual who can't forgive."

The officer said, "I was only joking. I know you wouldn't do anything like that."

But I drew a conclusion from the conversation and attitude of those present (without them actually coming out and saying it) that I had a right to be upset for how I was treated in Santa Maria. And if they believed that then it meant others had also come to the same conclusion. So, maybe we did get the truth out after all.

Promotion to Lieutenant

The statewide CHP Lieutenant's examination was announced and the new Captain, Bob Cummings, asked me if I was going to take it. I had been acting Lieutenant in the absence of Lieutenants George House and John O'Brien.

Cummings noted that I had received a commendable incident report from the previous Captain, Gerald Clemons, when I was acting Field Operations Lieutenant and another commendable incident report for "attaining a score of 100% on the final exam" during the last In-Service Training Class at Sacramento.

On November 6, 1970, I received a Certificate of Award that read,"In appreciation of your constructive suggestion for improving the efficiency of the State Government" signed by Governor Ronald Reagan.

The day after I told Captain Cummings that I was interested in being promoted to Lieutenant, he removed me from being an active field sergeant and gave me a special assignment in the office to review all of the Area Standard Operational Procedures and make sure all of the Department Manuals were up to date.

"By the time you complete this project it will be just in time to take the Lieutenant's exam," Cummings said, with a sly smile.

At about this same time, I found out Commissioner Sullivan was now Mr. Sullivan and Governor Reagan was appointing Walter Pudinski the new Commissioner. Given the timing of the change and the fact that it was done in the middle of a term, caused me to think that the negative publicity generated by our hearings and Nancy's Reagan's role, had led to Sullivan's removal.

PART 1: *Chapter 14:* Big Win in Santa Maria   305

Pudinski had the distinction of being the first Commissioner appointed from the CHP ranks. And that selection process has continued throughout the years.

I studied very hard for the Lieutenant's examination and fortunately passed with a high score. On May 10, 1972, Captain Cummings called me into his office and said, "I've been informed they have an opening for Lieutenant at Headquarters in Sacramento and your name came up. It's in Planning Section and working at Headquarters will really broaden your experience. It's a real opportunity for you."

He said I would need to let him know within 48 hours, but I told him the next day I would take it.

Chapter 15
Assigned to CHP Headquarters

I left the family in Van Nuys and drove to Sacramento. The next morning I reported to Headquarters and went to my new assignment in Planning and Analysis Section. Planning and Analysis Section was just what one would expect. We were given projects requiring in-depth research and made recommendations. We were located on the top floor and were neighbors with the Office of Internal Affairs and the Commissioner's office. Every workday I would pass the interview room where Klippness and I had our "final interview" before being fired three years and eleven months earlier.

After about a year and a half, Inspector Harold Jones, who was now heading Planning and Analysis Section, told me that the California Highway Patrol was going to send two administrators to the next FBI National Academy in Quantico, Virginia, for a 3-month training session. I applied, along with other lieutenants and above, to the statewide selection committee.

Captain William Schilling, Commander of the Santa Fe Springs Area, and I were selected to attend the 98th Class and we drove back to Quantico in the Spring of 1974. There were law enforcement administrators from all 50 states and other countries attending the Academy located on the Marine Base in Quantico, Virginia.

In addition to advanced training in administrative and investigative techniques, one has an opportunity to exchange ideas with other law enforcement agencies. It gave me an excellent opportunity to discuss how other states and countries enforced DUI and their attitude toward the DUI problem although that was not a scheduled part of our training.

The training was excellent and a great experience. I did learn, however, there is a great difference in how laws are enforced in different parts of the United States. Although I found the officers to be dedicated and well-intentioned toward enforcement of driving under the influence, DUI was still looked upon as a high grade traffic offense as opposed to the senseless killing machine that it is.

With fairness to the officers, the majority were not State Troopers and didn't have the experience of investigating fatal DUI crashes. DUI is not just another traffic offense. On occasion it is murder and quite often it is manslaughter.

Challenge to Remove 200,000 Abandoned Cars

Shortly after returning from the FBI Academy, Commissioner Pudinski (who had replaced Sullivan) called me to his office and said, "I've got a special assignment I want to give you if you think you can handle it."

"Here's what I've got," he told me. "The Legislature has given us a $15.5 million dollar fund and directed us to put together a program to abate abandoned vehicles throughout the state. We have had three attorneys working on this for almost a year and we still don't have a program. One attorney representing the Highway Patrol, one the Division of Highways and the other from the Department of Transportation. They can't seem to agree on how it should be done and we can't wait any longer. It's a new program and you will have to start from scratch."

I asked Pudinski who else would be working on the project and he said, "Just you."

I told him I would like to do it, but asked if he could at least give me one sergeant to do some of the leg work and research. He said, "OK, I'll see that you get a sergeant, but I want the program up and running in 90 days."

I told him I would meet the deadline, even though I didn't know exactly what was involved at the time. It also concerned me that three lawyers couldn't do it in a year and I was expected to do it in three months. I reasoned that maybe they had too many personalities involved when sometimes a project like this calls for only a "benevolent dictator."

The Commissioner meant it when he said I would have to start from scratch. We did not get one piece of paper from the attorneys. In fact, I never met nor talked with them. I had five sections of the California Vehicle Code telling me what I could do and couldn't do. As long as the program complied with those guidelines, who could complain?

The next day the Inspector in charge of Planning Section called me to his office. It was obvious that he didn't know the Commissioner had already discussed the project with me and I wasn't about to volunteer it.

He said, "I've got a special assignment for you and I'm going to give you 90 days to complete it. The Commissioner requested that you handle the assignment. I'm also going to assign a sergeant to work with you."

I requested Sergeant Doc Wright, a friend of mine from Kentucky, and someone who was always good for a laugh even when we were handling serious matters.

The assignment was to develop a statewide program in all 58 counties and 412 incorporated cities whereby all derelict and abandoned vehicles were to be removed from the landscape. To accomplish this I was given a $15.5 million fund. The only source of information or directions would come from five newly enacted sections of the vehicle code and my ability to interpret them as the legislators intended. Success of the program would also require that I write an abandoned vehicle abatement manual that would be distributed to other states requesting them.

At the time I didn't even know, nor did anyone else, how many derelict and abandoned vehicles we had in California. We later determined there were 200,000, with an additional 80,000 more abandoned annually. The first year we abated 28,000 vehicles and signed up seven counties and 31 cities. The program was a tremendous success and is still very active today.

The following article appearing in the Sacramento Union, July 5, 1974, summarizes what happened after one year of operation:

"CHP Clearing the California Landscape" by Earl C. Waters.

"Have you an abandoned old clunker making your neighborhood blighted? If not, you are fortunate for it is estimated that there are over 200,000 discarded vehicles strewn along the California landscape. Recognizing the problem as one fast destroying the state's scenic beauty, Sen. Randolph Collier authored legislation to rid California of Detroit's outmoded products.

It called for a one-time assessment on every vehicle registration of $1 and was collected in 1973. This raised $15.5 million for the recovery and disposal of the mechanical outcasts. The funds were turned over to the California Highway patrol, which was assigned the job of carrying out the program. CHP created a vehicle abatement unit with the function of encouraging local government participation in the program, coordinating the activities, training personnel, negotiating with salvagers, and administering the fund. It named Lt. Bob Mitchell to head the unit.

"It appears they picked the right boy.

"Mitchell started with caution in July 1973, by launching pilot programs in three counties to iron out the procedures.

"By May of this year, some 28,000 vehicles had been cleared away as a direct result of the state's efforts.

"During the same period, contracts with 80 per cent of the cities and counties have been successfully negotiated for their participation.

"An unanticipated bonanza in the furtherance of the program has been inflation. Because of this, the price of junk rose to the point where salvagers have found it profitable in the urban areas to remove abandoned cars, either voluntarily or through contracts, at no cost to the state or local governments.

"One county, Napa, has lucked out with a contract by which salvagers will actually pay for the privilege of removing the cars.

"Another benefit has been the accrued interest on the initial fund which, because of Mitchell's studied approach in developing an untried program, has grown to more than $17 million.

"As a result of the two things—inflation in junk prices and interest accruals, the fund raised by the one-time assessment, which had been estimated to last only five years, now appears to be good indefinitely.

"In working out the contracts with local governments Mitchell negotiated a unit cost averaging $16 to reimburse for administrative expenses only. Removal costs were not included and it now appears there will be none due to increased prices for junk.

"Mitchell showed great wisdom in his approach to the payments. By establishing that funds would only be paid on the basis of reimbursement for cars actually removed, he avoided the kind of boondoggle which often occurs when money is merely parceled out on the basis of estimated needs.

"Past experience has shown that in many such cases the money is dissipated without achieving its purpose.

"Another interesting fact about Mitchell's operation is that he has operated his program with a headquarters staff of only himself and three others.

"And, his crew to operate the pilot programs in three counties numbered only eight, all of which are now being decommissioned and assigned back to other duties.

"Mitchell's record of conserving funds, refraining from empire building, and admirable progress in getting the program rolling is as unusual as it is remarkable. The state could use more administrators of his caliber."

When this article appeared in the newspaper I was as surprised as anyone else. But rumors started circulating at headquarters that I knew the columnist, Earl Waters, and had planted the story.

The truth is, not only did I not know the columnist, I had never met him nor was I ever interviewed by him or anyone else for this article. There were hundreds of articles about the abandoned vehicle abatement program in newspapers and magazines throughout the United States. The Highway Patrol has a public relations employee at Headquarters who searches newspapers and magazines every day for articles that pertain to the California Highway Patrol. She cuts out the articles and makes them into a book. I have three books of newspaper clippings in reference to the abandoned vehicle abatement program during the time I had it.

Being appointed the Section Commander of the AVA program, I traveled frequently throughout the state meeting with mayors and city officials. Doc Wright and I named the program AVA so we wouldn't have to spell it out each time. I was told that the legislators were becoming displeased because I was not spending enough of the $15.5 million and it was becoming an embarrassment to them. Especially, since it had grown to $17 million. I was told, "If you don't get rid of the money, they're going to give it to Parks and Recreation."

We did have some abandoned and derelict cars in some difficult locations, such as forests, Catalina Island and the Santa Monica beach.

The abandoned cars on the Santa Monica beach were those left by the movie industry after making movies like the "Keystone Cops" where they drove the cars off of the cliffs and just left them there.

I had an adage on my office desk that I lived by that read, "There's always a better way." So, I thought I would try something new: using helicopters. Back then you could rent a helicopter for about $200 an hour. This way we could spend more money, remove derelict vehicles from the environment in places that were inaccessible to tow trucks and create some favorable publicity.

When the news media discovered what we had planned they were there to cover it. Removing the vehicles from the Santa Monica beach generated the most excitement. ABC, CBS and NBC were there covering it nationally.

It was a spectacular sight seeing a helicopter pulling the damaged and abandoned vehicles from the sand at the bottom of the cliffs with cables more than 100 feet long and then the cars dangling from the helicopter over the blue Pacific ocean. Surprisingly, there were more abandoned vehicles there than first thought. They were stacked one upon the other. I couldn't help but reflect back to when I was a youngster in Fort Smith, Arkansas, watching the movies and not knowing someday I would be responsible for removing those very cars from the bottom of the cliffs. I also wondered how the movie producers got by with just leaving them where they landed.

I met with the officials on Catalina Island. They only had a couple of dozen abandoned cars so we came to the conclusion it would be more economical to barge them to the mainland than to rent a helicopter. We also cleaned out the forests and national parks using helicopters but the tow companies were paying us for the junk cars so we weren't spending much of the fund.

Later, after I left for another assignment, there was $17.5 million in the fund or $2 million more than what I started with and the legislators were not happy. They ended up giving most of the AVA fund to the Parks & Recreation Department.

I only wish that I had gotten an assignment to put together a more aggressive DUI program for the Department.

Representing the CHP Commissioner

During the time I was heading the AVA program, Commissioner Pudinski phoned and said, "If you're free come over to my office, I've got a special detail for you."

I thought to myself, here we go again.

The first thing Pudinski said was, "You play golf, don't you?"

I said, "Yes sir, when I have time."

"Well, how would you like to take my place in Palm Springs for a couple of days? You can take your wife."

I knew it was going to be more than just golf, so I said, "What else will I be expected to do?"

He said, "I'm scheduled to speak to about 300 tow truck operators and their wives at their annual convention explaining the abandoned vehicle abatement program. I'm going to be busy those two days and, besides, I don't know enough details about the operation to answer their questions. I think it would be best that you take my place and just tell them I would like to be there but I have another commitment. You can also take my place at the Rancho Mirage Golf course if you want to take your clubs."

I thanked the Commissioner and told him I would be delighted to take his place at the convention and at the golf course.

A few days later, as we were flying to Palm Springs, I reminded Laura (as if she needed reminding) that less than 5 years ago I was fired for incompetency, inefficiency, inexcusable neglect of duty, insubordination, willful disobedience and now, for the next two days, we would be representing the Commissioner in Palm Springs.

But then I also remembered that shortly before I was fired for refusing to stop arresting drunk drivers, I had put my trust in the Lord, and that it was His battle and that He would see us through. Now that the battle was over, Proverbs 3:5 came to mind, "Trust in the Lord with all your heart; and lean not on your own understanding. In all your ways acknowledge Him, and He shall direct your paths." I was thankful the battle was His and not mine. I'm not sure the Highway Patrol was aware of who they were up against.

20/40 Program

Normally, Officers assigned CHP Headquarters are rotated out after two years and I had been there two years so I was surprised when I was chosen for another special assignment. The Highway Patrol on occasion would select officers, usually lieutenants and above, to attend college on state time. It was referred to as a 20/40 program. It was a program for officers that the Department planned on promoting so it was considered a choice assignment.

It worked this way: The Highway Patrol would pay an officer full salary plus all college expenses to attend, in this case, California State University Sacramento, until the officer obtained his degree. The one requirement was for the officer to have enough units so that he could graduate with a Bachelor of Arts Degree within two semesters.

I would go to class 20 hours a week and work in Planning and Analysis Section 20 hours a week for a total of 40 hours. I appreciated the assignments and I have always suspected that Commissioner Pudinski had a lot to do with me getting them. I can't prove this, but I think he knew the truth of what happened in Santa Maria and he was making up for it and the $6,300 I lost in salary.

I graduated from California State University, January 14, 1975.

Commissioner Pudinski Retires

In 1975, Edmund "Jerry" Brown Jr., son of Edmund "Pat" Brown Sr., became Governor of California and appointed Glenn Craig, Commissioner of the California Highway Patrol. That was not good news because Craig was from Visalia where Thobe had been transferred and he was not all that friendly. He also played on a softball team that I managed—so I knew him more than just casually.

Pudinski invited Laura and me to come to his retirement dinner. There were a fairly large number of people attending, but one person in particular stood out. As we were being seated at the table for dinner, Commissioner Pudinski and one of his friends approached us. Pudinski said, "Thank you for coming and I would like to introduce you to a friend of mine. This is Richard Turner. He works for the Attorney General's office."

Out of respect for Pudinski, I restricted my comment to, "We've met before." During the entire event, we both sat at the same table. Although it was difficult, I had a peace of mind because I had forgiven him. Nevertheless, we didn't say one word to each other the entire evening.

Assigned to Operational Dispatch Section

On August 15, 1975, I was assigned as Section Commander of the Operational Dispatch Center from the Abandoned Vehicle Abatement Section. The Dispatch Center was in the basement of the same building for security reasons. I supervised one sergeant, four state traffic officers, and 18 non-uniform personnel. I was just waiting for the South Sacramento Area office to have an opening for a lieutenant so I could transfer there and get back to DUI enforcement. There was supposed to be an opening in 37 days and I had seniority over all of the lieutenants who had requested there. We owned a home in Sacramento and wanted to remain here. Bob Jr. our youngest son, was a sergeant on the Sacramento Police Department and Cheryl was working for the Department of Justice. But now there were individuals at Headquarters that had other plans for me. They hadn't forgotten Santa Maria so it was "pay back time."

Skulduggery Used in Transfer and Captain's promotional Exam

While working at the Operational Dispatch Center I took the Captain's examination on September 11, 1976, and was told confidentially (by a key person I knew in Personal Section) that I had placed Number 13 on the list and would be promoted. In fact, she said she wanted to be the first to congratulate me.

But about 10 days later, the same person phoned and said, "Your Management Assessment score was changed and other things are going on with the Employee Development Appraisal (EDA) Rating Committee and that's all I can tell you."

She added, "I want you to know that I had nothing to do with it. I just want you to know that."

I was disappointed but not surprised. I knew things had changed since Glenn Craig had taken over as Commissioner. This would never have happened while Pudinski was in charge. But I wasn't going to sit idly by either.

In the meantime, I was asked by Inspector Ben Killingsworth if I would mind being transferred back to Operational Planning Section because, "We've got a lieutenant in there that is incompetent. We've got to get him out of there."

PART 1: *Chapter 15:* Assigned to CHP Headquarters 317

I thought to myself, if they want me back in Planning Section then I can just wait until the Sacramento Area opens and transfer from there. So I agreed and was transferred to Operational Planning Section on December 1. The "incompetent" lieutenant was still there but he told me he was being transferred to the Sacramento Area in a couple of weeks. I suddenly realized that I had been had.

I had been working at Planning Section for only one day when I was advised that Assistant Commissioner Bob Smith wanted to talk with me in his office.

"Mitchell, I just want you to know we are going to transfer you to Los Angeles in about 45 days."

I said, "I don't want to go to Los Angeles. Sacramento is open and I have the most seniority . . . "

Smith cut me off and said, "If Clemons (Assistant Commissioner and brother-in-law of Killingsworth) doesn't say you get the area, you're not going to get the area. You're going to go where we send you so you might as well prepare yourself."

I responded, "Well, I don't think this is right. I've been waiting here for five years for this. I have the most seniority and the supposedly incompetent lieutenant I replaced in Planning Section is now taking my place in Sacramento."

Smith said, "Well, think it over."

I told him I was filing a grievance against the Department.

Ed Maghakian said the California Association of Highway Patrolmen (CAHP) would support me on both the changing of my Captain's test scores and the unlawful transfer to Los Angeles.

At Maghakian's request, Commissioner Craig and Chief Watkins agreed to meet with us on January 17, 1977, and tell us why I was being transferred in violation of the Department's General Order 10.7, which prohibits arbitrary transfers of lieutenants and below.

Maghakian told them, "I don't want to see the men in my Association being transferred around like they are cattle. I think you owe it to Lieutenant Mitchell to tell him why he is not getting the Sacramento area."

Chief Watkins would only say, "He'll be told."

But Maghakian pushed for an answer, telling Watkins that getting an answer was the whole reason for the meeting.

Finally, Craig gave one reason and cited three examples. He said I had used "poor judgment" by not selecting his friend, Sergeant Hyatt, to work with me in Planning Section. I chose Sergeant Curt Harjo who went on to make Assistant Chief while Hyatt retired as sergeant.

And Craig said I used poor judgment when I worked the Baldwin Park area. It was in the Baldwin Park Area where I was commended for my "outstanding contribution in training and directing officers" and was responsible for an average monthly increase of over 200 % in DUI arrests (119 vs. 255).

Then, in desperation, Craig mentioned Santa Maria, which, in my opinion, was the real reason for his actions.

Craig knew he had put his foot in his mouth by mentioning Santa Maria and later tried to justify his slip at the appeals hearing. He told the Hearing Officer James Waller, "I did mention Santa Maria; I told him immediately thereafter that that punitive action was behind us. I should not have made reference to it, but in my personal knowledge trying to immediately grasp a particular point where I knew that he had been talked to in regard to his judgment, I used that example. It was not a good example and probably should not have been used."

Since Craig could not come up with any valid reason for not granting the local transfer and his blunder in mentioning Santa Maria, so he said, "I'm going to direct Chief Clemons to meet with you immediately and explain fully why you are being transferred."

I was anxious to meet with Chief "Jerry" Clemons, who I had known for years, to see what phony excuse he would come up with and I wasn't disappointed.

PART 1: *Chapter 15:* Assigned to CHP Headquarters

I asked Clemons, "Would you tell me why I'm not being transferred to the Sacramento area?"

He said he didn't want to get into it and I said, "Well, just give me some type of reason."

And he said, "You agree with the boss too much."

I said, "I agree with the boss too much?"

Clemons said, yes, and I said, "Are you saying that I'm supposed to disagree with the boss?"

And he replied, "Well, maybe at times."

I said, "Well, Chief, there's a way of disagreeing with people without being offensive. I'm not the type of person that raises my voice or displays emotion. I like to sit down and reason things out."

Clemons said, "Well, that's it, you've got your reason."

I said, "Well, you'd have to concede, I'm not agreeing with the boss on my transfer."

Clemons laughed and that was the end of the conversation. Shortly thereafter, I was transferred to Monterey.

I was officially notified on December 14th, that I had been "disqualified" as a candidate for State Traffic Captain. I filed an appeal three days later with the State Personnel Board and immediately contacted Officer Ed Maghakian, President of the California Association of Highway Patrolman and told him what was going on.

Maghakian, a real straight shooter, said, "Bob, I'm not surprised. We'll do what we can to help you." and then made arrangements through the Association for an attorney, Richard Romanski, to handle the appeal.

The appeal hearing was set for February 16, 1977, at the State Personnel Board, to be heard by Hearing Officer Gianelli.

If it had gotten to the news media that the Captain test scores had been changed, that two lists existed and one was "lost," and that the Employee Appraisal (EDA) Rating Committee was given a list of who the Department wanted promoted prior to the interviews, there would have been a statewide scandal of major proportions.

This was the last thing the Department wanted to happen, so I was given a new EDA interview in San Francisco and placed number two on the Captain's list. But I was warned, "You may have won the battle but you lost the war."

No further captains were appointed and the list expired.

The lieutenant that was number one on the list was told "not to worry," he would be "taken care of" on the next list.

Chapter 16
Transferred to Monterey

On February 1, 1977, I was transferred to the Monterey Area, which was actually located between Salinas and Monterey.

Monterey County is one of the most beautiful places in California. Carmel By the Sea, Big Sur, Seventeen Mile Drive, Pebble Beach, Carmel (inland), and the Laguna Seca Raceway make up the area. We had a large area of responsibility: Highway 1 running next to the Pacific Ocean from Santa Cruz almost to Hearst Castle in San Simeon and then Hwy 101 from King City almost to San Juan Bautista. It included the small town of Soledad where the Soledad State Correctional Facility is located. Inland is mostly farming with a large sugar factory made famous by writer John Steinbeck, who was born in Salinas.

This is an area steeped in history. Steinbeck, whose home is now part of downtown Salinas, was known for writing numerous books including "The Grapes of Wrath" in 1939 and "East of Eden." James Dean, who starred in the "East of Eden" film that was shot in the area in 1954, was killed the next year, on September 30, 1955, in a solo accident in nearby King City en route to Laguna Seca Raceway. He had a speeding ticket in his pocket that he had received only a few minutes earlier from the California Highway Patrol. The cause of the accident was determined to be excessive speed.

In my new position I would be supervising 7 sergeants, 61 traffic officers and 12 non-uniform radio dispatchers. I was also told that I would be working for the most difficult captain in the state.

I had never met Captain Dan Lyons, but when I did meet him, I found there was nothing phony about him. He said he had been told a lot of things about me. Some good and some bad, but that he didn't really care what somebody else thought about me. He'd "make up his own mind."

Lyons said, "I've had my disagreements with them myself so I know what's going on. They're not fooling anybody. I'm glad you're here and I know you'll do a good job."

"But there is one thing," he said, "No one uses a green felt pen in the office but me. Write with any color you want but *no* green."

I was in my office putting things away, organizing the desk, and emptying boxes when one of the sergeants came in to meet and welcome me to the Monterey Area office. I had some felt pens laying on the desk and the sergeant pointed toward them and said, "You better get rid of the green one."

I said, "It's OK as long as I don't use it."

The sergeant said, "No. He doesn't want one in the office. Someone might pick it up by mistake."

When I went home that evening, I was laughing when I told Laura about it, but it wasn't long before I thought it was a good idea.

Captain Lyons and I each had a cruiser that we kept all of the time.

He said "When you get called out at night, I don't want you to have to drive to the office and pickup a cruiser. You can respond straight from your home."

We actually lived in an apartment because I had no intention of staying there. As new cruisers were assigned to the office, I would get one to break-in before it was put on regular patrol.

Lyons also told me I could work any hours I wanted as long as I put 40 hours in a week: "You decide when you want to work days or nights. I don't care as long as you get the job done."

Of course, I recorded the actual times I worked on an Official Time Sheet. Most of the time I chose to work evenings.

Doing the Job You're Hired to Do

I didn't have to tell the troops that DUI was a high priority because they already knew. Some of the officers were not all that enthused about arresting DUIs but this wasn't Santa Maria and Dan Lyons wasn't Don Thobe. It was time to go to work.

Checking the officers' monthly activity forms, I noticed that one sergeant in particular didn't have much enforcement activity. He appeared disinterested in the job and came across extremely liberal. I was beginning to wonder what he was doing when he was supposed to be working, so I called him into the office one day after briefing.

I asked him about his lack of activity and no DUI arrests.

He said, "I write what I see."

I said, "I wonder why the other sergeants consistently see more violations than you do?"

He said, "I don't know. Maybe they write things I wouldn't write and arrest people I wouldn't arrest."

"Do you believe they're making bad arrests?" I asked.

The sergeant said, "It all depends on how you look at it."

I shifted gears and asked, "Do you believe in the Department's policy of enforcement?"

And he said, "No. Lieutenant, I don't think we are accomplishing anything by writing tickets. The only reason we write tickets is for the revenue. It doesn't have a thing to do with preventing accidents."

I asked him how he arrived at that conclusion?

He said, "Do you think some one is going to slow down just because you write them a ticket? Just as soon as you're out of sight, they're going to speed again."

I asked him what his solution was to reducing accidents and he said, "Being in view. As long as they see a black and white they're going to obey the law. That's all we can do."

I told the sergeant that we were going to have to have "a meeting of the minds."

"You are paid a fairly good salary to go out here and enforce the law. Not the law the way you see it, but the law the way the State of California sees it. If you don't believe in the department's policy of enforcement then you better get another job, because you're not going to be working here."

About a month later the sergeant came in to the office and wanted to talk. First he said, "Did you know that I have lived in Salinas all of my life. I was fortunate to be able to transfer here out of the Academy. I have a family and a home almost paid for and I planned on retiring here."

I was beginning to wonder where we were going with the conversation when he said, "I'm transferring to the Santa Rosa area this month and do you know why?"

I said, "I have no idea."

He said very emphatically, "To get away from you."

I responded, "Are you sure it's not to get away from working?" He would not be the last officer to transfer because he didn't want to do his job.

Coast Highway 1 is Unique

Highway 1, which is often referred to as the Coast Highway, is unique in many ways. In most of its 72 miles, it follows the California Coast with its rugged canyons and steep cliffs, majestic redwood forests and pristine coastline. Highway 1, except for a short freeway portion as it passes through Monterey, is a winding two-lane highway with pleasant bends and curves and sheer rocky cliffs on one side and the blue Pacific Ocean with crashing waves on the other.

It's not an area where you would want to get involved in a pursuit. Responding to an emergency call was an experience.

On the third day at work, while I was still organizing my new office, one of the dispatchers stuck her head in the room and said, "We just got a call of a motor home going over the cliff on Highway 1 north of Big Sur. We have a unit on the way."

I dropped everything I was doing and responded. Traveling code three, it still took about 25 minutes to get there.

In this rare case, there were no serious injuries and the motor home stopped before it reached the water. Most of the coastline is not that forgiving. Normally, when a car went over one of the cliffs it landed in the ocean and the tide quickly took it out to sea, which made it a popular highway for suicides.

One lady drove all the way from Beverly Hills to plunge her Mercedes into the ocean. One reason it was so popular for suicides is that loved ones could always speculate it was an accident. And without witnesses, how could one know? A Rule of Thumb we used was the physical evidence at the scene and, in the case of possible suicides, we are talking about tire markings, lack of skid marks, angle of entry, how far the vehicle traveled through the air and several other telltales. Of course, following up on a person's state of mind prior to the "accident" helped in most cases. If it's a suicide, it's not an accident, and the reports are forwarded to the Sheriff's Department. Properly determining the cause is important because it may have an effect upon an insurance settlement.

I think I Hit Something

One night near midnight I was working late in the office when one of the female dispatchers came into my office and told me someone was knocking on the front door. I could see it was a small elderly woman as I opened the door.

Instead of entering, she calmly stood there and said, "I think I hit something."

I asked, "Why do you think that?"

She said, "I just do."

As I started walking out of the door, I said, "Let's look at your car."

Her car was parked a few feet from the front door and it was well illuminated by the street lights.

I was thinking I might need a flashlight until I looked at the right front windshield. There was a hole the size of an adult head and extensive damage to the front part of the car. Even without a flashlight I could see human hair and blood around the hole.

I said, "You hit something alright. And it was probably a human being."

The hole in the windshield was so large it would not have surprised me to find a head in the right front seat.

First priority was to find the victim, and second, was to find out if this little old lady was DUI.

I asked, "Where were you when you thought you hit something?"

She pointed in an easterly direction and said she thought she was on Highway 68. "It was only a mile or two down the road."

I told the dispatcher to have any units in the area check for a possible body in the roadway on Highway 68. With the elderly lady in my cruiser, I asked her to direct me to the spot where she thought she "hit something." But before we even drove out of the lot, one of the units said they had found a male body lying in a ditch, obviously deceased.

The lady asked if it would be possible for us not to go over there because she didn't want to see the body. I saw no need to go to the scene because she had openly, and without hesitation, answered all of the questions concerning the accident.

It was my opinion that the lady was not under the influence of alcohol, drugs or medication but was possibly suffering from shock. She was transported to a hospital and checked by a doctor who came to the same conclusion.

Physical evidence at the scene indicated the deceased was walking in a lane of traffic when he was hit, his clothing was dark (almost the same color as the pavement) and he had been drinking. Lighting was poor and there were no witnesses.

The lady was technically guilty of hit-and-run, but no court would ever convict her since she drove directly to the Highway Patrol Office, only minutes away, and was in a state of shock. The conclusion of the investigating officers was the deceased was the primary cause of the accident. There were no charges brought against the driver.

Police Brutality—ACLU Style

The clerk-typist at the front desk "buzzed" my office and said there was an attorney from the ACLU that wanted to file a police brutality case against two of our officers. The attorney was in her late 20's, petite, formal, and carrying an attache case as well as her purse. She handed me her business card and then got right down to business.

"I'm here to get a copy of an arrest report involving two of your officers. They arrested two of my clients for kidnapping and attempted rape and, in doing so, used excessive force amounting to police brutality." I asked the clerk-typist to bring us two copies of the arrest report because I wanted to go over the details of the arrest with the attorney.

After handing her a copy of the arrest report, I said, "I'm familiar with this incident because I have already talked with the arresting officers."

She said, "Yes, did they tell you that they smashed one of my client's heads down on the hood of the patrol car and bloodied his nose?"

I told her, "They didn't use the word 'smashed' but they did say he received a bloody nose during a scuffle when they were trying to handcuff him."

"Yes, and they also treated the second young man very roughly and I want to make an official charge against them for police brutality now," she said. "They had no right to treat them so badly."

"Do you have any other complaint against the officers other than what you have already mentioned?" I asked.

She replied, "Nothing else other than they put the handcuffs on too tight."

I then asked her, "Are you interested in hearing the officers' side of the story?"

She indicated she was not there to defend the officers but the arrestees.

I said," Well, would you be interested in hearing what your clients did to the 14 and 15 year old girls?"

She commented, "It's immaterial what they did to the girls. That has nothing to do with the brutality charges. That's a separate matter."

I told her I understood where she was coming from and that technically she was right, but "what about the human element?"

She said, "What do you mean?"

"We have two young teenage girls who jumped out of a car, ran for their lives, were caught and thrown down on a gravel road, skinned, bruised and crying hysterically. They were in the process of being raped when two of our officers rolled up in a cruiser. You, being a woman, can't you relate to that?"

She said, "I've talked to my clients and that's not what they told me happened."

"Did they by any chance tell you that after they bailed out, they called the rape victims' homes and threatened to kill them if they testify against them in court?"

For the first time the attorney got serious and said, "No they didn't tell me that. I didn't know they knew them."

"I'll bet they didn't tell you they fought with the officers either," I added.

I said, "I want you to know that I take police brutality very serious. I've investigated several cases for the Department where an officer has used excessive force that resulted in the officer being fired or resigning. I have

PART 1: *Chapter 16:* Transferred to Monterey 329

no sympathy for an officer who uses excessive force, even to the point of filing criminal charges against him." In this case, the officer admitted that he pushed the subject's head down on the hood of the car that resulted in him getting a bloody nose but the little girls he was trying to rape had more serious injuries. Whose looking out for them?"

The attorney didn't say anything and appeared to be thinking about what I had said, and at the same time, studying me to see if I was "for real." She didn't want someone "conning" her and I wasn't trying.

I continued, "I've got a proposal for you. You're a woman and I know you can relate to what these young teenagers went through and are still going through by being threatened. Would you take 24 hours to think it over, now that you have heard the other side of the story, and if you still want to file against the officers who saved these young girls from being raped, then we'll do the paperwork and I won't say another word."

The attorney put the report in her attache case and said, "That's fine with me and thank you for your time."

I never heard from or saw the ACLU attorney again.

Police Brutality for Real

As the only Lieutenant in Monterey, I was always on call but I really didn't mind. All I had to do was put on my uniform and get in the cruiser downstairs. Laura and I were living in a 2-story apartment and just waiting for an opportunity to get back to Sacramento.

About three o'clock one morning I got a call from dispatch that there was a multi-agency pursuit that finally ended in a "spin-out" in Seaside, a small city north of Monterey. The pursuit involved four separate law enforcement agencies, in addition to our two CHP officers in a single cruiser. The vehicle was recently stolen and was driven by a 21-year old male who was arrested and booked by our officers.

About a month later, I got a phone call from Assistant Chief W.E. Costello advising me that the Department wanted me to investigate a charge of police brutality against the two officers involved in the pursuit. Most of the time the Highway Patrol brought investigators in from Sacramento or from Zone Headquarters—especially if an investigation may result in dismissal. I told Chief Costello I had no problem doing the investigation

The first thing I did was talk to the complainant who was an attorney in downtown Monterey. He told me his client had suffered injuries from a beating that he had received at the time of the arrest. He gave me a copy of photographs of the injuries and copies of hospital bills, as well as other documents.

The first thing I discovered was there were officers from five different agencies including the Highway Patrol. And it's no secret that officers don't like to testify against other officers. But, fortunately, most officers are honest.

The attorney cooperated with me in every respect except for one request. "You can't talk to my client," he said, "If you have any questions of him, just call me and I'll get the answer for you."

The next step was interviewing the two CHP officers separately, one right after the other, on tape. Of course, they already had more than a month to get their story together.

But as far as I was concerned, both officers were innocent unless there was evidence to the contrary. I had an officer at Headquarters tell me one day: "If I was innocent I would want you doing the investigation but if I was guilty, I wouldn't want you anywhere around."

After questioning the officers, I came to the conclusion they were not leveling with me and were hiding something. They both did agree the arrestee was injured, as the photographs depicted, but they weren't the ones responsible.

"There were a lot of officers there and a lot of commotion going on," they both said. They both also said they didn't see who hit him. The next step was to interview the witnesses, who were all police officers, and find out what they may have seen.

I had to get permission from each Police Department Chief to interview the officers. I had to convince them I would conduct a fair and honest

PART 1: Chapter 16: Transferred to Monterey

investigation. All of the Chiefs agreed and directed the officers to be cooperative and forthright. All the officers basically said that when the pursuit ended there was a lot of "turmoil" and "excitement," but three of them said the CHP officers actually made the physical arrests and may have hit him a couple of times.

To help the witnesses remember and to get a clearer picture of what happened, I came up with an idea I had never used before. I drew a diagram to scale of the scene and then made ten copies of the diagram. Then I re-interviewed everyone and gave each officer their own copy of the diagram and asked them to put down their time of arrival and departure. To draw where they parked their patrol car and the positions of all of the other patrol cars they could remember. And lastly, where they, and anyone else they could remember, were standing when the suspect was taken from the vehicle. After I put it all together on one color-coded diagram, the picture became very clear.

Upon completion of the investigation (about 150 pages plus annexes) and based upon the witnesses saying unnecessary force was used, and after being confronted with overwhelming evidence of their guilt, the officers finally admitted they may have struck the arrestee. I recommended the officers be dismissed and they were. Had the Officers been honest about the arrest they would only have gotten time off.

A month later the officers filed an appeal and volunteered to take a polygraph test to prove they had been honest. A polygraph technician from the Department of Justice administered the tests at the Salinas Police Department. I was informed the Officers had passed the polygraph tests and I asked to speak with the technician before he left to return to Sacramento. When I arrived at the Police Department, the polygraph technician was packed and ready to leave.

I asked him how it was possible that the officers passed the polygraph tests.

He said, "They said they didn't hit the suspect and I believe they were telling the truth."

I said, "They admitted to me that they hit him, so something's wrong."

The technician said, "That's my finding," and started walking away.

I said, "Now, you know why polygraph tests are not admissible in court. They're only as reliable as the person giving the test."

Both officers were returned to the job.

Despite the reversal of the officers' dismissals, I received the following commendable incident report from the California Highway Patrol.

"You were the primary Investigating Supervisor in a Punitive Action case which resulted in the recommended dismissal of two members of the Department who were assigned to the Monterey Area.

"It was an extremely complex case, actually two cases being investigated concurrently and arising from the same incident, and was further complicated by the fact that the incident was not brought to the attention of the Department for some time after it occurred.

"The investigation was quite sensitive in that it necessitated contacting and re-contacting numerous members of several allied agencies, some of whom were to some degree involved in the incident themselves.

"You completed the investigation and prepared files which were complete, accurate, well-documented, and merited concurrence with Area's recommendations by both Division and the Office of internal Affairs.

"Your efforts are noted and appreciated."

W.E. Costello, Assistant Chief

Big Sur Life or Death Negotiation

Big Sur, a community located on Highway 1 overlooking the Pacific Ocean and nestled on the edge of the Los Padres National redwood forest, was handled by a resident officer assigned out of our Monterey Area office. Because of its location, about 40 miles south of Carmel by the Sea on Highway 1, I didn't get down there very often. The CHP officer lived there and because he was subject to "call out," he was assigned his own cruiser.

PART 1: Chapter 16: Transferred to Monterey 333

On occasion he would have to call for assistance and one of those times occurred at about noon one day.

I received a radio dispatch that the resident officer was requesting immediate assistance. An irate husband had forcibly taken his wife into the redwood forest and was threatening to kill her. He had a gun to her head and would not let anyone approach him. The CHP officer and two sheriffs were talking to him but he was becoming more agitated and threatening, telling them: "If anyone comes any closer, I'm going to kill her."

I advised I was en route to the location but I asked the dispatcher if she could call the Monterey Police Department and see if they had a SWAT team with a negotiator that could also respond. In just a few minutes she radioed, "You're not going to believe this but there is an Emergency Response Team (ERT) training class being held in Monterey right now. I had to convince them that my request was not part of the training. They are responding now."

As soon as I arrived, the CHP resident officer said, "We've got an idea that we think will work but I told the sheriffs I would have to get approval. The suspect said he will not talk to any law enforcement officer except a Highway Patrolman. One of the sheriffs suggested that we change uniforms. He believes he can talk him into giving up if he can get close enough to him."

I told him, "It sounds good to me. Go ahead."

They changed uniforms and the sheriff gradually worked his way into the wooded area and in about 10 minutes the suspect surrendered his weapon and they all three emerged without incident.

I had dispatch cancel the Emergency Response Team, which was only minutes away at the time. I'm not sure that the ERT was thoroughly convinced this wasn't a planned part of their training that day.

Officer Acting Strange

We had some very good officers working out of the Monterey area. One of those officers started complaining of headaches and not feeling well. I talked with him and asked him if he had gone to a doctor. He said he had but the doctor couldn't find anything wrong. The officer said he had not felt the same since he had investigated a DUI traffic accident where a car had gone over the side and ended up in some bushes.

As the days went on the officer started acting strange. His partner told me he was saying strange things and just acting different. His face would get flushed at times. As a last resort, we finally decided that the officer might be having mental problems so we suggested that he take a few days off and visit his family in the Los Angeles area. We thought they might be able to help him.

I got a phone call the next day from the officer from San Luis Obispo where he had gone to an emergency hospital while en route to Los Angeles.

He said, "I got to feeling so bad I thought I was going to die. While the doctor was examining me, one of the nurses saw a spider crawling out of my ear. The doctor thinks that when I worked that traffic accident in the bushes I got these spiders in my ear. What a relief. You can't imagine how happy I am to find out what was causing this"

The officer had no further problems and returned to his same high level of performance.

President Gerald Ford Security

The 17-Mile Drive, part of the Monterey area of responsibility, runs inland past Spanish Bay, then adjacent to beaches, providing scenic viewpoints. The most famous being the Lone Cypress Tree, the official symbol of Pebble Beach where the National Pro-AM golf games are played.

In February, 1978, President Gerald Ford was playing golf at Pebble Beach and I was assigned to work with the Secret Service providing security and other protective services. Without revealing any security details, the Former President was adequately protected and we spent most of the day with him. There was some joking about protecting the spectators from him during some of his drives off of the tee, but it was all done in fun.

After President Ford finished his round of golf around 4 pm, we transported him to the Monterey Peninsula Airport on Highway 68. We drove into the airport and stopped near the runway where a private plane was scheduled

PART 1: *Chapter 16:* Transferred to Monterey 335

to pick up him and his daughter and take them to his home in Rancho Mirage, in Southern California. One of the Secret Service agents asked me to remain with the President and said he and the others would be right back.

It took me a couple of seconds to realize that there was just the two of us, President Ford and I, standing on the Tarmac alone waiting for an airplane to arrive. There were two things I noticed about him.

The first was his size. I knew that he was an outstanding football player for the University of Michigan so I had pictured him to be pretty big. But I noticed that he and I were almost the same size, 6 foot, 200 lbs. He might have been a little smaller.

Secondly, after standing there and talking with him, I came to the conclusion that he was one of the friendliest, most down-to-earth persons I have ever met. He asked me how long I had been on the Highway Patrol, about my family and if I played golf.

After we had talked for a few minutes he said, "Would you like to meet my daughter?"

I said, "Sure."

He turned around and motioned for his daughter to come over where we were and said, "Susan, this is Lieutenant Mitchell." We greeted each other and then she walked back were she had been. Most of our conversation was about golf and whether he would be returning the next day to Pebble Beach. He said he didn't know because he had a party he had to go to that night. Shortly thereafter, the Secret Service returned and the plane arrived.

Jack Nicklaus Not Having a Good Day

Jack Nicklaus was playing golf at Pebble Beach one day and ran out of gas on his way to the golf course. One of our officers, Don Scott, stopped to assist him.

While Scott was driving him to a gas station, Nicklaus mentioned he was playing in a golf tournament at Pebble Beach. Scott, knowing absolutely nothing about golf or golfers, asked Nicklaus how he was doing.

Nicklaus said, "I'm not playing very well." Then Nicklaus assuming the officer played golf, gave him three golf balls in a packet, in appreciation for the officers assistance.

Scott said, "Thank you but I don't play golf. My lieutenant does though."

Nicklaus said, "Then give them to him."

I was in my office when Scott came in, put the packet of golf balls on the desk and said, "Here's some golf balls for you."

I inquired, "Where did you get them.?"

Scott said this golfer had run out of gas and wanted to give him the golf balls for assisting him. I asked, "Who was he? He must have been a pretty good golfer if he was playing in a tournament at Pebble Beach."

Scott said, "No. He told me he wasn't playing very well. He told me his name but I can't remember what it was."

I reached over and opened the packet and took out one of the golf balls. In gold lettering on the ball it read, "Jack Nicklaus."

I said, "Was his name Jack Nicklaus?"

He said, "Yeah. That's who it was."

I told Scott if Nicklaus said he wasn't having a good game that meant he was probably shooting a 68 or more." Of course, Scott didn't know what that meant so I said, "Jack Nicklaus is probably the best golfer in the world." I thanked Scott for his thoughtfulness but also reminded him that Highway Patrolmen are not suppose to accept gifts for doing their job.

Filing Another Grievance Against the Commissioner

Most of the officers, especially the lieutenants, throughout the state had heard about my problems at Headquarters—changing the scores on a Captain's promotional examination and then transferring a lieutenant without the authority. Needless to say, there was a hue and cry because they knew if it could happen to me then it could happen to them.

The fact I had fought the Department and beat them in Santa Maria only added more credibility to what was happening.

In addition, I was telling everyone I could, in person and by phone, what the Department had done and was still doing. I believe when you are being wronged, you should tell the world. Officers were finding out for the first time what some administrators are capable of doing.

The California Association of Highway Patrolmen (CAHP) was representing me and their area representatives were going back to their areas and telling officers what was happening. Again, Ed Maghakian, their president, was making sure the CAHP funds were being well spent and the officers knew that he could be trusted.

During all of this communication, I was notified that the Sacramento area was going to be divided and there was going to be a North and, now, a new South area. I immediately went to work and filed a grievance against the Department (Commissioner Craig) requesting a transfer to the new South Sacramento area office based upon my qualification and seniority. There were a lot of officers throughout the state who were following this grievance very closely.

About three weeks later, Assistant Chief Costello came to the Monterey area office and said he wanted to speak with me in private.

He said, "I know you want to transfer to Sacramento and there is going to be an opening very soon. I think I can arrange for you to get transferred there but under one condition.

"I'm doing this on my own. The Department has nothing to do with what I'm proposing."

I said, "OK"

Costello continued, "There's a lot of dissension throughout the state and it's mainly because of what you are saying about Commissioner Craig. You've got to make me a promise that if you get transferred to South Sacramento that you will not say another word about the Commissioner even if you're asked. If you will do that, you will get the transfer."

First and most importantly, I trusted Chief Costello. He was one of the "good guys." Secondly, I wanted the transfer to Sacramento mainly for Laura's sake. She wanted to be back with the family as I did. Thirdly, I had no reason to continue bad-mouthing Craig as long as he was doing the right thing. Lastly, that would resolve the grievance and it would improve morale throughout the state. I gave Costello my word and he knew he could trust me.

About one week later, I was notified I was being transferred to the South Sacramento area office effective January 8, 1979, where I would take Maury Hannigans place as Field Lieutenant. Hannigan, a friend of mine, went on to become Commissioner of the Highway Patrol.

A couple of days later, Sergeant Mert Baarts, my racquetball partner in Monterey, said he wanted to take me to lunch as a going away present. We went to this large Italian restaurant and they directed us to the back room. When I opened the door, almost the entire office was present and shouted, "Surprise!"

They gave me a nice engraved pen set for the new office in South Sacramento. I was caught totally by surprise. The last time something like this happened was when I left the Montebello Police Department twenty years earlier. It was a nice ending to my stay in Monterey.

Chapter 17
Attitude Toward DUI Enforcement Hasn't Changed

The South Sacramento area office was created because of the large population increase in the Capitol city. When I reported to the area, the new office at Mack Road and Stockton Blvd was still under construction and we were being housed in temporary quarters. All the officers were transfers from different areas of the state and there was a noticeable diversity in their attitudes toward the job. As my brother use to say, "It takes all kinds and we've got 'em." Sometimes the only thing uniform about a police officer is his uniform.

I could always tell the attitude of an officer toward a DUI by his response to seeing a vehicle weaving down the road. The professional officer would say, "It looks like we have a possible drunk driver." An unprofessional officer or dead-beat, seeing the same weaving vehicle would say, "He's probably sleepy or using a cell phone." Comments can be revealing. A police officer should always expect the worst and hope for the best.

There were two officers, who I could see from the very beginning, that were going to need some serious training. They were "old timers" with very bad attitudes. They didn't like the "brass" and they thought too highly of themselves. They would go around boasting they had 20 years experience when they really only had 1 year experience 20 times.

They were always trying to influence "rookie" officers to adopt their demeanor and made fun of those who followed the rules. These types of individuals always try to become friends with the highest ranking officer possible so they can run to him when a supervisor below their rank did something they didn't like.

It was amazing how often this was done on the job successfully. Ideally, if they could get something on the Commander, then they could blackmail him and become untouchables. This tactic was quite common and was used very successfully in Santa Maria.

But there are other reasons why officers are not disciplined. Some supervisors are incompetent, some afraid and some who want to be accepted, so they can hang out with the officers they supervise.

In the case of the two officers in South Sacramento, they had been operating in this fashion their entire career and none of their supervisors had the guts to do anything to correct the situation. It was just accepted conduct on their part. The problem with letting this type of conduct continue is that it's like a disease. Pretty soon every officer in the area has it.

I noticed the two officers were very close friends and always rode partners when they worked other than the day shift. Their favorite shift seemed to be either days or graveyard. On day shifts they could take care of personal business and on graveyard they could hide. Both of those things are difficult to do on the evening shift, which was my favorite—and another reason they didn't want to work it.

My first brush with them was at briefing. They would meander in late and then sit in the back where they could talk while briefing was going on. They also liked to play games by researching a Headquarter General Order the night before and then asking the sergeant, during briefing in front of all the other officers, a question about the order. This was designed to embarrass the sergeant and impress the younger officers.

I was present one day at briefing when they "played their little game" on a new sergeant in the area. The sergeant attempted to answer their question and one of them said, "You're wrong. That's not what the order says."

I intervened and said, "How do you know that's not how the order reads? And if you already know how it reads then why are you asking the sergeant? And, furthermore, your question doesn't have anything to do with briefing."

PART 1: *Chapter 17:* Attitude Toward DUI Enforcement Hasn't Changed   341

Embarrassed, but looking for an opportunity to save face, he said, "Well, I just wanted to know if the sergeant knew what it said."

I told him if he had any further personal questions that were unrelated to the group as a whole, he should ask the sergeant after briefing and not waste the time of the other officers who could be out on their beat.

One of the rookies jokingly said, "Yeah. Quit wasting our time."

When I first went into a new area office I just sat back and observed. I have always followed the principle that before one acts he should have all of the facts. And that includes human behavior.

Quite often there are dead-beat officers that are promoted to sergeant and they become part of the problem and that was the case here. For example, there was one sergeant who liked to party and hang out with the officers he was suppose to be supervising, another sergeant who just wanted to be a "nice guy" and like the first sergeant, would cover for the officers rather than discipline them. Then there was another sergeant who was lazy and just didn't care. The rest of the sergeants wanted to do their job. One of those sergeants was Richard Skipper. He didn't like what he saw either. He was from the old school where he thought a person should do the job they were getting paid to do.

The first thing we did was to check the two "prima donnas" activity work sheets. And that didn't take long because there was just a smattering of numbers on it. Most importantly, there were no DUI arrests; mainly mechanicals and verbal warnings.

It was time to call the first officer into the office to talk.

"Yeah. Sergeant Skipper said you wanted to talk with me. What's this all about?"

I said, "It's about your activity or lack there of."

He said, "I write what I see. I've been through this with other supervisors and they didn't get anywhere and you're not either. A person can only write what they see."

I agreed, but I told him, "We're going to help you so you can start seeing better."

"And just how are you going to do that?" he asked.

"By providing training. Beginning tomorrow you will be riding with a sergeant. If you don't see a violation. then he will point it out to you and then you will write the citation."

The officer did not like this idea at all because that meant he had to knock off any personal business during his shift. The officer's activity increased considerably to an acceptable level.

After the month was over, the officer returned to working solo and his activity dropped back down to almost no activity.

He was called back into the office, and with a slight smile on his face, said, "Things have been a little slow out there this month."

I said, "Oh! That's alright. We've come to the conclusion that you need additional training so I've made arrangements for you to attend the next cadet class."

He responded in an angry tone, "I'm not going to no cadet class. I'm one of the senior officers in this area and I went through the cadet class 20 years ago."

I said, "Apparently you didn't learn from the first one so you're going to have to do it again."

The officer said, "What if I refuse to go?"

"Then you'll be fired. But that's not the end of the story. If you do take the cadet class again and your activity doesn't increase then you'll be fired anyway. It's time to go to work, Charlie. You've been cheating the public for over 20 years. And this time you can't transfer to another area office because you are under investigation that could result in punitive action."

Charlie chose to resign from the Highway Patrol rather than go through cadet training.

And before we could turn our attention to his partner, he did a very stupid thing. His wife divorced him and moved to Oakland. He made an explosive device (I hope it had nothing to do with the training I had provided years before) and mailed it to his ex-wife. He was no more competent making an explosive device than he was performing his job. While the US Post Office was handling the box, one of the wires worked loose which prevented it from detonating. The package was easily traced back to the officer and he was fired.

Oakland Police Department was so far behind prosecuting murders and other similar crimes that it took two years for the officer to come to trial. He was convicted and served 5 years in prison and died shortly after being released.

It didn't take long for the officers to realize we meant business and that we weren't going to "let the inmates take over the prison." Some officers took that as a signal for them to transfer to another area office more compatible to their style of doing nothing. But we also had some very reliable, hard working officers who put in a solid days work and conducted themselves professionally. Morale picked up and the office took on a friendly environment.

Bob Mitchell Jr. Makes a Tough DUI Call

My youngest son, Bob Jr., had decided he wanted to be a police officer from day one and I knew he would make a good one because of his logic and qualities. He was raised in the 60's and 70's during the drug and hippie culture but never bought into that stupidity. As far as that goes, neither did Steve or Cheryl.

When Bob was 21, he became a police officer for the City of Sacramento. Six years later he was promoted to sergeant. He shares my belief that the DUI is the number one terrorist in America and he arrested them at every opportunity. But not all DUI arrests are routine.

Not too long after being promoted to sergeant he got one of those non-routine calls. Two of his officers requested he meet with them at Broadway and 9th Street. Usually, when an officer doesn't tell a supervisor why he wants the "11-98" the supervisor can expect something of a sensitive nature awaiting him. Or at least something they don't want to broadcast over the radio.

Upon arriving at the scene, one of the officers said, "Here's what we've got sarge. This state police officer saw this DUI driving westbound in the eastbound lane of Broadway at 5th Street. He turned the DUI over to us. There's no doubt about him being under the influence, but there is one problem, and that's why we called you. He's a Sacramento Police officer."

Bob did what the department policy calls for—he notified the lieutenant. When the lieutenant got there, he notified the Captain.

After hearing all of the details, the Captain called Bob over to the side and said, "You called for a decision and I have made that decision. And it is, the decision is yours." The Captain then got in his cruiser and left. The officers said, "Well, sarge what do you want us to do?" Bob said, "Book him just like you would anyone else."

The next day, while Bob was conducting briefing, a few of the officers wanted to know why "one of their own" had been booked for DUI. "Whose decision was this? The Captain said it was yours."

Bob explained that the officer tested over a .20% BAC and was driving on the wrong side of the road, facing opposing traffic head-on. But some officers didn't care about the details. And as hard as it is to believe, there are many officers throughout the United States with the same attitude.

Arresting DUIs, to them, is like advocating prohibition. Their motto is, "You've got the right to drink and you've got the right to drive. And on occasion you just do both." I've even had people tell me they are better drivers when they've had a couple of drinks. "I'm more cautious."

Bob phoned me at home and told me what was going on and what he planned on doing. "The Captain isn't backing me on my decision so I'm going to file a grievance against him."

I told him that was exactly what I would do.

I added, "He can't afford a grievance. There's no way he could talk his way out of this, especially if it got to the newspaper."

Bob went straight to the Captain, who was working at the time, and after saying "Good afternoon" he said, "I've decided I'm going to file a grievance against you."

The Captain said, "Now wait a minute. Let's talk this over."

Bob told the Captain, "My decision to book the officer was made based upon departmental policy and you should have supported that decision when asked by the other officers. Instead, you made it sound like you thought it was the wrong decision."

After a few more minutes of discussion, the Captain said Bob was correct and that he would be at the next briefing and explain that he supported Bob's decision. So, the grievance ended there at the verbal first step. That's the way grievances are supposed to be handled.

Bob had a distinguished career and retired from the Sacramento Police Department as a Captain. Steve recently retired as a Kern County Deputy Sheriff. Cheryl worked for the Department of Justice before switching to California Consumer Affairs where she is presently employed.

Same Old DUI Enforcement Problems

As a Field Operation Lieutenant in the South Sacramento area office and after the DUI battle in Santa Maria and then challenging and winning two more battles with the Highway Patrol (the Captain's promotional test and transfer to Sacramento), I had no problem from any source within the Department. I took a CHP cruiser home, because I was on 24 hour call, and just did my job as defined in Departmental orders. I never slowed in my efforts to rid the highways of DUIs and to actively see that other CHP Officers were doing the same.

I give credit to the Highway Patrol for assigning me as a Field Operations Lieutenant in such a key area as the Capital City, knowing I would continue to enforce DUI. I believe all law enforcement agencies would like to see DUIs removed from the highways, but the problem lies with individual officers who are not willing to do what it takes. And the present system of enforcement is inadequate. There's going to have to be a major change in attitude of officers as well as the public.

I experienced a perfect example of this in South Sacramento.

In each area where I worked there were always a few officers who were dedicated to doing their job. They believed in the Highway Patrol and they wanted to make a difference in saving peoples lives. Richard Skipper was one of those officers. He and his wife, Juanita, were a couple that Laura and I got to know because Skipper had no hidden agenda—what you see is what you get. I was pleased when they made him Acting Sergeant because I knew I could trust him and he knew he could trust me.

On the surface it appears everyone is doing their job, but all kinds of things may be going on behind the scenes and if someone doesn't break the code of silence—and if supervisors refuse to investigate and take action—then it's one cover-up after another.

A good example occurred on November 20, 1980, at 2:15 am. CHP Officer Wayne Pierce and his partner received a radio call to meet a CHP sergeant from the North Sacramento area office who was holding Thomas Moore, a DUI suspect. Pierce gave Moore a FST and found him to be well under the influence. The sergeant gave Pierce a summary report of the DUI's driving and Moore was transported to the Sacramento County jail for testing and booking.

En route to the jail DUI Moore told Officer Pierce that he (Moore) was on the CHP list to be hired and was scheduled to attend the next CHP Academy class in one month.

Moore said, "My wife just had a baby and I was out celebrating. Will this arrest affect my starting at the academy?"

Pierce would later say, "Moore appeared to be good CHP material so I asked Sergeant Skipper if I could release him."

Another CHP officer got involved and said they could report him as a low blow (on the breathalyzer). Pierce phoned the North Sacramento sergeant who made the original arrest and asked him if it would be alright to release Moore. The sergeant said he had no objections to releasing the subject, but Pierce would have to destroy his supplemental report.

PART 1: *Chapter 17:* Attitude Toward DUI Enforcement Hasn't Changed

A Sacramento Deputy Sergeant suggested that they report Moore as being "ill" and release him on those grounds. Skipper did not get involved and left the jail facilities believing Moore was going to be booked for DUI. Pierce said he thought Skipper left so that arrangements could be made to release Moore. Moore was never given a chemical test and, after two hours, was transported to his car and released without being charged for DUI.

When Skipper came to work the next day he started searching for the arrest report on Moore and couldn't find it. He asked Pierce's partner if he knew where the report was and his partner lied and said it had "gone forward."

Sergeant Carr, another no-nonsense sergeant, became suspicious, as well. He called the sergeant in the north area and quizzed him on the arrest. The sergeant told Carr, as far as he knew, Moore was released without being booked. Once it was confirmed that Moore had not been booked, Skipper contacted me and told me what had been going on. I requested memos from everyone involved and started an investigation.

When conducting an investigation, I always asked parties involved for memorandums concerning their involvement before doing anything else. Usually, if a person is going to lie they will do it at the beginning of an inquiry. The memo tells an investigator a lot by just its wording. Usually, if the memo is brief then the writer has something to hide. The very nature of the wording also tells an investigator a great deal.

It is very important to find out as quickly as possible who is involved. I always found that the more people involved the better. And every investigation always starts with a cover-up. Also, remembering a "friend" will only go so far to cover for his partner.

After all the memos were in, I started putting the event together. In this case, the driver, Thomas Moore, was stopped by a CHP Sergeant for DUI. Officer Pierce and his partner were dispatched to handle the DUI arrest. Pierce gave the FST and concluded, along with his partner and the sergeant, that Moore was well under the influence of alcohol and should not be driving. He was arrested and transported to the Sacramento County Jail.

So far, so good.

But during the trip to the jail, Moore said he was scheduled to go to the CHP Academy the following month so Pierce decided he wanted to "give him a break and not book him."

It apparently never entered his mind, or the minds of the other officers who were also involved in releasing Moore that, at that very time, they were booking other drivers for DUI. But Pierce said he thought Moore would make "a high caliber CHP officer." Unbelievably, this is the mentality of some officers. But soon after this occurred, Officer Pierce got his "wakeup call."

Unfortunately, this is not an isolated case. The real question is, how many DUIs have been "kicked loose" and then later killed some innocent person or persons in a DUI accident? It's inevitable.

Klippness and I ran into similar situations in East Los Angeles. We stopped a DUI who said he was scheduled to go to the next Academy, and besides booking him for DUI, we also had his arrest report flagged to make sure the Academy got a copy of the report.

On another occasion, it turned out that the DUI had not even applied. It is not uncommon for a DUI to tell you anything your gullible little mind will accept to get out of being arrested. "I just found out I have terminal cancer, my son was killed yesterday in the military, my wife divorced me today" and so on. Most of the time they are lying and if they're telling the truth then that's no reason for them to be allowed to kill someone.

The next step in the Officer Pierce case was to interview everyone in person and tape record the proceedings. When I knew an officer under investigation was lying, I always warned him before questioning him in person. "You are expected to tell the truth. If you do, then you will probably save your job and only get some time off. But if you lie, then you will be charged with dishonesty and will probably lose your job."

Pierce not only went on to lie about this case, but two months after this incident, he and another partner stopped a female DUI (who worked at one of the local restaurants) and decided not to book her but to take her home instead. This particular incident was more revealing of the problems with DUI enforcement than the Moore incident.

It's the CHP's Duty to Arrest DUIs, Not Drive Them Home

On December 16, 1980, at about 1:30 am, Officer Pierce stopped a Teri Thornton, 23, for DUI. Instead of arresting her, even though she was obviously under the influence of alcohol, he decided to transport her to her apartment several miles out of his assigned area. This decision was made even though his unit had been requested to cover a traffic accident.

While en route to Thornton's apartment and with her in the back seat of the CHP unit, another female (Manley) was observed and stopped for DUI. As Pierce was getting out of the cruiser, Manley placed her car in reverse and backed into the cruiser causing minor damage and knocking Pierce back into the door post as he was opening the driver's door. Pierce claimed he received a back injury and requested a sergeant come to the scene.

Of course, Pierce had a problem. Thornton was DUI and in the back seat of the cruiser and the sergeant was on his way to the scene. Pierce persuaded his partner to support his (Pierce) story that Thornton was a disabled motorist who had flagged them down and they were giving her a ride home. Pierce then asked Thornton to tell the sergeant the same thing and also be a witness for him that Manley, the other DUI, had backed into the cruiser and injured him.

Officer Sabo arrived at the scene to investigate the traffic accident between Manley and the cruiser.

When the sergeant arrived, Pierce lied to him about Thornton being a DUI and asked the sergeant to take Thornton to her apartment, which the sergeant reluctantly did. The sergeant later testified that Thornton was so intoxicated that she could have been arrested for plain drunk. Manley was booked for DUI. The sergeant also told Pierce that he did not believe he (Pierce) was injured and was upset over having to take Thornton to her apartment. The sergeant was incompetent and should have received punitive action for his part, but the Department thought otherwise.

In my investigation of this incident, the first person I investigated and taped was Pierce's partner, Harris. Harris readily admitted Thornton was a DUI and answered all questions clearly and without hesitation. Officer Pierce insisted Thornton was a disabled motorist and described how she was standing by the car with her hood up and her four-way flashers on. Thornton was contacted and admitted to being a DUI and further stated Pierce had called her on the job urging her to lie about being a disabled motorist.

There's No Such Thing as a Borderline DUI

In still another incident, on January 17, 1981, at 3:00 am, Officer Pierce was dispatched to meet with a Sheriff's unit that had stopped a Mrs. Tsumura, 49, for possible DUI. Tsumura was later released and Pierce lied that he had gotten permission from the shift sergeant to release Tsumura.

It was during these investigations that Officer Pierce made some disturbing statements that represent some serious problems in DUI enforcement that I believe is prevalent today throughout the United States.

Pierce was being interrogated by me and the Area Commander with his CAHP counsel present. He said he had stopped Thornton for possible DUI. He said, "She was a borderline and I didn't think it was safe for her to continue driving. We were taking her to the nearest phone so she could call someone to pick her up."

I said, "You said she was a borderline and you decided to have her lock her vehicle and accompany you to a phone for her own safety since she had been drinking. And you said you didn't think it was safe for her to continue driving? It sounds like she was a DUI."

Pierce said: "Wrong. As far as I was concerned, if I had taken her down and put her on a breathalyzer, she would probably have been in the area of a .08—.09. Okay, she's in the gray zone and she can't operate a motor vehicle safely."

I replied, "That's all it takes to constitute a DUI—to be under the influence to such an extent that they can't safely operate a motor vehicle."

Pierce: "The thing that I'm looking at is she wasn't driving erratically and I didn't want her to drive any farther. It's a common practice . . ."

Captain: "You were saying it's a common practice to do what?"

PART 1: *Chapter 17:* Attitude Toward DUI Enforcement Hasn't Changed

Pierce: "It's a common practice, we have done it many, many times in the past, and I can bring almost every traffic officer in here and he would say the same thing, that we have done it many times in the past."

I thought at this point the Captain would point out that an officer has no authority to stop someone, tell them they can't continue driving their car, take them to the nearest telephone and drop them off. I expected the Captain to say, "What in the world are you talking about and what do you mean it's common practice?"

Instead, the Captain said, "What you have explained to me might be a common practice, that you have a borderline and you try for their security, but don't you agree with me that it seems unusual that you went beyond those limits? That you're explaining to me insofar as passing several telephones, several locations, and you did not go to the nearest spot you could have deposited her for a cup of coffee or something like this. And this differs from what the normal practice is."

In essence, the Captain was agreeing that there is such a thing as a borderline drunk driver, that it's OK to stop a woman, remove her from her car and drop her off at the nearest telephone booth or take her to a coffee stop.

The Captain was dead wrong. First, anyone who is not safe to drive a car because of their intoxication should go *directly* to jail. Secondly, can you hear the hue and cry if a "borderline DUI" female was dropped off at a phone booth, then raped or maybe murdered. And lastly, the Captain's response was jeopardizing our case. He was in essence agreeing with Pierce.

I couldn't say what I wanted to say, because we were on tape and this was an official investigation, but I did say, "I just would like to go on record, and I'm sure not every Highway Patrolman would agree with this, I do not believe that a person can be a borderline. I believe it's like saying a woman is partly pregnant. She's either pregnant or not pregnant—this woman was either not under the influence and she continues on her way down the road or she is under the influence and arrested and booked for DUI. I do not agree with how you handled it."

Pierce replied, "I have ridden with sergeants who have done the same thing that I did."

I said, "I'm saying this is my opinion of how it should be handled and that is how the CHP enforcement manual says it should be handled."

Pierce said: "I'm telling you, that's the way we handle it in the field. As a matter of fact, in another office where I worked, the Captain gave us a direct order that Captains or above in the Air Force were not to be booked. They were to be transported. I know this is not the issue, but I'm just telling you. Do you understand what I'm trying to say to you?"

I replied, "I don't know what anybody else has told you anywhere else. I don't know what your practice was anywhere else, I'm only concerned with what you do at the South Sacramento area office."

Officer Pierce was charged with inexcusable neglect of duty, dishonesty, and willful disobedience and was fired on May 19, 1981. Pierce appealed the dismissal but lost the appeal on August 27, 1981.

On October 16, 1981, less than two months later, the Mountain View Police Department notified us that Wayne Pierce and his wife, Darlene, were arrested for grand theft and conspiracy in their city.

Reckless Driver has Heart Attack, or Does He?

In October of 1986, the California Highway Patrol was experimenting with "souped-up" Ford Mustangs as pursuit cruisers. They were light-weight with a powerful engine and when you pressed down on the accelerator, the body would raise up as the vehicle accelerated forward. They were so powerful and difficult to handle that an officer had to get certified by the Academy before he could drive one. As Field Lieutenant, I got the new cars when they first arrived in the Area so I was driving one of the new Mustangs when I was working one day.

I was traveling southbound on the Highway 99 freeway before stopping on the Fruitridge Road on-ramp to observe traffic. It was about 3:00 pm and conditions were right for a speeder, providing he cut in and out of traffic.

Of course, there's always a chance a DUI would "show his face." I had only been there about 5 minutes when I saw a blue Chevrolet speeding southbound and being driven recklessly. Even though I had to start from a

PART 1: *Chapter 17:* Attitude Toward DUI Enforcement Hasn't Changed 353

"stand still" it only took a short time before I was on the Chevrolet, which was changing lanes repeatedly. In response to the red light and siren, the driver suddenly pulled off on the shoulder and came to a skidding stop.

As I was getting out of the cruiser and walking toward the violator's car, passing motorists were honking and waving in appreciation for the apprehension. But just as I got to the suspect's car, his body went to the right and I could no longer see him. I put my hand on my revolver and went to the passenger's side of the car knowing he would be looking for me to approach on the driver's side.

To my surprise, the driver was holding his chest and screaming that he was having a heart attack. I opened the passenger door and he kept screaming, "Help me. I've got a bad heart." I knew that Methodist Hospital was only about a mile south of our location, so I decided to take him in the cruiser instead of waiting on an ambulance.

As I was half carrying him back to the cruiser, a concerned citizen stopped and helped me put him in the right front seat. I radioed dispatch and told them to alert Methodist Hospital that I would be there in about five minutes with a "possible heart attack victim," so there would be no delay in treating him. All the time, the driver was expressing how severe the pain was.

When I arrived at the Emergency entrance to the hospital, they placed the driver on a gurney and rolled him into the operating room. I gave the hospital the information on the driver but I kept his driver's license. As soon as he was out of danger, I wanted to talk to him about his reckless driving.

I told the hospital personnel the circumstances and asked them to contact me as soon as the driver was out of danger and could answer some questions, and that I was going to the South Sacramento area office, only about 5 minutes away, and would return and take him into custody.

No sooner did I get to the office than I received a phone call from the Methodist Hospital Emergency room. "Lieutenant, can you come over here and take care of this guy? He won't let the doctor examine him and he wants to leave right now. The doctor says there is nothing wrong with him. He was faking the heart attack."

The driver was arrested for reckless driving and delaying and obstructing a public officer in the discharge of his duties. His vehicle was stored and he had to pay a hospital bill. I assume he pled guilty to the charges because I didn't receive a subpoena.

Retiring Knowing Very Little Had Changed

That was my last arrest on the Highway Patrol. I left the job one week later, October 8, 1986, and officially retired, February 26, 1987.

It seemed strange to go home that last day, take off my uniform which was a part of me for 34 years and 2 months (except for the six months and 20 days I was fired) and put it in the closet, never to wear it again.

It was also discouraging to know that after more than 30 years fighting the hidden forces protecting America's Domestic Terrorists—drivers under the influence—very little had really changed. Klippness and I fought the good fight in Santa Maria and put our livelihoods on the line along with our families but drunk driving was still just as prevalent.

Today, more than four decades later, a DUI is still killing a person on an average of every 40 minutes in the United States. And now you know why.

Chapter 18
How to Defeat America's Domestic Terrorists—Drunk Drivers

The reason that driving under the influence is considered a traffic violation is probably because it occurs on the highways and involves motorists. Unfortunately, the wording undermines the seriousness of the act, when in fact, it is a major crime that kills far more innocent people than any other criminal act in the United States.

Murder and manslaughter are in the Penal Code and both of these charges are sometimes used in prosecuting DUIs. They need to be used more often.

If someone took a high-powered rifle and said he was going to aim it down the highway at windshield level and fire it, regardless of who might be driving a car in his direction, he would be arrested or overpowered and taken to the psychiatric ward. But a DUI can get into a 4,000-pound automobile and aim it at opposing traffic at high speed and no one gives it much thought.

Ironically, a person's chances of survival are much better facing the high-powered rifle.

America cannot continue to take 13,000 casualties a year. It's time to get serious. Drastic steps must be taken to end this highway slaughter now. It only makes sense that resources should be allocated on the basis of priority. That is not being done. There is no higher priority than ending DUI killings. We don't set idly by and let a sniper kill motorists as they drive down the highway but we'll let a DUI do the same thing with a 4,000-pound automobile. It's important to remember that DUI is a crime, not an accident.

The good news is DUI can be eradicated. That's right. We don't have to live with this highway plague. It's time to declare war on DUIs. They have killed enough. The problem with the DUI terrorist is the same as other terrorists—They are almost impossible to identify until they kill someone. This will not be a conventional war, because, as difficult as it may be to believe, there is a segment of society that supports DUI. Likewise, billions of dollars are made from DUIs and they have strong lobbies. And legislators listen to lobbyists. That's how some legislators get into office and are able to stay there.

This blueprint for winning the war against DUIs will save at least one thousand lives the first year. But it means a fundamental change from what we are doing now.

Establish a DUI Enforcement Agency in Every State.

These agencies' sole duty would be the eradication of DUI. They would have no other responsibilities. The enforcement personnel would have peace officer powers and have their own training academy. State highway patrol, county sheriffs and city police would still make arrests for DUI, but they would book their arrestee into the DUI jail/detention centers.

Why?

The present law enforcement agencies cannot adequately enforce DUI. It's impossible. They have too many other responsibilities. Some of the officers are doing the best they can, but that's not good enough.

Most law enforcement officers can recognize an intoxicated driver, but identifying a DUI is something else. It could be compared to a doctor. There are general practitioners who can treat a basic illness and then there are surgeons who specialize in certain types of surgery. They're both doctors but they have different duties. You can't expect the general practitioner to do a heart transplant. Nor can you expect the average beat officer to handle all of his other responsibilities and effectively enforce DUI.

The California Highway Patrol is the leader in DUI enforcement, but even the CHP has many other responsibilities. Using the words of former Commissioner Mike Brown, "The CHP patrols more miles of highways, provides protection and service to more drivers and vehicles than many countries. Over the years, we've acquired additional responsibilities such as protecting state officials, investigating criminal activity in state government and providing homeland security protection throughout the state. It's not surprising, then, the wide variety of jobs and responsibilities we have within our CHP family."

Those assignments don't include a CHP officer's regular duties of commercial enforcement, special drug eradication, variety of helicopter assignments, transportation of life saving organs to hospitals, stolen vehicle detail, assisting other agencies, and so on.

Now realistically, how can an officer be trained in all of those duties and still be an expert in DUI detection and enforcement? And this applies to all law enforcement agencies throughout the nation. I can tell you from experience, they can't. It's not the officer's fault that they have all these duties and don't have the time and expertise to arrest DUIs. Most people (and officers) are not aware that DUI is a special field and it takes more training than provided in the Academy. And it can't be a part time assignment.

As proof, 72 percent of alcohol-impaired drivers involved in crashes are never charged with DUIs, according to MADD.

The proposed DUI Enforcement Agency would be very similar to establishing a police SWAT team. SWAT teams have proven themselves over and over. The California Highway Patrol has a MAIT team that specializes in investigating multiple fatal accidents. They are both very proficient in what they do.

In 2007 (latest figures), an estimated 12,998 people died in alcohol-impaired traffic crashes—an average of one every 40 minutes. These deaths constitute 31.7 percent of the 41,059 total traffic fatalities.

It should be noted that the basic measurement of DUI fatalities changed in 2006. Before that date, DUI fatals were calculated using the "alcohol-related" standard. In 2006, the measurement became "alcohol-impaired" fatalities. Alcohol-related meant the driver had been drinking at any level. Alcohol-impaired means the driver's BAC is .08% or greater.

In 2002, surveys estimated that DUIs took more than 159 million alcohol-impaired trips. And that number has grown. Just 5 years earlier in 1997, DUIs took 116 million alcohol-impaired trips, according to the American Journal of Preventative Medicine.

Very few of those drivers were arrested on their DUI trips—1,141,378 in 2002. That means the DUIs made almost 158 million alcohol-impaired trips without being arrested. How dangerous is that? Too bad you can't ask the 13,472 people who died because of the DUIs in 2002.

To combat this problem we need an agency whose only responsibility is to stop DUI.

Some will say we can't afford State DUI Agencies. In 2000, alcohol-related crashes in the United States cost the public (taxpayers) an estimated $114.3 billion including $51.1 billion in monetary costs and an estimated $63.2 billion in quality of life losses. People other than the drinking driver paid $71.6 billion of the alcohol-related crash expenses. That was 63 percent of the total cost of the crashes. Wouldn't it be better to use the money to prevent the devastation caused by DUIs?

In California in August of 1929, traffic was handled by the county sheriffs department. This included sheriff deputies riding motorcycles and enforcing traffic laws. But some wise legislators realized the need for a separate agency to handle traffic. It became apparent, the sheriffs could not adequately handle it and still manage the other criminal activities that were their responsibility. So, the legislature created the California Highway Patrol (CHP).

Eugene Biscailuz, Undersheriff, Los Angeles County, was appointed to head the Department. Some of the officers employed by various counties made up motor squads that were absorbed into the CHP. Creating the CHP was an excellent decision. Now it's time to realize that the different law enforcement agencies throughout the state, including the CHP, have too many responsibilities to adequately enforce DUI. We need State DUI Agencies in all 50 states, with officers sole or primary responsibility to rid the highways of DUIs, if we are going to stop this carnage.

We've lost over 4,500 brave men and women in Iraq over the past five years and most of the casualties were from terrorists. And there is a

PART 2: *Chapter 18:* How to Defeat America's Domestic Terrorists—Drunk Drivers

hue and cry throughout the nation, and rightfully so, concerning these losses even though war casualties are inevitable, as terrible as that may be. Yet during this same time more than 66,266 Americans were killed and 1,375,000 maimed and disfigured in the United States by local DUI terrorists and the victims were just using our highway system. It's ironic that both foreign and domestic terrorists use cars to kill most of their victims.

There are numerous advantages to having a State DUI Agency and it is the only way we can win this war against the drinking driver. The DUI officers would be trained specialists and their sole job would be to win the battle against DUIs. If present law enforcement agencies stopped a DUI then they could continue to book the DUI as they presently do or contact the DUI Agency and they would handle it. This is the same principle that is being practiced by law enforcement agencies throughout the nation today. For example, if a sheriff observes a traffic accident he calls the highway patrol. If an illegal alien is stopped, then Immigration is contacted and so on. If an officer chooses to book a DUI, then a report would need to be forwarded to the State DUI Agency. Again, similar practices are already being used between existing law enforcement agencies.

A DUI Agency would spend 100 percent of their time concentrating on the elimination of DUIs through planning, developing, organizing, coordinating, and controlling. I doubt right now if any law enforcement agency spends more than 25 percent of their time on DUI enforcement. They can't with all of their other responsibilities. From some of the statistics I have been reviewing, it doesn't appear that Illinois, New York or Washington D.C even have a DUI program. If they do, judging from arrests, it's pathetic.

A State DUI enforcement agency would also greatly minimize the politics and favoritism that presently permeate the rural communities. I would strongly recommend that no State DUI officer be allowed to work in the same community where he lives.

Klippness and I started special DUI enforcement in East Los Angeles and accidents started dropping almost immediately. Felony DUIs (a traffic crash where a DUI kills or injures someone) dropped 25% almost immediately. I know, from experience, this type of enforcement program will save over a 1,000 lives the first year.

An additional benefit is the Special DUI Team officers will have the training and confidence to make the arrests and their training will help increase conviction rates. With DUI special teams, all an officer in any other enforcement agency will have to do is call them to the scene.

Supervisors Must Make Sure Officers are Enforcing DUI Laws

On the Police Department, as opposed to the California Highway Patrol, an officer has different duties, ranging from barking dog complaints to a shootout with an armed felon. But one of the duties common to both is traffic enforcement.

Although I liked police work, I realized that if I learned how to ride a motorcycle and was assigned traffic enforcement, I would have more of an impact on saving lives and, at the same time, enjoy the job more. After I had been on the Department for several months, one of the more experienced Motorcycle Officers, Paul Beard, who I had become friends with, volunteered to teach me how to ride a motorcycle.

He told me that a motorcycle officer is primarily involved in traffic enforcement, doesn't work graveyard shifts, the work is dangerous but exciting and the officer takes the motorcycle home. (For safety purposes, officers are assigned a motorcycle that they keep until it's traded in. Every motorcycle rides just a little different.)

Also, I realized that if I learned how to ride a motorcycle and was assigned traffic enforcement then I could have more of an impact on saving lives. In less than a month, I was a motor officer.

Of course, investigating traffic accidents can be painful and horrifying because of what you see and need to do. A part of the job is seeing people horribly maimed and in severe pain. Some are dead and others burned beyond recognition. This is something that one never gets "use to seeing." And, of course, children and babies are always the most devastating sights.

After being a motorcycle officer for several months and seeing the results of traffic accidents, I realized the most important section in the Vehicle Code was the violation of driving under the influence of alcohol or other drugs.

Most people are not aware that driving under the influence is so devastating and even joke about it. How many times have we heard some driver boast about how drunk he was but still made it home without having an accident. Most people never have to see the blood, mangled bodies and hear the screams coming from the children trapped in crushed cars. That's reality. It's not a movie or video game.

Emergency doctors and nurses know how real it is, and so do the coroners.

So I decided that if DUI is that important then why not concentrate my enforcement efforts toward that violation. Not to the exclusion of other violations or duties, because they are also important and necessary. So, from that point on, my priority was arresting DUIs.

But not all officers agreed—then, or now.

Very early in my career with the Montebello PD, I began to notice that not all of the officers agreed with DUI enforcement. In fact, I noticed that some of them never made arrests for that violation. I've always been curious and when I see something that I don't understand, I investigate until I find out the reason.

I first discovered that some of the officers were not knowledgeable enough in the field of DUI enforcement and had no desire to learn. In their defense, DUI enforcement is complicated and requires special training. This is one of the problems with DUI enforcement that must be dealt with if we are going to ever win this battle in America.

And as difficult as it is to believe, some officers do not believe in DUI enforcement unless the driver is obviously intoxicated.

Why?

A CHP Officer in East Los Angeles confided that he did not arrest drunk drivers because every time he pulled one over "he saw his father."

"My father was an alcoholic," he said.

I asked him, "But what about the innocent people that are killed by drunk drivers?"

The officer, angered by the question, said, "Don't start that stuff."

I told him if I ever found out he let a DUI go I would report him and I advised him to find another line of work.

But he is not alone in his reluctance. Other officers have said they are reluctant to arrest DUIs because they have "a couple" of drinks and drive and don't think it's "that big of a deal." But almost every driver that I ever stopped for DUI told me that he had had "only a couple of drinks" regardless of how drunk he was.

The truth of the matter is that it takes training and skill to detect a person that has had *more* than a couple of drinks but has not yet reached the level of being *obviously* under the influence (a blood alcohol level between .08% and .18%). I have found that range accounts for at least two-thirds of the DUIs on the road. And this is the DUI range that most officers are either inefficient in identifying or they don't have the confidence to make the arrest.

In law enforcement, not unlike other occupations, there are levels of competency. We are not talking about individuals who are promoted because not all promotions are based upon competency. We are talking about level of skills. Some officers only have the basic knowledge and ambition and do only what they have to do. That's O.K. in some occupations but not in law enforcement because people's lives hang in the balance. This is another reason why DUI fatalities continue to exist.

One veteran officer I knew was almost criminally incompetent.

I had noticed he never arrested DUIs and acted like it bothered him when others did. It didn't take long to figure out the reason: He didn't want the Department to find out how incompetent and lazy he was. It was much easier for him to drive around, eat donuts and not see anything. He knew he was still going to get his paycheck at the end of the month.

He also had the reputation of not arresting anyone, not just DUIs, and he became very skillful in finding excuses for his shortcoming. He was a master at avoiding the handling of complaints. He would use the old standard, "This is a he says, she says, so I'll have to take you both in if you insist on making a report." Officers like that exist today on every department

PART 2: *Chapter 18:* How to Defeat America's Domestic Terrorists—Drunk Drivers

throughout the nation. They usually hide on the graveyard shift. However, there are outstanding, dedicated officers working graveyard shifts.

One night I saw this officer standing on the sidewalk alongside his patrol car with his flashing red lights activated and his spot light shinning into the car in front. This told me that he had made a stop and was not just conversing with a friend. The driver appeared to be inebriated, or at least a DUI. Knowing the officer's proclivity to "kiss off" arrests to avoid work, I decided to stop a distance away on my motorcycle and watch.

As expected, after a couple of minutes, the drunk got into his car and drove off and the officer returned to his patrol car and turned off his emergency lights.

In a little over a block, I was able to overtake the DUI and signal him to stop. Of course, he wanted to know why I was stopping him. He told me that "another officer had just stopped (him) and let (him) go."

His wording, "and let me go," was very appropriate for his condition. I gave him a field sobriety test even though he was obviously under the influence. After the test was complete, I arrested him for driving under the influence, and he logically demanded, "If I'm drunk then why didn't the other officer arrest me?"

Good question. I wish I could have told him but, somehow, I don't think he would have understood. I did explain that, "I'm not accountable for what another officer does or doesn't do but you have no business driving a car in your condition."

Needless to say, this type of an arrest can have its problems. It's difficult to go to court and try to explain what happened. The Deputy DA wouldn't want to prosecute a case under these conditions.

But whether he would be prosecuted or not, he would be removed from the road. Justifiably, he should have been arrested. So, that's what I did.

Secondly, I had no obligation to report that the other officer had let him go. My report started as soon as I saw the DUI pull away from the curb and ended with the details of the arrest. Now, if I was in court and was asked about what preceded the "pulling away from the curb," then I would have had a moral and lawful obligation to report everything that I had seen and I would not have hesitated to do so.

The report was written as it occurred. The DUI suspect pled guilty. The officer was unable to explain away his actions and resigned several months later when the supervisors started taking a closer look at his work.

Unfortunately, this type of officer is often impossible to retrain to effectively arrest DUIs—or any other offender—and should be weeded out of law enforcement.

In two other cases, incompetent officers' decisions caused both death and serious injury.

You can't just leave a drunk to forge for himself just because you would rather not book him. That decision has ended in tragedy many times.

Here is a CHP report of one such incident:

> "The officer made a stop on a vehicle being driven erratically and gave the driver field sobriety tests. As a result of these tests, the officer concluded the suspect was not under the influence and told him he was free to go. The suspect was embarrassed about being stopped and didn't want to risk being stopped again. He told the officer he would call a friend to take him home and insisted the officer lock the car keys in the trunk.

"The officer complied. Shortly thereafter, the suspect was struck and killed by a vehicle while walking from the scene. His blood alcohol level, as determined by the coroner, was .24%. Further, the Officer failed to record the drunk driver check on his CHP Form 415 (activity sheet)."

What nonsense! The driver was driving erratically and had a .24% alcohol reading and the officer told him he was free to go? The officer also chose not to give the DUI a traffic citation and for good reason. If an officer is going to let a DUI continue on his way, he doesn't want the DUI to have a citation in his possession in case he crashes the car a few minutes later.

That's another reason for not entering the stop on the CHP Form 415. All that "garbage" about the suspect being embarrassed and wanting his keys locked in the trunk, you can forget.

A more likely scenario would be that the officer told him, "I'm not going to book you, but you're in no condition to drive a car. I'm not going to write you a ticket because I don't want anybody to know I stopped you. But to make sure you don't come back tonight, I'm going to lock your keys in the trunk. That way you'll have to go home to get a second key."

Then the officer let the drunk walk away and he was struck and killed. No mention is made, but it would not be unreasonable to think that he staggered into a lane of traffic. Many DUI's lives have been saved because they were arrested.

What did this Officer get for all of this? A five-working-day suspension. He should have been fired.

Another situation that involved an officer not doing his job occurred on the Ventura Freeway near the city of Camarillo. An officer stopped a female for DUI in the early morning hours. On her own admission, she was well under the influence of alcohol and had no business driving. For reasons known only to the officer, the female DUI was not arrested and permitted to drive away. Several miles down the road, she had a solo traffic collision and was seriously injured.

She sued the officer and CHP for allowing her to drive in an intoxicated condition and was awarded a large settlement. I'm not aware of any Departmental action that may have been taken against the officer, but anything less than fired was too lenient.

It is not unheard of for a department to protect an officer, even knowing that he is wrong, because they need him as a witness in a civil suit. If they do the right thing and fire the officer, then that could be taken as an overt admission that he (and the Department) are culpable and could result in the State paying out millions of dollars.

The main reason for mentioning these cases is not because they are unique, because unfortunately they are not. I have absolutely no doubt that similar situations in large numbers take place *every day and night* throughout the nation. This is a major problem and one that must be faced if we are going to stop this violence.

DUIs Should Have Their Own Incarceration Facilities

DUIs should not be incarcerated with other prisoners unless they are being charged with a felony. They should have their own facilities. In fact, I think the present prison system of mixing murderers, child molesters, burglars, auto thieves, and rapists together in the same prison is thoughtless and foolish.

I have very little sympathy for anyone who harms someone else, and criminals, without doubt, are the stupidest human beings in the world. But, that aside, there's no reason to punish them unnecessarily and prison officials have told us over and over they can't protect prisoners from each other.

Rapes and murders occur regularly. So since the inmates are running the prisons, why don't we at least separate the violent from the non-violent? There should be a prison solely for sex offenders. Let them violate each other. Have a prison for murderers. Let them kill each other. But don't mix car thieves and DUIs in with them, especially, if you can't assure them of being protected. This should also apply to both jails and prisons.

That is one reason jurors don't want to convict DUIs. If DUIs had their own incarceration facilities, convictions and sentencing would increase notably.

Keeping DUIs in the present prison system will mean most will serve little or no time for their crimes.

The Sacramento Bee newspaper reported in 2008, "Gov. Arnold Schwarzenegger made it official—he really does intend to open the prison gates next fiscal year to 22,159 lower-risk inmates and enact new parole policies that could result in some 6,249 fewer re-incarcerations the year after that."

He is proposing this as a way of reducing the state budget.

Assemblyman Todd Spitzer, R-Orange, said, "It's a betrayal. Now some people will be doing less time if they're sentenced to prison than if they're sentenced to county jail."

In other words, low-risk criminals will not be incarcerated if their sentence is less than two years. And those low-risk prisoners with 2 years or less to serve, will be released. Because a DUI is defined as a low-risk offender, then under this law, they would never serve one day in jail.

That's telling DUIs to go right on killing someone every 40 minutes and seriously injuring someone every 30 seconds and all you're going to get is a fine, and maybe some public service.

DUI Detention facilities would mean DUI offenders would actually serve time for their crimes.

And, there is no reason to incarcerate most DUIs in regular prisons. DUIs are only violent when they are under the influence and behind the wheel of an automobile. They don't need to be locked up in a jail cell like most other criminals unless they have killed someone or are repeat offenders. Facilities constructed like military bases, with guards and fencing would suffice.

With only DUI prisoners, these facilities could institute mandatory training classes and graphic films. Expenses for housing these very low-risk prisoners could probably be covered by a stiff fine. If the DUI doesn't have any money then he could pickup trash on the roadways when he wasn't in a class. Training should also include the type of program being used in Los Angeles. It is the "Scared Straight" hospital and morgue program.

If separate facilities for DUIs were available, it would help reduce outrageous sentencing such as the following. Consider actress Rebecca Broussard. She was recently sentenced to five days in jail and three years of probation after pleading no contest to a *felony* DUI. Los Angeles Superior Court Judge Katherine Mader also ordered Broussard, mother of Jack Nicholson's two teenage children, to also undergo an alcohol treatment program and state highway cleanup.

This is the type of sentence a first time misdemeanor DUI should receive, NOT a felony DUI.

The DUI Detention facilities would free the regular jails and ensure DUIs were receiving some type of punishment and training as a deterrent. Right now they pay a small fine and are placed on probation.

We need to deliver a message that, "You better not do this again *period*."

This type of incarceration does not minimize the punishment for a DUI. These facilities should be for first-time offenders and for those not injuring or grossly endangering others' lives. There should be a minimum mandatory five-day incarceration for first offenders.

DUI jails and prisons would provide a much less expensive—and much more effective—way of dealing with offenders who, when returned to society, would have a deeper awareness of the tragic effects of DUIs in America.

DUIs Should Have Their Own Court System

About 85 per cent of DUI arrests are misdemeanors, meaning there were no injuries or fatalities involved in the arrests. The object is to arrest a DUI before he strikes a pedestrian or crashes into another vehicle. This is one of the most important statistics pertaining to DUI and I do not believe any departments keep them.

Every DUI arrest should be categorized either "DUI arrest non-collision" or "DUI arrest collision." It's a figure that reveals either success or failure. They should not be treated the same. Some officers have the audacity to claim a DUI on their activity form when they have driven the DUI to the nearest phone or taken him home. Some officers never arrest a DUI unless the DUI is involved in a collision.

Misdemeanor DUIs should not be crowding our courts. Based upon the latest figures available (2002) 1,141,384 persons were arrested for DUI throughout the 50 states plus the District of Columbia. Although this figure is several years old, I don't believe more current figures would make a difference in the conclusions.

For example, California had, by far, the largest number of arrests, 178,688 (15.6 % of the total arrests nationwide). If just 10% "asked for their day in court," which they should do if they truly believe they are innocent, that would be 17,686 trials each year.

PART 2: *Chapter 18:* How to Defeat America's Domestic Terrorists—Drunk Drivers

Misdemeanor DUIs should have their own court similar to our present small claims court, which is a tremendous success. The case could be heard by a Hearing Officer or a Justice and if the DUI defendant did not believe he got a fair ruling or finding, he could appeal to the Municipal or Superior court. Of course, he would have to show cause before the case could advance.

It would free our present overburdened courts, which is the reason there are so many deals behind closed doors on DUI cases. If DUIs had their own court system, that type of adjudication (usually involving favors to someone or celebrities) could no longer be used.

There are many more advantages of a special court hearing only DUI cases. There would be more uniformity in sentencing.

A DUI couldn't shop around for a liberal judge. It would be much more difficult to "cut a deal." The court would be comparing a DUI with a DUI and not a DUI with an armed robber or murderer in deciding a sentence. It would be more difficult for a DUI to hide his priors and hopefully there would be no more pleading to a reckless driving violation to avoid a DUI conviction. DUI arrests would be taken far more seriously by the public if they had their own court.

Punishment must be more consistent with the offense.

A good example of justice in sentencing occurred Oct. 8, 2008, in Sacramento. Clinton Colon, 21, had been racing a car on Highway 99 before exiting on Franklin Boulevard and weaving through traffic at speeds of up to 110 mph in a 35 mph zone. He T-boned a car at an intersection, immediately killing Anthony Mondragon, a 15-year-old passenger.

Prior to sentencing, Colon read a letter to the court (my experience is that many of these letters are written by the defense attorneys): "Every day that I wake up, I ask for forgiveness from God for the young man's life that I took. There is no greater pain than knowing you took someone's baby."

Superior Court Judge Steve White sentenced Colon to 15 years and six months in state prison and he required that 85 % of the sentence be served before Colon was eligible for parole.

What is the difference in killing someone while traveling 110 miles per hour, or killing someone while DUI? Both are deliberate acts with the same result.

It is a joke to sentence someone who has killed or maimed another to probation or several hours of public service. Probation really means, "Don't do this again for six months or a year." That's not a penalty. We need a judicial system that penalizes a DUI for what he has done.

"Public service" is an even bigger joke. It's primarily for celebrities and is totally worthless and it's a mockery to those victims killed or maimed. Forget probation and public service; we need to institute real prison time and add several thousands of dollars to their fine.

The DUI should be required to reimburse all of the victims' medical costs, lost time on the job and for pain and suffering. The court should have the obligation of collecting the reimbursement; this should not be left to the victims.

The DUI should also be required to reimburse the insurance company for all damages. Otherwise, others will have to pay for it in the form of higher insurance premiums.

And, what if the DUI cannot pay the fines and restitution? Then he loses some of his possessions, such as his car. If he still doesn't have enough money to pay for restitution, and if he has not been convicted of a felony, he should be required to work it off at the new DUI Detention Centers.

A part of the sentencing and rehabilitation should also include periodic mandatory visits to the coroners to look at some of the mangled bodies left by other DUIs. It wouldn't hurt for judges to periodically make the same visit, to keep the crime in perspective.

Monitor Court Decisions

Our judicial system is one of the weakest links in combating DUI carnage. They have all kinds of excuses for doing what they do.

The favorite excuses are:

PART 2: *Chapter 18:* How to Defeat America's Domestic Terrorists—Drunk Drivers   371

> "We don't have enough judges,"
>
> "Not enough court rooms are available"
>
> "We have to plea away some cases because we would never get through all of them."

Well, why don't we have enough judges and courtrooms? Whose fault's that? Could it be because we don't care that much about reducing or, heaven forbid, eliminating DUI?

It is easier to play "let's make a deal" if there's too many cases for the court to handle. And why is it so many celebrities and politicians have their cases dismissed or reduced? And what about judges giving out public service instead of jail time? I don't know of one case where a privileged individual, doing public service, has ever prevented one DUI violation and isn't that supposed to be our goal?

Why don't we have a law requiring the courts to make public the disposition on all DUIs and the reason for their actions? After all, it is public record. Maybe an organization like MADD could monitor them. But don't expect this to ever happen.

Courts should be held accountable for their decisions: they should not be made in private for the benefit of the privileged few.

Vote Legislators and Judges into Office who Support DUI Enforcement

It is surprising the number of our present legislators who do not support stronger measures to reduce DUIs.

Their mentality, apparently, is that this is the price we must pay for the enjoyment of drinking and socializing.

They also argue that driving automobiles result in about the same number of deaths each year "and we're not going to do away with the automobile are we?"

But they fail to take into account that traffic accidents are just that, accidents. DUI is not an accident, it's a crime. It's a stupid and selfish act. It's like playing Russian roulette but instead of putting the gun up to one's own head, they put it up to an innocent person's head.

Over the past several decades, the people who make the laws have changed, but the elitist attitude of those in power has not. In too many cases, these legislators refuse to support bills that may affect them personally. Driving under the influence laws are prime examples: they are afraid they will be the ones stopped and arrested.

The legislators have significant support from a sizable segment of the public that also drinks and drives. The proof, of course, is in the sheer number of DUIs arrested. And that number represents only a small portion of the people who drink and drive.

But when the number of people who are killed and maimed reaches the millions, it is time for the public to recognize the problem and bring it into the open so that it may be properly addressed.

How does the public send a message to legislators that it is time to aggressively fight DUIs?

The average person has only a few means of fighting back. We can protest and we can write letters and make phone calls. Getting the news media involved can be effective. But the most powerful tool we have is our vote. This is the most effective power we have.

There is an innate potential unfairness in the fact that a small number of legislators can very easily make changes behind closed doors and the public can only make changes in large numbers, over time, and in the open.

All laws affecting the general public should only be passed by the voters. Permitting legislators to pass controversial laws they know the public does not want passed is nothing short of criminal.

That's the problem we are experiencing with changes in DUI laws. Legislators don't want DUI laws passed because they may be caught in them. We need to let the voters make the decision and not just a handful of party boozers behind closed doors who don't want to change their lifestyle.

Having said that, legislators do pass some good laws. One law that passed the California Legislature in 2009 included the Zero Tolerance Law (AB1165), which prohibits a convicted DUI offender from driving with a BAC of .01% while on probation. If the driver refuses to submit to a breathalyzer or if the driver submits and has a BAC .01% or greater, he will be cited and his license will be suspended.

A second law, Alcohol-Related Reckless Driving (AB2802), requires the court to order a person convicted of this offense to participate in a licensed DUI program for at least 9 months. The court is required to revoke a person's parole if he fails to register and attend a licensed program.

Let's get the legislation we need or vote those opposing it out of office. We have that power.

Major Awareness Campaigns

If we are going to stop the senseless slaughter of innocent people then the first step is to raise the level of awareness. We need a campaign at least as intense as the "No Smoking" campaign.

Let it be known that more than 13,000 innocent people are killed and 250,000 seriously injured each year. We've got to make this our number one priority and it's going to take thousands of individuals getting involved to be able to do this.

This is not an anti-drinking campaign. We're not trying to bring Prohibition back. People will still be able to drink, even get drunk if they like. And people will still be able to drive. This campaign is simply designed to prevent people from drinking AND driving.

What's more important than saving thousands of innocent lives? This is far worse than the terrorist attack of September 11 and it is continuing unabated.

Maybe it's time that all of the newspapers publish the names of those persons arrested for DUI and the disposition of their case in court at least once a week. Have a column of "America's Number One Terrorists for this week". This would also put the pressure on the courts to do the right thing. Don't we have a right to know who is responsible for killing 13,000 of our citizens each year?

Increased DUI Awareness Training in Our Schools and Colleges

Education is always a major part of a solution and a companion to awareness. It could be argued that we have always had notices and slogans about not drinking and driving. Now let's get serious. We need more than slogans.

We need to educate our children and our college students. We can teach alternative lifestyles that involve less than 10% of our population, but we have no time for DUI education that involves 100% of our population. Who is deciding our educational priorities?

One reason given for not teaching about the effects of alcohol and other drugs in our class rooms is "it is a moral issue."

It is not a moral issue; it is a basic human right issue. We just want the schools to teach young people why they should not drink and drive. It has nothing to do with religion or morals. It has to do with saving lives.

Encourage the Public to Become More Involved

During my entire career in law enforcement, I have heard the news media, and the general public—and even the police—refer to individuals who provide information as "snitches."

"Snitch" and "ratting on someone" no doubt started in the prisons, then was picked up by the guards and, then somehow, the general public started using it, probably as the result of seeing movies. If we want good citizens to help us in our fight against crime, it's time we stopped using the prison jargon. We should use "informant" or "witness" when referring to individuals who are providing us information.

Law enforcement could not survive without informants, so lets stop talking like "ex-cons."

An "informant" is a person who provides truthful information primarily for the good of others.

PART 2: *Chapter 18:* How to Defeat America's Domestic Terrorists—Drunk Drivers

A "snitch" is a person who provides information, which may or may not be true, for his own personal gain. Webster defines "snitch" as an "informer" and then defines informer as "a person who secretly accuses, or gives evidence against, another, often for a reward." "Witness" is a good word but sometimes an informant is not always a witness.

One of the most proactive actions by the California Highway Patrol has been asking people to report DUIs by calling 911. This message appears on Division of Highway alert signs on the freeways. Almost everyone now has a cell phone and a 911 call is free, so there is no conceivable reason for not making that call.

If a driver sees a DUI he should continue to follow the suspect vehicle at a safe distance and speed and advise the radio operator of his changing locations. Of course, only follow the DUI if it can be done safely.

Hopefully, people can discard the notion of being a "snitch," especially when public safety is involved.

Simon Kasperoff represents the very best example of how a citizen can provide information to thwart crime.

Just before dusk, and while working as a Montebello Police motorcycle officer on Whittier Blvd next to the Montebello public park, I was waved over by Kasperoff, a local businessman.

He said, "There may not be anything to this but just about a block from here, on a baseball diamond, I saw a man with a little girl and he was walking her to his car, parked in the field. It just didn't look right."

I thanked him for the information and immediately went to the field, which was only a couple of minutes away. When I arrived I saw a male derelict, who was about 55 years old, with a small 5-year-old girl. He was placing her in the front passenger seat of an old model car. When the suspect saw me, he quickly closed the door and rushed around to the driver's side.

At this point, I "jumped the curb" with the motorcycle and accelerated to the suspect's car before he had an opportunity to start the engine.

The little girl had been kidnapped from the adjoining park and probably had not yet been missed by her mother. The suspect admitted that he had taken the child but had done nothing else. He was arrested and he and the little girl were taken to the police department in a cruiser. Shortly, the mother called the police station, frantically looking for her daughter.

A check with the National Criminal Identification Center (NCIC), a national central database maintained by the FBI (since its creation in 1967), revealed the suspect had a twelve page "rap sheet." The suspect had been arrested for almost every felony in the book including child molestation, rape, and murder. His first arrest was as a teenager for stealing chickens. At the time I arrested him he was working as a cook at a local restaurant. He was charged with kidnapping and received a life sentence.

Witnesses' Home Addresses should be Protected

One reason why citizens don't want to get involved in the arrest procedure is the requirement that their name and address be recorded on the arrest report, which is accessible to the criminal and his attorney. A witness to any crime should not have to have their home address on a document that is accessible to the suspect.

Witnesses should be protected from possible intimidation and threats. The witness should be able to use the police department's address, just like an officer does. Not having a person's home address is not a violation of a defendant's rights.

Be Aware There is Opposition to DUI Enforcement

The average citizen would be shocked to know how much opposition there is to DUI enforcement. There is a portion of the general public that think it's all right to drink and drive "as long as you don't drink too much."

The alcohol beverage industry has billions of dollars at stake, and even though they would prefer that no one gets killed by DUIs, it is not their main objective—selling liquor is their main objective. Also, consider how many million people depend on the DUI for their livelihood: Breweries, lawyers, bars, auto repair shops, lobbyists, Bar Owners Associations, and many more.

PART 2: *Chapter 18:* How to Defeat America's Domestic Terrorists—Drunk Drivers 377

For example, the alcohol industry spent $6.6 billion for 2,033,931 product advertisements that aired on television between 2001 and 2007.

When I was fighting for my job in Santa Maria, I got the following letter from Robert Malkin, a very influential Canadian living in Vancouver, B.C. His son was killed by a DUI in Palo Alto and Malkin spent a fortune (and five years of his life) working with the Federal Minister of Justice, John Turner, in Ottawa, trying to get stronger DUI laws in Canada. At one time, Malkin got 23,000 signatures in 56 hours to get one measure on the ballet.

In support of my situation in Santa Maria, he wrote:

> "I was very sorry to hear about your bad luck [being fired]. I tried to phone Ex Gov Brown but his office said he was in Europe, so I wrote to various sources I have in your state. You will hardly believe this, but they clammed up and/or told me to keep out—the door is closed. I could do little or nothing. I have to be frank and I won't go into details as I don't want to involve you."

Later in his letter he wrote of his sacrifices in fighting DUI and then gave me a serious warning, "The Bar Owners Association—a strong lobby—is against you, and you can't lick it. And please don't try."

He ended with, "Courage my friend, it's not the end of the world, but I know how you feel and I'm sorry."

Bob Malkin never learned that I won, but his letter gives some insight into what we were up against in Santa Maria and those same opposing forces are still alive and well today.

Lower the Alcohol Impaired Law to .04% BAC

In 1988, former US Surgeon General Koop reported unequivocally that everyone is impaired at .04% BAC and should not be driving an automobile. January 1, 1982, California made it unlawful for any person to drive a commercial vehicle at a .04% BAC. If it's unsafe for an experienced commercial driver than why is it safe for an amateur driver to drive at twice that impairment level? Most countries have a .05% BAC with Japan, Russia and Sweden at .02% BAC.

When Belgium and France lowered their limit in 1994 to .05% BAC, they experienced a 14% reduction in fatal accidents the following year. That represents a saving of 1,820 American lives and over 1 million injured.

No one can successfully argue that a person is not impaired at .04%. They can only argue to what degree.

Chapter 19
Resources for Combating DUIs

DUI Vans and RVs

Having DUI vans is a great means of processing DUIs on a busy night. And every night should be a busy night for DUIs.

While I was working the South Sacramento Area, we had a large motorcross event in the North Sacramento area. We knew there were going to be hundreds or thousands of fans attending the weekend event. We also knew there was going to be a lot of drinking and driving so we wanted to be prepared. The Sacramento County Sheriffs had a large DUI recreational vehicle that had been converted into a mobile booking unit. They also had a DUI van to make trips back and forth to their jail facilities. It was a joint effort between the CHP and SCS.

We got DUIs coming and going. They were lined up outside the mobile unit waiting for their BAC test and as soon as the DUI van was full the deputy sheriff would make a trip to the jail.

The special enforcement detail was very successful. No traffic collisions occurred, and surprisingly, there were no complaints. Well, other than some of the DUIs who thought it was "poor sportsmanship."

Pursuit Intervention Technique

One of the most effective methods of safely ending pursuits is the Pursuit Intervention Technique (PIT).

The method originated over 20 years ago with the California Highway Patrol and has a long history of success. Today there are more law enforcement agencies than ever before utilizing the PIT. By ending the pursuit as soon as possible, there is less chance of innocent people becoming involved. And if the maneuver is performed properly the only person in danger of being injured is the "bad guy" and he has less chance of being injured than by letting him continue to flee.

The PIT stop is not a bumping or ramming but a precision maneuver, and although it requires special training, it is not difficult to perform. The training can be completed in one day, with updates taking as few as 4 hours a year.

The maneuver involves the pursuing cruiser deliberately spinning-out the pursued suspects vehicle and ending the chase. There is a possibility the suspect may be injured, but that's better than letting him continue until he kills an innocent family at an intersection.

Courts have ruled that PIT is not deadly force.

"In Adams v. St. Lucie County Sheriff's Department, the court ruled that, while fatalities may result from intentional collisions between automobiles, they are infrequent, and therefore deadly force should not be presumed to be the level of force applied in such incidents," reported Captain Travis Yates, Tulsa, Oklahoma Police Department.

"When used correctly along with adequate training an officer can place a suspect vehicle to a predetermined point," said Yates. "Injuries are rare and the success is very high. By considering the Pursuit Intervention Technique an intermediate force, officers can utilize it much more to stop dangerous police pursuits."

The first time I experienced the PIT stop was during academy training in January 1958, when it was used on me. Our training consisted of pursuits on oil slick tracks and if a cadet did not lose control of his cruiser during the pursuit, an instructor would come up behind him and do a PIT, causing the cadet to spin out of control. It was all part of training.

PIT is one of the best tools an officer has and the Los Angeles Police Department should use it. LAPD follows the suspect around until he runs out of gas or gets tired or crashes. Of course, during these "pursuits" there are numerous times LAPD could easily use the PIT, but they let the suspect continue on endangering peoples lives.

I'm not blaming the officers because I use to work with them and I know they would be the first to use a PIT. Someone who knows nothing about liability and law enforcement has tied their hands.

But this will change the first time someone gets seriously injured or killed in an LAPD just-tag-along-behind pursuit. All the survivors will have to do is subpoena the pursuit tape and point out the different locations where the pursuit could have been easily terminated by the PIT and the City of Los Angeles will be out millions of dollars.

Using Preliminary Alcohol Screening Devices

The PAS device is a hand-held breath-testing device, weighing six ounces and about the size of a cell phone. It's designed to analyze a person's blood alcohol concentration (BAC). There is also a Preliminary Breath Testing (PBT) device. The CHP reports the PAS devices used by them as "accurate and highly reliable instruments, which meet stringent federal guidelines for evidentiary breath-testing instruments."

The device is used to augment an officer's probable cause to arrest a person for driving under the influence (DUI) and related offenses. In California, an officer must advise the suspected driver that he may refuse to take the test, that it is not an implied consent test. The officer must further advise the driver, "If arrested, you will be required to submit to another test of either your blood, breath or urine (if applicable) to determine the alcoholic and/or drug content of your blood."

This is a valuable tool for law enforcement that was authorized by the California legislators in January 1994.

The PAS device is especially valuable for persons under the age of 21 who are prohibited from having a BAC of .01% or a person driving a commercial motor vehicle at .04%.

Even with all of the new laws and devices, the CHP sometimes is slow to act.

In February 2008, while I was writing this book, my granddaughter, Heidi Row, 27, came to the house and said there was a drunk driver stuck in a ditch a couple of miles away. She had called the CHP on her cell phone, but was afraid the driver would get back on the road before the CHP arrived. So we went to the location to make sure he didn't leave. There were no streetlights and his car was partially in the roadway sideways. I used my van's warning lights to protect the scene and kept the DUI busy talking about the situation until the CHP arrived. The next day I filed a citizen's complaint against the CHP for taking an hour to respond.

Ignition Interlock Device

An ignition interlock device (IID) is a mechanism similar to a breathalyzer installed in a vehicle's dashboard. A driver must blow a sample of his breath into a hand-held alcohol sensor unit, that is attached to a vehicle's dashboard, before turning on the ignition. The device analyzes a programmed blood alcohol concentration (BAC) and the vehicle cannot be started if a BAC is above a present preset level.

Even if the driver has not been drinking and the ignition is activated, the IID will require another breath sample at random times while the vehicle is being operated. The purpose being to prevent another person from breathing into the device enabling the DUI to continue driving. If the breath sample isn't provided or the sample exceeds the IID present BAC level, the device will log the reading, warn the driver and then set off an alarm such as flashing lights, horn sounding, etc., until the ignition is turned off.

A misconception is that interlock devices will simply turn off the engine, which is incorrect because that could easily result in an unsafe situation and expose IID makers to liability suits.

The driver's activities are recorded on the IID and printed out or downloaded each time the device's sensors are calibrated, usually at one-month intervals. If violations are detected, then additional sanctions can be implemented by the court. Installation, maintenance and calibration are usually paid by the offender at a cost of $60 to $75 a month.

The newer IID's use an ethanol-specific fuel cell for a sensor. A fuel cell sensor is an electrochemical device in which alcohol undergoes a chemical

PART 2: *Chapter 19:* Resources for Combating DUIs 383

oxidation reaction on a catalytic electrode surface (platinum) to generate an electrical current. This current is then measured and converted to an alcohol equivalent reading.

At present, 46 states and the District of Columbia require DUI offenders to use vehicles equipped with ignition interlocks. Alabama, Hawaii, South Dakota, and Vermont do not.

However, only one out of eight convicted DUIs presently get the device. About 100,000 IIDs are being used in the United States, compared to approximately 1.4 million DUI arrests made annually. People with previous DUI convictions make up approximately one-third of the DUI problem in America.

Assemblyman Mike Feuer, D-Los Angeles, introduced an IID law requiring any motorist found guilty of a first DUI offense in Sacramento county will be required to install an IID device in their car for five months. Gov. Arnold Schwarzenegger signed it into law to become effective July 1, 2010.

It is a six year pilot project in four counties—Sacramento, Alameda, Los Angeles and Tulare. The American Beverage Institute, a restaurant trade association, had urged Schwarzenegger not to sign the bill, calling the locks intrusive and saying the state should target repeat offenders.

Mother's Against Drunk Drivers (MADD) reports that 65% of the public favors mandatory interlocks for first-time offenders and 85% favor mandatory interlocks for repeat offenders. MADD strongly supports having IID installed on a DUIs first conviction.

Not everyone supports the Ignition Interlock Devices.

One critic, the director of the American Beverage Institute, writes, "Applying a single response to a complex issue, such as ignition interlock devices for all charged with driving under the influence, indicates the focus has moved from an anti-drunk driving campaign to one of anti-drinking."

No system is perfect but there are still valid reasons for requiring the IID that cannot be disputed. If the DUI is caught cheating then he runs the risk of a more severe penalty but if there is no requirement for a DUI to have an IID then he can continue to drive with impunity without the worry of getting caught cheating. In other words, I would rather have an imperfect system than no system at all.

In support of the devices, MADD reports there are 12 high-quality studies on IID for repeat offenders. All of those reports showed decreases in repeat offenses while the IID was on the vehicle. In Maryland, Alberta, California and elsewhere, offenders who were assigned interlocks had 50 percent to 90 percent fewer repeat offenses than offenders who didn't receive the device.

MADD goes on to report, "Interlocks fail when the supporting judicial infrastructure is weak—usually when mandatory interlock laws aren't enforced or offenders who are sentenced to receive interlocks don't have them installed or receive little oversight."

I agree with MADD but I'll put it in stronger words. Our DUI enforcement and punishment programs are only as good as the agencies enforcing them and here lies the problem. Legislators should seriously look at MADD's model interlock law.

The Federal Government supports the use of the ignition interlock. The Transportation Equity Act for the 21st Century (TEA-21) "Requires that all motor vehicles of repeat intoxicated drivers be impounded or immobilized for some period of time during the license suspension period, or require the installation of an ignition interlock system on all motor vehicles of such drivers for some period of time after the end of the suspension."

All states were required to have such repeat intoxicated driver laws in place by October 1, 2000, or have a portion of their Federal-aid highway construction funds redirected into other state safety activities, beginning in fiscal year 2001.

A Drivers License just for DUIs

There is one piece of legislation I would like to propose and it is relatively affordable. When a DUI is convicted then he should receive a new drivers license identifying him as a DUI. The drivers license should be distinct and include all prior arrests. Likewise, on a second offense, the Department of Motor Vehicles (DMV) should be directed to issue a DUI license plate that the DUI would have to display for 3 years.

New Laws Requiring Doctors to Report Alcohol Abuse

All states should have a law requiring physicians to report potentially dangerous medical conditions to the Department of Transportation until such time as the DUI Enforcement Agency is established. This is a proactive way of removing potential drug and alcohol addicts and problem drivers from the highways without waiting to discover them after they are involved in traffic collisions.

Pennsylvania is one of only six states in the nation that direct physicians to report drivers with potentially dangerous medical conditions, and it is the only state to list alcohol abuse as a problem that should be brought to official attention.

"About 230 Pennsylvania drivers lost their licenses last year after doctors reported their drug or alcohol addiction," the Pennsylvania Department of Transportation said.

Limiting Car Speed

No car manufacturer should be permitted to assemble a car that can exceed a maximum speed of 75 mph except for special cars such as police cruisers and emergency vehicles. There is no reason the public should have a car that exceeds that speed. This would give the advantage to police during pursuits (almost eliminating them), reduce the severity of collisions, and reduce traffic collisions in general.

High-Tech OK Fighting Thieves, But No High-Tech for DUIs

In a month-long operation by a multi-agency task force identified as the Delta Regional Auto Theft Team (Delta RATT), bait cars netted 105 auto thieves. There's no doubt about its success. The task force was made up of CHP officers, personnel from San Joaquin County Sheriff's Department, Lodi Police Department, a San Joaquin County District Attorney's officer and a special agent with the national Insurance Crime Bureau.

As reported in CHP publication, Vol. 54, No. 1: "High-tech is a vital player in the CHP's successful bait car stings. Thieves are under constant monitoring with audio, satellite and infrared video from the moment they open the car door until they're apprehended. All the data can be stored in the computer for evidence."

The thieves are tracked in real time, on a laptop, with a street map display. The sting includes an ignition kill-switch, preventing high-speed chases, and a door locking mechanism foiling escapes. The laptop sounds an alarm when the bait car is entered.

"Bait cars are one of the CHP's most successful auto theft programs ever. The conviction rate in some jurisdictions is 99 percent, "commented CHP Officer Blake Schnabel. CHP Officer Will Inskip added, "Some days, we made six to eight arrests."

Their efforts paid off. In the first 10 months of 2006, auto thefts in the county dropped 14 percent compared to the same period in 2005. "The bait car operation also illustrates how proactive enforcement can yield unexpected results," Anne Da Vigo reported in her article.

Court TV now airs the program.

Catching auto thieves is a necessity and the different departments should be congratulated for their proactive enforcement and innovative means of catching them. Also notable, is the high-tech equipment they were able to obtain.

Now, if this can be done successfully with auto thieves, then the same effort and high tech should be used for apprehending DUIs. Auto thefts are important but someone dying every 40 minutes by the hand of a DUI is a much higher priority.

But most people know that.

The public wants auto thieves and similar criminals caught because the general public doesn't steal cars. They want bank robbers caught because they don't rob banks.

But the public as a whole does drink and does drive and sometimes they do both.

So, many people do not want laws or high-tech programs in place that will result in *their* getting caught. As long as DUI enforcement is random, and only about 10 percent of the DUIs are being arrested, then one has a

PART 2: *Chapter 19:* Resources for Combating DUIs

90 percent chance of not getting caught. Even after a person is arrested for DUI, the justice system makes it unlikely that they will get more than a slap on the wrist.

That is why it is acceptable to stake out auto thieves but not DUIs.

For as long as I can remember, it has been against the California Highway Patrol's policy to stake out bars, and I know the California legislators are opposed to it.

Even though Klippness and I didn't stake out bars on the CHP, we thought the prohibition was stupid. However, we were catching so many DUIs patrolling our assigned beats that we weren't looking for other methods of apprehension—and that was when .15% BAC was the legal limit.

If the BAC had been .08%, as it is today, we would have had to have a portable booking van immediately available. Even back then, on one occasion we had to handcuff a DUI to a parking meter while we arrested a second DUI.

But there is nothing wrong with staking out bars. I don't think it's necessary to have a plainclothes officer inside the bar, but they could certainly be waiting outside the bar for a DUI to drive out of the parking lot. Many people have told me, "That's not fair." But this is NOT a game. The only unfair thing about it is the selfish DUI killing or maiming innocent people because he wants to have a few drinks and socialize.

If we knew someone was going to rob a bank, would it be fair to stake out the bank? Or, if we knew someone was going to steal a car, would it be fair to stake out the car?

DUIs cause more damage than bank robbers or car thieves in terms of injuring and killing innocent people. It is time we aggressively pursue a policy of staking out bars, especially at closing time, because this is when most of the DUI-involved crashes occur.

Fresno is bucking public pressure and setting a great example in doing exactly that. See Chapter 22 for details.

License Plate Scanner

More high-tech equipment is being created to catch criminals. Law enforcement agencies, including the California Highway Patrol, and cities of Lincoln and Roseville, now have a device installed on a few of their cruisers that automatically reads license plates, telling the officer immediately whether a vehicle has been listed as stolen or has an invalid plate.

The software will also register whether the vehicle's driver is wanted by law enforcement for a crime, a warrant or another reason. They are updated daily by the California Department of Justice.

Four small cameras are mounted inside and atop of the cruiser that read license plates on vehicles behind and in front of the squad car. The device also reads licenses of parked vehicles. The cameras at the front of the cruiser are infrared, allowing an officer to get a clear read on a license plate after dark.

PlateScan, one of the manufacturers, will beep to let the officer know when a suspect license plate has been detected, and an image of the plate will be displayed on the patrol car's computer. A moment later the computer's automated voice will provide an audible description such as "stolen vehicle," "stolen plate," or "felony vehicle."

These devices are made by several companies and cost between $21,000 and $31,000 each. The Roseville Police Department has three. The Department paid for one, a grant from a statewide Indian gaming task force paid for one and the last one will be paid with a federal Homeland Security grant. Even Arden Fair Mall, in Sacramento, has two license plate scanners on their security vehicles, which they purchased with a $42,000 federal grant from Homeland Security.

Lincoln Police Chief Brian Vizzusi said the license plate readers are "a great new technology that will help us put bad guys in jail."

Again, the departments are to be commended for their proactive enforcement and use of high-tech equipment.

Just imagine what could be done using high-tech equipment to apprehend DUIs or to prevent a person under the influence from driving at all. By priority, 90 percent of our resources should be used for the removal of DUIs from our highways. Right now, it's more like 10 percent.

Chapter 20
Celebrities: The Privileged Get a Free Pass

Justice is not always blind. Everyone is not treated the same regardless of race, creed, or standing in the community. There are exceptions—and it often depends on your class in society.

As far as the American law enforcement and justice systems are concerned, there are two basic classes of society: the privileged and all others, who generally include the middle class and the poor.

The laws of the land are pretty consistently applied to the middle class and the poor. But the privileged class, which includes celebrities, has its own "justice system" and many individuals in positions of power, being in the privileged class themselves, support and carry out this system of injustice.

Why?

In addition to basic self-preservation, people in positions of power want to be able to drink and drive without worrying about normal consequences. They (prosecutors, judges, juries and law enforcement officers) also seem to be mesmerized by celebrities. I saw this firsthand for years while working in the Hollywood area.

If you have enough money or fame and know the right people, you can make things happen. This is a basic corruption of our justice system. In order to stop it, there needs to be a change in our system.

Consider just a few recent cases in which celebrities received special treatment:

Paris Hilton's Reduced Sentence

Now, Paris Hilton is another thing altogether. Hilton was arrested in 2006 for DUI and responded, "It was nothing."

"Paris Hilton being arrested just makes her more famous," veteran publicist Michael Levine told the press. "She has devoted her entire adult life to appearing to be the princess of parties."

Hilton, who didn't even bother to appear in court, pled "no contest" to a reduced charge of alcohol-related reckless driving (instead of DUI) and was placed on 36 months probation, ordered to pay about $1,500 in fines and attend some alcohol-education programs.

Just for reference, the maximum penalty for a first misdemeanor DUI offense is a $1,000 fine and six months in jail.

Finally, after being stopped two more times for driving with a suspended license, Hilton was ordered to spend 45 days behind bars for violating probation in the alcohol-related, reckless-driving case.

Then, the 45 days were reduced to 23 days for "good time" for days served. How could it be for days served since she hadn't served any time yet?

And then she only served 3 days because the jail was "over-crowded."

How many other prisoners were released with her that day because of the "over-crowded" condition? And in regards to the "undisclosed health condition," could it have been she got homesick? Whatever that undisclosed health condition was, it didn't seem to affect her nightlife after being released.

This kind of favoritism degrades the judicial system and should not be tolerated by the public, who wants to know why she didn't serve her time like everyone else.

Lost Star Serves 10% of DUI Sentence

In January 2008, former "Lost" TV star, Michelle Rodriguez, was released from a Los Angeles County women's jail in Lynwood after serving 18 days of a 180-days sentence for violating probation in a drunken driving case.

She was released early under a program that deals with jail overcrowding by allowing non-violent female inmates to serve as little as 10 percent of their sentences.

This wasn't the first time Rodriguez got out early. A similar thing happened two years ago when Rodriguez served just one day of a 60-day jail sentence for probation violation.

The jails get crowded when celebrities are locked up. This type of favoritism, is disgusting to the average citizen who knows that's not the real reason they were released.

Lindsay Lohan's Sentencing a Joke

In 2007, Lindsay Lohan, 22, was arrested for DUI after crashing her Mercedes-Benz into a tree in Beverly Hills. She was arrested for DUI again, in Santa Monica in July 2008 for reportedly chasing a former personal assistant in her SUV.

Lohan pled guilty in, August 2008, to two counts of being under the influence of cocaine, two counts of driving under the influence of alcohol, and one count of reckless driving. There is no way of knowing how many lives she endangered by her selfish and reckless conduct. Now, it was up to the court to be fair and impartial in sentencing.

The ordinary person would be expected to spend some serious time in prison. Lohan spent a total of 84 minutes in jail. That is less time than it normally takes to book a person and a lot less time than it takes to get sober.

It was also reported that she completed "community service." Community service is the court's way of letting celebrities beat the system—and it never reduces DUIs.

And if that were not enough punishment, Lohan had to undergo (or attend) drug-rehabilitation treatment. Attending a group discussion is not punishment.

So, our present justice system failed us again. Not surprisingly, Judge Marsha N. Revel had to admonish Lohan in March 2009 that she needed to show better documentation of her treatment program. Does anyone really believe that this sort of coddling and pampering is going to have any effect upon reducing the deaths that are occurring on our highways every 40 minutes?

Singer Brandy Kills on Freeway, Walks Away

Drinking isn't always involved in these cases, but separate justice certainly is; especially when a celebrity kills an ordinary person.

On December 29, 2007, the Los Angeles city attorney's office decided not to prosecute Grammy-winning singer-actress Brandy on criminal charges for a deadly freeway crash. Prosecutors decided there was "insufficient evidence" for a jury to find Brandy Norwood guilty beyond a reasonable doubt of vehicular manslaughter.

The decision ran counter to a California Highway Patrol recommendation that she be charged in the December 30 crash. Vehicular manslaughter carries a maximum sentence of a year in jail and a $1,000 fine.

Brandy was driving her Range Rover on Interstate 405 when she failed to slow with traffic and hit the back of a Honda at about 65 mph, according to a CHP report. The Honda, driven by Awatef Aboudihaj, 38, of Los Angeles, hit another vehicle, slid sideways and struck the center divider, then was hit by an oncoming car.

Aboudihaj was killed.

There's got to be some kind of check and balance on the courts. Some of the city attorney's and district attorney's decisions could only be described as insane. How could any logical human being say that she was not responsible for Aboudihaj's death? If she had stayed home that day, Aboudihaj would still be alive. She had to be a contributing factor.

Brandy was sued for more than $50 million in separate actions filed by Aboudihaj's parents, children and wife.

Mike Tyson Gets 1 Day, Instead of 4 Years

On November 20, 2007, Mike Tyson, former heavyweight boxing champion, was arrested for cocaine possession and driving under the influence and almost striking a sheriff deputy's vehicle.

Tyson was realistically looking at more than four years in prison. Instead, Judge Helene Abrams, had her own idea of justice by sentencing him to one day in an open-air jail, three years of probation for the cocaine charge, a fine and 360 hours of community service.

Her justification for this slap on the wrist was, "You worked to address your addiction and self-destructive behavior."

I wonder how she was able to say that with a straight face.

Vivica Fox Dances Out of Trouble

On December 8, 2007, "Dancing with the Stars," Vivica A. Fox, entered a "no contest" plea deal with prosecutors to settle a drunken driving case and was given three years probation, 90-day alcohol education program and a $390 fine. A "no contest" amounts to a guilty plea.

The "90-day alcohol education program" sounds impressive but it doesn't really mean a thing without knowing the program. For example, it could require meeting once a month for one hour. Or she could be handed some material and be asked to read it over the next 90 days.

And with her money, the $390 means she might have to skip dinner out one night.

These judges are getting as creative as the loan companies did in the recent housing market. Possibly the answer is going to have to be mandatory sentencing.

Tony La Russa Gets Warning

Another celebrity who pled outright guilty in 2007 was Tony La Russa, manager of the St. Louis Cardinals. The newspaper reported that eight months before his court appearance, police found him asleep inside his running sport-utility vehicle, at a stoplight and smelling of alcohol, in Jupiter, Florida.

There's a thin line between being asleep and passed out. Normally, a person doesn't go to sleep, sitting in a car, in the middle of a lane of traffic at a stoplight. That's something you usually do at home in bed.

The newspaper reported he "will serve at least six months probation."

His penalty for passing out in his car was "Don't do that again for at least six months."

Mel Gibson Arrest Badly Handled

Sometimes, but not often, celebrities get less justice. Take Mel Gibson's DUI arrest in 2006 in which his anti-Semitic tirade caught worldwide attention.

As much as we may disagree with the remarks, they were not pertinent to the charge of DUI.

Gibson was arrested for driving under the influence. The arrest report is supposed to include the elements of the offense that support the arrest. How much did he have to drink? How did he perform the FST?

What does a DUI making anti-Semitic remarks have anything to do with being under the influence? I've heard Louis Farrakhan, acting head of the Nation of Islam, make anti-Semitic remarks and he wasn't accused of being under the influence because of his remarks. The only purpose it served was to embarrass Gibson and possibly damage his reputation.

A statement, "I know I shouldn't be driving" or "I'm not that drunk" would be appropriate statements on a DUI arrest report.

The Sheriff's Department came under widespread criticism when Sheriff Baca was accused of ordering details of the outburst eliminated from the deputy's report. Then it was reported, "Baca denied that the report was sanitized." What's wrong with sanitizing a report? Reports aren't final until a supervisor reviews, approves and signs them.

Princess Diana Pays Ultimate Price for Driver's DUI

Sometimes celebrities don't get a second chance and die as a result of someone driving under the influence. The world was shocked in August of 1997 when Princess Diana and her boyfriend, Dodi Fayed, were killed in an automobile accident in Paris.

It was a shock but it shouldn't necessarily have been a surprise, with a driver under the influence of alcohol, driving at a high rate of speed while trying to negotiate curves. This driver was reported to have been a heavy drinker and had been drinking that evening, so what were they doing in the car with him?

The news media seemed to play down the DUI part and blame the accident more on the paparazzi. What's wrong with making sure your driver is sober and requiring him to drive the speed limit? So, a few paparazzi take a few extra pictures of you. So what? The issue was not the paparazzi but the DUI.

Evidence showed that Henri Paul, deputy director of security, was driving twice the speed limit and had three times the legal blood alcohol limit when the crash occurred. Pure and simple, that was the problem.

Most people only take DUI serious when someone gets killed or injured. If DUI was taken more seriously, then maybe people would be more likely to say, "Wait a minute. I'm not going to get in this car with this driver. He's been drinking."

But if a DUI conviction only amounts to six months probation, community service (which is a joke) and $350 fine, then it is only slightly more serious than running a stop sign.

Even the light sentences handed down by most judges reveal the complacency of society, otherwise, those judges would be voted out of office the next election.

Chapter 21
Victims of DUI

The numbers of the victims of DUIs are overwhelming, especially when you consider the pain and anguish inflicted on people who were completely random—and completely innocent.

In other words, it could happen to any of us at any time.

Victims of DUIs had every right to assume that they would return home safely, as they had their entire lives. Instead, suddenly and without warning, a DUI either killed them or mangled their bodies in just a split second, changing their lives forever.

Their loved ones must bury them or those who survive must live the remainder of their lives in pain and despair. All because some unaware and uncaring individual wanted to have a few drinks and drive—and because drinking and driving is not recognized as the true menace it represents.

One thing about DUIs, they don't discriminate. They will—and do—kill anyone without regard to their nationality or standing in the community. If you drive a car, you could be the next victim.

In fact, some of you reading this will be killed or maimed by a DUI. That is reality.

Here are just a few examples of the tragedy spawned by DUIs.

Just a Few Beers Can Send You to Prison

"I'll just have a couple of drinks and that's all," and the next thing you know you are on your way to prison. It is estimated that DUI arrests cost an average of $10,000 when all expenses are totaled. But that's just part of the story. There are thousands of well-meaning individuals who just want to have a good time but end up spending years of their life in prison.

Former "Prison Break" actor Lane Garrison was sentenced to three years and four months in prison for a DUI crash that killed a 17-year-old Beverly Hills High student in December 2006.

Before the sentencing, Garrison, 27, apologized to the family of Vahagn Setian. Setian was a passenger in the 2001 Land Rover that Garrison rammed into a tree. Two 15-year-old girls, who also were in the vehicle, survived.

These senseless deaths have been happening for decades.

So many people were being killed by DUIs in the 1960s that a few conservative courts decided to start charging the DUIs with manslaughter if they killed someone. That was a safe charge because the law defines manslaughter "as the killing of a human being."

As the DUI killings continued, some wises souls in the judicial system decided that if a DUI deliberately got into an automobile, drove in such a reckless manner that it could be deemed he knew there was a high probability that he may kill someone, then, according to the law, he could be charged with murder. As a result, some DUIs are getting big-time sentencing for "a night out with the boys" followed by a stupid decision to drive.

Prosecutors won DUI murder convictions in Washington State in 1996 and California in 1995, but did not seek the death penalty.

The first case in the nation in which prosecutors pushed for the death penalty in a DUI trial took place in Winston-Salem, North Carolina in May 1997. Thomas Richard Jones, 39, was convicted of murder in the deaths of two young women who were passengers in a car hit by Jones' pickup. Four others in the car were injured.

PART 2: Chapter 21: Victims of DUI 399

Jurors deliberated only 1½ hours before returning a verdict of guilty of first-degree murder and Jones was sentenced to two life sentences. The prosecutor, Vincent Rabil, had sought the death penalty, but said the verdict would still send a strong message to people who drink and drive.

During his testimony, Jones wept as he described how his pickup crossed the median and struck the student's car while he was trying to insert a tape into his stereo.

The victims were Maia Witzl, 19, of Arlington, Texas, and Julie Hansen, 19, of Rockville, Maryland. Both attended Wake Forest University, in Winston-Salem.

Maia's father, Bob, said, "My wife and I are in sort of a prison and will be for the rest of our natural lives, and we feel Mr. Jones should be, too." The parents said they favored Jones getting life sentences and not the death penalty.

DUI Causes Fiery CHP Crash

Several years ago a CHP officer stopped a DUI in the San Francisco Bay Area on a highway near a bridge, with water flowing under it. The officer was completing the arrest and was seated in the CHP cruiser when it was struck by another DUI.

The CHP cruiser burst into flames, trapping the CHP officer. Seriously burned and wanting to extinguish the flames, the officer jumped off of the bridge into the water below. A citizen, who had seen the crash, jumped into the water and saved the officer from drowning.

The officer, with very serious burns over his entire body, was rushed to a hospital. The courageous officer lived but found it necessary to retire.

Don't tell this officer or his family that DUIs aren't terrorists.

Four Killed After 3-Martini Lunch

Sometimes even people from the privileged class can't escape the consequences.

On March 26, 2007, Roberto Vellanoweth, 64, a prominent California State executive and gubernatorial appointee, stopped by a local bar for a three-martini lunch with friends.

He had done it before, but this time when he got into his Jeep Grand Cherokee, he sped over rain-slick city streets and crashed head-on into another car, killing 4 people and seriously injuring one.

Vellanoweth was traveling at 72 miles per hour when his car smashed head-on into the car carrying Brizchelle Rice-Nash, 21, her 19-month-old son Kamall Osby, Shanice Carter, 18, Brittanaya Rice-Nash, 17, and Tanisha Jackson. Only Jackson survived, and she suffered extensive internal injuries.

Vellanweth became an ultimate symbol of a "power sleaze" during his trial, as he used high-priced attorneys to claim that a friend of his (who died before the trial) had given him a mysterious drink before he drove, that his wife was actually driving, and finally, that he had a "temporary abdominal problem that kept him sober at the time of the fatal crash, but healed in time for him to test .16% BAC after the crash."

Immediately after the crash, Vellanoweth was belligerent and had to be restrained. He never apologized to the victims' families until after he was convicted and before he was sentenced.

This time, his privileged status of a power-broker in California couldn't help him. A disgusted Judge Patrick Marlette gave him the maximum sentence of 17 years and 6 months, telling Vellanoweth that he made a "conscious decision" to drive drunk after he got "gassed up" on martinis.

Vellanoweth would have had to drink more than three martinis to have a .16% BAC four hours after the killings.

Pregnant Woman and Unborn Son Die in Gutter

In 2006, families were arriving to celebrate a Passover dinner in the normally quiet Sacramento neighborhood of Arden Arcade.

Jessica Plaut-Cappon had just arrived and was unstrapping her infant son from his car seat. Her friend, Annette Brodovsky, 33, who was five months pregnant with a son, was waiting for her on the front lawn.

At that moment, Brandon Bowman, a 26-year-old drunk driver, came screeching around the corner and into their lives. Bowman lost control of his car on the curve.

The car slammed into Plaut-Cappon, then ran onto the front lawn where it hit Brodovsky. The force of the impact threw Brodovsky, a mother of two young girls, in the air, flung her onto Bowman's windshield and then tossed her body between another car and a gutter.

"Both Mrs. Brodovsky and her unborn son died in that gutter," Deputy District Attorney Nancy Cochrane told the court.

After the collision, Bowman got out of his wrecked car, uttered some profanities and then ran away. He was found a short time later, hiding in a drainage ditch. His BAC surpassed .20%, more than twice the legal limit.

On April 2, 2007, Bowman, pled "no contest" to DUI, gross vehicular manslaughter, DUI causing death or injury and hit-and-run that caused death or serious injury. Bowman received 8 years in prison

Why Hasn't My Daughter Gotten Home Yet?

A very good friend (who I played tournament softball with for years,) Bill Petrelli, and his family, lost a 21-year-old vivacious daughter to a DUI one Saturday night as she was driving home from work. One minute she was laughing and joking on the phone with him and the next time the phone rang it was from the coroner.

The judge sentenced the DUI to a few months in jail and the Petrelli family was left to bury their daughter and with an agonizing lifetime of sorrow. The DUI didn't have any money to pay for the funeral expenses, and that's understandable, because mixed drinks are pretty expensive especially when you drink a lot of them.

I asked Bill how he could cope with such a tragedy and, looking forlorn, he said, "What can you do?"

DUI Ruins the Life of a Good Man

Most of the time the effects of a DUI's actions are felt long after the crash.

When I was working as a plainclothes detective in Montebello, my partner and I were assigned to bring a man back to a mental institution from which he had escaped.

The man's wife had called the police station asking for our help in returning him to the institution. Her husband told her that he was never going back.

She said he was sitting on the front porch and she described his appearance. She also said he had a gun in the house. She said she would be sitting on the front porch with him to discourage him from going in the house. She also recommended that we bring a straight-jacket because she was sure he would put up a fight.

We drove by the house in an unmarked cruiser to make sure everything was as described. Then we parked about three doors down and began walking toward the house with a large clothes bag with the straight jacket in it. We were hoping we could pass ourselves off as salesmen.

We stopped in front of their house and asked them if they would like to buy a magazine. Everything was going on schedule until we took one step toward the porch and the suspect jumped up and said, "You're cops and you've come to get me."

He turned and ran for the front door and just as he got into the front room, we were able to tackle him. All the time we were wrestling with him he was screaming, "I'm not going back," and pleading with his wife to help him.

We were able to get the straight jacket on him without hurting him but he continued to plead with us to let him go.

Now, the sad part.

Why was this gentleman in a mental institute in the first place? Well, he was driving down the street one day, Greenwood Avenue going through the intersection of Whittier Blvd. to be exact, when a DUI terrorist ran a red light and smashed into his car.

He received a serious head wound and was never able to function normally again. He had to spend the rest of his life in a mental institution away from his loving wife.

The DUI terrorist? His penalty was a $350 fine and six months probation. Back then DUIs didn't go to jail for injuring and killing people. That still applies today.

The DUI incidents mentioned here are just every day occurrences throughout the United States and will continue as long as the public tolerates it.

DUIs Subject of Civil Suits

Besides the possibility of going to prison, the DUI must also worry about being sued. Bar owners, who serve patrons who go out and get involved in DUI collisions, are not strangers to civil suits either.

In 2003 in Riverside County, Charles Giordano was convicted of DUI vehicular manslaughter and sentenced to four years in prison after he struck and killed Kenneth Armstrong, who was riding a motorcycle.

Armstrong's wife, Patricia, requested restitution "based on the her husband's modest earnings of approximately $35,000 per year." A lower court granted her $167,700. The California Supreme Court ruled: "Spouses of victims may receive restitution from convicted killers [in this case a DUI] based on the lost earning potential of the person slain."

Those Serving DUIs Arrested

Culpability does not always end with the driver. Some statues extend the element of control to one who owns or is in custody of the vehicle, such as the passenger. The owner is in violation as long as he knows, or reasonably should know, the driver is DUI.

And people who serve alcohol to DUIs are also held responsible.

Four University of California, Davis, students were arrested in 2007 for serving beer at a keg party that resulted in a fatal DUI crash. The driver in that crash, another student, was sentenced to state prison for six years.

Sergei Andres, 19; Conor Tekautz, 19; and Brian Soest, 20; all were taken into custody at their apartment complex in Davis. Timothy Gereg, 21, who lived at the same complex, had already left for a crew team practice but turned himself in later.

All four were accused of furnishing alcohol to 19-year-old Eric James Holmes, who on Feb. 7th caused a head-on collision on Interstate 5 in Sacramento that killed Amanda LeGrand, 34, of Washington State.

Authorities said Holmes, a UCD student who lives in Auburn, was driving home from a keg party at a Davis apartment. Holmes reportedly had a blood-alcohol level of .15%—nearly twice the legal limit of .08%—when he entered I-5 going the wrong direction, colliding with LeGrand's car in a crash that also injured the woman's aunt.

Holmes was sentenced to six years in state prison after pleading guilty to a charge of gross vehicular manslaughter while intoxicated.

The arrests were made by officers from the California Department of Alcoholic Beverage Control, with assistance from Davis police officers, as part of the state's TRACE (Target Responsibility for Alcohol Connected Emergencies) program. The program seeks to determine the sources of alcohol provided to minors who are involved in serious or fatal traffic collisions.

The protocol for the TRACE program was developed by a coalition of California law-enforcement groups and other agencies, including ABC, the Attorney Generals Office, the California Highway Patrol, Office of Traffic Safety, Mothers Against Drunk Driving and the California Police Chiefs and Sheriffs associations.

Arrested 4 Times for DUI Before Killing

Lyle Norbert, 41, of Suisun City, California, had his driver's license suspended six times and had been arrested four times on suspicion of DUI, plus he liked to run from the police. Norbert only had one DUI conviction,

PART 2: Chapter 21: Victims of DUI   405

a misdemeanor. According to his long-time attorney, Pam Herzig, of San Francisco, that's because he "never hurt anybody."

His first arrest for DUI was on Halloween 1997 when he crashed a white Ford Mustang into five parked cars near 26th and Noe streets in San Francisco and fled the scene, according to police. Although he was arrested for DUI, he was allowed to plead guilty to reckless driving and was placed on three years probation.

Then, on January 24, 1999, Norbert was spotted by the CHP driving a Mustang and speeding on Eastbound Interstate-80 in Crockett. Once again, he was arrested on suspicion of drunken driving.

He made bail and, seven days later, led the CHP on a 16 mile, 12-minute pursuit on I-80, in a rented 1999 Pontiac Grand Am, at speeds up to 90 mph. Norbert, allegedly DUI, whizzed past the toll booth at the Carquinez Bridge and was stopped near his home.

In July 1999, Norbert pled guilty to a reduced charge of reckless driving for the January 24, 1999, incident and was fined $275.

On November 3, 2000, Norbert was arrested again for DUI while driving a rented Daewoo Leganza. He failed to make a court appearance, and a $30,000 warrant was issued for his arrest. He also failed to show up in court for the January, 1999, incident. A no-bail warrant was issued and his probation was revoked.

Norbert told California Highway Patrol officers, after leading them on the chase, that he "always runs from the police but I always get caught because I'm slow. I'm just too drunk."

The inevitable happened in March 2001, when Norbert once more failed to stop for CHP officers near El Cerrito, this time leading them on a high-speed chase into Berkeley. It ended when Norbert's rented 2001 Pontiac Bonneville ran a red light and crashed into a car driven by Theodore Kesnick, 33, of San Francisco, killing Kesnick instantly. Norbert's only injuries were described as abrasions from an airbag.

Norbert, who also had previous convictions for weapons and drugs, was able to drive after four drunken-driving arrests because he either made bail, or failed to show up in court or for counseling sessions. In at least two cases, Norbert was permitted to plead guilty to lesser charges of reckless driving, resulting in only fines and probation.

On May 18, 2004, Norbert was convicted of second-degree murder, possession of hashish and marijuana.

An Oakland traffic officer, echoing sentiments by others in law enforcement, said there was just no way an overburdened criminal justice system could deter a problem driver who persisted in driving. I don't accept that defeatist attitude. The criminal justice system needs to be overhauled *now*.

Chapter 22
Fresno: A case example of how to fight DUIs

In 2006, in response to an alarming increase in DUI fatalities in Fresno, the sixth largest city in California with a population of almost one-half million, the Police Department's Traffic Bureau decided they had to be more aggressive and creative in their fight against DUIs.

To make this happen, they would have to go to the source of the problem and that meant the bars.

Captain Andy Hall knew by taking the enforcement of drunken driving to a new level would bring both success and outrage. Traffic Detective Mark Van Wyhe said that while he expected some people to be upset, community safety had priority. Ignoring the inevitable public outcry, the Fresno Police Department had the courage to implement a new program that they call the "Bar Watch."

Captain Andy Hall, who heads the traffic bureau, said he came up with the idea for undercover bar surveillance in December, 2005, while traffic officers were teaming with the Department of Alcoholic Beverage Control (ABC) to send minors into bars or stores to try to buy alcohol. It is a common practice for ABC to put undercover officers in bars.

The bars were targeted based on alcohol-related incidents. Those incidents included alcohol-related crashes, arrests and calls for service. Some of the fatal DUIs were identified as coming from the bars that would now be part of the "Bar Watch."

Barry Gleeson, a Fresno man who serves on the state's executive board for Mothers Against Drunk Drivers, summed it up this way, "What the police were trying to do was take irresponsible people and keep them from killing themselves and other people."

Two plainclothes officers, usually a male and female, were positioned inside the bar where they could observe the customers firsthand and report to officers outside in unmarked police cars when a person under the influence was leaving the bar. If the bar was packed it was sometimes necessary for the plainclothes officers to move around to observe the clientele.

The undercover officers looked for three potential levels of intoxication, according to the Fresno police Department's Traffic Bureau publication:

> "The first level of impairment is the obvious drunk, one who can't care for himself could pose the most serious danger to the public. He is detained prior to his getting into his car and either arrested for public intoxication or turned over to a responsible adult.
>
> "The second level is a person that has demonstrated some signs of intoxication, but has not committed a crime. The crime occurs when they attempt to drive their car from the parking lot where they are stopped and arrested.
>
> "The last level is the driver leaving the establishment who exhibits no obvious signs of intoxication. This person may be followed a short distance to determine if further investigation is warranted."

The officers in the unmarked cars follow the questionable driver and if his driving indicates he might be DUI, then marked police cars are called to pull him over.

Van Wyhe and a task force of officers conducted its first bar surveillance operation on February 10, 2006. Six people were arrested on DUI charges from the El Molino Rojo and El Dorado nightclubs the first Saturday.

PART 2: *Chapter 22:* Fresno: A case example of how to fight DUIs 409

The following Saturday was even more productive as the task force hit several bars including the Dirty Olive.

At the Dirty Olive, one of Fresno's most popular bars, the undercover officers set up camp in a corner after getting some drinks at the bar. Gerardo Franco, manager of the Dirty Olive, said he supported police efforts to get drunken drivers off the road although "it completely made our patrons feel uncomfortable." He didn't believe it would hurt his business because he said the Dirty Olive was doing its best to ensure patrons got home safely.

Whatever Franco was doing to ensure his patron's safety appeared wildly unsuccessful.

Before operation "Bar Watch" even started at 10:30 on the first night, an undercover officer observed a DUI "stumbling to his car" in the Dirty Olive parking lot. But that's only the beginning.

Later, as the bar neared its closing time around midnight, a Fresno Bee article describes it this way: "The next half-hour is the busiest of the night. The plainclothes officers flooded Van Wyhe with phone calls, describing patrons who appeared visibly drunk as they walked out. Van Wyhe and Owen, in turn, keep tabs on the cars and their direction of travel, while dispatching patrol units to go after them."

"It's like someone opened the floodgates," Van Wyhe said, "Everybody was just running crazy in the parking lot being blatantly drunk." One of the DUIs arrested that night was Nicole Gonzalez who said she worked at the Dirty Olive but it was her night off. She said she had two "shooters" before leaving but refused to take a Breathalyzer test. Maybe someone should tell the manager of the Dirty Olive his "Operation Safe Home" is not working.

Tony Brisceno, co-owner of Veni Vidi Vici nightclub, told The Bee that he believed bar profits would be affected by the Bar Watch program. "It'll keep people from staying out so late, having more drinks," he said, "They might just stay home and buy some alcohol."

"Like this is a bad thing?" was the response of one of the local columnists. The columnist, Eddie Jimenez, also commented, "It's amazing that despite all the statistics trotted out routinely on the dangers of drunken driving and despite our supposed awareness of the problem, we are still in a drunken stupor of denial on this issue."

Public reaction was fast and furious.

Before most of the DUIs had time to post bail after the second night of the operation, a segment of the public was up in arms. The newspaper headlined, *"Fresno police initiate DUI sting"* and *"Police strategy called 'underhanded."* Then more headlines, *"Fresno DUI stings on hold"* and *"Public has strong reaction to officers in bars."*

The newspaper reported that Fresno Police Chief Jerry Dyer announced that he would review the new drunken-driving enforcement operation that placed undercover officers in bars before the department conducted another sting.

The police chief also said he didn't know his traffic bureau had been conducting undercover bar stings until Monday, but he commended their creativity while saying he had some concerns. He added, "I have encouraged our traffic unit to explore new and creative ways to address drunk driving."

Members of the community that had strong feelings both for and against the new procedure were calling talk shows and finding outlets where they could be heard.

Michael Levine, a retired college professor, said he supported police cracking down on drunken drivers but considered the bar stings to be entrapment. "I just find that to be inappropriate behavior," Levine said. "They're trying to entrap people, and I don't think that's the function of a police officer."

He also said he believed police could be liable if a drunken person who was allowed to leave the parking lot hurt someone in a car crash.

"What would they have said if one of those individuals got into an accident before they stopped them?" Levine asked. "That police officer, in my opinion, would have been as guilty as the person behind the wheel."

Professor Levine was actually wrong on all counts.

PART 2: *Chapter 22:* Fresno: A case example of how to fight DUIs   411

Number one, the bar surveillance program had nothing to do with entrapment. Entrapment is "the act of officers or agents of the government inducing a person to commit a crime not contemplated by him, for the purpose of instituting a criminal prosecution against him." (Black's Law Dictionary, revised 4th edition). Entrapment means putting the intent in someone's mind.

To be entrapment an officer would have to talk someone into getting drunk, when that was not their intention, and then persuade them to drive an automobile, when that was not their intention, for the purpose of arresting them.

Secondly, the officers were trying to prevent the professor, his family and others in the community from being killed by a drunk driver.

Thirdly, an officer letting an obviously drunk person get into a car and drive away, when the officer had an opportunity to arrest him sooner, would create some liability but it would be extremely difficult to prove. But who said these drivers were obviously drunk? We're talking about individuals under the influence.

There would be three people liable under the professor's scenario: the DUI, the bar owner and bartender. Ironically, he didn't mention any of them.

The professor's opinion shows just why it is so difficult to change laws to effectively combat DUIs. He even called the Fresno officer's behavior "inappropriate." What part of getting intoxicated people off the road to prevent them from killing innocent people is "inappropriate?" The professor should think about that the next time he's on the road because DUIs don't discriminate. They're random killers.

A few days later, Chief Jerry Dyer announced that the undercover bar stings targeting drunken drivers would continue but some changes were made to the program. The decisions were made after a series of meetings with high-ranking officers, members of the traffic bureau, Mayor Alan Autry, city officials and the police department's legal adviser.

He said undercover officers would not be positioned inside bars or restaurants. They would only be outside the bars in parking lots. He also said, officers, preferably uniformed, would approach people who appear to be intoxicated to dissuade them from driving.

At least one bar owner said the changes were an improvement. My question to this bar owner is—when is he going to get together with all of the other bar owners and initiate a program that would stop putting DUIs out on the road? That would also be an improvement.

In fact, it's against the law for a person (which includes bartenders, waitresses and owners) to serve an intoxicated person. They're putting the DUIs on the road and then complaining about methods of catching them before they kill someone.

I commend Chief Jerry Dyer for supporting a DUI program that concentrates on bars but I know from my experience in Santa Maria that DUI enforcement is extremely political and there are billions of dollars involved. Opposition comes from all directions the more successful the program becomes. Many livelihoods depend upon DUIs, such as breweries, bar associations, defense lawyers, tow operators, and even body and fender shops.

And then there is the social issue. Consider that in the United States 79% of the men and 63% of the women over 21 drink. This obviously is a major factor.

So is the fact that people often are treated differently.

"People with juice—be it money, political connections or simply a badge—have been cut so many breaks by Fresno police it was big news a few months back when the head of the city's traffic unit said anyone suspected of drunken driving would be arrested," wrote local Fresno columnist Bill McEwen about the program. "What's more, there was evidence of teeth in Capt. Andy Hall's declaration that officers were treating citizens one and the same: the arrests of a sheriff's deputy, a prison lieutenant and a federal investigator on DUI charges."

McEwen is right, a DUI enforcement program is only going to be successful if everyone is treated the same. When I spoke with Chief Jerry Dyer he brought up the need for treating everyone fair regardless of their position in life.

"That's the only way a drunk driving program like this will work. We need passionate officers in the field but they must not show favoritism," Dyer said.

One of the many Letters to the Editor of the Fresno Bee illustrate how many people write off DUIs as an unfixable problem of alcohol in society.

Chris Jarvis wrote: "The Fresno DUI operation is controversial because it affects everyone who drinks . . . people drink and drive in massive numbers every day. Is this good? No. Is it a fact of life? Yes. You can't have alcohol entrenched in society and not have the consequence of accidents. Parking lots of bars and clubs are filled with cars, and about 99% of them are driven home by someone who was drinking."

"But to set up shop outside businesses whose main source of revenue is alcohol sounds like entrapment to me, or worse, easy revenue. It doesn't take many drinks to be legally drunk."

We've already addressed entrapment—and does anyone really believe this program is about generating revenue? Get real. But Jarvis is right in saying it doesn't take many drinks to be legally DUI.

I'm sure Fresno police know that bar owners have to walk a tight rope. They know they produce DUIs who eventually get on the roadway. And getting people under the influence, and in many cases drunk, is their livelihood. Police, on the other hand, don't want DUIs on the road and they arrest individuals for being under the influence and drunk. To say the least, there is a conflict of interest.

From my 32 years of experience, I have found that bar owners will do what they can to protect their patrons—and their livelihood. In East Los Angeles bar owners gave patrons directions on what side-streets to use to avoid getting arrested on their way home. It sounded like a good idea but it wasn't fool proof. From time to time we would find out their route and be waiting for them along the way.

Fresno has already discovered that bars have been circumventing their DUI checkpoints through the use of cell phone text messages. I think it was Shakespeare who said, "Know thine enemy."

In its fight to keep DUIs off the road, Fresno officers approached patrons leaving bars who appeared to be intoxicated to dissuade them from driving. While it is certainly commendable to keep them off the road and prevent them from killing innocent people, there is a very real problem: the warning is only good for that moment in time. It won't change the drunk's conduct in the future.

There is no clear-cut answer to this dilemma. I would always make a physical arrest of the obvious drunk and I would send a copy to the Alcoholic Beverage Control (ABC) so they could investigate and find out if the bar was serving obviously drunk patrons. Or better yet, catch them serving obvious drunks.

Maybe legislators can come up with a law whereby it can be assumed a drunk intends to drive a vehicle if he has his keys in his hand and has opened the driver's door. This is not as extreme as it may sound. In California (Section 40300.5 Cal. Vehicle Code) authorizes an officer to make an arrest "when the officer has reasonable cause to believe that the person <u>had been driving</u> while under the influence of an alcoholic beverage" and (a) "The person is observed <u>in or about</u> a vehicle that is obstructing a roadway" and (b) "The person is involved in a traffic accident." Section 40300.6 CVC adds for clarification "Section 40300.5 shall be <u>liberally</u> interpreted to further safe roads and the control of driving while under the influence of an alcoholic beverage or any drug in order to permit arrests to be made pursuant to that section within a reasonable time and distance away from the scene of a traffic accident."

How about including a <u>liberal</u> interpretation before they have an opportunity to get on the road?

Of course, that can cause problems in court. Deputy district attorneys often allow DUIs to plea down to reckless driving because *there wasn't enough driving observed by officers.* It's one of the commonly used excuses for not going to trial or showing favoritism.

Chief Dyer mentioned another progressive method being used by his department to assist in curbing DUI offenses that was not available when I was on the road—the Global Positioning System (GPS).

Chief Dyer explained it this way, "Anyone with four or more convictions for drunk driving or felony drunk driving is monitored so we can keep track of them. It's part of a court order and we go to their home and inform them that they are being monitored." The device is planted on the criminal's car as opposed to being "hardwired." This is just another method being used by Fresno Police to protect the public.

The Fresno Police Department deserves all of their recognition, awards and acclaims for their DUI enforcement programs. They are being proactive and not just sitting back and clearing the wreckage and bodies from the highway.

Since 2002, traffic fatalities in Fresno are down 28.8%. This represents 53 fewer families that had to bury a loved one and 1,447 people who weren't transported to the hospital with missing limbs and other serious injuries. Between May and December 2006, Fresno police conducted 24 Bar Watch Operations resulting in 143 arrests. And the first six months of 2007, DUI fatalities were down 50% (4 deaths versus 8 deaths) and DUI collisions are down 19.3%. Chief Dyer told me that his department tries to conduct a Bar Watch activity at least once a month.

Fresno County Coroner David Hadden, said he believes the decline is significant, and that the 50% reduction very likely stems from the Police Department's traffic enforcement, which is a striking accomplishment. Hadden said, "Traffic fatalities in the county have remained steady. There were 133 and 127 deaths in the county in 2005 and 2006." Actually, the reduction in deaths in the county could be attributed to Fresno's DUI enforcement. If a DUI is arrested before he drives into the county then it does have an effect upon county statistics. Not every DUI lives in the area where they are arrested.

In September 2005, Mothers Against Drunk Drivers gave Fresno police its Outstanding Law Enforcement award. In 2008, the department was recognized by the International Association of Chiefs of Police for having the nation's best impaired-driving program. In 2003 and 2004 they received the CHP Commissioner's Award for their enforcement. This year Fresno Police is again in line to take number one in the nation in enforcement. A part of their annual publication is this reminder, "Although we can quantify the tens of millions of dollars saved from traffic collisions, the saving of just a single human life is priceless."

Remember, if you're not part of the solution then you're part of the problem.

PART 2: *Chapter 23:* Schemes Used by Lawyers in Court   417

Chapter 23
Schemes Used by Lawyers in Court

As difficult as it may be to believe, there are people who make their living from people driving under the influence of alcohol and drugs. Their livelihood depends on it. Large breweries will advertise "responsible driving" but that's just a blatant public relations move. The companies know it has no real effect in reducing DUIs.

But the worst offenders are the lawyers who use schemes and forms of deceit to knowingly distort the truth. They say they are protecting the innocent, but they often know, without a doubt, they are protecting the guilty. I truly do not know how they sleep at night. They try to clear their conscience by saying that everyone has a right to be defended. And everyone does have a right to be defended but not by lies and deceit.

The judicial system was founded on the principle of "a search for the truth." There isn't even a slight semblance of that today. In fact, the court will not even accept a guilty plea in some cases. Many times, the lawyer is actually searching for a loophole so that his client can avoid justice, truth can be ignored and the lawyer can live a lavish lifestyle.

When I was actively arresting DUIs and working in the East Los Angeles Area, there was a lawyer who was very successful defending DUIs. He wasn't successful against Klippness and me because we had a 96% conviction rate in court. And a large number of our DUI arrestees pled guilty, rather than go to trial, when the lawyers discovered we were the arresting officers. But one night this attorney had a life changing experience and, as a result, he would no longer defend a DUI. The attorney was involved in a very serious accident with a DUI that hit him head-on and he was paralyzed from the waist down.

In that same time period there was a judge in the Los Angeles area who had lost a child to a DUI and lawyers would use every means available to get a change of venue. It's a shame individuals have to experience these personal tragedies before realizing what damage DUIs are doing. This is not to say that a DUI arrestee should not have his day in court. I'm talking about lawyers who use devious tactics to get them off. That also includes judges who, by their liberal decisions, are responsible for putting DUIs back on the road.

One reason some officers don't arrest DUIs is their fear of being embarrassed in court by a devious lawyer. And this is almost always the case. Take an officer who arrests and removes one of America's terrorists from the road, very possibly preventing some innocent person or persons from being killed, only to go to court and be falsely accused and humiliated by a lawyer who uses any means available to clear a DUI of the charges. He knows the DUI is guilty but is more interested in what he is going to get paid than the number of innocent people that will later be endangered.

Lawyers will argue, and rightfully so, that everyone has a right to be defended in court. And I would be one of the strongest defenders of that right. But that does not give someone the right to conspire to help a guilty person escape justice. The judicial system was designed for a guilty person to be found guilty and an innocent person to be found innocent. The lawyer who knowingly perverts justice to get a guilty client off, is just as guilty as if he, the lawyer, had committed the crime.

Over time, lawyers have come up with different ways of helping DUIs avoid justice. The first move is to contact the Deputy District Attorney's office and play "let's make a deal." If that doesn't work then the next maneuver is to find the most liberal judge and try to get the case assigned to his court. That's done by continuations, vacations, etc. Once the lawyer gets the most liberal judge available then he tries a couple of court tactics that sometimes work, but if they don't, they at least impress their client.

The most popular one is:

PART 2: *Chapter 23:* Schemes Used by Lawyers in Court 419

The Officer Did Not have Probable Cause for the DUI Arrest.

The lawyer can claim there was not enough evidence for the officer to believe a crime had been committed. The lawyer will then ask for a special court proceeding called a "suppression hearing" or "1538.5 hearing." At this hearing the judge decides if the officer had enough probable cause to arrest the DUI. In practice, judges usually side with the prosecution at the suppression hearing but if they don't, the results of the chemical test can be excluded from evidence and there is always a chance the entire case can be dismissed.

But even if the judge rules there is probable cause, the hearing provides the lawyer with an opportunity to question the officer and discover any problems the officer may have experienced with the DUI arrest. This questioning will also assist the lawyer in preparing a defense, also a tactic lawyers sometimes use to point out weaknesses in the prosecutor's case, in hopes they can get a dismissal or a reduction to reckless driving.

There are five other major approaches lawyers use to try to keep DUIs from being convicted. An officer should be aware of these practices so the officer can successfully testify in court.

1. *Defending DUI's Driving*

First, the defense attorney will claim that weaving in a lane does not constitute being under the influence, even if the DUI drifts or weaves into another lane. The defense attorney will argue the weaving must be "pronounced weaving" for a "substantial distance." This argument is totally without merit. An officer should not let a possible DUI drive any farther than it takes to stop him. Weaving in a lane of traffic can be an indication that the driver is possibly a DUI but, of course, weaving can be for other reasons. But it's not something to be ignored.

And to let a possible DUI drive for a "substantial" distance is insane even though some deputy district attorneys have used that excuse to dismiss DUI cases. Usually an officer will have more indications of the driver being DUI than just weaving (window down in cold weather, driving too slow, jerky motion, etc.) Usually no one single act constitutes a person being under the influence and the arresting officer should make that clear when testifying.

The defense attorney will also try to minimize his client's weaving by asking, "Isn't it true that sober drivers sometime weave and drift because of inattentive driving such as using a cell phone or eating?" Suggested answer: "Yes. But that was not what caused the weaving in this case." If the lawyer makes the mistake of asking you what it was then you can reply, "His lack of sobriety."

Separate from the suppression hearing, the lawyer will most likely question an officer during the trial concerning his probable cause for making the DUI traffic stop and that is a fair question. Most of the time the stop is made for a traffic violation but it can be as a result of a citizen's report or if the officer has reasonable cause to believe the driver is DUI. It can't just be done arbitrarily.

The lawyer may try to pull the officer into the trap of testifying that he, the officer, based the DUI's sobriety, to some degree, upon the fact the DUI was speeding. The lawyer would then argue successfully that people speed all the time and that doesn't make them a DUI.

The officer should agree with the lawyer, but add, "The fact he was speeding didn't necessarily mean he was under the influence. But it is one of the traits of a DUI. Nevertheless, other tests showed that he was under the influence."

2. Attacking the Field Sobriety Test (FST)

The lawyer will ask the officer how his client performed on the field sobriety tests. When the officer replies, "He failed it" or "Did poorly," the lawyer is going to ask, "Compared to what? Have you ever met my client before?"

Officer, "No."

"Then how do you know how he should have performed the test? Did you know my client has always had poor balance even as a child?"

It's important to remember that there are many factors that contribute to how a person performs a balance test, such as his natural level of coordination, equilibrium, fitness level, nervousness, age, and so on.

Avoid testifying that the DUI "failed the tests." Just testify how the DUI did on the test and let the jury or court decide how he performed.

PART 2: *Chapter 23:* Schemes Used by Lawyers in Court

A defense attorney can have a field day asking an officer what constitutes failing a test. An officer can testify the DUI didn't perform the test as it was demonstrated and that cannot be contested by the defense attorney, except to ask, "Did you know the defendant has a problem from an old injury that prevents him from walking a street line without losing his balance?"

Answer: "I asked Mr. Jones, 'Is there any reason why you can't perform the field sobriety tests and he said no."

A sharp defense attorney will probably counter with, "Where does that question and answer appear in your arrest report?" The officer should be prepared to show the defense attorney. Always record the DUI's answers verbatim. However, keep in mind that the DUI may have a legitimate reason for not being able to perform the tests and that should be noted on the arrest report.

An officer's first priority should be to ensure he does not arrest an innocent person. But not being able to administer a FST, for good cause, will not prevent prosecution of a DUI if the DUI has a good reason for not being able to take the tests and the officer has properly explained this in the arrest report. I never lost a case in court due to a DUI not being able to take a FST.

In East Los Angeles Municipal Court, a lawyer used the excuse his client failed the FST because he had a problem with equilibrium and had never been able to walk a line or stand with his feet together and head back without losing his balance. I testified, as well as having it recorded in the arrest report, that he told me there was nothing to prevent him from taking the test.

The judge said, "Well, lets see how he does in court. We'll let the jury make that decision."

The judge then asked me to step down from the witness stand and give the defendant a FST. I demonstrated the walking heel to toe and then the defendant was asked to do it. It became very obvious, almost laughable, the defendant was trying to purposely lose his balance. There's one thing harder than maintaining your balance and that is trying to make out like you are losing your balance. The jury didn't buy it and found the defendant guilty.

An officer must make sure he gives a FST in a fair manner. The surface must be level, smooth, and clear of debris. Other considerations are weather, standing close to passing traffic, glaring lights or problems with darkness, nervousness or footwear, to mention the most obvious. Anything that would cause a person to lose their balance should be avoided. Regardless what lawyers will try to convey in court, the officer's purpose for giving a FST is to satisfy his mind concerning the subject's sobriety. It is for that reason and that reason only. If the subject is not under the influence and safe to drive, that's all the officer should try to determine.

Never give a FST in front of a patrol car that is parked on or near the roadway. **Never** stand between the patrol car and the violator's car even if you have a stationary camera filming the stop. **Never** turn your back to traffic. **Never** stand in a location where a violator can shove you into a lane of traffic. These warnings will save your life. I cringe every time I see an officer do this on television. An officer who does this is also at the mercy of the next drunk driver that comes along. It can happen. On one occasion, Klippness and I had *three* DUIs approach the scene after we had stopped and was arresting a DUI.

It happened in East Los Angeles, but believe me, it can happen anywhere. Klippness and I arrested four DUIs at the same intersection—Arizona Ave and Third St. It's true that one DUI stopped and asked us directions, the first DUI was a regular stop and the other two were flagged in with our flashlights as they approached. All of this occurred while we were trying to process the first DUI. We were on our motorcycles so we ended up calling two transportation units who hauled two DUIs in each cruiser. They didn't have far to go because the East Los Angeles County jail was only three blocks away.

And, yes, we joked about being close enough to walk them to the jail.

There's a law firm in Southern California that contends in their advertisements that, "Arresting officers are bias and frequently do slipshod DUI investigations. Their claims and opinions should never be taken at face value."

I agree if an arresting officer is bias and does slipshod investigations, his claims and opinions should be questioned, but not every officer fits that

PART 2: *Chapter 23:* Schemes Used by Lawyers in Court 423

description. And that is what the law firm is implying so DUIs will plead not guilty and use their services. They believe they can discredit the officer in court. Once the DUI is in court and finds out the arresting officer is not bias, but is competent and professional in his investigation, it's too late.

The National Highway Traffic Safety Administration (NHTSA) standardized the Horizontal Gaze Nystagmus Test, the Walk-and-Turn Test and the One-Leg-Stand Test as the most effective tests for determining a sobriety.

I only used the Nystagmus test (eye test) when I was suspicious of drugs.

Almost exclusively, I used the Walk-and-Turn Test, walking a straight line touching the toe to the heel and then turning around, as well as the One-Leg-Stand Test. The eyes closed, finger-to-nose test is of value but an officer should not close his eyes when demonstrating it to the DUI. He may end up getting shot or punched in the jaw.

I never used the hand pat test or alphabet test nor the "Rhomberg test" (tilting head back for an estimated 30 seconds). I've really never had a problem testifying in court concerning a FST. Just relate your observations.

As previously mentioned, avoid saying a DUI failed or passed a Field Sobriety Test (FST) because of the many issues the defense attorney can raise as to what constitutes passing and what constitutes failing the test.

And I never testified that I had decided the driver was under the influence until I informed him he was under arrest and placed the handcuffs on him. "Testing his balance and ability to perform the tests only assisted me in making the decision. There is no passing or failing." Imagine trying to explain how a person passes or fails a FST. It's not something that can be easily measured. It's kind of like pornography as described by a Supreme Court Judge. "You can't define it but you know it when you see it."

A Southern California law firm specializing in DUI defense reports the following; "Even when the standardized field sobriety tests are administered perfectly (which is rare), they still provide a very inaccurate measure of whether a DUI suspect is impaired. According to NHTSA, for example, the one leg stand test has a 65% accuracy rate and the walk-and-turn test a 68% accuracy rate."

I have absolutely no idea what they are talking about. There is no possible way a meaningful accuracy rate could be measured on these tests. Each person has different skills, it would also depend on the degree of intoxication and numerous other factors.

They go on to say: "This means that if people were convicted based on these roadside tests, one-third of them would be innocent and wrongly convicted. Or, viewed another way, when officers arrest DUI suspects based on failing these tests, one in three suspects is wrongfully arrested."

Talk about gobbledygook. No one is ever convicted upon "failing" one of these tests. A person's guilt or innocence for DUI is based upon numerous factors, not just a single standing-on-one-leg test. So the "one-in-three wrongfully arrested" analogy is not reality.

Video Taping a FST

Should a Field Sobriety Test be videoed so it can be used in court as evidence? I'm all for using videos in law enforcement, but video taping the FST tests is not one of them.

A large number of law enforcement officers would not recognize a person under the influence unless the DUI had reached an intoxication level of about a .20%. So, why would anyone think it was a good idea to video tape a FST and show it to a jury made up of individuals that have absolutely no knowledge or experience in recognizing a person under the influence? Most citizens can only recognize a person who is falling down drunk. And to the average citizen, if a person is not falling down drunk, then that person must be sober. It takes expert training and experience to recognize a DUI at a level of .08%, which is now the law in every state. Showing a videotape of a DUI taking a Field Sobriety Test could be equivalent to video taping doctors performing a major operation and then later asking the jury if the doctors made a mistake during the operation.

3. Trying to Explain Away a DUI's Intoxicated Condition

An attorney may say that many of the "typical" symptoms associated with DUI can easily be explained. For example, fatigue is one condition. They report that exhaustion often causes a person to drive a vehicle poorly, have bloodshot and watery eyes, respond slowly to some of the officer's questions and struggle with the field sobriety tests. They also mentioned drowsy driving causing the same condition.

In my 32 years of law enforcement experience and years of testifying in court, this situation was never an issue. I have never heard of an officer being accused of arresting someone for DUI because they were fatigued or exhausted. A person going to sleep, which happens occasionally, has the same driving patterns as a DUI, but you don't arrest a sleepy person for DUI.

Smelling alcohol on a DUI's breath

When I was a rookie police officer in Montebello, I saw an officer on a DUI stop ask the suspect DUI to blow his breath in his face so he could smell for alcohol. I don't think anyone does that anymore—at least, I sure hope not. People are much more conscious of germs and diseases now. But I had an experience in regards to this that will stay with me for life.

I stopped a young man who had run a red light and I was issuing him a citation. Every time I asked him a question or he had something to say to me, he would turn his head in the other direction and talk. Then he would turn back and face me while I answered. It was a real irritant and finally I asked him why he didn't look me in the eye when he spoke.

He said, "I have active tuberculous and I don't want to spread it." He had no reason to be lying and there was no advantage in revealing it. He was only subjecting himself to being reported to the Health Department. But I couldn't help but think back about the officer asking the DUI suspect to blow his breath in his face.

Even when I testified in court in regards to the odor of alcohol on a defendant's breath, I would only mention that he had an odor of alcohol present. Whether an odor is strong or weak, in my opinion, is not that significant. On occasion, I have had an attorney ask if I smelled the defendant's breath.

My answer was, "I smelled an odor of alcohol when he was talking but I didn't attempt to smell his breath."

One day in East Los Angeles, I was questioned by an attorney who thought he was going to score big points with the jury by asking, "Officer Mitchell, you testified that you smelled alcohol on my client's breath. Isn't that correct?"

I answered to the affirmative.

The attorney said, "Did you know that alcohol has no odor and it would be impossible for you to smell it?"

I replied, "Yes."

He said, "So, you didn't smell alcohol on his breath, did you?"

I said, "No, I was actually smelling the ingredients, if you want to be technical about it."

"But you testified that you smelled the odor of alcohol, didn't you?"

I said, "I was testifying to the odor that is associated with a person who has been drinking alcohol." Alcohol (ethanol) is odorless and it is the mixing agent or flavoring that produces the odor associated with alcohol that we smell.

This is a favorite tactic an attorney likes to "spring" but I don't think the jurors are ever impressed with technicalities. I know they weren't in this case, because they found the defendant guilty.

The only importance I ever put on a DUI having an odor of alcohol (actually the ingredients) on his breath was that he had been drinking. That's all it really tells you. There are many intoxicants and drugs that have no detectable odors so an odor, in and of itself, is limited to the fact the suspect has been drinking, but is no indication of how much.

4. Claim that Officer is Not Qualified to Determine Intoxicated Condition

A defense attorney will sometimes use the tactic that the officer's special training and experience makes him no more qualified than anyone else to determine whether a person is DUI. They will cite a controlled study by Rutgers University's Alcohol Behavior Research Laboratory to support their statement. They will contend that social drinkers and bartenders were just as accurate as experienced police officers and that all three correctly judged the level of intoxication only 25% of the time.

Probably the only time this defense would come up in court would be if the client's attorney asked the officer if he was familiar with the study, and then just repeat the findings of the study, in an effort to influence the jury. It would be up to the prosecutor to challenge the creditability of the study which I don't believe he would have any trouble doing.

It is conceivable that being under the influence involves two types of impairment—mental and physical.

So if the defense attorney can get an officer to testify the defendant was coherent, alert and responsive, then it can be assumed there was no "mental impairment." If this is accomplished, then the defense attorney will proclaim that any toxicologists will tell you "mental impairment" always precedes "physical impairment" so if there is no mental impairment present then, presumably, there is no physical impairment.

I can never recall a DUI that I arrested that was alert. As far as a DUI being coherent and responsive, it would depend on the degree. As far as coherent, a DUI is usually not consistent in his actions, does not clearly articulate, and is normally slow to respond. In regards to a DUI being responsive, he will eventually respond to directions but in a slow, unsteady, and inconsistent manner. If a person is under the influence, there is going to be some mental impairment so I can't imagine an officer letting a defense attorney lead him down that path.

5. Claim that Officer Preconceived DUI's Guilt

One of the best known ploys of a defense attorney is to attempt to convince the jury that the officer was premature in concluding that his client was under the influence. That seems to be every defense attorney's primary goal. It's a good maneuver and serves two major purposes. First, the defense attorney can argue that the officer made up his mind without probable cause and, as a result, the officer was no longer objective but looked only for reasons to arrest his client and, if necessary, write his report in such a fashion as to justifying his contention.

Secondly, the definition of an "arrest" can get very technical and defense attorneys like for things to get technical so they can confuse the jurors. An officer should be just the opposite and keep his testimony clear and simple.

As for as the actual arrest, an officer should never make a decision that a person is under the influence until he has completed his entire investigation. To put it another way, it should not be any one thing that leads to the decision the DUI is under the influence, such as driving, intoxicated physical appearance, incriminating statements, results of FST, and witnesses' statements. It should be all of them combined that convinces an officer the suspect is under the influence.

By waiting until the investigation is complete before concluding there is a violation and arresting the suspect, all of the statements the DUI makes can be used against him. An officer does not have to advise a suspect of his Miranda Rights until he is placed under arrest or in a custodial situation. Meaning the suspect's freedom of movement is restrained, although he is not under arrest.

At the same time, the defendant has no obligation or requirement to answer an officer's questions at any time except to provide proof of his identity, including address and place of birth and provide an officer with his vehicle registration and evidence of insurance.

Of course, the defense doesn't like for an officer to wait until the investigation is complete before deciding the defendant is under the influence. He might say, "You mean to tell me you didn't think my client was under the influence when he kept losing his balance?"

My response was always: "No, but I was becoming more suspicious that he was."

Then the attorney would say, "What about his blood shot eyes and slurred speech?"

My response, "That made me even more suspicious."

PART 2: *Chapter 23:* Schemes Used by Lawyers in Court   429

Another ploy of the defense is to ask the officer when he decided to arrest the defendant. My response was, "As soon as I determined he was under the influence and that was after completing the investigation."

The defense will then counter with, "Well, was he free to walk away at any time?" (Knowing that if the defendant was not free to leave then he was, by definition, technically under arrest.)

I would answer, "No. I was suspicious that he was guilty of driving under the influence. If he had attempted to leave then I would have had to arrest him at that time. But he was not under arrest because he didn't attempt to leave."

However, if a DUI is obviously under the influence and you have already made that determination then you should advise him of his constitutional rights at that time.

Officer Has Right to Explain His Answer in Court

It is very important for an officer to remember that he has a legal right to explain his answer. Don't let a defense attorney use the old ploy of, "Do you still beat your wife? Yes or No?"

When it comes to testifying in court, the prosecution will always advise a witness to limit his answers to "yes" or "no." They will tell you that if you have to explain, keep it brief and don't volunteer anything. That is excellent advise for 90 per cent of the public and certainly good advise for an inexperienced witness, but there are exceptions.

I think every officer should prepare himself to testify as an expert witness. The Superior Court declared me an expert witness and the district attorney's office never expressed a disagreement with any of my testimony.

In fact, as I related in another portion of this book, I had a prosecutor ask me while I was testifying in Superior Court, "Officer, is there any thing that I have not asked you, that you would like to tell the jury?" I mention this to encourage officers to be prepared for defense attorneys using the old ploy, "Do you still beat your wife? Yes or no." An officer should always be prepared and ready to explain his answer,

Here's an example of a "yes" or "no" answer that should be explained: "Isn't it true you arrested my client because you didn't like his attitude?"

The officer should answer, "No. That isn't true. In fact, I thought Mr. Jones was a nice person and I didn't want to see him involved in an accident."

If a defense attorney asks an officer a question and then adds, "I want only a yes or no answer to this question."

The officer may reply, "I can't answer your question with a simple yes or no." The judge will usually intervene and say, "The officer has a right to explain his answer."

Naturally, there are many questions that can be answered by a simple "yes" or "no," such as "Did you advise my client of his constitutional rights?"

On more than one occasion I have had a defense attorney ask me, "You want my client to be found guilty, don't you?" This being a trick question. The attorney wants to catch the officer off guard. Of course, the officer can reply, "I'm willing to abide by the decision of the court."

Defense Attorney's Will Try to Explain Away Symptoms

The usual symptoms of a person under the influence of alcohol are: (1) bloodshot eyes, (2) slurred speech, (3) flushed face and (4) an unsteady gait.

The defense attorney will contend that fatigue, allergies and eye strain also cause bloodshot eyes and that nervousness and anger can also cause a flushed face. He may even attempt to contend his client's slurred speech was caused because he was confused, nervous or befuddled.

Of course, all of the reasons stated above are possibilities, but if the defense attorney is putting this information in the form of a question then the officer should respond, "Yes, that's a possibility but it's also the symptoms of a person that has had too much to drink."

The defense attorney is trying to justify each of his client's symptoms as something other than being under the influence. His objective is to eliminate each symptom until there is nothing left to conclude but that his client is innocent.

PART 2: *Chapter 23:* Schemes Used by Lawyers in Court 431

If the officer agrees with the defense with a simple "yes" or "no" then that's sending the wrong message to the jury. All answers by the officer should point to the guilt of the defendant as long as the officer can answer truthfully.

It's a game. And one of the rules of the game is to put the officer on trial. If the officer comes across as honest, sincere, compassionate (that's right, compassionate, forget the authoritative cop image) and competent (it's not enough just to be a nice guy, you've got to know what you're doing) then the jury will support the officer. Again, remember, *you're* on trial not the defendant. It all comes down to who the jury believes. Before jurors will put their confidence in the evidence, they must be convinced that the prosecution, which includes the arresting officer, can be trusted. Although they won't admit it, that's why some juries find a defendant not guilty in spite of the evidence.

Getting a DUI conviction can be a "hard sell" because it's quite possible some of the jurors are driving under the influence on occasion and they are sitting there thinking, "Only by the Grace of God am I sitting in the jury box and not the defendant's chair."

But if the officer is respectful toward the defendant and convinces the jurors that the defendant could have killed or injured himself or others, then the jurors do not relate to that and will find him guilty.

Intoxication Symptoms Should be Consistent with BAC

Lawyers for DUIs use three strategies when it comes to their client taking mandatory chemical tests.

The first one is advising the DUI to refuse to take the chemical test if the DUI knows he's under the influence. Even though his client's license will be suspended, it's easier to get a "not guilty" verdict when there is no chemical test. In some cases, if the attorney knows a liberal deputy district attorney, the lawyer may even get the DUI charge dismissed without going to trial. Almost all DUIs prefer a license suspension over a DUI conviction.

The second strategy is to advise his client to take the breathalyzer test because it's easier to attack the validity of the equipment.

The strategy behind the blood and urine tests is basically the same. Even though they are considered the most reliable tests, the results are not immediately known. The lawyer hopes the officer's arrest report will not be consistent with the alcohol concentration reading. The lawyer, if he can convince the jury the arrest report is inconsistent with the BAC results, can discredit the officer and win his case.

Of course, if the officer writes a complete and thorough report, being careful to record all pertinent information and statements just as they happened, then his report will be consistent with the BAC results. I discovered over the years while testifying in court that the jury was more interested in the defendant's unique statements such as,"I'm not that drunk"and "I'm not use to drinking," than they were with the standard, slurred speech, unsteady gait, bloodshot eyes, etc. testimony.

Challenging Chemical Tests in Court

The main chemical test the defense attorney likes to challenge is the breathalyzer. Not because it's not accurate but it's the easiest to cast doubt about. An officer should be aware of these possible challenges so he will be better prepared in court.

Acid reflux or heartburn can cause an inaccurately high reading.

California regulations require the officer to watch the DUI suspect continuously for at least 15 minutes prior to administering the breath alcohol test to ensure the DUI suspect does not drink anything, burp, belch, hiccup or regurgitate.

There are numerous other challenges a defense attorney may try, but the prosecutor will need to have an expert witness testify on the operation of the breathalyzer to dispute those claims. An officer is not expected to answer technical questions about the operation or maintenance of a breathalyzer machine.

Defense attorneys don't normally attack the readings of blood-alcohol tests unless it involves a serious felony. If they do, it is the job of an expert to defend the test, not the officer.

PART 2: *Chapter 23:* Schemes Used by Lawyers in Court 433

However, there is one area where the defense attorney will most certainly question the officer and that is regarding when the DUI suspect had his last drink. Then he will ask the officer if he knows how long it takes for the alcohol to absorb in the blood stream and what effect it may have on the driver. The prosecutor will object at this point and offer to "produce an expert if this line of questioning is going to continue."

I did find that social drinkers displayed more evidence of the effects of alcohol than longstanding drinkers. Such as cockiness, unusual cheerfulness, nervousness, and reluctant to comply with instructions. This is another reason why the BAC reading does not always correlate with the DUI's performance.

The following information is right out of the CHP Enforcement manual. "The habitual drinker while consuming large amounts of alcohol, may have so conditioned his actions that he appears to be merely slow and deliberate or exhibits no apparent external manifestations on his intoxication.

"The important thing to remember is, regardless of the various individual rates of absorption, oxidation, or elimination, we are interested in the measurement of the concentration of alcohol in the brain. People with the same percentage reading will suffer similar loss of judgment but may or may not exhibit outward manifestations.

"Because the human body does not always react the same way in exhibiting those outward manifestations for the same percentage reading of blood alcohol, the officer must exercise a fine degree of observation in noting all actions of the subject suspected of being 'under the influence.'"

Chapter 24
The Substances Behind DUI

One of the few alcohols made for consumption is ethyl alcohol, or ethanol, a clear, thin, odorless liquid. It never exists full-strength in any alcoholic beverage. In this article it will be referred to simply as "alcohol."

Alcohol affects human behavior when it reaches the brain and central nervous system. The extent of influence depends upon the concentration of alcohol present in the blood. Blood-alcohol concentration (BAC) is determined by such factors as the amount of alcohol consumed relative to the amount of water in the body, the duration of drinking, and the competing rates of absorption and elimination.

Here is the California Highway Patrol's definition: "A person is considered under the influence of an alcoholic beverage, drug, or combination of alcohol and drugs when his/her physical or mental abilities are impaired to such a degree that he/she no longer has the ability to drive a vehicle with the caution characteristic of a sober person of ordinary prudence, under the same or similar circumstances." (California Highway Patrol Manual HPM 70.4, 1995 revision)

There are numerous factors involved in alcohol absorption. How long one takes to drink, as well as the size and weight of the individual, food in the stomach, to name a few factors. The effects of alcohol are directly related to the concentration (percentage) of alcohol in the blood; however, the effects vary among individuals and even in the same individual at different times. The standard weight used by most sources is 150 pounds. A standard drink consists of 12 ounces of beer, 1 ounce of 100-proof alcohol or 4 ounces of table wine.

When someone drinks an alcoholic beverage it flows into the stomach. While in the stomach, the drinker does not feel the effects of the alcohol, but alcohol does not remain in the stomach very long. Some of it is absorbed through the stomach walls into the bloodstream but most alcohol passes into the small intestine and then into the bloodstream and this circulates throughout the body.

Once alcohol is in the bloodstream it reaches the brain and the drinker begins to feel its effects. The reason that a large person does not feel the effects of a drink as quickly as a small person is because the large person has more blood and other body fluids and will not have as high a level of alcohol in the blood after drinking the same amount of alcohol. (Gail Gleason Milgram, Ed. D, Rutgers University, Center of Alcohol Studies, 1996)

Most of the alcohol a person drinks is eliminated by chemical oxidation in the liver. A small portion (approximately 2-10 percent) of the alcohol consumed is not metabolized and eliminated through other pathways such as urination, respiration, and perspiration. The rate of elimination (excretion) varies between individuals, and can even very from time to time for the same person.

However, after reaching its peak, an average person's BAC will decline approximately 0.015 percent per hour. This general elimination rate is roughly equivalent to the consumption of two-thirds of a standard drink per hour. (National Highway Traffic Safety Administration, DWI Detection and Standardized Field Sobriety Testing—HS 178 R1/02)

The California Highway Patrol (CHP Manual 70.4, Revised August 1995) provides the following guidelines to their officers in regards to the California presumptive-limit law: "Pursuant to Section 23610(a) VC, if there was at the time of a chemical test less than 0.05 percent by weight of alcohol in the person's blood, it shall be presumed that the person was not under the influence of an alcoholic beverage at the time of the alleged offense." and "Officers should feel secure in the knowledge that no injustice is involved when arresting a person with a BAC of 0.08 percent or greater despite the

PART 2: *Chapter 24:* The Substances Behind DUI

absence of physical manifestations or the opportunity for observing them. Likewise, an officer is justified in arresting a subject with a BAC <u>below</u> 0.08 percent if they meet the definition of 'under the influence.'"

This is an outstanding guideline and should be part of every law enforcement officer's thought process throughout the nation. And any officer that doesn't accept and follow this directive should be a member of the "unemployed."

California Department of Motor Vehicles, Alcohol Impairment Chart, DL 606 (Rev. 10/2004) put it this way:

.01% to .04% possible DUI-Definitely unlawful if under 21 years old;

.05% to .07% likely DUI Definitely unlawful if under 21 years old;

.08% and up, Definitely DUI.

Standardized Field Sobriety Tests (FST)

From 1975 through 1998, major scientific studies have been conducted in an effort to identify the most reliable FSTs and study their relationship to intoxication and driving impairment. The studies were conducted under contract from the National Highway Traffic Safety Administration (NHSTA). The first study conducted by the Southern California Research Institute (SCRI) identified three reliable FSTs.

1. **Horizontal Gaze Nystagmus (HGN)**, which is defined as the involuntary jerking of the eyes occurring as the eyes gaze toward the side. The CHP manual HPM 70.4 advises "it should be used only by officers who have received formal training in its administration." I would hope that the lack of training and ability to use this test would not discourage an officer from making a DUI arrest. Klippness and I used it as early as the 1960s on a limited basis and were never asked to explain in court its use or correlation in relation to the subject's blood alcohol level.

2. **Walk and Turn**. "Based on scientific research, the Walk and Turn FST is considered to be the most sensitive psychophysical test. The test requires the subject to stand in a heel-to-toe fashion with the

arms at the sides while a series of instructions are given. It requires the subject to divide attention among mental tasks and physical tasks." When giving a field sobriety test, the objective is to give clear and simple directions and, in no way, confuse the subject.

3. **One-Leg-Stand.** "The test requires the subject to stand on one leg while the other leg is extended in front of the subject in a 'stiff-legged' manner with the foot held approximately six inches above the ground. The subject is to stare at the elevated foot and count out loud in a designed fashion for 30 seconds."

Based upon the exhaustive studies regarding the three tests, the reliability rate for identifying drivers with a blood alcohol level at or above the legal limit is at least 90%.

The California Highway Patrol uses the 3 tests and the Preliminary Alcohol Screening (PAS) device to assist an officer in identifying the impaired driver.

The CHP also recognizes five alternative FSTs and accepts additional FSTs that may be requested by local district attorneys.

Those five tests are.

1. Romberg Balance (Requiring the subject to stand with his/her feet together, head tilted slightly back, eyes closed while estimating the passage of 30 seconds).

2. Finger-to-nose (Requires touching the tip of the nose, with eyes closed and head tilted backward).

3. Hand Pat (Patting the bottom hand, while rotating the top hand 180 degrees and counting out loud, "1,2,1,2.")

4. Finger Count (Touching each finger in sequences with the tip of the thumb and then reversing while counting).

5. Alphabet (Requires the subject to recite the English alphabet out loud).

As reported in the CHP manual, "Officers should not rely on one test as the sole criteria for making a DUI arrest. It is imperative that an officer base his/her opinion to arrest a suspected DUI driver on the totality of the circumstances presented. **It is important to note that a subject does not pass or fail a field sobriety test.** As the subject performs the FST, an officer makes note of the observable signs of impairment."

This last paragraph is extremely important and I'm not sure all law enforcement officers are aware of this. When I testified concerning the FST, I would say, "Based upon how Mr. Jones performed the tests, I determined he was under the influence."

One test I never used was asking the subject, to recite the alphabet. I always thought of this as more of an educational question than a test of a person's sobriety. Just recently I saw a video of a female officer in a southern state ask an obviously intoxicated driver to recite the alphabet backwards. And he did. I don't know anyone, including myself, who can do that sober. Then she had him do a "rumba" while walking an imaginary line. Which he did. Then she asked him if he could "dance" for her and he said, "I could if I wasn't drunk." She pointed at him and said, "I gotcha," and arrested him.

This would all be humorous if we weren't talking about innocent people being killed and maimed because our officers are not properly trained. All a lawyer would have to do is subpoena the tape and play it for the jurors. Or the attorney could ask the officer to demonstrate the tests in court for the jury—especially, the alphabet backwards and the "rumba."

Other Intoxicating Substances

There are other intoxicating substances that people use as a substitute for alcohol. Sometimes they are very difficult to detect, but the officer must be aware of the possibility of their presence for several reasons. To prove his case in court he must be aware of the symptoms and, if possible, identify the drug, sedative or intoxicant. It is not uncommon for a defendant's attorney to "muddy the water" by confusing the officer and/or jury by bringing in other substances as an issue.

Here is a guide on other substances from the California Highway Patrol's "Drinking Driving Manual" (Revised 1966):

Glue, an adhesive component, commonly used by teenagers. The most common is model airplane cement. It is sniffed from a handkerchief and recovery is generally quick. However, a chemical analysis of either blood or urine, while the odor is still on the suspects breath, may be obtained. Sniffing glue can cause severe brain damage. However, this would be a non-narcotic drug offense

Amphetamine, a restricted, dangerous drug, is a stimulant used in combination with other drugs. It is the basic ingredient in Benzedrine. If taken excessively, it may cause symptoms of intoxication similar to alcohol. It can be detected by a urine analysis.

Barbiturates, a family of restricted, dangerous drugs. Various barbiturate preparations can cause acute intoxication. Addicts and chronic alcoholics are prone to their use. Alcohol intensifies the effects so a person using medically prescribed barbiturates should avoid alcohol consumption. A laboratory test will reveal the drugs.

Bromides. Intoxication is characterized by drowsiness with impairment of mental functions such as difficulty remembering. Many of the bromide drug products are available to the public at drug stores and may be purchased without a prescription.

My first experience with bromide intoxication was during an enforcement stop around midnight in East Los Angeles. The car had been weaving all over the roadway and all the symptoms of a DUI were present. When I approached the driver, I recognized him immediately as a western singer I had heard over the years. He was staring straight ahead and, frankly, appeared to be "stoned out of his mind." He didn't have much to say and was obviously under the influence of something. (When you put a cowboy's hat on crooked and he doesn't straighten it, you know he's drunk).

Because my partner and I were on motorcycles, we radioed for a car unit to transport the suspect to the East Los Angeles Sheriff's sub-station.

The suspect was given a breathalyzer test and we got a reading of "zero." Our next step was to ask the suspect to take a blood or urine test because he had all of the symptoms of intoxication. After the tests we were going to take the suspect to the hospital for a doctor's medical diagnosis. But about this time we got an urgent phone call at the Sheriff's Station from the CHP Officer storing and inventorying the suspect's car.

The Officer said, "I don't know what's going on but there are empty bromide bottles all over this guy's car." The bromide bottles were circumstantial evidence but we got a blood test and advised the laboratory what to look for. Driving under the influence of bromide is very unusual.

Chloroform produces symptoms similar to alcohol. Consumption is accomplished by inhalation and the effects are rapid and the duration of "under the influence" is short. A person highly intoxicated may be completely sober in less than five minutes after the last inhalation. A blood test to determine chloroform is possible if taken while subject still has obvious symptoms. I never ran into a chloroform capper.

Cocaine, a narcotic, is a white crystalline, odorless powder, with a bitter taste. It is a strong stimulant and attacks the central nervous system. It may be used either by sniffing or by intravenous injections. The subject has intense euphoria and fear, with hallucinations. Possession of the drug is a felony.

Gasoline and By-Products are probably the most dangerous and easiest means of getting intoxicated. In rare cases it has been drunk, but juveniles have been known to sniff fumes to get intoxicated. Intoxication may be a result of carbon monoxide poisoning. Gasoline and its by-products are not drugs or alcohols, so a charge of reckless driving may be appropriate if the other elements of the violation are present.

Diabetic Ketosis is caused by excessive food or insufficient insulin. Prosecution for this condition is not possible as it is the result of an individual afflicted with diabetes who has been without proper medical care for a long period.

Insulin Shock very closely resembles an individual under the influence of alcohol. It is the result of a diabetic receiving too much insulin or insufficient food. They are usually in need of medical care and should be taken to a doctor. Insulin is a drug, and depending upon the circumstances, may be in violation of DUI.

Nutmeg used in large quantities may cause the appearance of being intoxicated. Smell is the only means of detection, so a charge of reckless driving may be appropriate if the other elements of the violation are present.

Other toxicity drugs are paraldehyde, tranquilizers, and marijuana. Marijuana is an addicting drug and users develop some tolerance. The effects are usually lightness, a false feeling of power and distortions of time and space. These sensations are usually regarded as pleasurable and symptomatic of mild inebriation. Chemical tests of body fluids will not reveal its presence so the officer must go by physical appearance and the marijuana itself as evidence.

Cold Medicines Abused

About 3.1 million people between the ages of 12 and 25 have used cough and cold medicine to get high, the government reported recently.

The number of young people who abused over-the-counter cold medicines is comparable to use of LSD. And much greater than that for methamphetamines among the age group, according to the federal Substance Abuse and Mental Health Services Administration.

The agency's 2006 survey on drug abuse and health found that more than 5 percent of teenagers and young adults had misused cough and cold medicines. The survey also indicated that these people also had experimented frequently with illicit drugs.

Chapter 25
How to Identify a DUI

If we are going to succeed in removing DUI terrorists from the road then we are going to have to have a "zero tolerance" toward DUIs. And who better can assist us than the public—you?

The following information is being provided to assist you in recognizing a DUI. It is important to keep in mind that every characteristic a DUI displays can also be attributed to something else, but several symptoms would indicate the driver is probably driving under the influence.

Even if you're not sure, contact the police so they can check them out. Dialing 911 will get the quickest response.

Look for:

1. Unreasonable speed. I have found that a DUI will either drive unreasonably slow or unreasonably fast. Seldom will he drive at a normal speed. You can eliminate about 90 percent of the drivers because if the car is being driven at a normal speed then the driver is probably not under the influence. Remember you are looking for the exception.

2. Weaving. A normal traffic lane is 12-feet wide, although some are 10-feet wide. A DUI will have trouble keeping his vehicle in a straight line. Weaving is probably the most common trait of a DUI. The weaving doesn't have to be frequent or exaggerated for you to

take a closer look. If you see other traits then it's time to call 911. If he is weaving over a single line or the double line that's bad news and you should make sure you stay a safe distance.

3. Drifting. This is a very good sign of DUI, drugs, or going to sleep. If this occurs more than once then there is reason to be concerned.

4. Improper passing with insufficient clearance. This is a very dangerous trait because it can result in head-on collisions. My wife and I were driving on a two-lane highway in Colorado several years ago and as we approached two cars coming from the opposite direction, the second car appeared to be weaving and that tipped me off that he might pull into our lane, which he did. To avoid a head-on collision I swerved completely onto the gravel shoulder, almost spinning out, avoiding the collision. I made a 911 call to the Colorado Highway Patrol.

5. Stopping at the last minute, overshooting or disregarding traffic control signals. Failing to go when the light turns green. Approaching signals unreasonably fast or slow and stopping at the last minute.

6. Driving at night without lights. Delay in turning lights on when starting from a parked position.

7. Failure to dim lights to oncoming traffic.

8. Driving in lower gears without an apparent reason or clashing gears. This is the characteristic of a drunk driver. In other words, he's past the point of DUI.

9. Jerky or uneven starting or stopping.

10. Driving unreasonably slow. Some DUIs reveal themselves by trying to be too cautious. This same driver will probably drive too close to shoulders or curbs or appear to hug the edge of the road.

11. Driving with windows down in cold weather. In some cases driving with the head partly out of the window.

PART 2: *Chapter 25:* How to Identify a DUI

Remember it is out-of-the-ordinary driving that indicates a possible DUI.

It is not recommended that a person make a citizen's arrest because of the danger involved and other complications that can arise. Nevertheless, if you can prevent a DUI from driving or leaving the scene without getting physically involved or placing yourself in danger, you may save someone's life.

As a concerned citizen, it is best to notify the police immediately and provide them with as much information as possible to identify the violator.

CPSIA information can be obtained at www.ICGtesting.com
Printed in the USA
LVOW041608311011

252873LV00002B/7/P

DOWNTOWN CAMPUS LRC

J.S. Reynolds Community College

3 7219 001645822

```
HE 5620 .D72 M538 2009
Mitchell, Bob.
Drunk driving and why the
 carnage continues
```

DISCARDED